Auditing, Assurance Services, and Forensics

Felix I. Lessambo

Auditing, Assurance Services, and Forensics

A Comprehensive Approach

palgrave
macmillan

Felix I. Lessambo
School of Business
Central Connecticut State University
New Britain, CT, USA

ISBN 978-3-030-08034-1 ISBN 978-3-319-90521-1 (eBook)
https://doi.org/10.1007/978-3-319-90521-1

Softcover re-print of the Hardcover 1st edition 2018

Cover illustration: Laurent Hamels, PhotoAlto Agency RF Collections/Getty Images

Printed on acid-free paper

This Palgrave Macmillan imprint is published by the registered company Springer International Publishing AG part of Springer Nature
The registered company address is: Gewerbestrasse 11, 6330 Cham, Switzerland

Acknowledgements

Writing a book is always a challenge. But writing a book on "Auditing, Assurance Services, and Forensics" a more daring intellectual exercise for twofold reasons: (i) because of the hard choice of topics to cover, and (ii) audit is part science and part art.

I would like to express my gratitude to those who motivated me all along the project, knowing my dedication to the subject, and thought I am more than able to complete this project: Dr. Gordon Marsha, Dr. Linda Sama, and Jerry Izouele.

Several goods friends provided me with needed guidance and materials to complete this book, while others took from their busiest time to review and comb the manuscripts: Reverend Pastor Roland Dalo, Aline Kabongo.

Disclaimer

While the author has made every effort to ensure that the information in this book is correct at the time of publication, he does not assume and hereby disclaims any liability to any Party for any loss, damage, or disruption caused by errors or omissions, whether such errors or omissions result from negligence, accident, or any other cause.

This publication is designed to provide accurate and authoritative information in regards to the subject matter covered. It is sold on the understanding that the publisher is not engaged in rendering professional services. If professional advice or other expert assistance is needed, the services of a competent professional should be sought.

Contents

Abbreviations

AICPA	American Institute of Certified Public Accountants
CAG	Consultative Advisory Group
CAQ	Center for Audit Quality
CISA	Certified Information Systems Auditor
CMA	Certifies Management Accounting
CPA	Certified Public Accountant
FASAB	Federal Accounting Standards Advisory Board
FASB	Financial Accounting Standards Board
FIFO	First In First Out
FINRA	Financial Industry Regulatory
GAAP	Generally Accepted Accounting Principles
GAAS	Generally Accepted Auditing Standards
IAASB	International Auditing and Assurance Standards Board
IAG	International Auditing Guidelines
IAPC	International Auditing Practices Committee
ISA	International Standards on Auditing
ISB	Independence Standards Board
LIFO	Last In First Out
PCAB	Public Company Accounting Oversight Board
PIOB	Public Interest Oversight Board
QC	Quality Control
SEC	Securities and Exchange Commission
SOX Act	Sarbanes-Oxley Act
SQCS	Statement on Quality Control Standards
SRTPs	Statements on Responsibilities in Tax Practice
SSARS	Statements on Standards for Accounting and Review Services

SSTS	Statements on Standards for Tax Services
SSVS	Statements on Standards for Valuation Services

List of Cited Cases

- James Thomas McCurdy v. SEC, US Court of Appeals for the District of Columbia Circuit, No. 04-1047, February 8, 2005.
- SEC, In the Matter of the Application of Wendy McNeeley, CPA, AAER No. 3427, at 15 (December 13, 2012), http://www.sec.gov/litigation/opinions/2012/34-68431.pdf.
- SEC Settles Civil Fraud Charges Filed Against Richard A. Causey, Former Enron Chief Accounting Officer; Causey Barred From Acting as an Officer or Director of a Public Company (U.S. Securities and Exchange Commission ("SEC" or "Commission") Litigation Release No. 19996, February 9, 2007).
- World Radio v. Coopers & Lybrand, 251 Neb. 261, 557 N.W.2d 1 (1996).
- Ryan v. Kanne, 170 NW 2d. 395 [Iowa].
- Larsen v United Fed. Sav. & Loan Assn., 300 NW2d 281 [Iowa].
- Shatterproof Glass Corp. v James, 466 SW2d 873 [Tex Civ App].
- Coleco Indus. v Berman, 423 F Supp 275 [ED Pa].
- Rosenblum v. Adler, 93 N.J 324 (1983) 461 A.2d 138.
- AHERF Creditors' Comm v. PwC, No. 2000 cv 684 (W.D. Pan. January 17, 2007).
- National Surety v. Lybrand, 256 A.D. 226 (1939).
- Shapiro v. Glekel, 380 F. Supp. 1053, 1056 (S.D.N.Y. 1974).
- Reves et al. v. Ernst & Young, 507 US 170 (1993).
- Continental Vending [U.S. v. Simon, 425 F.2d 796 (2d Cir. 1969)].

- Safavian, 435 F. Supp. 2d at 40.
- Taylor Bean & Whitaker Plan Trust v. PricewaterhouseCoopers LLP, case number 2013-33964-CA-01, in the 11th Judicial Circuit Court of the State of Florida.

List of Figures

PART I

Audit Framework, Profession, and Standards

CHAPTER 1

Overview, History, and Overall Objectives of Auditing

1.1 General

The word "audit" comes from the Latin word audire, which means "to hear". The ancient "audit-checking" activities can be traced back to ancient civilizations, such as of China, Egypt, and Greece. The ancient checking activities found in Greece (around 350 B.C.) appear to be closest to the present-day auditing.[1] Auditing is a systematic process of objectively obtaining and evaluating the evidence regarding assertions about economic actions and events to ascertain the degree of correspondence between the assertions and established criteria and communicating the results to interested users.[2] The role assured by audit firms is crucial to our financial markets. Information is the lifeblood of the market. For the market to operate efficiently—indeed, for it to operate at all—information must have some measure of reliability. Investor confidence is bolstered by the knowledge that public financial statements have been subjected to the rigors of independent and objective investigation and analysis.[3]

[1] LEE Teck-Heang, Azham Md. Ali (2008): The Evolution of Auditing: An Analysis of the Historical Development, *Journal of Modern Auditing and Accounting*, Volume 4, No. 12, p. 2.

[2] American Accounting Association Committee on Basic Auditing Concepts (1973): *A Statement of Basic Auditing Concepts*, American Accounting Association (Sarasota, FL).

[3] American Institute of Certified Public Accountants, Code of Professional Conduct, Paragraph 53, at http://www.aicpa.org.

F. I. Lessambo, *Auditing, Assurance Services, and Forensics*,
https://doi.org/10.1007/978-3-319-90521-1_1

1.2 Attestations and Assurance Services

1.2.1 Attestation Services

Attestation involves an engagement resulting in the issuance of a report on subject matter or an assertion about the subject matter that is the responsibility of another party. Attestation services include: (i) audit, (ii) internal control over financial statements, (iii) review, (iv) information technology, and (v) others.[4] There are four types of audit services:

- Operational audit

Operational Audit is a systematic review of effectiveness, efficiency, and economy of operation. Operational audit is a future-oriented, systematic, and independent evaluation of organizational activities. The process is very similar to the processes for other forms of audits, such as the financial audit, but the operational audit process is a much more in-depth review of the business. It usually does not focus on a single department or project, because each department plays a role in the overall operational process and is interconnected. It aims to determine whether the internal controls of the business (i.e., policies and procedures) are sufficient to produce an optimum level of efficiency and effectiveness. Operational audit is often praised as a process which provides a company with objective opinions enabling it to generate quicker production or sales turnaround, better allocation of costs, improved control systems, the location of areas of delay and an overall streamlined workflow. However, like any audit process, operational audit can be time-consuming and costly.

- Compliance audit[5]

A compliance audit is a comprehensive review of an organization's adherence to regulatory guidelines. Independent accounting, security, or IT consultants evaluate the strength and thoroughness of compliance

[4] Include services such as compliance with trading policies and procedures, environmental audit. They can be extended to include assurance services, such as internal audit support, agreed upon procedures, and IT consulting.

[5] AU Section 801.

preparations. A compliance audit is based on the premise that management is responsible for the entity's compliance with compliance requirements. Management's responsibility for the entity's compliance with compliance requirements includes the following:

a. Identifying the entity's government programs and understanding and complying with the compliance requirements
b. Establishing and maintaining effective controls that provide reasonable assurance that the entity administers government programs in compliance with the compliance requirements
c. Evaluating and monitoring the entity's compliance with the compliance requirements
d. Taking corrective action when instances of noncompliance are identified, including corrective action on audit findings of the compliance audit.

The auditor's objectives in a compliance audit are to: (a) obtain sufficient appropriate audit evidence to form an opinion and report at the level specified in the governmental audit requirement on whether the entity complied in all material respects with the applicable compliance requirements; and (b) identify audit and reporting requirements specified in the governmental audit requirement that are supplementary to GAAS and Government Auditing Standards, if any, and perform procedures to address those requirements.

The auditor should determine which of those government programs and compliance requirements to test in accordance with the governmental audit requirement. The auditor should assess the risks of material noncompliance whether due to fraud or error for each applicable compliance requirement and should consider whether any of those risks are pervasive to the entity's compliance because they may affect the entity's compliance with many compliance requirements. The auditor should report noncompliance as well as other matters that are required to be reported by the governmental audit requirement in the manner specified by the governmental audit requirement.

- Financial statement audit

A financial statement audit is the examination of an entity's financial statements and accompanying disclosures by an independent auditor.

The result of this examination is a report by the auditor, attesting to the fairness of presentation of the financial statements and related disclosures. It aims to add credibility to the reported financial position and performance of a business, and is required for all publicly traded entities. The audit process is based upon management assertions. The auditor may base his or her work on financial statement assertions that differ from those in this standard if the assertions are sufficient for the auditor to identify the types of potential misstatements and to respond appropriately to the risks of material misstatement in each significant account and disclosure that has a reasonable possibility of containing misstatements that would cause the financial statements to be materially misstated, individually or in combination with other misstatements. Those assertions can be classified into the following categories:

1. Existence or occurrence—Assets or liabilities of the company exist at a given date, and recorded transactions have occurred during a given period.
2. Completeness—All transactions and accounts that should be presented in the financial statements are so included.
3. Valuation or allocation—Asset, liability, equity, revenue, and expense components have been included in the financial statements at appropriate amounts.
4. Rights and obligations—The company holds or controls rights to the assets, and liabilities are obligations of the company at a given date.
5. Presentation and disclosure—The components of the financial statements are properly classified, described, and disclosed.

1.2.2 Assurance Services

Assurance services are independent professional services that improve the quality of information, or its context, for decision makers. Assurance services include many areas of information, including nonfinancial areas. They may include process documentation, control testing, development of entity-level and activity level controls and documentation review, or an agreed-upon procedure, or IT assurances.

The needs of for assurance and related services on various types of financial information often are addressed through assurance and related services (other than audits) and through combinations of services that satisfy a particular entity's specific needs.[6]

1.3 Audit Objectives

The objectives of the audit have also evolved through time from the detection of fraud to its by prevention through adequate safeguards and principles.[7] An audit function plays a critical role in maintaining the welfare and stability of the society.[8] Today, it is well accepted that the role or function of an audit consists of providing credibility to the financial statements prepared and released by company managers for their shareholders, including the detection, the report, as well as the assessment of the business' risks.

1.4 Overall Objectives[9]

The overall objectives of the auditor, in conducting an audit of financial statements, are:

- To obtain reasonable assurance about whether the financial statements as a whole are free from material misstatement, whether due to fraud or error, thereby enabling the auditor to express an opinion on whether the financial statements are presented fairly, in all material respects, in accordance with an applicable financial reporting framework; and
- To report on the financial statements, and communicate as required by GAAS, in accordance with the auditor's findings.

In all cases when reasonable assurance cannot be obtained and a qualified opinion in the auditor's report is insufficient in the circumstances

[6]IAASB (March 2010): Assurance and Related Services on Financial Statements Other Than Audits, p. 2.

[7]Yolanda and Cathy (2010): Developments in Auditing and Assurance, Corporate Financial Reporting, NJ, p. 93.

[8]LEE Teck-Heang, Azham Md. Ali (2008): The Evolution of Auditing: An Analysis of the Historical Development, *Journal of Modern Auditing and Accounting*, Volume 4, No. 12, p. 1.

[9]AU 200.

for purposes of reporting to the intended users of the financial statements, GAAS require that the auditor disclaim an opinion or withdraw from the engagement, whenever withdrawal is possible under applicable law or regulation. The auditor's opinion on the financial statements addresses whether the financial statements are presented fairly, in all material respects, in accordance with the applicable financial reporting framework. Such an opinion is common to all audits of financial statements. The auditor's opinion, therefore, does not assure, for example, the future viability of the entity nor the efficiency or effectiveness with which management has conducted the affairs of the entity. In some circumstances, however, applicable law or regulation may require auditors to provide opinions on other specific matters, such as the effectiveness of internal control. Although GAAS include requirements and regarding such matters to the extent that they are relevant to forming an opinion on the financial statements, the auditor would be required to undertake further work if the auditor had additional responsibilities to provide such opinions.

The requirements for audits of the financial statements of governmental entities may be broader than those of other entities. As a result, the premise, relating to management's responsibilities, on which an audit of the financial statements of a governmental entity is conducted, may include additional responsibilities, such as the responsibility for the execution of transactions and events in accordance with law, regulation, or other authority (Fig. 1.1).

1.5 Reasonable Assurance

Reasonable assurance refers to the auditor's degree of satisfaction that the evidence obtained during the performance of the audit supports the assertions embodied in the financial statements. The auditor's standard report on the audit of financial statements explicitly asserts in the scope paragraph that the audit was conducted in accordance with professional standards and states that "those standards require that we plan and perform the audit to obtain *reasonable assurance* about whether the financial statements are free of material misstatement." The exercise of due professional care allows the auditor to obtain reasonable assurance that the financial statements are free of material misstatement, whether caused by error or fraud. Absolute assurance is not attainable because of the nature of the audit evidence and the characteristics of fraud. Therefore, an audit

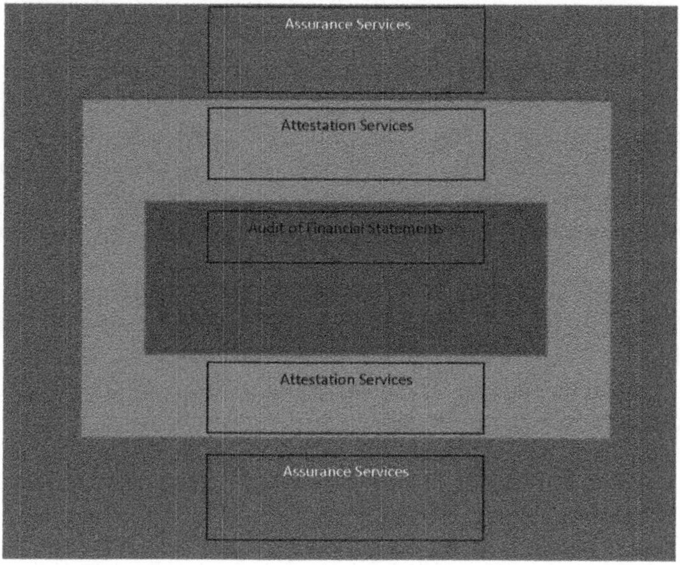

Fig. 1.1 Relationship between audits, attestations services, and assurances (*Source* The Author)

conducted in accordance with generally accepted auditing standards may not detect a material misstatement.[10]

PCAOB Auditing Standard No. 2, paragraph 17 describes reasonable assurance as follows:

> Management's assessment of the effectiveness of internal control over financial reporting is expressed at the level of reasonable assurance … Reasonable assurance includes the understanding that there is a remote likelihood that material misstatements will not be prevented or detected on a timely basis. Although not absolute assurance, reasonable assurance is, nevertheless, a high level of assurance.[11]

[10]AU Section 230.10.

[11]PCAOB Auditing Standard No. 2, An Audit of Internal Control Over Financial Reporting Performed in Conjunction With an Audit of Financial Statements.

1.6 Terms Engagement[12]

The objective of the auditor is to accept an audit engagement for a new or existing audit client only when the basis upon which it is to be performed has been agreed upon through: (a) establishing whether the preconditions for an audit are present and (b) confirming that a common understanding of the terms of the audit engagement exists between the auditor and management and, when appropriate, those charged with governance.

The auditor should agree upon the terms of the audit engagement with management or those charged with governance, as appropriate. The agreed-upon terms of the audit engagement should be documented in an audit engagement letter or other suitable form of written agreement and should include the following:

- The objective and scope of the audit of the financial statements
- The responsibilities of the auditor
- The responsibilities of management
- A statement that because of the inherent limitations of an audit, together with the inherent limitations of internal control, an unavoidable risk exists that some material misstatements may not be detected, even though the audit is properly planned and performed in accordance with GAAS
- Identification of the applicable financial reporting framework for the preparation of the financial statements
- Reference to the expected form and content of any reports to be issued by the auditor and a statement that circumstances may arise in which a report may differ from its expected form and content

Before accepting an engagement for an initial audit, including a re-audit engagement, the auditor should request management to authorize the predecessor auditor to respond fully to the auditor's inquiries regarding matters that will assist the auditor in determining whether to accept the engagement. If management refuses to authorize the predecessor auditor to respond, or limits the response, the auditor should inquire about the reasons and consider the implications of that refusal in deciding whether to accept the engagement. The auditor should evaluate the predecessor

[12] AU 210.

auditor's response, or consider the implications if the predecessor auditor provides no response or a limited response, in determining whether to accept the engagement.

On recurring audits, the auditor should assess whether circumstances require the terms of the audit engagement to be revised. If the auditor concludes that the terms of the preceding engagement need not be revised for the current engagement, the auditor should remind management of the terms of the engagement, and the reminder should be documented. The auditor should not agree to a change in the terms of the audit engagement when no reasonable justification for doing so exists. If, prior to completing the audit engagement, the auditor is requested to change the audit engagement to an engagement for which the auditor obtains a lower level of assurance, the auditor should determine whether reasonable justification for doing so exists. If the terms of the audit engagement are changed, the auditor and management should agree on and document the new terms of the engagement in an engagement letter or other suitable form of written agreement. If the auditor concludes that no reasonable justification for a change of the terms of the audit engagement exists and is not permitted by management to continue the original audit engagement, the auditor should:

- withdraw from the audit engagement when possible under applicable law or regulation,
- communicate the circumstances to those charged with governance, and
- determine whether any obligation, either legal, contractual, or otherwise, exists to report the circumstances to other parties, such as owners, or regulators.

Example of an Audit Engagement Letter

[The objective and scope of the audit]

You 2 have requested that we audit the financial statements of ABC Company, which comprise the balance sheet as of December 31, 20XX, and the related statements of income, changes in stockholders' equity, and cash flows for the year then ended, and the related notes to the financial statements. We are pleased to confirm our acceptance and our understanding of this audit engagement by means of this letter. Our audit will be conducted with the objective of our expressing an opinion on the financial statements.

[The responsibilities of the auditor]

We will conduct our audit in accordance with auditing standards generally accepted in the United States of America (GAAS). Those standards require that we plan and perform the audit to obtain reasonable assurance about whether the financial statements are free from material misstatement. An audit involves performing procedures to obtain audit evidence about the amounts and disclosures in the financial statements. The procedures selected depend on the auditor's judgment, including the assessment of the risks of material misstatement of the financial statements, whether due to fraud or error. An audit also includes evaluating the appropriateness of accounting policies used and the reasonableness of significant accounting estimates made by management, as well as evaluating the overall presentation of the financial statements.

Because of the inherent limitations of an audit, together with the inherent limitations of internal control, an unavoidable risk that some material misstatements may not be detected exists, even though the audit is properly planned and performed in accordance with GAAS.

In making our risk assessments, we consider internal control relevant to the entity's preparation and fair presentation of the financial statements in order to design audit procedures that are appropriate in the circumstances but not for the purpose of expressing an opinion on the effectiveness of the entity's internal control. However, we will communicate to you in writing concerning any significant deficiencies or material weaknesses in internal control relevant to the audit of the financial statements that we have identified during the audit.

[The responsibilities of management and identification of the applicable financial reporting framework]

Our audit will be conducted on the basis that [management and, when appropriate, those charged with governance] 3 acknowledge and understand that they have responsibility

a. for the preparation and fair presentation of the financial statements in accordance with accounting principles generally accepted in the United States of America;
b. for the design, implementation, and maintenance of internal control relevant to the preparation and fair presentation of financial statements that are free from material misstatement, whether due to fraud or error; and
c. to provide us with
   (i) access to all information of which [management] is aware that is relevant to the preparation and fair presentation of the financial statements such as records, documentation, and other matters;
   (ii) additional information that we may request from [management] for the purpose of the audit; and
   (iii) unrestricted access to persons within the entity from whom we determine it necessary to obtain audit evidence.

As part of our audit process, we will request from [management and, when appropriate, those charged with governance], written confirmation concerning representations made to us in connection with the audit.

[Other relevant information]

[Insert other information, such as fee arrangements, billings, and other specific terms, as appropriate.]

[Reporting]

[Insert appropriate reference to the expected form and content of the auditor's report. Example follows:]

> We will issue a written report upon completion of our audit of ABC Company's financial statements. Our report will be addressed to the board of directors of ABC Company. We cannot provide assurance that an unmodified opinion will be expressed. Circumstances may arise in which it is necessary for us to modify our opinion, add an emphasis-of-matter or other-matter paragraph(s), or withdraw from the engagement.
>
> We also will issue a written report on [Insert appropriate reference to other auditor's reports expected to be issued.] upon completion of our audit.
>
> Please sign and return the attached copy of this letter to indicate your acknowledgment of, and agreement with, the arrangements for our audit of the financial statements including our respective responsibilities.

1.7 Quality Control of Engagement[13]

Quality control systems, policies, and procedures are the responsibility of the audit firm. Under QC section 10, A Firm's System of Quality Control, the firm has an obligation to establish and maintain a system of quality control to provide it with reasonable assurance that (a) the firm and its personnel comply with professional standards and applicable legal and regulatory requirements and (b) reports issued by the firm are appropriate in the circumstances. Engagement teams have a responsibility to implement quality control procedures that are applicable to the audit engagement and provide the firm with relevant information to enable the functioning of that part of the firm's system of quality control relating to independence. Engagement teams are entitled to rely on the firm's system of quality control, unless the engagement partner determines that it is inappropriate to do so based on the information provided by the firm or other parties. The engagement partner may use the

[13]AU 220.

assistance of other members of the engagement team or other personnel within the firm in meeting the requirements under QC section 10. These requirements do not relieve other members of the engagement team of any of their professional responsibilities.

Appendix

- Auditor Independence: Evidence on the Joint Effects of Auditor Tenure and Non-audit Fees, by Ferdinand A. Gul, Bikki L. Jaggi, and Gopal V. Krishnan; *AUDITING: A Journal of Practice & Theory*, November 2006, Vol. 25, No. 2, pp. 1–23.

Practice

Question 1

Docilo LLC is an audit firm based in Tarrytown, NY. Docilo has accepted a new engagement to perform audit services for Danger T, Inc. The auditor professional responsibilities is to:

(a) The client only
(b) The state of New York
(c) The public
(d) The client, the public, and the shareholders

Question 2

Management's responsibility for the entity's compliance with compliance requirements includes the following:

(a) Identifying the entity's government programs and understanding and complying with the compliance requirements
(b) Establishing and maintaining effective controls that provide reasonable assurance that the entity administers government programs in compliance with the compliance requirements
(c) Evaluating and monitoring the entity's compliance with the compliance requirements
(d) Taking corrective action when instances of noncompliance are identified, including corrective action on audit findings of the compliance audit
(e) All of the above

Question 3

The following are types of assurance services with the exception of:

(a) Training engagement
(b) Due diligence engagement
(c) Compliance engagement
(d) Financial engagement

Question 4

The following are types of assurance services with the exception of:

(a) Legal counsel engagement
(b) Facilitation engagement
(c) Advice engagement
(d) System security engagement

Question 5

An accountant's objective of a review of the financial statements of a non-issuer (nonpublic company) is to provide what type of assurance?

(a) Absolute assurance
(b) Limited assurance
(c) No assurance
(d) Reasonable assurance

CHAPTER 2

The Audit Profession: The US Sarbanes-Oxley Act

2.1 General

The Sarbanes-Oxley Act of 2002 (the "SOX") was enacted to fix a string of auditing scandals in the United States. US corporations engage often in massive financial statements' frauds with the help or assistance of big auditing firms. The number of audit failures implicating top audit firms grew significantly over the last three decades. To quote just some well-known scandals: (i) in 2000, Ernst & Young settled for a record $335 million; (ii) in 2001, an SEC investigation revealed over 8000 violations at PricewaterhouseCoopers, with top partners owning stocks in their audit client firms; and (iii) in 2002, Arthur Anderson destroyed it work pursuant to Enron and disappeared or cease to exist.[1] Four theories have been proposed to explain the occurrence of audit frauds in the US: (i) the de-professionalization of the auditing or a loss of the capacity to detect fraud[2]; (ii) the sale of consulting services to the same client firms they are called to audit[3]; and (iii) the reduced liability by auditing firms

[1] John C. Coates IV (2007): The Goals and Promise of the Sarbanes-Oxley Act, *Journal of Economic Perspectives*, Volume 21, No. 1, p. 94.

[2] Paul Healy and Krishna G. Palepu (2003): How the Quest for Efficiency Undermined the Market, *Harvard Business Review*, July 1, 2003.

[3] Levitt Arthur, Jr. (2002): Accounting and Investor Protection Issued Raised by Enron and Other Public Companies, available at http://www.iasplus.com/resource/levitt.pdf.

F. I. Lessambo, *Auditing, Assurance Services, and Forensics*,
https://doi.org/10.1007/978-3-319-90521-1_2

to face up their mishaps,[4] unfettered deregulation, which started in the 1980s.[5]

Prior to the SOX Act, the auditing profession was self-regulated, with light state and federal oversight. A Public Oversight Board did exist since 1978, but the board was hijacked by accountants, funded by auditors, with no inspection at all. When the series of audit scandal hit the media, the Public Oversight Board resigned in 2002, leaving an auditing profession without any watchdog.

The SOX Act filled the blank with the creation of the Public Company Accounting Oversight Board (PCAOB). The SOX Act provides rules concerning the oversight of the auditors, the responsibility of corporate officers for the accuracy and completeness of corporate financial statements, the relationship between public company auditors and auditor-client, the enhancement of corporate financial statements disclosure, the enhancement of corporate governance standards. It extends the Securities and Exchange Commission powers, criminalizes auditing frauds, and protects whistleblowers against retaliation.

2.2 The Public Company Accounting Oversight Board

The United States PCAOB is a private sector, nonprofit corporation, created by the Sarbanes-Oxley Act of 2002, to oversee the auditors of public companies in order to protect the interests of investors and further the public interest in the preparation of informative, fair, and independent audit reports.

The PCAOB is neither a pure private body nor a governmental agency. Rather it is a nonprofit corporation with a mandate to oversee public company auditors and protect investors. It is to many a 'sui-generis'[6] private body with a public mandate. It is private in a sense that its charter clearly states that it not a government or public agency and its employees are not government agents. It is public in a sense that its board is appointed by the Security and Exchange Commission, and its budget funded by the SEC. The hybrid nature of the PCAOB would

[4] John C. Coffee IV (1999): *Gatekeepers: The Professions and Corporate Governance*, Oxford University Press.

[5] Felix Lessambo (2013): *The International Banking System: Capital Adequacy, Core Businesses, and Risk Management*, Palgrave Macmillan, Chapter 1.

[6] Constituting a class alone, unique, peculiar.

not sustain the auditing crisis to come, and the PCAOB would better become a public agency under the straight oversight of the Treasury. The PCAOB employs 500 persons, including 300 full-time inspectors who audit firms with more than 100 public company clients.

2.2.1 PCAOB Standards and Rules

PCAOB Rule 3100, Compliance with Auditing and Related Professional Practice Standards, requires registered public accounting firms and their associated persons to comply with all applicable auditing and related professional practice standards. PCAOB auditing and related professional practice standards include the following: (i) auditing standards; (ii) attestation standards; (iii) ethics and independence standards and rules; and (iv) quality control standards.

Additionally, PCAOB Rule 3101 defines specific terms that are used to describe the auditor's responsibilities when complying with PCAOB auditing and related professional standards (among others: "must," "should," and "may"). In short, PCAOB Rule 3100 describes three categories of responsibilities:

- Unconditional Responsibility: The words "must," "shall," and "is required" indicate unconditional responsibilities. The auditor must fulfill responsibilities of this type in all cases in which the circumstances exist to which the requirement applies. Failure to discharge an unconditional responsibility is a violation of the relevant standard and PCAOB Rule 3100.
- Presumptively Mandatory Responsibility: The word "should" indicates responsibilities that are presumptively mandatory. The auditor must comply with requirements of this type specified in the Board's standards unless the auditor demonstrates that alternative actions he or she followed in the circumstances were sufficient to achieve the objectives of the standard. Failure to discharge a presumptively mandatory responsibility is a violation of the relevant standard and PCAOB Rule 3100 unless the auditor demonstrates that, in the circumstances, compliance with the specified responsibility was not necessary to achieve the objectives of the standard.

In the rare circumstances in which the auditor believes the objectives of the standard can be met by alternative means, the auditor, as part of documenting the planning and performance of the work, must document the information that demonstrates that the objectives were achieved.

- Responsibility to Consider: The words "may," "might," "could," and other terms and phrases describe actions and procedures that auditors have a responsibility to consider. Matters described in this fashion require the auditor's attention and understanding. How and whether the auditor implements these matters in the audit will depend on the exercise of professional judgment in the circumstances consistent with the objectives of the standard.

If a Board standard provides that the auditor "should consider" an action or procedure, consideration of the action.

2.2.2 *The PCAOB Responsibilities*

The PCAOB has four main responsibilities which include:

- Registration of accounting firms (including non-US firms) that audit public companies (including non-US issuers) trading in US securities markets;
- Inspections of registered public accounting firms;
- Establishment of auditing and related attestation, quality control, ethics, and independence standards for registered public accounting firms; and
- Investigation and discipline of registered public accounting firms and their associated persons for violations of specified laws or professional standards.

1. Registration of Accounting Firms
   Public accounting firms engaged in the preparation or issuance of any audit with respect to an issuer must be registered with the PCAOB. Further the registrant must consent to cooperate with the Board and pay a registration fee as well as annual fees. The registration form shall provide the following information:

   (a) The names of all issuers for which the firm prepared or issued audit reports during the immediately preceding calendar year, and for which the firm expects to prepare or issue audit reports the current calendar year;

(b) The annual fees received by the firm from each issuer for audit services, other accounting services, and non-audit services;

(c) Such other current financial information from the most recently completed fiscal year of the firm as the Board may reasonably request;

(d) A statement of the quality control policies of the firm for its accounting and auditing practices;

(e) A list of all accountants associated with the firm who participate in or contribute to the preparation of audit reports, stating the license or certification number of each such person, as well as the State license numbers of the firm itself;

(f) Information relating to criminal, civil, or administrative actions or disciplinary proceedings pending against the firm or any associated person of the firm in connection with any audit report;

(g) Copies of any periodic or annual disclosure filed by an issuer with the Commission (SEC) during the immediately preceding calendar year which discloses accounting disagreements between such issuer and the firm in connection with an audit report furnished or prepared by the firm for such issuer; and

(h) Such other information as the rules of the Board or the Commission shall specify as necessary or appropriate in the public interest or for the protection of investors.

2. Inspections of Registered Public Accounting Firms
Registered firms are subject to the rules and program inspections by the PCAOB.[7] The inspection program extends to every SEC-registered brokers dealer, which must have their financial statements certified by the SEC. The inspections shall be conducted: (a) annually with respect to each registered public accounting firm that regularly provides audit reports for more than 100 issuers; and (b) not less frequently than once every three years with respect to each registered public accounting firm that regularly provides audit

[7] The Sarbanes-Oxley Act of 2002, Section 104.

reports for 100 or fewer issuers. In conducting its inspections, the PCAOB shall:

- Inspect and review selected audit and review engagements of the firm;
- Evaluate the sufficiency of the quality control system of the firm;
- Perform such other testing of the audit, supervisory, and quality control procedures of the firm.

At the end of each inspection, a written report of findings is given to the inspected firm. Violations may include: civil monetary penalties, the revocation of the firm registration, and the barring of an associated person from participating or sharing in the benefits of audits for public companies.
The procedural steps of the PCAOB inspections can be summarized as follow:

- Notification
  At the start of an inspection, the PCAOB notifies the accounting firm about the date(s) scheduled to conduct the inspection, and provides a detailed request of information about the firm's public company engagements, the personnel performing those audits, and the firm's quality control program.

- Selection of Audit Engagements to be Reviewed
  The PCAOB generally takes a risk-based approach in selecting the audit engagements to be reviewed. As a result, inspections do not involve a random or representative sample of a firm's public company practice. The PCAOB has developed a variety of tools to identify audits that may pose difficult or complex/challenging issues. The PCAOB risk factors include, inter alia, the nature of the company, its market capitalization; the audit issues likely to be encountered; the type and range of its public company engagements, the results of prior PCAOB inspections.

- The Field Inspection
  The field inspection aims to assess whether (i) the firm has complied with all PCAOB's auditing standards, and (ii) the firm quality control is effective.

(i) PCAOB Standards
A field inspection does not cover the entire engagement, but rather concentrates on areas that appear to the inspectors to present significant challenges or difficulties. The Registered firm is required to cooperate with the inspection and provide all requested information. The team auditors of the selected engagements must provide the firm work papers thereon.

(ii) Firm Quality Control
A firm quality control review is tailored to the size of the firm and the nature of its practice. The PCAOB's review focuses on how these systems operate in practice and on how they impact audit engagements. PCAOB inspectors consider issues such as the review of management structure and processes, review of partner management, review of engagement acceptance and retention, review of the use of audit work performed by foreign affiliates, review of the firm's processes for monitoring audit performance.

- Dialogue between the PCAOB and Audit Firm
A dialogue follows between the Inspector(s) and the team auditor(s) concerning the firm compliance with the PCAOB audit standards and the firm quality control. For any aspect of the audit that the inspector believes to be in departure from the PCAOB standard the team auditor would have to respond and provide explanation. The firm has the opportunity to present its views on any aspects of the audit that the inspectors needed further explanations.

- The Issuance of the Report of Inspection
At the conclusion of the inspection fieldwork and the review of the firm' explanations the PCAOB will send a final inspection report to the firm. The PCAOB report has two-components or parts. Part I addresses findings related to compliance with the Board auditing standards, and Part II treats firm quality control findings. At that juncture, the firm can either address within a requested time or seek for the SEC review.

- The Remediation
  A firm is given a time to remediate all audit deficiencies and quality control identified in the report. Most the time, the firm would respond and comply with the Board finding before even the issuance of the report. As to quality control findings, the firm has 12 months to satisfactorily remediate the issues. The PCAOB remains in contact with the firm within these 12 months to respond to any query that the firm may have. After 12 months, if the PCAOB is not satisfied with a firm's remediation, it will publish on its website the portion of the inspection report that discusses the quality control criticism that has not been satisfactorily remediated. Again, the firm can reach out to the SEC to reconsider the Board determination.

3. Establishment of Auditing Standards
   The Sarbanes-Oxley Act has vested in the PCOB the right to set up specific auditing standards. The PCAOB has adopted, so far, 14 principles which have been approved by the Securities and Exchange Commission.[8]

AS No. 1	References in Auditors' Reports to the Standards of the Public Company Accounting Oversight Board
AS No. 3	Audit Documentation
AS No. 4	Reporting on Whether a Previously Reported Material Weakness Continues to Exist
AS No. 5	An Audit of Internal Control over Financial Reporting that is Integrated with An Audit of Financial Statements
AS No. 6	Evaluating Consistency of Financial Statements
AS No. 7	Engagement Quality Review
AS No. 8	Audit Risk
AS No. 9	Audit Planning
AS No. 10	Supervision of the Audit Engagement
AS No. 11	Consideration of Materiality in Planning and Performing an Audit

[8] PCAOB (2012).

AS No. 12	Identifying and Assessing Risks of Material Misstatement
AS No. 13	The Auditor's Responses to the Risks of Material Misstatement
AS No. 14	Evaluating Audit Results
AS No. 15	Audit Evidence

4. Investigation and Discipline of Registered Public Accounting
The PCAOB conducts in-depth selected reviews of individual audit engagements performed by registered public account firms to determine compliance with the GAAS, the GAAP, the SEC, and other mandatory rules. The procedures and conduct of these reviews are covered under Section 105 of the SOX Act. Under section 105 (b)(2), the board may:

(a) Require the testimony of the firm or of any person associated with a registered public accounting firm, with respect to any matter that the Board considers relevant or material to an investigation;
(b) Require the production of audit work papers and any other document or information in the possession of a registered public accounting firm or any associated person thereof, wherever domiciled… and the board may inspect the books and records of such firm or associated person to verify the accuracy of any documents or information supplied;
(c) Request the testimony of, and production of any document in the possession of, any other person, including any client of a registered public accounting firm that the Board considers relevant or material to an investigation, subject to a proper notice;
(d) Provide for procedures to seek issuance by the SEC, in a manner established by the SEC, of a subpoena to require the testimony of, and production of any document in the possession of, any person, including any client of a registered public accounting firm that the Board considers relevant or material to an investigation.

It is worthy to note that the investigation exercise is flawed in a sense that when the PCAOB publishes the conclusions of its findings, the opinion certifying the financial statements is already published and both the Markets and the investors relied upon to make their decisions. Big public accounting firms are not even impressed by the PCAOB reviews for several reasons:

(i) the reviews will covered a miniscule portion of their auditing engagements;
(ii) the PCAOB finding are not automatically made available to the public, therefore they can play the commitment game to comply;
(iii) the PCAOB is understaffed with only 300 full-time inspectors;
(iv) public accounting firms provide non-auditing services that have come to bring more revenue than the core auditing services, and the PCAOB inspectors do not possess polyvalent skills to link the tax considerations to the underpinning accounting. Failure to cooperate with the Board investigation entails sanctions such as suspension or revocation of the license and other sanction that the Board consider appropriate.

2.2.3 The PCAOB Enforcement Role

The PCAOB is authorized to impose sanctions or penalties to deter possible violations in order to enhance the quality and reliability of auditing. These sanctions range from revoking a firm's registration to barring a delinquent auditor of a public accounting firm from practicing auditing.

2.3 The Audit Committee

The SOX Act gives some specific powers to the audit committee of a public company. The audit committee is a subsection of the board of directors, composed of independent directors. From its independent status, a member of an audit committee shall not (i) accept any consulting, advisory, or other compensatory fee from the issuer; or (ii) be an affiliated person of the issuer or any subsidiary thereof. Under the SOX Act of 2002, section 301(2), the audit committee of a public company is responsible for:

- Direct appointment, compensation, and oversight of the work of a registered public accounting firm retained or employed by the firm management;

- Resolving any disagreements that may arise between the management and the external auditor regarding financial reporting, the audit or any related work or report;
- Establishing procedures for: (a) the receipt, retention, and treatment of complaints received by the issuer regarding accounting, internal accounting controls, or auditing matters; and (b) the confidential, anonymous submissions by employees of the issuer of concerns regarding questionable accounting or auditing matters.

More, under section 204 of the SOX Act each registered public accounting firm that performs for any issuer any audit assignment should report the following to the audit committee of the issuer:

- All critical accounting policies and practices to be used;
- All alternative treatments of financial information within GAAPs that have been discussed with management official and the public accounting firm and the public accounting firm preferences thereon;
- Other material written communication between the registered public accounting firm and the management of the issuer, such as any management letter or schedule of unadjusted differences.

Finally, section 407 of the SOX Act of 2002 requires that at least one member of the audit committee be a financial expert.

2.4 Use of IT in SOX Compliance (Auditboard)

It automates the firm entire SOX program in one simple tool, empowering auditors to scale their SOX compliance operations. It fully integrates platform for SOX, operational audits, IT compliance, and ERM, all united by a powerful, intuitive workflow.

Appendix

- SOX 404, Auditor Effort, and the Prevention of Financial Report Misstatements by Yuping Zhao, Jean C. Bedard, and Rani Hoitash; *AUDITING: A Journal of Practice & Theory*, November 2016, Vol. 35, No. 4, pp. 1–22.
- The Association between Audit Partner Rotation and Audit Fees: Empirical Evidence from the Australian Market by Jenny Stewart,

Pamela Kent, and James Routledge; *AUDITING: A Journal of Practice & Theory*, November 2015, Vol. 34, No. 4, pp. 1–32.
- PCAOB Quality Control Inspection Reports and Auditor Reputation by Albert L. Nagy; *AUDITING: A Journal of Practice & Theory*, May 2014, Vol. 33, No. 2, pp. 111–139.
- An Analysis of SEC and PCAOB Enforcement Actions against Engagement Quality Reviewers by William F. Messier, Jr., Thomas M. Kozloski, and Natalia Kochetova-Kozloski; *AUDITING: A Journal of Practice & Theory*, May 2010, Vol. 29, No. 1, pp. 207–220.
- Audit Committee Financial Expertise, Litigation Risk, and Corporate Governance by Jagan Krishnan and Jong Eun Lee; *AUDITING: A Journal of Practice & Theory*, November 2008, Vol. 27, No. 2, pp. 231–252.

Further Reading

PUBLIC COMPANY ACCOUNTING OVERSIGHT BOARD

In the Matter of)

PricewaterhouseCoopers LLP's)

Quality Control Remediation)

Submissions)

PCAOB Release No.104-2013-054

March 7, 2013

The Public Company Accounting Oversight Board ("Board" or "PCAOB") has evaluated the submissions of PricewaterhouseCoopers LLP ("the Firm") pursuant to PCAOB Rule 4009(a) for the remediation periods ended March 25, 2010 and August 12, 2011 concerning the Firm's efforts to address certain quality control criticisms included in the nonpublic portions of the Board's March 25, 2009 and August 12, 2010 inspection reports on the Firm ("the Reports"). The Board has determined that as of March 25, 2010 and August 12, 2011, respectively, the Firm had not addressed certain criticisms in the Reports to the Board's satisfaction. Accordingly, pursuant to Section 104(g)(2) of the Sarbanes-Oxley Act of 2002 ("the Act") and PCAOB Rule 4009(d), the Board is making public the portions of the Reports that deal with those criticisms.

The Firm has notified the Board that it will not seek Securities and Exchange Commission review of the determination, which the Firm has a right to do under the Act and Commission rules. The Firm has requested that a related statement by the Firm be attached as an Appendix to this release, and the Board has granted that request. By allowing the Firm's statement to be attached as an Appendix to this release, however, the Board is not endorsing, confirming, or adopting as the Board's view any element of the Firm's statement.

II

The quality control remediation process is central to the Board's efforts to cause firms to improve the quality of their audits and thereby better protect investors. The Board therefore takes very seriously the importance of firms making sufficient progress on quality control issues identified in an inspection report in the 12 months following the report. Particularly with the largest firms, which are inspected annually, the Board devotes considerable time and resources to critically evaluating whether the firm did in fact make sufficient progress in that period. The Board makes the relevant criticisms public when a firm has failed to do so to the Board's satisfaction.

It is not unusual for an inspection report to include nonpublic criticisms of several aspects of a firm's system of quality control. Any Board judgment that results in later public disclosure is a judgment about whether the firm made sufficient effort and progress to address the particular criticisms articulated in the report on that firm in the 12 months immediately following the report date. It is not a broad judgment about the effectiveness of a firm's system of quality control compared to those of other firms, and it does not signify anything about the merits of any additional efforts a firm may have made to address the criticisms after the 12-month period.

ISSUED BY THE BOARD.

/s/ Phoebe W. Brown

Phoebe W. Brown

Secretary

March 7, 2013

Statement of PricewaterhouseCoopers LLP on the PCAOB's March 7, 2013, Release No. 104-2013-054

The execution of quality audits in full compliance with PCAOB standards is the top priority of our practice and something in which our professionals take a significant amount of personal and professional pride. We continue to support the mission of the Public Company Accounting Oversight Board.

The Board issued a Release today making public certain portions of Part II of our 2008–2009 Inspection Reports (the "Part II comments"). The Release is based on the Board's determination that we did not address the matters contained in the Part II comments to the Board's satisfaction during the 12 month period following issuance of the reports. We believe that our actions in response to the Part II comments were significant, but we acknowledge the Board's determination with a view toward continued cooperation with the Board and in furtherance of our commitment to audit quality.

The Part II comments relate to some of the most complex, judgmental and evolving areas of auditing. Our actions relating to those areas, during the 12 months following issuance of the comments and thereafter, have included providing our audit professionals with enhanced audit tools, training and additional technical guidance to promote more consistent audit execution. We believe that these efforts have been important positive contributors to audit quality at our firm. We are proud of our focus on continuous improvement and of the dedication and high-quality audit work performed by our partners and other professionals.

As the Board has explained, "[i]t is not unusual for an inspection report to include nonpublic criticisms of several aspects of a firm's system of quality control. Any Board judgment that results in later public disclosure is a judgment about whether the firm made sufficient effort and progress to address the particular criticisms articulated in the report on that firm in the 12 months immediately following the report date. It is not a broad judgment about the effectiveness of a firm's system of quality control compared to those of other firms, and it does not signify anything about the merits of any additional efforts a firm may have made to address the criticisms after the 12-month period."

We are one of the world's largest audit practices and a leader in the profession, and we are committed to maintaining our leading role in promoting further improvements in auditing and financial reporting and delivering the highest quality audits in the profession. We look forward to continuing our dialogue with the Board in support of our commitment to audit quality.

Source: PCAOB.

Practice

Question 1

The PCAOB auditing and related professional practice standards include the following, except:

(a) Auditing standards
(b) Attestation standards
(c) Ethics and independence standards and rules
(d) Quality control standards
(e) All the above

Question 2

The PCAOB main responsibilities include the following, except:

(a) Registration of accounting firms (including non-US firms) that audit public companies (including non-US issuers) trading in US securities markets
(b) Inspections of registered public accounting firms
(c) Providing a letter grade to public accounting firms
(d) Establishment of auditing and related attestation, quality control, ethics, and independence standards for registered public accounting firms
(e) Investigation and discipline of registered public accounting firms and their associated persons for violations of specified laws or professional standards

Question 3

In conducting its inspections, the PCAOB shall perform these below-mentioned except:

(a) Inspect and review selected audit and review engagements of the firm
(b) Assess the qualification of the partners
(c) Evaluate the sufficiency of the quality control system of the firm
(d) Perform such other testing of the audit, supervisory, and quality control procedures of the firm

Question 4

Under the SOX Act of 2002, section 301(2), the audit committee of a public company is responsible for, except:

(a) Direct appointment, compensation, and oversight of the work of a registered public accounting firm retained or employed by the firm management
(b) Providing clear and sound guidelines to the Chief Financial Officer
(c) Resolving any disagreements that may arise between the management and the external auditor regarding financial reporting, the audit or any related work or report
(d) Establishing procedures for the receipt, retention, and treatment of complaints received by the issuer regarding accounting, internal accounting controls, or auditing matters; and the confidential, anonymous submissions by employees of the issuer of concerns regarding questionable accounting or auditing matters

Question 5

Under section 204 of the SOX Act each registered public accounting firm that performs for any issuer any audit assignment should report the following to the audit committee of the issuer, except:

(a) All critical accounting policies and practices to be used
(b) All alternative treatments of financial information within GAAPs that have been discussed with management official and the public accounting firm and the public accounting firm preferences thereon

(c) The salaries of the top executives
(d) Other material written communication between the registered public accounting firm and the management of the issuer, such as any management letter or schedule of unadjusted differences

CHAPTER 3

The International Auditing and Assurance Standards Board

3.1 General

The International Auditing and Assurance Standards Board (IAASB) is an independent standard-setting body that serves the public interest by setting high-quality international standards for auditing, assurance, and other related standards, and by facilitating the convergence of international and national auditing and assurance standards. The IAASB aims to enhance the quality and consistency of practice throughout the world and to strengthen public confidence in the global auditing and assurance profession.

Founded in March 1978, the IAASB was previously known as the International Auditing Practices Committee (IAPC), which initial work focused on three areas: object and scope of audits of financial statements, engagement letters, and general auditing guidelines. In 1991, the IAPC's guidelines were recodified as International Standards on Auditing (ISAs).[1] In 2001, a comprehensive review of the IAPC was undertaken, and in 2002, the IAPC was reconstituted as the IAASB. In 2004, the IAASB began the Clarity Project, a comprehensive program to enhance the clarity of its ISAs.[2] This program involved the application of new conventions to all ISAs, either as part of a substantive revision or

[1] http://www.iaasb.org/about-iaasb.

[2] http://www.iaasb.org/about-iaasb.

F. I. Lessambo, *Auditing, Assurance Services, and Forensics*,
https://doi.org/10.1007/978-3-319-90521-1_3

through a limited redrafting to reflect the new conventions and matters of clarity generally.

The Audit Directive of May 17, 2006 enforces the use of the International Standards on Auditing for all statutory audits to be performed in the European Union.

3.2 List of the Standards

Since its inception, the IAASB has published a series of ISAs:

- ISA 200: Overall Objectives of the Independent Auditor and the Conduct of an Audit in Accordance with International Standards on Auditing
- ISA 210: Agreeing the Terms of Audit Engagements
- ISA 220: Quality Control for an Audit of Financial Statements
- ISA 230: Audit Documentation
- ISA 240: The Auditor's Responsibilities Relating to Fraud in an Audit of Financial Statements
- ISA 250: Consideration of Laws and Regulations in an Audit of Financial Statements
- ISA 260: Communication with Those Charged with Governance
- ISA 265: Communicating Deficiencies in Internal Control to Those Charged with Governance and Management
- ISA 299: Responsibility of Joint Auditors
- ISA 300: Planning an Audit of Financial Statements
- ISA 315: Identifying and assessing the risks of material misstatement through understanding the entity and its environment
- ISA 320: Materiality in planning and performing an audit
- ISA 330: The auditor's responses to assessed risks
- ISA 402: Audit Considerations Relating to an Entity Using a Service Organization
- ISA 450: Evaluation of Misstatements Identified during the Audit
- ISA 500: Audit Evidence
- ISA 501: Audit Evidence—Additional Considerations for Specific Items
- ISA 505: External Confirmations
- ISA 510: Initial Engagements—Opening Balances
- ISA 520: Analytical Procedures
- ISA 530: Audit Sampling and Other Means of Testing

- ISA 540: Auditing Accounting Estimates, Including Fair Value Accounting Estimates, and Related Disclosures
- ISA 550: Related Parties
- ISA 560: Subsequent Events
- ISA 570: Going Concern
- ISA 580: Written Representations
- ISA 600: Special Considerations—Audits of Group Financial Statements (Including the Work of Component Auditors)
- ISA 610: Using the Work of Internal Auditors
- ISA 620: Using the Work of an Auditor's Expert
- ISA 700: Forming an Opinion and Reporting on Financial Statements
- ISA 705: Modifications to the Opinion in the Independent Auditor's Report
- ISA 706: Emphasis of Matter Paragraphs and Other Matter Paragraphs in the Independent Auditor's Report
- ISA 710: Comparative Information—Corresponding Figures and Comparative Financial Statements
- ISA 720: The Auditor's Responsibilities Relating to Other Information in Documents Containing Audited Financial Statements
- ISA 800: Special Considerations-Audits of Financial Statements Prepared in Accordance with Special Purpose Frameworks
- ISA 805: Special Considerations-Audits of Single Financial Statements and Specific Elements, Accounts or Items of a Financial Statement
- ISA 810: Engagements to Report on Summary Financial Statements

3.3 IAASB Due Process

The IAASB follows a rigorous due process in developing its pronouncements. Input is obtained from a wide range of stakeholders including the IAASB's Consultative Advisory Group national auditing standard setters, IFAC member bodies and their members, regulatory and oversight bodies, firms, governmental agencies, investors, preparers, and the general public. Exposure drafts of proposed pronouncements are posted on the website and comments are invited; final pronouncements are accompanied by a basis of conclusions with respect to comments received.

The Public Interest Oversight Board (PIOB) oversees the work of the IAASB and its CAG to ensure that the activities of the IAASB follow due process and are responsive to the public interest. The IAASB is dedicated to operating as transparently as possible. IAASB meetings are open to the public and meeting agendas, agenda papers, and meeting highlights are posted on the website. In addition, the website includes project histories, audio recordings of the IAASB meetings, IAASB exposure drafts and all comments made on those drafts by stakeholders.

Practice

Question 1

Which of the following assertions is accurate concerning the IAASB?

(a) The International Auditing and Assurance Standards Board (IAASB) is an independent standard-setting body that serves the public interest
(b) The IAASB sets up high-quality international standards for auditing, assurance, and other related standards
(c) The IAASS facilitates the convergence of international and national auditing and assurance standards
(d) The IAASB aims to enhance the quality and consistency of practice throughout the world and to strengthen public confidence in the global auditing and assurance profession
(e) All of the above

Question 2

Which of the following is accurate concerning the IAASB due process?

(a) The IAASB follows a rigorous due process in developing its pronouncement
(b) Input is obtained from a wide range of stakeholders including the IAASB's Consultative Advisory Group national auditing standard setters, IFAC member bodies and their members, regulatory and oversight bodies, firms, governmental agencies, investors, preparers, and the general public
(c) Exposure drafts of proposed pronouncements are posted on the website and comments are invited

(d) Final pronouncements are accompanied by a basis of conclusions with respect to comments received
(e) All of the above

CHAPTER 4

Generally Accepted Auditing Standards, Audit Planning and Engagement Quality Review

4.1 General

An independent auditor plans, conducts, and reports the results of an audit in accordance with generally accepted auditing standards (GAAS). Auditing standards provide a measure of audit quality and the objectives to be achieved in an audit. Auditing procedures differ from auditing standards. Auditing procedures are acts that the auditor performs during the course of an audit to comply with auditing standards.

Planning the audit includes establishing the overall audit strategy for the engagement and developing an audit plan, which includes, in particular, planned risk assessment procedures and planned responses to the risks of material misstatement. Planning is not a discrete phase of an audit but, rather, a continual and iterative process that might begin shortly after (or in connection with) the completion of the previous audit and continues until the completion of the current audit.

The objective of the engagement quality reviewer is to perform an evaluation of the significant judgments made by the engagement team and the related conclusions reached in forming the overall conclusion on the engagement and in preparing the engagement report, if a report is to be issued, in order to determine whether to provide concurring approval of issuance.

F. I. Lessambo, *Auditing, Assurance Services, and Forensics*,
https://doi.org/10.1007/978-3-319-90521-1_4

4.2 AICPA Auditing Standards

The general, field work, and reporting standards (the 10 standards) approved and adopted by the membership of the AICPA, as amended by the AICPA Auditing Standards Board (ASB), are as follows:

4.2.1 General Standards

- The audit is to be performed by a person or persons having adequate technical training and proficiency as an auditor.
- In all matters relating to the assignment, an independence in mental attitude is to be maintained by the auditor or auditors.
- Due professional care is to be exercised in the performance of the audit and the preparation of the report.

4.2.2 Standards of Field Work

- The work is to be adequately planned and assistants, if any, are to be properly supervised.
- A sufficient understanding of internal control is to be obtained to plan the audit and to determine the nature, timing, and extent of tests to be performed.
- Sufficient appropriate evidential matter is to be obtained through inspection, observation, inquiries, and confirmations to afford a reasonable basis for an opinion regarding the financial statements under audit.

4.2.3 Standards of Reporting

- The report shall state whether the financial statements are presented in accordance with generally accepted accounting principles (GAAP).
- The report shall identify those circumstances in which such principles have not been consistently observed in the current period in relation to the preceding period.
- Informative disclosures in the financial statements are to be regarded as reasonably adequate unless otherwise stated in the report.
- The report shall contain either an expression of opinion regarding the financial statements, taken as a whole, or an assertion to the

effect that an opinion cannot be expressed. When an overall opinion cannot be expressed, the reasons therefor should be stated. In all cases where an auditor's name is associated with financial statements, the report should contain a clear-cut indication of the character of the auditor's work, if any, and the degree of responsibility the auditor is taking.

The auditor should have sufficient knowledge of the SASs to identify those that are applicable to his or her audit. The nature of the 10 standards and the SASs requires the auditor to exercise professional judgment in applying them. Materiality and audit risk also underlie the application of the 10 standards and the SASs, particularly those related to field work and reporting. The auditor should be prepared to justify departures from the SASs.

4.3 Interpretive Publications

Interpretive publications consist of auditing Interpretations of the SASs, appendixes to the SASs, auditing guidance included in AICPA Audit and Accounting Guides, and AICPA auditing Statements of Position. Interpretive publications are not auditing standards. Interpretive publications are recommendations on the application of the SASs in specific circumstances, including engagements for entities in specialized industries. An interpretive publication is issued under the authority of the ASB after all ASB members have been provided an opportunity to consider and comment on whether the proposed interpretive publication is consistent with the SASs.

The auditor should be aware of and consider interpretive publications applicable to his or her audit. If the auditor does not apply the auditing guidance included in an applicable interpretive publication, the auditor should be prepared to explain how he or she complied with the SAS provisions addressed by such auditing guidance.

4.4 Other Auditing Publications

Other auditing publications include AICPA auditing publications not referred to above; auditing articles in the Journal of Accountancy and other professional journals; auditing articles in the AICPA CPA Letter; continuing professional education programs and other instruction materials, textbooks, guidebooks, audit programs, and checklists; and other auditing publications from state CPA societies, other organizations, and individuals. Other auditing publications have no authoritative status; however, they may help the auditor understand and apply the SASs. If an auditor applies the auditing guidance included in another auditing publication, he or she should be satisfied that, in his or her judgment, it is both relevant to the circumstances of the audit, and appropriate. In determining whether another auditing publication is appropriate, the auditor may wish to consider the degree to which the publication is recognized as being helpful in understanding and applying the SASs and the degree to which the issuer or author is recognized as an authority in auditing matters. Other auditing publications published by the AICPA that have been reviewed by the AICPA Audit and Attest Standards staff are presumed to be appropriate.

4.5 PCAOB Auditing Standard

The PCAOB standards have been classified as either definitive standards or interim standards.

4.5.1 Professional Standards

The Sarbanes-Oxley Act of 2002 authorized the Public Company Accounting Oversight Board ("PCAOB") to establish auditing and related professional practice standards to be used by registered public accounting firms. PCAOB Rule 3100, Compliance with Auditing and Related Professional Practice Standards, requires the auditor to comply with all applicable auditing and related professional practice standards of the PCAOB. The professional qualifications required of the independent auditor are those of a person with the education and experience to practice as such.

The independent auditor has the responsibility to comply with the standards accepted by his fellow practitioners. In recognition of the importance of such compliance, the American Institute of Certified Public Accountants has adopted, as part of its Code of Professional Conduct, rules which support the standards and provide a basis for their enforcement.[1]

[1] AU Section 110—Responsibilities and Functions of the Independent Auditor.

4.5.1.1 The General Standards[2]

The general standards are personal in nature and are concerned with the qualifications of the auditor and the quality of his work as distinct from those standards which relate to the performance of his field work and to his reporting. These personal, or general, standards apply alike to the areas of field work and reporting.

- The first general standard is that audit is to be performed by a person or persons having adequate technical training and proficiency as an auditor. Capable a person may be in other fields, including business and finance, he cannot meet the requirements of the auditing standards without proper education and experience in the field of auditing.
- The second general standard is that in all matters relating to the assignment, an independence in mental attitude is to be maintained by the auditor or auditors. However, independence does not imply the attitude of a prosecutor but rather a judicial impartiality that recognizes an obligation for fairness not only to management and owners of a business but also to creditors and those who may otherwise rely (in part, at least) upon the independent auditor's report, as in the case of prospective owners or creditors. To be independent, the auditor must be intellectually honest; to be recognized as independent, he must be free from any obligation to or interest in the client, its management, or its owners.
- The third general standard is "due professional care" is to be exercised in the planning and performance of the audit and the preparation of the report. Due professional care imposes a responsibility upon each professional within an independent auditor's organization to observe the standards of field work and reporting. An auditor should possess "the degree of skill commonly possessed" by other auditors and should exercise it with "reasonable care and diligence" (i.e., with due professional care). Due professional care requires the auditor to exercise professional skepticism, which is an attitude that includes a questioning mind and a critical assessment of audit evidence.

[2]AU Section 150.

The Standards of Field Work[3]

a. Communications Between Predecessor and Successor Auditors

An auditor should not accept an engagement until he communicates with the previous auditor. The initiative for communicating rests with the successor auditor. The communication may be either written or oral. Both the predecessor and successor auditors should hold in confidence information obtained from each other. This obligation applies whether or not the successor auditor accepts the engagement.

Inquiry of the predecessor auditor is a necessary procedure because the predecessor auditor may be able to provide information that will assist the successor auditor in determining whether to accept the engagement. The successor auditor should bear in mind that, among other things, the predecessor auditor and the client may have disagreed about accounting principles, auditing procedures, or similarly significant matters. The successor auditor should request permission from the prospective client to make an inquiry of the predecessor auditor prior to final acceptance of the engagement. Except as permitted by the Rules of the Code of Professional Conduct, an auditor is precluded from disclosing confidential information obtained in the course of an engagement unless the client specifically consents. Thus, the successor auditor should ask the prospective client to authorize the predecessor auditor to respond fully to the successor auditor's inquiries. If a prospective client refuses to permit the predecessor auditor to respond or limits the response, the successor auditor should inquire as to the reasons and consider the implications of that refusal in deciding whether to accept the engagement.

The successor auditor should make specific and reasonable inquiries of the predecessor auditor regarding matters that will assist the successor auditor in determining whether to accept the engagement. Matters subject to inquiry should include:

- Information that might bear on the integrity of management.
- Disagreements with management as to accounting principles, auditing procedures, or other similarly significant matters.

[3]AU Section 300—The Standards of Field Work.

- Communications to audit committees or others with equivalent authority and responsibility regarding fraud, illegal acts by clients, and internal-control-related matters.
- The predecessor auditor's understanding as to the reasons for the change of auditors.

The predecessor auditor should respond promptly and fully, on the basis of known facts, to the successor auditor's reasonable inquiries. However, should the predecessor auditor decide, due to unusual circumstances such as impending, threatened, or potential litigation; disciplinary proceedings; or other unusual circumstances, not to respond fully to the inquiries, the predecessor auditor should clearly state that the response is limited. If the successor auditor receives a limited response, its implications should be considered in deciding whether to accept the engagement.

The successor auditor should request that the client authorize the predecessor auditor to allow a review of the predecessor auditor's working papers. The predecessor auditor may wish to request a consent and acknowledgment letter from the client to document this authorization in an effort to reduce misunderstandings about the scope of the communications being authorized. It is customary in such circumstances for the predecessor auditor to make himself or herself available to the successor auditor and make available for review certain of the working papers. The predecessor auditor should determine which working papers are to be made available for review and which may be copied. The predecessor auditor should ordinarily permit the successor auditor to review working papers, including documentation of planning, internal control, audit results, and other matters of continuing accounting and auditing significance, such as the working papers containing an analysis of balance sheet accounts, those relating to contingencies, related parties, and significant unusual transactions. Also, the predecessor auditor should reach an understanding with the successor auditor as to the use of the working papers. The extent, if any, to which a predecessor auditor permits access to the working papers is a matter of judgment.

The successor auditor must obtain sufficient appropriate evidential matter to afford a reasonable basis for expressing an opinion on the financial statements he or she has been engaged to audit, including evaluating the consistency of the application of accounting principles. The audit evidence used in analyzing the impact of the opening balances on the current-year financial statements and consistency of accounting principles is a matter of professional judgment. Such audit evidence may include the most recent audited financial statements, the predecessor auditor's report thereon, the results of inquiry of the predecessor auditor, the results of the successor auditor's review of the predecessor auditor's working papers relating to the most recently completed audit, and audit procedures performed on the current period's transactions that may provide evidence about the opening balances or consistency. For example, evidence gathered during the current year's audit may provide information about the realizability and existence of receivables and inventory recorded at the beginning of the year. The successor auditor may also apply appropriate auditing procedures to account balances at the beginning of the period under audit and to transactions in prior periods.

The successor auditor's review of the predecessor auditor's working papers may affect the nature, timing, and extent of the successor auditor's procedures with respect to the opening balances and consistency of accounting principles. However, the nature, timing, and extent of audit work performed and the conclusions reached in both these areas are solely the responsibility of the successor auditor. In reporting on the audit, the successor auditor should not make reference to the report or work of the predecessor auditor as the basis, in part, for the successor auditor's own opinion.

b. Audits of Financial Statements That Have Been Previously Audited

If an auditor is asked to audit and report on financial statements that have been previously audited and reported on (henceforth referred to as a re-audit), the auditor considering acceptance of the re-audit engagement is also a successor auditor, and the auditor who previously reported is also a predecessor auditor. The successor auditor should state that the purpose of the inquiries is to obtain information about whether to accept an engagement to perform a re-audit.

If the successor auditor accepts the re-audit engagement, he or she may consider the information obtained from inquiries of the predecessor auditor and review of the predecessor auditor's report and working papers in planning the re-audit. However, the information obtained from those inquiries and any review of the predecessor auditor's report and working papers is not sufficient to afford a basis for expressing an opinion. The nature, timing, and extent of the audit work performed and the conclusions reached in the re-audit are solely the responsibility of the successor auditor performing the re-audit.

The successor auditor should plan and perform the re-audit in accordance with GAAS. The successor auditor should not assume responsibility for the predecessor auditor's work or issue a report that reflects divided responsibility. If, in a re-audit engagement, the successor auditor is unable to obtain sufficient appropriate evidential matter to express an opinion on the financial statements, the successor auditor should qualify or disclaim an opinion because of the inability to perform procedures the successor auditor considers necessary in the circumstances.

The successor auditor should request working papers for the period or periods under re-audit and the period prior to the re-audit period. However, the extent, if any, to which the predecessor auditor permits access to the working papers is a matter of judgment.

c. Discovery of Possible Misstatements in Financial Statements Reported on by a Predecessor Auditor

If during the audit or re-audit, the successor auditor becomes aware of information that leads him or her to believe that financial statements reported on by the predecessor auditor may require revision, the successor auditor should request that the client inform the predecessor auditor of the situation and arrange for the three parties to discuss this information and attempt to resolve the matter. The successor auditor should communicate to the predecessor auditor any information that the predecessor auditor may need to consider in accordance with Section 561, Subsequent Discovery of Facts Existing at the Date of the Auditor's Report, which sets out the procedures that an auditor should follow when the auditor subsequently discovers facts that may have affected the audited financial statements previously reported on. If the client refuses to inform the predecessor auditor or if the successor auditor is not satisfied with the resolution of the matter, the successor auditor should evaluate (a) possible implications on the current engagement and (b) whether to resign from the engagement. Furthermore, the successor auditor may wish to consult with his or her legal counsel in determining an appropriate course of further action.

Illustrative Client Consent and Acknowledgment Letter

[Date]
ABC Enterprises
[Address]

You have given your consent to allow [name of successor CPA firm], as successor independent auditors for ABC Enterprises (ABC), access to our working papers for our audit of the December 31, 19X1, financial statements of ABC. You also have given your consent to us to respond fully to [name of successor CPA firm] inquiries. You understand and agree that the review of our working papers is undertaken solely for the purpose of obtaining an understanding about ABC and certain information about our audit to assist [name of successor CPA firm] in planning the audit of the December 31, 19X2, financial statements of ABC.

Please confirm your agreement with the foregoing by signing and dating a copy of this letter and returning it to us.
Attached is the form of the letter we will furnish [name of successor CPA firm] regarding the use of the working papers.

Very truly yours,
[Predecessor Auditor]

By: ______________________

Accepted:

ABC Enterprises

By: ______________________ Date: ________________

Illustrative Successor Auditor Acknowledgment Letter

[Date]
[Successor Auditor]
[Address]

We have previously audited, in accordance with auditing standards generally accepted in the United States of America, the December 31,

20X1, financial statements of ABC Enterprises (ABC). We rendered a report on those financial statements and have not performed any audit procedures subsequent to the audit report date. In connection with your audit of ABC's 20X2 financial statements, you have requested access to our working papers prepared in connection with that audit. ABC has authorized our firm to allow you to review those working papers.

Our audit, and the working papers prepared in connection therewith, of ABC's financial statements were not planned or conducted in contemplation of your review. Therefore, items of possible interest to you may not have been specifically addressed. Our use of professional judgment and the assessment of audit risk and materiality for the purpose of our audit mean that matters may have existed that would have been assessed differently by you. We make no representation as to the sufficiency or appropriateness of the information in our working papers for your purposes.

We understand that the purpose of your review is to obtain information about ABC and our 19X1 audit results to assist you in planning your 19X2 audit of ABC. For that purpose only, we will provide you access to our working papers that relate to that objective.

Upon request, we will provide copies of those working papers that provide factual information about ABC. You agree to subject any such copies or information otherwise derived from our working papers to your normal policy for retention of working papers and protection of confidential client information. Furthermore, in the event of a third-party request for access to your working papers prepared in connection with your audits of ABC, you agree to obtain our permission before voluntarily allowing any such access to our working papers or information otherwise derived from our working papers, and to obtain on our behalf any releases that you obtain from such third party. You agree to advise us promptly and provide us a copy of any subpoena, summons, or other court order for access to your working papers that include copies of our working papers or information otherwise derived therefrom.

> Please confirm your agreement with the foregoing by signing and dating a copy of this letter and returning it to us.
>
> Very truly yours,
>
> [Predecessor Auditor] [Successor Auditor]
>
> By: _______ Date: _______ By: _______ Date: _______
>
> Accepted:

Even with the client's consent, access to the predecessor auditor's working papers may still be limited. Experience has shown that the predecessor auditor may be willing to grant broader access if given additional assurance concerning the use of the working papers. Accordingly, the successor auditor might consider agreeing to the following limitations on the review of the predecessor auditor's working papers in order to obtain broader access:

- The successor auditor will not comment, orally or in writing, to anyone as a result of the review as to whether the predecessor auditor's engagement was performed in accordance with GAAS.
- The successor auditor will not provide expert testimony or litigation support services or otherwise accept an engagement to comment on issues relating to the quality of the predecessor auditor's audit.
- The successor auditor will not use the audit procedures or results thereof documented in the predecessor auditor's working papers as evidential matter in rendering an opinion on the 20XX financial statements of ABC Enterprises, except as contemplated in Statement on Auditing Standards No. 84.

The following paragraph illustrates the above:

> Because your review of our working papers is undertaken solely for the purpose described above and may not entail a review of all our working papers, you agree that (1) the information obtained from the review will not be used by you for any other purpose, (2) you will not comment, orally or in writing, to anyone as a result

of that review as to whether our audit was performed in accordance with generally accepted auditing standards, (3) you will not provide expert testimony or litigation support services or otherwise accept an engagement to comment on issues relating to the quality of our audit, and (4) you will not use the audit procedures or results thereof documented in our working papers as evidential matter in rendering your opinion on the 19X2 financial statements of ABC, except as contemplated in Statement on Auditing Standards No. 84.

4.5.1.2 Standards of Reporting[4]

- The three first standard of reporting is that the report shall state whether the financial statements are presented in accordance with GAAP.

When an auditor reports on financial statements prepared in accordance with a comprehensive basis of accounting other than GAAP, the first standard of reporting is satisfied by disclosing in the auditor's report that the statements have been prepared in conformity with another comprehensive basis of accounting other than GAAP and by expressing an opinion (or disclaiming an opinion) on whether the financial statements are presented in conformity with the comprehensive basis of accounting used.

- The fourth standard of reporting is that the report shall either contain an expression of opinion regarding the financial statements, taken as a whole, or an assertion to the effect that an opinion cannot be expressed. When an overall opinion cannot be expressed, the reasons therefor should be stated. In all cases where an auditor's name is associated with financial statements, the report should contain a clear-cut indication of the character of the auditor's work, if any, and the degree of responsibility the auditor is taking.

An independent auditor's report contains an opinion as to whether the financial statements present fairly, in all material respects, an entity's

[4] AU Section 400 and AU Section 500.

financial position, results of operations, and cash flows in conformity with GAAP. An identification of the country of origin of those GAAP also is required. The independent auditor's judgment concerning the "fairness" of the overall presentation of financial statements should be applied within the framework of GAAP. Without that framework, the auditor would have no uniform standard for judging the presentation of financial position, results of operations, and cash flows in financial statements.

4.5.2 Interim Standards

In April 2003, the Board adopted certain preexisting standards as its interim standards. Pursuant to Rule 3200T, Interim Auditing Standards consist of GAAS, as described in the AICPA's Auditing Standards Board's Statement of Auditing Standards No. 95, as in existence on April 16, 2003, to the extent not superseded or amended by the Board.

- Interim Ethics standards

Pursuant to Rule 3500T, Interim Ethics Standards consist of ethics standards described in the AICPA's Code of Professional Conduct Rule 102, and interpretations and rulings thereunder, as in existence on April 16, 2003, to the extent not superseded or amended by the Board.

- Interim Independence standards

Pursuant to Rule 3500T, Interim Independence Standards consist of independence standards described in the AICPA's Code of Professional Conduct Rule 101, and interpretations and rulings thereunder, as in existence on April 16, 2003, to the extent not superseded or amended by the Board, and certain standards, and interpretations, of the Independence Standards Board, to the extent not superseded or amended by the Board.

- Interim Quality Control standard

In April 2003, the Board adopted certain preexisting standards as its interim standards. Pursuant to Rule 3400T, Interim Quality Control Standards consist of the AICPA's Auditing Standards Board's Statements on Quality Control Standards, as in existence on April 16, 2003, to the extent not superseded or amended by the Board, and (for those firms that were members of the AICPA SEC Practice Section (SECPS)) certain AICPA SEC Practice Section's membership requirements, as in existence on April 16, 2003, to the extent not superseded or amended by the Board.

- Attestation Interim standard

In April 2003, the Board adopted certain preexisting standards as its interim standards. Pursuant to Rule 3300T, Interim Attestation Standards consist of the AICPA's Auditing Standards Board's Statements on Standards for Attestation Engagements, related interpretations, and statements of position as in existence on April 16, 2003, to the extent not superseded or amended by the Board.

4.6 Audit Planning

The auditor should properly plan the audit. This standard describes the auditor's responsibilities for properly planning the audit. Prior to the audit, per se, the auditor should perform the following activities: (i) perform procedures regarding the acceptance of the client relationship and the specific audit engagement; and (ii) communicate with the predecessor auditor in situations in which there has been a change of auditors. At the beginning of the audit, the auditor should (i) perform procedures regarding the continuance of the client relationship and the specific audit engagement, (ii) determine compliance with independence and ethics requirements, and (iii) establish an understanding of the terms of the audit engagement with the audit committee in accordance with Auditing Standard No. 16.

4.6.1 Planning Activities

The nature and extent of planning activities that are necessary depend on the size and complexity of the company, the auditor's previous experience with the company, and changes in circumstances that occur during the audit. When developing the audit strategy and audit plan, the auditor should evaluate whether the following matters are important to the company's financial statements and internal control over financial reporting and, if so, how they will affect the auditor's procedures:

- knowledge of the company's internal control over financial reporting obtained during other engagements performed by the auditor;
- matters affecting the industry in which the company operates, such as financial reporting practices, economic conditions, laws and regulations, and technological changes;
- matters relating to the company's business, including its organization, operating characteristics, and capital structure;
- the extent of recent changes, if any, in the company, its operations, or its internal control over financial reporting;
- the auditor's preliminary judgments about materiality, risk, and, in integrated audits, other factors relating to the determination of material weaknesses;
- control deficiencies previously communicated to the audit committee or management;
- legal or regulatory matters of which the company is aware;
- the type and extent of available evidence related to the effectiveness of the company's internal control over financial reporting;
- preliminary judgments about the effectiveness of internal control over financial reporting;
- public information about the company relevant to the evaluation of the likelihood of material financial statement misstatements and the effectiveness of the company's internal control over financial reporting;
- knowledge about risks related to the company evaluated as part of the auditor's client acceptance and retention evaluation; and
- the relative complexity of the company's operations.

4.6.2 Audit Strategy

The auditor should establish an overall audit strategy that sets the scope, timing, and direction of the audit and guides the development of the audit plan. In establishing the overall audit strategy, the auditor should take into account:

a. The reporting objectives of the engagement and the nature of the communications required by PCAOB standards,
b. The factors that are significant in directing the activities of the engagement team,

c. The results of preliminary engagement activities and the auditor's evaluation of the important matters in accordance with paragraph 7 of the auditing standard No. 9,[5] and
d. The nature, timing, and extent of resources necessary to perform the engagement.

4.6.3 Audit Plan

The auditor should develop and document an audit plan that includes a description of:

- the planned nature, timing, and extent of the risk assessment procedures;
- the planned nature, timing, and extent of tests of controls and substantive procedures; and
- other planned audit procedures required to be performed so that the engagement complies with PCAOB standards.

In an audit of the financial statements of a company with operations in multiple locations or business units, the auditor should determine the extent to which audit procedures should be performed at selected locations or business units to obtain sufficient appropriate evidence to obtain reasonable assurance about whether the consolidated financial statements are free of material misstatement. This includes determining the locations or business units at which to perform audit procedures, as well as the nature, timing, and extent of the procedures to be performed at those individual locations or business units. The auditor should assess the risks of material misstatement to the consolidated financial statements associated with the location or business unit and correlate the amount of audit attention devoted to the location or business unit with the degree of risk of material misstatement associated with that location or business unit. Factors that are relevant to the assessment of the risks of material misstatement associated with a particular location or business unit and the determination of the necessary audit procedures include:

[5] The nature and extent of planning activities that are necessary depend on the size and complexity of the company, the auditor's previous experience with the company, and changes in circumstances that occur during the audit.

a. The nature and amount of assets, liabilities, and transactions executed at the location or business unit, including, e.g., significant transactions that are outside the normal course of business for the company or that otherwise appear to be unusual due to their timing, size, or nature ("significant unusual transactions") executed at the location or business unit;
b. The materiality of the location or business unit;
c. The specific risks associated with the location or business unit that present a reasonable possibility of material misstatement to the company's consolidated financial statements;
d. Whether the risks of material misstatement associated with the location or business unit apply to other locations or business units such that, in combination, they present a reasonable possibility of material misstatement to the company's consolidated financial statements;
e. The degree of centralization of records or information processing;
f. The effectiveness of the control environment, particularly with respect to management's control over the exercise of authority delegated to others and its ability to effectively supervise activities at the location or business unit; and
g. The frequency, timing, and scope of monitoring activities by the company or others at the location or business unit.

In determining the locations or business units at which to perform audit procedures, the auditor may take into account relevant activities performed by internal audit, the Auditor's Consideration of the Internal Audit Function in an Audit of Financial Statements, or others requirements regarding using the work of internal audit and others, respectively. The auditor should modify the overall audit strategy and the audit plan as necessary if circumstances change significantly during the course of the audit, including changes due to a revised assessment of the risks of material misstatement or the discovery of a previously unidentified risk of material misstatement. Further, the auditor should determine whether specialized skill or knowledge is needed to perform appropriate risk assessments, plan or perform audit procedures, or evaluate audit results. If a person with specialized skill or knowledge employed or engaged by the auditor participates in the audit, the auditor should have sufficient knowledge of the subject matter to be addressed by such a person to enable the auditor to: (a) communicate the objectives of that person's work; (b) determine whether that person's procedures meet the auditor's objectives; and (c) evaluate the results of that person's procedures as they relate to the nature, timing, and extent of other planned audit procedures and the effects on the auditor's report.

4.6.4 Use of IT in Planning Audit (Verse Audit Management)

Verse Audit Management software allows you to create audit plans, with multiple audits throughout the year. It enables firms to set up profiles for each audit, with integrated checklists and question data based on keywords from the audit process. Questions, checklists, and scoring methods are all configurable within the system. Audit Management Software, as with any other Verse application, can be integrated to other processes, such as Verse Corrective Actions, in order to launch a corrective action directly from the audit findings.

4.7 Engagement Quality Review

An engagement quality review and concurring approval of issuance are required for the following engagements conducted pursuant to the standards of the PCAOB: (a) an audit engagement; (b) a review interim financial information; and (c) an attestation engagement performed pursuant to Attestation Standard No. 1—Examination Engagements Regarding Compliance Reports of Brokers and Dealers, or Attestation Standard No. 2—Review Engagements Regarding Exemption Reports of Brokers and Dealers.

The engagement quality reviewer must be an associated person of a registered public accounting firm. An engagement quality reviewer from the firm that issues the engagement report (or communicates an engagement conclusion, if no report is issued) must be a partner or another individual in an equivalent position. The engagement quality reviewer may also be an individual from outside the firm. An engagement quality reviewer must have competence, independence, integrity, and objectivity.

- Competence

The engagement quality reviewer must possess the level of knowledge and competence related to accounting, auditing, and financial reporting required to serve as the engagement partner on the engagement under review.

- Independence, integrity, and objectivity

The engagement quality reviewer must be independent of the company, perform the engagement quality review with integrity, and maintain objectivity in performing the review. The reviewer may use assistants in performing the engagement quality review. Personnel assisting the engagement quality reviewer also must be independent, perform the assigned procedures with integrity, and maintain objectivity in performing the review.

To maintain objectivity, the engagement quality reviewer and others who assist the reviewer should not make decisions on behalf of the engagement team or assume any of the responsibilities of the engagement team. The engagement partner remains responsible for the engagement and its performance, notwithstanding the involvement of the engagement quality reviewer and others who assist the reviewer. The person who served as the engagement partner during either of the two audits preceding the audit subject to the engagement quality review may not be the engagement quality reviewer.

Moreover, the documentation of an engagement quality review should be included in the engagement documentation.

4.7.1 Engagement Quality Review for an Audit

In an audit engagement, the engagement quality reviewer should evaluate the significant judgments made by the engagement team and the related conclusions reached in forming the overall conclusion on the engagement and in preparing the engagement report. To evaluate such judgments and conclusions, the engagement quality reviewer should, to the extent necessary to satisfy: (i) hold discussions with the engagement partner and other members of the engagement team, and (ii) review documentation.

In an audit, the engagement quality reviewer should:

a. Evaluate the significant judgments that relate to engagement planning, including:
   - The consideration of the firm's recent engagement experience with the company and risks identified in connection with the firm's client acceptance and retention process,

   - The consideration of the company's business, recent significant activities, and related financial reporting issues and risks, and
   - The judgments made about materiality and the effect of those judgments on the engagement strategy.

b. Evaluate the engagement team's assessment of, and audit responses to:
   - Significant risks identified by the engagement team, including fraud risks, and
   - Other significant risks identified by the engagement quality reviewer through performance of the procedures required by this standard.

c. Evaluate the significant judgments made about (1) the materiality and disposition of corrected and uncorrected identified misstatements and (2) the severity and disposition of identified control deficiencies.

d. Review the engagement team's evaluation of the firm's independence in relation to the engagement.

e. Review the engagement completion document and confirm with the engagement partner that there are no significant unresolved matters.

f. Review the financial statements, management's report on internal control, and the related engagement report.

g. Read other information in documents containing the financial statements to be filed with the Securities and Exchange Commission ("SEC") and evaluate whether the engagement team has taken appropriate action with respect to any material inconsistencies with the financial statements or material misstatements of fact of which the engagement quality reviewer is aware.

h. Based on the procedures required by this standard, evaluate whether appropriate consultations have taken place on difficult or contentious matters. Review the documentation, including conclusions, of such consultations.

i. Based on the procedures required by this standard, evaluate whether appropriate matters have been communicated, or identified for communication, to the audit committee, management, and other parties, such as regulatory bodies.

The engagement quality reviewer should evaluate whether the engagement documentation that he or she reviewed when performing the procedures required: (a) indicates that the engagement team responded appropriately to significant risks, and (b) supports the conclusions reached by the engagement team with respect to the matters reviewed. Further, the engagement quality reviewer may provide concurring approval of issuance only if, after performing with due professional care the review required by this standard, he or she is not aware of a significant engagement deficiency. A significant engagement deficiency in an audit exists when (1) the engagement team failed to obtain sufficient appropriate evidence in accordance with the standards of the PCAOB, (2) the engagement team reached an inappropriate overall conclusion on the subject matter of the engagement, (3) the engagement report is not appropriate in the circumstances, or (4) the firm is not independent of its client.

4.7.2 *Engagement Quality Review for a Review of Interim Financial Information*

In an engagement to review interim financial information, the engagement quality reviewer should evaluate the significant judgments made by the engagement team and the related conclusions reached in forming the overall conclusion on the engagement and in preparing the engagement report, if a report is to be issued. To evaluate such judgments and conclusions, the engagement quality reviewer should, to the extent necessary (i) hold discussions with the engagement partner and other members of the engagement team, and (ii) review documentation. In a review of interim financial information, the engagement quality reviewer should:

a. Evaluate the significant judgments that relate to engagement planning, including the consideration of:
   - The firm's recent engagement experience with the company and risks identified in connection with the firm's client acceptance and retention process,
   - The company's business, recent significant activities, and related financial reporting issues and risks, and
   - The nature of identified risks of material misstatement due to fraud.
b. Evaluate the significant judgments made about the materiality and disposition of corrected and uncorrected identified misstatements

and any material modifications that should be made to the disclosures about changes in internal control over financial reporting.

c. Perform the procedures aforementioned.
d. Review the interim financial information for all periods presented and for the immediately preceding interim period, management's disclosure for the period under review, if any, about changes in internal control over financial reporting, and the related engagement report, if a report is to be issued.
e. Read other information in documents containing interim financial information to be filed with the SEC and evaluate whether the engagement team has taken appropriate action with respect to material inconsistencies with the interim financial information or material misstatements of fact of which the engagement quality reviewer is aware.
f. Evaluate whether appropriate matters have been communicated, or identified for communication, to the audit committee, management, and other parties; or evaluate whether appropriate matters have been communicated, or identified for communication, to the audit committee, management, and other parties.

The engagement quality reviewer should evaluate whether the engagement documentation that he or she reviewed when performing the procedures required under the review supports the conclusions reached by the engagement team with respect to the matters reviewed. The engagement quality reviewer may provide concurring approval of issuance only if, after performing with due professional care the review required by this standard, he or she is not aware of a significant engagement deficiency. A significant engagement deficiency in a review of interim financial information exists when (1) the engagement team failed to perform interim review procedures necessary in the circumstances of the engagement, (2) the engagement team reached an inappropriate overall conclusion on the subject matter of the engagement, (3) the engagement report is not appropriate in the circumstances, or (4) the firm is not independent of its client. Further, in a review of interim financial information, the firm may grant permission to the client to use the engagement report (or communicate an engagement conclusion to its client, if no report is issued) only after the engagement quality reviewer provides concurring approval of issuance.

4.7.3 Engagement Quality Review for an Attestation Engagement Performed Pursuant to Attestation Standard No. 1, Examination Engagements Regarding Compliance Reports of Brokers and Dealers, or Attestation Standard No. 2, Review Engagements Regarding Exemption Reports of Brokers and Dealers

In an attestation engagement performed pursuant to Attestation Standard No. 1, Examination Engagements Regarding Compliance Reports of Brokers and Dealers, or Attestation Standard No. 2, Review Engagements Regarding Exemption Reports of Brokers and Dealers, the engagement quality reviewer should evaluate the significant judgments made by the engagement team and the related conclusions reached in forming the overall conclusion on the attestation engagement and in preparing the engagement report. To evaluate such judgments and conclusions, the engagement quality reviewer should, taking into account the procedures performed in the engagement quality review of the financial statement audit, (1) hold discussions with the engagement partner and other members of the engagement team, (2) read the engagement report and the document containing management's assertions, and (3) review the engagement completion document and other relevant documentation. The engagement quality reviewer may provide concurring approval of issuance only if, after performing with due professional care the review required by this standard, he or she is not aware of a significant engagement deficiency. A significant engagement deficiency exists when (1) the engagement team failed to perform attestation procedures necessary in the circumstances of the engagement, (2) the engagement team reached an inappropriate overall conclusion on the subject matter of the engagement, (3) the engagement report is not appropriate in the circumstances, or (4) the firm is not independent of its client. Further, the firm may grant permission to the client to use the engagement report only after the engagement quality reviewer provides concurring approval of issuance.

4.7.4 Documentation of an Engagement Quality Review

Documentation of an engagement quality review should contain sufficient information to enable an experienced auditor, having no previous connection with the engagement, to understand the procedures performed by the engagement quality reviewer, and others who assisted the reviewer, to comply with the provisions of this standard, including information that identifies:

a. The engagement quality reviewer, and others who assisted the reviewer,
b. The documents reviewed by the engagement quality reviewer, and others who assisted the reviewer,
c. The date the engagement quality reviewer provided concurring approval of issuance or, if no concurring approval of issuance was provided, the reasons for not providing the approval.

4.7.5 Integration of IT

Nowadays, auditors are using technology in their daily activities. Some new technological tools enable them to collect, process and analyze large volumes of structured and unstructured data related to their clients' financial information. Such a capability may allow auditors to test 100% of a company's transactions instead of only a sample of the population.

According to a recent report, the accounting profession spends approximately $3 billion to $5 billion a year on technology and it is now part of the new baseline of operational costs for the major firms.

SAS no. 94 offers guidance on how technology use affects the independent audit.

Under SAS 94, information technology (IT) encompasses automated means of originating, processing, storing, and communicating information, and includes recording devices, communication systems, computer systems (including hardware and software components and data), and other electronic devices. SAS 94 recognizes the distinction between application controls and general controls auditors have commonly used for many years and describes aspects of these controls that are relevant to the audit.

SAS 94 states that an organization's IT use may affect any of its five internal control components as well as how businesses initiate, record, process and report transactions.

Where a significant amount of information supporting one or more financial statement assertions is electronic, the auditor has to decide whether it is practical or not to limit detection risk to an acceptable level by performing only substantive tests for one or more financial statement assertions. In so doing, the auditor should gather evidence about the effectiveness of both the design and operation of controls intended to reduce the assessed level of control risk.

SAS no. 94 clarifies what the auditor needs to know to understand the automated and manual procedures an entity uses to prepare its financial statements and related disclosures. Included are the procedures an entity uses to

1. Enter transaction totals into the general ledger.
2. Initiate, record and process journal entries in the general ledger, including the procedures for standard entries required on a recurring basis and nonstandard entries to record nonrecurring or unusual transactions and adjustments.
3. Record in the financial statements recurring and nonrecurring adjustments, such as consolidating adjustments, report combinations and reclassifications that are not reflected in formal journal entries.

Under SAS 94 an auditor may need specialized skills to determine the effect of IT on the audit, to understand IT controls or to design and perform tests of IT controls and substantive tests. In some instances he or she might have to get help from someone who has such skills. The statement includes a number of factors the auditor might use to determine whether such skills are required, as well as the specific procedures someone with those skills might perform.

Practice

Question 1

The 10 AICPA Auditing Standards are organized under the below standards, except:

(a) The general standards
(b) The field standards
(c) The documentation standards
(d) The reporting standards

Question 2

Which of the following assertions concerning the interpretive publications is inaccurate:

(a) Interpretive publications consist of auditing Interpretations of the SASs, appendixes to the SASs, auditing guidance included in AICPA Audit and Accounting Guides, and AICPA auditing Statements of Position
(b) Interpretive publications are not auditing standards
(c) Interpretive publications are auditing standards
(d) Interpretive publications are recommendations on the application of the SASs in specific circumstances, including engagements for entities in specialized industries
(e) An interpretive publication is issued under the authority of the ASB after all ASB members have been provided an opportunity to consider and comment on whether the proposed interpretive publication is consistent with the SASs

Question 3

In establishing the overall audit strategy, the auditor should take into account the following:

(a) The reporting objectives of the engagement and the nature of the communications required by PCAOB standards
(b) The factors that are significant in directing the activities of the engagement team
(c) The results of preliminary engagement activities and the auditor's evaluation of the important matters
(d) The nature, timing, and extent of resources necessary to perform the engagement
(e) All of the above

CHAPTER 5

Other Engagements, Reports, and Accounting Services

5.1 General

In 1997, at the request of the AICPA, a Special Committee on Assurance released its report concerning the expansion of assurance services. The AICPA finally adopted a series of attestation services CPAs were allowed to accomplish. Further, the AICPA authorizes CPAs to perform other non-assurance services, including, inter alia: (i) consulting services, (ii) tax services, (iii) valuation services, and (iv) personal financial planning.

5.2 Other Attestation Services

5.2.1 *Forecasting Financial Statements' Analysis*

When a new corporation is envisioned, its founders will prepare pro forma financial statements for the information of prospective investors. Likewise, lenders and investors also require such statements to structure or confirm compliance with debt covenants, such as debt service reserve coverage and debt to equity ratios. They are also vital for any valuation exercises one might do in investment analysis or M&A evaluation/planning. The standard approach used in the compilation of financial statements is known as the "percent of sales forecasting."

F. I. Lessambo, *Auditing, Assurance Services, and Forensics*,
https://doi.org/10.1007/978-3-319-90521-1_5

5.2.2 *Management Discussion & Analysis (MD&A)*

MD&A is a narrative explanation of the financial statements and other statistical data that the registrant believes will enhance a readers' understanding of its financial condition, changes in financial condition and results of operation. The objectives of MD&A are:

a. To provide a narrative explanation of a company's financial statements that enables investors to see the company through the eyes of management;
b. To enhance the overall financial disclosure and provide the context within which financial information should be analyzed; and
c. To provide information about the quality of, and potential variability of, a company's earnings and cash flow so that investors can ascertain the likelihood that past performance is indicative of future performance.

5.2.2.1 Liquidity and Capital Resources [S-K 303(a)(1) and (2)]

These represent two separate requirements of S-K 303(a). A key objective of the liquidity and capital resources discussion is to provide a clear picture of the company's ability to generate cash and to meet existing known or reasonably likely future cash requirements.

Liquidity is the ability of the registrant to generate adequate amounts of cash to meet its needs for cash. Any known trends, or any known demands, commitments, events, or uncertainties that will result in or are likely to result in the registrant's liquidity increasing or decreasing in a material way should be discussed. To the extent a material deficiency is identified, the registrant should disclose the steps taken to remedy the deficiency. The discussion should also evaluate the amounts and certainties of cash flows, as well as whether there has been material variability in historical cash flows.

The requirements of the disclosures related to capital resources include a discussion of material commitments for capital expenditures, the general purpose of any commitments and how these commitments will be funded, and material trends in the registrant's capital resources, including expected changes in the mix (equity, debt and any off-balance sheet financing arrangements) and their relative cost.

- The liquidity and capital resources discussion should address:

  (a) Material cash requirements;
  (b) Sources and uses of cash, including cash provided by/used in operations, as well as cash provided by/used in investing and financing activities; and
  (c) Material trends and uncertainties related to a company's flexibility in determining when and how to use the available cash flows to satisfy obligations and make other capital expenditures.

  It may be necessary for the liquidity and capital resources discussion to address debt instruments, guarantees, and related covenants. Disclosure is likely to be necessary if:

  (a) The registrant is, or is reasonably likely to be, in breach of debt covenants or
  (b) Debt covenants impact the registrant's ability to obtain additional debt or equity financing.

- Improving Liquidity and Capital Resources

  (a) One of the most common deficiencies is when registrants simply repeat items reported in the statement of cash flows. Registrants should focus on the primary drivers of and other material factors necessary to an understanding of the registrant's cash flows and the indicative value of historical cash flows.
  (b) Registrants should describe cash flows from operating, investing and financing activities associated with discontinued operations separately from continuing operations if that information is not apparent from the cash flow statement. Additionally, registrants should describe how the company's liquidity is likely to be affected by the absence of cash flows (or negative cash flows) associated with discontinued operations.

5.2.2.2 Results of Operations [S-K 303(a)(3)]

The discussion that is provided with respect to the results of operations should not consist merely of numeric dollar and percentage changes measured from period to period of various line items on the income statement. The focus should be on an analysis of the factors that caused these changes to occur. In providing this analysis, registrants may find it helpful to include a discussion of key variables and financial measures management is utilizing in managing the business. These variables may be nonfinancial in nature or may represent industry-specific metrics.

- The following disclosures are required by S-K 303(a)(3):

  (a) Any unusual or infrequent event or transaction or any significant economic change that materially affected the amount of reported income from continuing operations;
  (b) Significant components of revenues and expenses that are necessary in order to understand the results of operations (e.g., segmental information);
  (c) Any known trends or uncertainties that have had or that the registrant reasonably expects will have a material favorable or unfavorable impact on net sales or revenues or income from continuing operations;
  (d) If events that are likely to cause a material change in the relationship between costs and revenues (increases in labor costs or raw materials for example), the change in the relationship should be disclosed; and
  (e) To the extent there is a material increase in net sales, discuss the price vs. volume mix (whether the overall increase is attributable to increases in prices or increases in the volume of goods and services being sold).

In order to comply with the requirement to discuss significant components of revenue and expenses, registrants will often provide a discussion along segmental lines (as determined under SFAS 131 [ASC 280]). Segment analysis is usually necessary to enable a reader to understand the consolidated amounts, but it should not result in repetitive disclosure that lengthens MD&A unnecessarily, or obscures salient information. The discussion and analysis of segments may be integrated with the discussion of the consolidated amounts to avoid unnecessary duplication. The discussion and analysis should be comprehensive. All components of the registrant's results of operations, including those that may not be allocated to the segments in determining the segmental profit or loss (such as certain corporate overhead items or income taxes for example) should be discussed.

Registrants should consider discussing and analyzing the tax implications related to material transactions, trends and other important items impacting their business as disclosed elsewhere in MD&A. A discussion of the nature and impact of significant tax rate reconciling items should also be considered. For example, discuss the tax rate reconciling item resulting from a change in assumptions related to an unrecognized tax benefit or a different final resolution related to the unrecognized benefit. Similarly, when uncertain tax positions are a critical accounting policy, MD&A should address why the assumptions were changed or why the actual resolution differed from management's assumption (Last updated: 9/30/2010).

Registrants should address the underlying reasons for changes in the price versus volume mix. For example, if sales declined because the volume of goods sold decreased by 20%, but this was offset by a 10% increase in price, the discussion in MD&A should not stop once it identifies the price and volume components. In this example, the underlying factors that contributed to the decline in volume as well as the increase in selling prices should also be discussed. In addition, discussions about changes in the price vs. volume mix should consider changes in foreign currency fluctuations.

The results of operations may not always be prepared on a consistent basis. This will occur, for example, when there has been a change in basis in the underlying financial statements. This might occur in the following situations:

a. When there has been a material acquisition (either the acquisition of a target entity that is significant to the registrant or predecessor/successor step-up in basis) during the period;
b. When pushdown accounting has been applied; or
c. When the registrant has adopted fresh-start accounting upon its emergence from bankruptcy.

When events such as those described in 9220.6 occur, registrants should consider whether the discussion of the results of operations and financial condition set forth in the audited financial statements included in the filing should be supplemented by a discussion based upon pro forma financial information. This supplemental discussion may be meaningful in the case of a material acquisition, but generally would not be appropriate in the case of fresh-start accounting. A determination as to whether a discussion of the audited financial statements should be supplemented by a discussion based on pro forma information should take into consideration all of the facts and circumstances surrounding the transaction, the nature of the pro forma adjustments to be made, and the overall meaningfulness of any such supplemental pro forma discussion.

If it is determined that a supplemental discussion in MD&A based on pro forma financial information is appropriate, then the pro forma financial information may be presented in a format consistent with S-X Article 11. Other formats, such as the footnote pro forma information specified by ASC 805, may also be appropriate depending on the particular facts and circumstances. It would be inappropriate to merely combine information for the pre- and post-transaction periods without reflecting all relevant pro forma adjustments required by S-X Article 11. Pro forma financial information should only be prepared for the most recent fiscal year and interim period prior to the transaction occurring (although the staff will not object to the registrant providing a pro forma income statement for the corresponding prior interim period). If pro forma results are discussed in MD&A, they should not be discussed in isolation. Supplemental discussions based on S-X Article 11 pro forma financial information should not be presented with greater prominence than the discussion of the historical financial statements required by S-K 303 (Last updated: 9/30/2010).

MD&A should fully explain the results of operations. For example, MD&A should not merely state that the increase in revenues and costs of revenues is due to a significant acquisition. Rather, the contribution of the recent acquisition to total revenues should be quantified to the extent possible, and any increase or decrease in the underlying revenues of the preexisting business should then be addressed.

MD&A should not consist of generic or boilerplate disclosure. Rather, it should reflect the facts and circumstances specific to each individual registrant. S-K 303 is a "principles-based" disclosure requirement. It is intended to provide management with flexibility to describe the financial matters impacting the registrant.

MD&A should fully explain the results of operations. For example, MD&A should not merely state that the increase in revenues and costs of revenues is due to a significant acquisition. Rather, the contribution of the recent acquisition to total revenues should be quantified to the extent possible, and any increase or decrease in the underlying revenues of the preexisting business should then be addressed. There are two assessments that management must make where a trend, demand, commitment, event, or uncertainty is known:

a. Is the known trend, demand, commitment event or uncertainty likely to come to fruition? If management determines that it is not reasonably likely to occur, no disclosure is required.
b. If management cannot make that determination, it must evaluate objectively the consequences of the known trend, demand, commitment, event or uncertainty, on the assumption that it will come to fruition. Disclosure is then required unless management determines that a material effect on the registrant's financial condition or results of operations is not reasonably likely to occur.

Note that "reasonably likely" is a lower threshold than "more likely than not" but a higher threshold than "remote". The concept of "reasonably likely" is used in the context of disclosure for MD&A purposes and is not intended to mirror the tests in SFAS 5 [ASC 450] established to determine when accrual is necessary, or when disclosure in the footnotes to the financial statements is required.

Very often the MD&A will provide some financial highlights. These are summary of major financially related happenings within the company, often provided in a publicly traded company's report to its shareholders. Highlights include various performance statistics depending on the specific industry. Below are some highlights from Walmart and Goldman Sachs.

5.2.3 *Internal Control Over Financial Reporting (ICFR)*[1]

Internal controls refer to those procedures within a company that are designed to reasonably ensure compliance with the company's policies. Under the framework developed in the early 1990s by the Committee on Sponsoring Organizations (COSO), there are three types of internal controls: (i) those that affect a company's operations; (ii) those that affect a company's compliance with laws and regulations; and (iii) those that affect a company's financial reporting.

[1] PCAOB (03/2006): A Layperson's Guide to Internal Control Over Financial Reporting (ICFR).

Since the enactment of the Foreign Corrupt Practices Act of 1977 (FCPA), every US-traded company, regardless of size and place of operations, has been required to create a system of internal accounting controls. In its rules implementing the FCPA, the SEC has explained that this responsibility requires that companies:

- maintain books, records, and accounts which, in reasonable detail, accurately and fairly reflect the company's transactions; and
- devise and maintain internal controls sufficient to provide reasonable assurance that:

  - Transactions are executed in accordance with management authorization;
  - Transactions are recorded as necessary to (a) permit preparation of financial statements in conformity with GAAP and (b) maintain accountability for assets;
  - Access to assets is permitted only in accordance with management authorization; and
  - Recorded accountability for assets is compared with the existing assets at reasonable intervals, and appropriate action is taken regarding any differences.

The Sarbanes-Oxley Act of 2002 enhanced this responsibility in two ways. First, §404(a) of the Act requires a large subset of these same companies to annually report on the company's own assessment of the effectiveness of these controls. Second, under §302 of the Act, certain corporate officers must, among other things, accept responsibility (as evidenced by individual signatures) for the content of the company's annual §404(a) report.

Under §404(b) of the Act, independent auditors are now required to "attest to, and report on" the company's §404(a) assessment. This requirement of public disclosure, by both the company and the auditor, now creates a strong incentive for company self-correction.

The audit of a company's financial statements and the audit of that company's ICFR must be performed by the same auditor, and the two audits should be integrated. With integrated audits, the tests that the auditor performs may serve two purposes. A material weakness in ICFR exists if there is some flaw within the company's overall control system such that it is at least reasonably possible that a material misstatement in the company's financial statements will not be prevented or corrected. Such a misstatement may occur on an annual basis (either before or after an audit, or through interim financial reporting. Under existing SEC and PCAOB rules, material weaknesses in ICFR must be publicly reported. Flaws in control systems that fall below "material" are reported within the company, either to company management or the audit committee—depending upon the severity of the flaw.

When an independent auditor issues a "clean" opinion on the company's financial statements, this is a representation to the public that the auditor has followed applicable auditing and related professional standards so as to allow the auditor to conclude with reasonable assurance that the financial statements are fairly presented in conformity with GAAP in all material respects. A "clean" audit opinion is not a guarantee of error-free financials, but is rather the conclusion by an auditor—using procedures and professional judgment that are reasonable to the circumstances—that the statements are fairly presented.

5.2.4 *Registration Statements & Other SEC Filings*

A company seeking to offer securities for public sale generally must file a registration statement with the Securities and Exchange Commission. These registration statements, in general, must include certain financial statements certified by an independent public or certified accountant. The end product of the auditor's work is, first and foremost, an expression of opinion as to whether the company's financial statements, taken as a whole, are in material compliance with GAAP.

5.2.5 *Miscellaneous Assurance Services*

Trust Services are defined as set of professional assurance and advisory services based on a common framework to address the risks and opportunities of IT.[2] In the development of Trust Services, the objective was to establish a core set of principles and related criteria for key areas related to IT, e-commerce, e-business, and systems. These form the measurement basis for the delivery of the related service(s).

The following principles and criteria have been developed by the AICPA/CICA for use by practitioners in the performance of Trust Services engagements, including SysTrust and WebTrust: (i) security[3];

[2] Overview of Trust Services (CICA), 2013.

[3] The system is protected against unauthorized access (both physical and logical).

(ii) availability[4]; (iii) processing integrity[5]; (iv) confidentiality[6]; and (v) privacy.[7]

Trust Services helps differentiate entities from their competitors by demonstrating to stakeholders that the entities are attuned to the risks posed by their environment and equipped with the controls that address those risks. Therefore, the potential beneficiaries of Trust Services assurance reports are consumers, business partners, creditors, bankers and other creditors, regulators, outsourcers, and those using outsourced services, and any other stakeholders who in some way rely on electronic commerce (e-commerce) and IT systems. A variety of factors have combined to make trust an issue. Factors such as globalization, the anonymity of e-commerce, and an increasing reliance on complex and powerful IT systems have caused concerns among business customers and partners leading to a decline in trust. These issues are addressed with the services provided by practitioners using the Trust Services framework. An important aspect of both the SysTrust and WebTrust brands is that they are designed to be sufficiently flexible to meet the needs of those entities wanting to be examined.

5.2.5.1 SysTrust Services

The SysTrust service is also comprised of a "family" of assurance services designed for a wide variety of IT-based systems as may be defined by the entity and, upon attainment of an unqualified assurance report, would entitle the entity to display a SysTrust Seal and accompanying auditor's report. The SysTrust family of branded assurance services includes the following, applied in the context of an entity's defined system:

a. SysTrust-Systems Reliability. The scope of the assurance engagement includes the Security, Availability, Processing Integrity or Confidentiality Principles and Criteria.
b. SOC 3 SysTrust for Service Organizations. The scope of the assurance engagement includes one or more combinations of

[4] The system is available for operation and use as committed or agreed.

[5] System processing is complete, accurate, timely, and authorized.

[6] Information designated as confidential is protected as committed or agreed.

[7] Personal information is collected, used, retained, and disclosed in conformity with the commitments in the entity's privacy notice and with the criteria set forth in Generally Accepted Privacy Principles issued by the AICPA/CICA.

the Security, Availability, Processing Integrity, Confidentiality or Privacy Principles and Criteria unique to service organizations.

SysTrust responds to this business need by providing suitable criteria and a process that enables a CPA to provide assurance that a system is, in fact, reliable.

5.2.5.2 WebTrust Services

The WebTrust service is actually comprised of a "family" of assurance services designed for e-commerce-based systems and, upon attainment of an unqualified assurance report, would entitle the entity to display a WebTrust Seal and accompanying practitioner's report on its Web site. During a WebTrust engagement, the practitioner "audits" a company's online business practices to verify compliance matters such as privacy, security, availability, confidentiality, consumer redress for complaints, and business practices. WebTrust provides suitable criteria for practitioners as well as a licensing process that enables CPAs to provide assurance on Web sites.

5.2.5.3 ElderCare Services

ElderCare is a service line designed to provide assurance to family members and the elderly themselves that care goals are achieved for family members who are no longer able to be totally independent. These services may include financial services such as paying bills, preparing tax returns, and estate work. In addition, a practitioner might coordinate and evaluate the provision of care, or deal with, unusual or unexpected occurrences.[8]

The Committee defines ElderCare Services as a service designed to provide assurance to family members that care goals are achieved for elderly family members no longer able to be totally independent. ElderCare Services can involve three kinds of services: direct services, assurance services, and consulting services. Direct services entail the more traditional aspects of accounting and financial services. Assurance services involve the measuring and reporting on prescribed goals against stated criteria. Consulting services include planning and evaluation of client needs.

[8]Steven E. Salterio (2000): Expanding Assurance Services: An Update from the Assurance Services Executive Committee, Volume 23, No. 3.

The wealth controlled by persons over the age of 65 is estimated to be $11 to $13 trillion in 1997. That number has significantly increased since then.[9]

5.2.5.4 Performance View Services
Whether employed during audits or tax engagements, performance measures can have a big effect on your clients' businesses. With performance view services, the auditor is assisting or aiding his or her clients develop an integrated set of financial and nonfinancial performance measures to employ in managing their businesses.

5.3 Advisory Services

The rise of the advisory and consulting services within accounting firms has become a major concern for regulators, both the PCAOB and the SEC. Mr. Harris who presides over both the PCAOB Investor Advisory Group and IFIAR's Investor and Other Stakeholders Working Group Provides a brilliant historical aspect of the long-time conflicts between core auditing and non-audit services as follows[10]:

- Starting in the 1950s, the SEC raised concerns about the rise of non-audit services in the largest firms.
- Congress looked into this issue in the 1970s, and while it seriously considered limiting the non-audit services that independent public accountants could provide, no action was taken.
- Congressional investigation continued in the 1980s, with then Chairman of the House Commerce Committee, John Dingell, conducting numerous oversight hearings directed principally to audit quality and independence.
- In the late 1990s, in response to an increasingly complex web of business and financial relationships between auditors and their audit clients and the dramatic increase in the revenues from non-audit services to clients, the SEC took action by imposing certain requirements for auditor independence.

[9] Robert K. Elliot and Don M. Pallais (1997): Are You Ready for New Services? *Journal of Accountancy*, p. 49.

[10] Steven B. Harris- PCAOB (Nov 24, 2014): The Rise of Advisory Services in Audit Firms.

– The link between the rise of non-audit services in the 1980s and 1990s to the financial reporting crises preceding the adoption of the Sarbanes-Oxley Act in 2002 is somewhat unclear. But, the rise of advisory services is generally considered to have fundamentally changed the culture and tone at the top at the firms and had firm leaders focusing more on offering broader services to audit clients.

Addressing these concerns, Section 201 of the Sarbanes-Oxley Act enumerates a number of prohibited non-audit services by auditors to audit clients and charged Board's independent audit committees with carefully monitoring these activities. Section 201 of the Sarbanes-Oxley Act prohibits the following services:

1. Bookkeeping or other services related to the accounting records or financial statements of the audit client;
2. Financial information systems design and implementation;
3. Appraisal or valuation services, fairness opinions, or contribution-in-kind reports;
4. Actuarial services; (5) internal audit outsourcing services;
5. Management functions or human resources;
6. Broker or dealer, investment adviser, or investment banking services;
7. Legal services and expert services unrelated to the audit; and
8. Any other service that the Board determines, by regulation, is impermissible.

Stop and Go

Following the passage of the Sarbanes-Oxley Act, three of the four major firms divested their advisory and consulting practices. Since then, however, each of these firms has rebuilt these practices.[11] A few examples of the many advisory and consulting services some of the largest firms now provide their non-audit clients include, but are certainly not limited to, enterprise strategy, marketing and sales, corporate finance, mergers and acquisitions, government consulting, legal services, immigration, and a wide variety of risk management services, including financial, insurance, and IT risk management, cybersecurity, human resources transformations

[11] Steven B. Harris- PCAOB (Nov 24, 2014): The Rise of Advisory Services in Audit Firms.

… and the list goes on. In fact, a Big Four firm's foreign affiliate announced in March its ambitions to become a global top 20 legal services player within the next five years.

Today, the advisory practices for the firms are growing much faster than the other service lines:

- At the four major global audit firms accounted for $51 billion in revenue in 2009 and $65 billion in 2013—a rise of $14 billion, or 27%, in four years. Contrast that with audit revenues, which only grew by $3 billion in those same four years. In 2013, revenues from non-audit services represented 57% of the global revenues at those firms.
- Domestically, advisory services alone represent 39% of total revenues across the major US firms, now larger than audit's 36% share. Since 2011, advisory services' prominence has risen while audit's has declined. To provide some perspective, audit revenues represented 70% of the firms' total revenues in 1977, 34% in 1998, and about 30% in 2000.
- Revenues for non-audit services have grown at an average rate of about 10% in recent years, while revenues for assurance services have grown at a modest 4%. Further, based on proxy statement fee disclosures, public company audit fees have been stagnant, so the growth in assurance revenue is coming from risk services or from audits in the nonpublic sectors.

- Risk Advisory Services

Risk Advisory Services provide the CPA with:

a. A common language and framework for understanding and communicating risk management issues; and
b. A series of practice guides describing tools, techniques, and training that support the risk management process.

The performance of these types of assurance services may or may not be subject to the attestation standards, depending on how an engagement is developed and performed. The attestation standards apply whenever a CPA is engaged to issue or does issue an examination, review, or agreed-upon procedures report on subject matter (or an assertion about the subject matter) that is the responsibility of another party. This definition is engagement-oriented and, therefore, the CPA must take care to define the nature of the services to be provided and whether they are intended to provide assurance.

- Potential threats to auditors' independence

A concern is that there may be greater risk of independence violations. This stems from two possibilities—insufficient monitoring of various services provided to audit clients and permissible tax consulting work that may cross the line. Investors' concerns stem from continued independence violations. For example, in 2014 the SEC concluded enforcement actions against several large accounting firms and individual audit partners relating to auditor independence matters. And I would think that these enforcement matters would be of considerable concern to board directors, audit committees and their counsel alike.

Audit firms have said that the acquisition and ownership of non-audit expertise benefits and supports audit expertise. He said those benefits need to be continually reexamined by firms and articulated.[12]

5.4 Non-assurance Services

A common characteristic of these non-assurance services is that the professional accountant's services are designed to provide technical skills, education, observations, experiences, and knowledge to subject matter for the direct use and benefit of the client. The services considered necessary are generally determined by agreement between the client and the practitioner, and the outcome of the work is not designed to provide any level of assurance to parties outside the client or responsible party. Examples of professional services typically provided by practitioners that would not be considered an attestation engagement include:

- Management consulting engagements whereby the practitioner provides advice or recommendations to a client;
- Engagements to advocate a client's position (e.g., tax matters being reviewed by the Internal Revenue Service);

[12] Ben Tysiac (Dec 9, 2013): Effects of Non-audit Services at Audit Firms Concern PCAOB, SEC Journal of Accountancy.

- Tax engagements involving the preparation of tax returns or providing tax advice;
- Compilations or reviews of financial statements;
- Engagements in which the practitioner's role is solely to assist the client (e.g., acting as the company's accountant in preparing information other than financial statements);
- Engagements to testify as an expert witness in accounting, auditing, taxation, or other matters; and
- Engagements to provide an expert opinion on certain points of principle, such as the application of tax laws or accounting standards, given certain stipulated facts provided by another party as long as the expert opinion does not express a conclusion about the reliability of the facts provided by another party.

5.4.1 Consulting Services

Consulting services possess fundamental differences from the engagements to provide assurance over assertions or subject matter of other responsible parties. In an assurance service (including attestation engagements), the practitioner expresses a conclusion about the subject matter or the reliability of a written assertion that is the responsibility of another party. In a consulting service, the practitioner develops the findings, conclusions, and recommendations based on the objectives of the engagement for the direct use and benefit of the client. The nature and scope of work is determined solely by the agreement between the practitioner and the client. Generally, the work is performed only for the use and benefit of the client rather than outside parties. The practitioner does not attest to someone else's assertion but is the one who develops the final presentation. The CPAs role is to assist the client or, on some occasions, to testify as an expert witness in accounting, auditing, taxation, or other matters, given certain stipulated facts.

In terms of the AICPA professional standards, consulting engagements are performed in accordance with Statements on Standards for Consulting Services (SSCS), and include consultations, advisory services, implementation services, transaction services, staff and other support services, and product services. An analytical approach and process is applied in a consulting service and typically involves some combination of activities relating to determination of client objectives, fact-finding, definition of the problems or opportunities, evaluation of alternatives, formulation of proposed action, results communication, implementation, and follow-up.

5.4.2 *Tax Services*

Non-audit tax services in general are not prohibited under the Sarbanes-Oxley Act because lawmakers believed that such traditional tax services were appropriate and, unlike advisory services, had not appeared to be the source of serious problems.

While many tax services do not impair independence, advising audit clients on certain kinds of tax structuring transactions and implementing certain tax structures could. Depending on the nature of the tax advisory service, auditor independence could be undermined in the following scenarios.

First, the auditor could effectively audit their own firm's work when he or she is auditing the company's tax accounts, which entails examining the effectiveness and accounting of the tax structures their firm designed and implemented.

Second, the firm may be perceived as part of the management team when the tax structures are complex or the implementation extensive.

Third, the firm may be advocating for its client when tax authorities challenge the tax structures the firm advised on.

A number of these concerns were raised in a report issued on April 1, 2014 by the Senate Permanent Subcommittee on Investigations relating to Caterpillar's Offshore Tax Strategy.

5.4.3 *Valuation Services*

Over the years, an increasing number of professional accountants have begun providing professional valuation services to meet a growing demand for such services. These services include valuations of businesses, business ownership interests, securities, or intangible assets that could be performed for a wide variety of purposes including the following:

1. Transactions or potential transactions, such as acquisitions, mergers, leveraged buyouts, initial public offerings, employee stock ownership plans and other share-based plans, partner and shareholder buy-ins or buyouts, and stock redemptions.

2. Litigation or pending litigation relating to matters such as marital dissolution, bankruptcy, contractual disputes, owner disputes, dissenting shareholder and minority ownership oppression cases, and employment and intellectual property disputes.
3. Compliance-oriented engagements, including (a) financial reporting and (b) tax matters such as corporate reorganizations; S corporation conversions; income, estate, and gift tax compliance; purchase price allocations; and charitable contributions.
4. Planning oriented engagements for income tax, estate tax, gift tax, mergers, and acquisitions, and personal financial planning.

There are generally two types of valuation services engagements as follows:

1. Valuation engagement: A valuation analyst performs a valuation engagement when (1) the engagement calls for the valuation analyst to estimate the value of a subject interest, and (2) the valuation analyst estimates the value and is free to apply the valuation approaches and methods he/she deems appropriate in the circumstances. The valuation analyst expresses the results of the valuation as a conclusion of value; the conclusion may be either a single amount or a range.
2. Calculation engagement: A valuation analyst performs a calculation engagement when (1) the valuation analyst and the client agree on the valuation approaches and methods the valuation analyst will use and the extent of procedures the valuation analyst will perform in the process of calculating the value of a subject interest (these procedures will be more limited than those of a valuation engagement), and (2) the valuation analyst calculates the value in compliance with the agreement. The valuation analyst expresses the results of these procedures as a calculated value. The calculated value is expressed as a range or as a single amount. A calculation engagement does not include all of the procedures required for a valuation engagement.

5.4.4 *Personal Financial Planning*

Personal financial planning engagements are only those that involve developing strategies and making recommendations to assist a client in defining and achieving personal financial goals. Personal financial planning engagements generally involve all of the following tasks:

1. Defining the engagement objectives;
2. Planning the specific procedures appropriate to the engagement;
3. Developing a basis for recommendations;
4. Communicating recommendations to the client;
5. Identifying the tasks for taking actions on planning decisions and making recommendations to assist a client in defining and achieving personal financial goals.

In addition, personal financial planning services could include:

1. Assisting the client to take action on planning decisions.
2. Monitoring the client's progress in achieving goals.
3. Updating recommendations and helping the client revise planning decisions.

However, personal financial planning does not include services that are limited to: (i) compiling personal financial statements; (ii) projecting future taxes; (iii) tax compliance, including, but not limited to, preparation of tax returns; and (iv) tax advice or consultations.

Practice

Question 1

Management's responsibility for the entity's compliance with compliance requirements includes the following:

(a) Identifying the entity's government programs and understanding and complying with the compliance requirements
(b) Establishing and maintaining effective controls that provide reasonable assurance that the entity administers government programs in compliance with the compliance requirements
(c) Evaluating and monitoring the entity's compliance with the compliance requirements
(d) Taking corrective action when instances of noncompliance are identified, including corrective action on audit findings of the compliance audit
(e) All of the above

Question 2

An auditor can accept an assurance engagement only where the practitioner's preliminary knowledge of the engagement circumstances indicates that:

(a) Relevant ethical requirements, such as independence and professional competence will be satisfied
(b) The subject matter is appropriate
(c) The criteria to be used are suitable and are available to the intended users
(d) The practitioner has access to sufficient appropriate evidence to support the practitioner's conclusion
(e) The practitioner's conclusion, in the form appropriate to either a reasonable assurance engagement or a limited assurance engagement, is to be contained in a written report
(f) All of the above

Question 3

Which of the following, is not an element of an assurance engagement?

(a) A three-party relationship involving a practitioner, a responsible party, and intended users
(b) An oral or written assurance report, at the convenience of the auditor, in the form appropriate to a reasonable assurance engagement or a limited assurance engagement
(c) An appropriate subject matter
(d) Suitable criteria
(e) Sufficient appropriate evidence

Question 4

Which of the following characteristics exhibit "Suitable criteria" under the assurance engagement?

(a) Relevance;
(b) Completeness;
(c) Reliability;
(d) Neutrality
(e) Understandability
(f) All of the above

Question 5

John Aristote LP is an audit firm based in Dublin (Ohio). In 2017, the firm was hired to compile the financial statements of Reggie Inc., a nonpublic entity based within the same state. Reggie Inc. financial statements omitted substantially all disclosures required by the GAAP. In its compilation report, John Aristote LP should indicate that the report is:

(a) Prepared in conformity with a comprehensive basis of accounting other than GAAP
(b) Not designed for those who are uninformed about the omitted disclosures
(c) Not compiled in accordance with Statements on Standards for Accounting and Review Services
(d) Only binding to those who are informed of the omitted disclosures

CHAPTER 6

Agreed-Upon Procedures

6.1 General

An agreed-upon procedures engagement is one in which a practitioner is engaged by a client to issue a report of findings based on the specific procedures performed on the subject matter. The client engages the practitioner to assist specified parties in evaluating subject matter or an assertion as a result of a need or needs of the specified parties. Because the specified parties require that findings be independently derived, the services of a practitioner are obtained to perform procedures and report his or her findings. The specified parties and the practitioner agree upon the procedures to be performed by the practitioner that the specified parties believe are appropriate. Because the needs of the specified parties may vary widely, the nature, timing, and extent of the agreed-upon procedures may vary as well; consequently, the specified parties assume responsibility for the sufficiency of the procedures since they best understand their own needs. In an agreed-upon engagement, the practitioner does not perform an examination or a review, and does not provide an opinion or negative assurance. Instead, the practitioner's report on agreed-upon procedures should be in the form of procedures and findings.

As a consequence of the role of the specified parties in agreeing upon the procedures performed or to be performed, a practitioner's report on such engagements should clearly indicate that its use is restricted to those specified parties.

F. I. Lessambo, *Auditing, Assurance Services, and Forensics*,
https://doi.org/10.1007/978-3-319-90521-1_6

To satisfy the requirements that the practitioner and the specified parties agree upon the procedures performed or to be performed and that the specified parties take responsibility for the sufficiency of the agreed-upon procedures for their purposes. Ordinarily, the practitioner should communicate directly with and obtain an affirmative acknowledgment from each of the specified parties. This may, for instance, be accomplished by meeting with the specified parties or by distributing a draft of the anticipated report or a copy of an engagement letter to the specified parties and obtaining their agreement. If the practitioner is not able to communicate directly with all of the specified parties, the practitioner may satisfy these requirements by applying any one or more of the following or similar procedures.

a. Compare the procedures to be applied to written requirements of the specified parties.
b. Discuss the procedures to be applied with appropriate representatives of the specified parties involved.
c. Review relevant contracts with or correspondence from the specified parties.

The auditor should not report on an engagement when specified parties do not agree upon the procedures performed or to be performed and do not take responsibility for the sufficiency of the procedures for their purposes.

The general, fieldwork, and reporting standards for attestation engagements together with interpretive guidance regarding their application as addressed throughout this section, should be followed by the practitioner in performing and reporting on agreed-upon procedures engagements.

6.2 Conditions for Engagement Performance

The auditor may perform an agreed-upon procedure attest engagement provided that:

a. The auditor is independent.
b. One of the following conditions is met:

(1) The party wishing to engage the practitioner is responsible for the subject matter, or has a reasonable basis for providing a written assertion about the subject matter when the nature of

the subject matter is such that a responsible party does not otherwise exist.

(2) The party wishing to engage the practitioner is not responsible for the subject matter but is able to provide the practitioner, or have a third party who is responsible for the subject matter provide the practitioner with evidence of the third party's responsibility for the subject matter.

c. The auditor and the specified parties agree upon the procedures performed or to be performed by the practitioner.
d. The specified parties take responsibility for the sufficiency of the agreed-upon procedures for their purposes.
e. The specific subject matter to which the procedures are to be applied is subject to reasonably consistent measurement.
f. Criteria to be used in the determination of findings are agreed upon between the practitioner and the specified parties.
g. The procedures to be applied to the specific subject matter are expected to result in reasonably consistent findings using the criteria.
h. Evidential matter related to the specific subject matter to which the procedures are applied is expected to exist to provide a reasonable basis for expressing the findings in the practitioner's report.
i. Where applicable, the practitioner and the specified parties agree on any materiality limits for reporting purposes.
j. Use of the report is restricted to the specified parties.
k. For agreed-upon procedures engagements on prospective financial information, the prospective financial statements include a summary of significant assumptions.

6.3 Subject-Matter and Related Assertions

The subject matter of an agreed-upon procedures engagement may take many different forms and may be at a point in time or covering a period of time. In an agreed-upon procedures engagement, it is the specific subject matter to which the agreed-upon procedures are to be applied using the criteria selected. Even though the procedures are agreed upon between the practitioner and the specified parties, the subject matter, and the criteria must meet the conditions set forth in the third general standard. The criteria against which the specific subject matter needs to be measured may be recited within the procedures enumerated or referred to in the practitioner's report.

Any declaration or set of declarations about whether the subject matter is based on or in conformity with is referred to as "assertion." A written assertion is generally not required in an agreed-upon procedures engagement unless specifically required by another attest standard. If, however, the practitioner requests the responsible party to provide an assertion, the assertion may be presented in a representation letter or another written communication from the responsible party, such as in a statement, narrative description, or schedule appropriately identifying what is being presented and the point in time or the period of time covered.

6.4 Establishing an Understanding with the Client

The practitioner should establish an understanding with the client regarding the services to be performed. When the practitioner documents the understanding through a written communication with the client (an engagement letter), such communication should be addressed to the client, and in some circumstances also to all specified parties. Matters that might be included in such an understanding include the following:

- The nature of the engagement
- Identification of the subject matter (or the assertion related thereto), the responsible party, and the criteria to be used
- Identification of specified parties
- Specified parties' acknowledgment of their responsibility for the sufficiency of the procedures.

Specified parties are responsible for the sufficiency (nature, timing, and extent) of the agreed-upon procedures because they best understand their own needs. The specified parties assume the risk that such procedures might be insufficient for their purposes. In addition, the specified parties assume the risk that they might misunderstand or otherwise inappropriately use findings properly reported by the auditor.

- Responsibilities of the auditor

The responsibility of the auditor is to carry out the procedures and report the findings in accordance with the general, fieldwork, and reporting standards. The auditor assumes the risk that misapplication of the procedures may result in inappropriate findings being reported. Furthermore, the auditor assumes the risk that appropriate findings may not be reported or may be reported inaccurately. The auditor's risks can be reduced through adequate planning and supervision and due professional care in performing the procedures, determining the findings, and preparing the report. For that purpose, the auditor should have adequate knowledge in the specific subject matter to which the agreed-upon procedures are to be applied. He or she may obtain such knowledge through formal or continuing education, practical experience, or consultation with others. However, the auditor has no responsibility to determine the differences between the agreed-upon procedures to be performed and the procedures that the auditor would have determined to be necessary had he or she been engaged to perform another form of attest engagement. The procedures that the auditor agrees to perform pursuant to an agreed-upon procedures engagement may be more or less extensive than the procedures that the auditor would determine to be necessary had he or she been engaged to perform another form of engagement.

The procedures that the auditor and specified parties agree upon may be as limited or as extensive as the specified parties desire.[1] However, mere reading of an assertion or specified information about the subject matter does not constitute a procedure sufficient to permit a practitioner to report on the results of applying agreed-upon procedures. In some circumstances, the procedures agreed upon evolve or are modified over the course of the engagement. In general, there is flexibility in determining the procedures as long as the specified parties acknowledge responsibility for the sufficiency of such procedures for their purposes. Matters

[1]Examples of appropriate procedures include the following:

- Execution of a sampling application after agreeing on relevant parameters
- Inspection of specified documents evidencing certain types of transactions or detailed attributes thereof
- Confirmation of specific information with third parties
- Comparison of documents, schedules, or analyses with certain specified attributes
- Performance of specific procedures on work performed by others
- Performance of mathematical computations.

that should be agreed upon include the nature, timing, and extent of the procedures.

The auditor should not agree to perform procedures that are overly subjective and thus possibly open to varying interpretations. Terms of uncertain meaning (such as general review, limited review, check, or test) should not be used in describing the procedures unless such terms are defined within the agreed-upon procedures. The auditor should obtain evidential matter from applying the agreed-upon procedures to provide a reasonable basis for the finding or findings expressed in his or her report, but need not perform additional procedures outside the scope of the engagement to gather additional evidential matter.

The agreed-upon procedures to be enumerated or referred to in the auditor's report are to be performed entirely by the auditor. However, internal auditors or other personnel may prepare schedules and accumulate data or provide other information for the auditor's use in performing the agreed-upon procedures. Also, internal auditors may perform and report separately on procedures that they have carried out. An auditor may agree to perform procedures on information documented in the working papers of internal auditors. However, it is inappropriate for the auditor to: (i) agree to merely read the internal auditors' report solely to describe or repeat their findings; (ii) take responsibility for all or a portion of any procedures performed by internal auditors by reporting those findings as the practitioner's own; and (iii) report in any manner that implies shared responsibility for the procedures with the internal auditors.

The auditor's education and experience enable him or her to be knowledgeable about business matters, in general, but he or she is not expected to have the expertise of a person trained for or qualified to engage in the practice of another profession or occupation. In certain circumstances, it may be appropriate to involve a specialist to assist the practitioner in the performance of one or more procedures. The auditor and the specified parties should explicitly agree to the involvement of the specialist in assisting an auditor in the performance of an agreed-upon procedures engagement. This agreement may be reached when obtaining agreement on the procedures performed or to be performed and acknowledgment of responsibility for the sufficiency of the procedures. The auditor's report should describe the nature of the assistance provided by the specialist. An auditor may agree to apply procedures to the report or work product of a specialist that does not constitute assistance by the specialist to the auditor in an agreed-upon procedures engagement.

An auditor should present the results of applying agreed-upon procedures to specific subject matter in the form of findings. The auditor should not provide negative assurance about whether the subject matter or the assertion is fairly stated based on the criteria. The concept of materiality does not apply to findings to be reported in an agreed-upon procedures engagement unless the definition of materiality is agreed to by the specified parties. Any agreed-upon materiality limits should be described in the practitioner's report. The auditor should avoid vague or ambiguous language in reporting findings.

6.5 Reporting

6.5.1 Required Elements

The auditor's report on agreed-upon procedures should be in the form of procedures and findings. The auditor's report should contain the following elements:

a. A title that includes the word independent
b. Identification of the specified parties
c. Identification of the subject matter (or the written assertion related thereto) and the character of the engagement
d. Identification of the responsible party
e. A statement that the subject matter is the responsibility of the responsible party
f. A statement that the procedures performed were those agreed to by the specified parties identified in the report
g. A statement that the agreed-upon procedures engagement was conducted in accordance with attestation standards established by the AICPA
h. A statement that the sufficiency of the procedures is solely the responsibility of the specified parties and a disclaimer of responsibility for the sufficiency of those procedures
i. A list of the procedures performed (or reference thereto) and related findings (the practitioner should not provide negative assurance)

j. Where applicable, a description of any agreed-upon materiality limits
k. A statement that the practitioner was not engaged to and did not conduct an examination of the subject matter, the objective of which would be the expression of an opinion, a disclaimer of opinion on the subject matter, and a statement that if the practitioner had performed additional procedures, other matters might have come to his or her attention that would have been reported
l. A statement of restrictions on the use of the report because it is intended to be used solely by the specified parties
m. Where applicable, reservations or restrictions concerning procedures or findings
n. For an agreed-upon procedures engagement on prospective financial information
o. Where applicable, a description of the nature of the assistance provided by a specialist
p. The manual or printed signature of the practitioner's firm
q. The date of the report.

The auditor also may include explanatory language about matters such as the following:

- Disclosure of stipulated facts, assumptions, or interpretations (including the source thereof) used in the application of agreed-upon procedures
- Description of the condition of records, controls, or data to which the procedures were applied
- Explanation that the practitioner has no responsibility to update his or her report
- Explanation of sampling risk.

The date of completion of the agreed-upon procedures should be used as the date of the practitioner's report.

Further, when circumstances impose restrictions on the performance of the agreed-upon procedures, the auditor should attempt to obtain agreement from the specified parties for modification of the agreed-upon procedures. When such agreement cannot be obtained (for example, when the agreed-upon procedures are published by a regulatory agency that will not modify the procedures), the auditor should describe any restrictions on the performance of procedures in his or her report or withdraw from the engagement.

6.5.2 *Miscellaneous Reporting Elements*

6.5.2.1 Adding Specified Parties

Subsequent to the completion of the agreed-upon procedures engagement, an auditor may be requested to consider the addition of another party as a specified party (a nonparticipant party). The auditor may agree to add a nonparticipant party as a specified party, based on the consideration of such factors as the identity of the nonparticipant party and the intended use of the report. If the auditor does agree to add the nonparticipant party, he or she should obtain affirmative acknowledgment, normally in writing, from the nonparticipant party agreeing to the procedures performed and of its taking responsibility for the sufficiency of the procedures. If the nonparticipant party is added after the auditor has issued his or her report, the report may be reissued or the auditor may provide other written acknowledgment that the nonparticipant party has been added as a specified party. If the report is reissued, the report date should not be changed. If the auditor provides written acknowledgment that the nonparticipant party has been added as a specified party, such written acknowledgment ordinarily should state that no procedures have been performed subsequent to the date of the report.

6.5.2.2 Written Representations

An auditor may find a representation letter to be a useful and practical means of obtaining representations from the responsible party. The need for such a letter may depend on the nature of the engagement and the specified parties.

Examples of matters that might appear in a representation letter from the responsible party include the following:

a. A statement acknowledging responsibility for the subject matter and, when applicable, the assertion
b. A statement acknowledging responsibility for selecting the criteria and for determining that such criteria are appropriate for their purposes

c. The assertion about the subject matter based on the criteria selected
d. A statement that all known matters contradicting the subject matter or the assertion and any communication from regulatory agencies affecting the subject matter or the assertion has been disclosed to the practitioner
e. Availability of all records relevant to the subject matter and the agreed-upon procedures
f. Other matters as the practitioner deems appropriate.

The responsible party's refusal to furnish written representations determined by the practitioner to be appropriate for the engagement constitutes a limitation on the performance of the engagement. In such circumstances, the practitioner should do one of the following.

a. Disclose in his or her report the inability to obtain representations from the responsible party, and withdraw from the engagement.
b. Change the engagement to another form of engagement.

6.5.2.3 *Knowledge of Matters Outside Agreed-Upon Procedures*

The auditor need not perform procedures beyond the agreed-upon procedures. However, in connection with the application of agreed-upon procedures, if matters come to the auditor's attention by other means that significantly contradict the subject matter (or written assertion related thereto) referred to in the practitioner's report, the auditor should include this matter in his or her report. For example, if, during the course of applying agreed-upon procedures regarding an entity's internal control, the auditor becomes aware of a material weakness by means other than the performance of the agreed-upon procedure, the auditor should include this matter in his or her report.

6.5.2.4 *Change to an Agreed-Upon Procedure Engagement*

An auditor who has been engaged to perform another form of attest engagement or a non-attest service engagement may, before the engagement's completion, be requested to change the engagement to an agreed-upon procedures engagement. A request to change the engagement may result from a change in circumstances affecting the client's requirements, a misunderstanding about the nature of the original services or the alternative services originally available, or a restriction on the performance of the original engagement, whether imposed by the client or caused by circumstances. Before an auditor who was engaged to perform another form of engagement agrees to change the engagement to an agreed-upon procedures engagement, he or she should consider the following:

a. The possibility that certain procedures performed as part of another type of engagement are not appropriate for inclusion in an agreed-upon procedures engagement
b. The reason given for the request, particularly the implications of a restriction on the scope of the original engagement or the matters to be reported
c. The additional effort required to complete the original engagement
d. If applicable, the reasons for changing from a general-use report to a restricted-use report.

If the specified parties acknowledge agreement to the procedures performed or to be performed and assume responsibility for the sufficiency of the procedures to be included in the agreed-upon procedures engagement, either of the following would be considered a reasonable basis for requesting a change in the engagement: (a) a change in circumstances that requires another form of engagement; and (b) a misunderstanding concerning the nature of the original engagement or the available alternatives.

If the auditor concludes, based on his or her professional judgment, that there is reasonable justification to change the engagement, and provided he or she complies with the standards applicable to agreed-upon procedures engagements, the auditor should issue an appropriate agreed-upon procedures report. The report should not include reference to either the original engagement or performance limitations that resulted in the changed engagement.

6.5.2.5 Combined Reports Covering Both Restricted-Use and General-Use Subject Matter

When a practitioner performs services pursuant to an engagement to apply agreed-upon procedures to specific subject matter as part of or in addition to another form of service, this section applies only to those services described herein; other Standards would apply to the other services. Other services may include an audit, review, or compilation of a financial statement, another attest service performed pursuant to the SSAEs, or a non-attest service. Reports on applying agreed-upon procedures to specific subject matter may be combined with reports on such other services, provided the types of services can be clearly distinguished and the applicable Standards for each service are followed.

Illustrative Report

Independent Accountant's Report on Applying Agreed-Upon Procedures

To the Audit Committees and Managements of ABC Inc. and XYZ Fund:

We have performed the procedures enumerated below, which were agreed to by the audit committees and managements of ABC Inc. and XYZ Fund, solely to assist you in evaluating the accompanying Statement of Investment Performance Statistics of XYZ Fund (prepared in accordance with the criteria specified therein) for the year ended December 31, 20X1. XYZ Fund's management is responsible for the statement of investment performance statistics. This agreed-upon procedures engagement was conducted in accordance with attestation standards established by the American Institute of Certified Public Accountants. The sufficiency of these procedures is solely the responsibility of those parties specified in this report. Consequently, we make no representation regarding the sufficiency of the procedures described below either for the purpose for which this report has been requested or for any other purpose.

[Include paragraphs to enumerate procedures and findings.]

We were not engaged to and did not conduct an examination, the objective of which would be the expression of an opinion on the accompanying Statement of Investment Performance Statistics of XYZ Fund. Accordingly, we do not express such an opinion. Had we performed additional procedures, other matters might have come to our attention that would have been reported to you.

This report is intended solely for the information and use of the audit committees and managements of ABC Inc. and XYZ Fund, and is not intended to be and should not be used by anyone other than these specified parties.

[Signature]

[Date]

6.6 Case Study: James Thomas McCurdy v. SEC[2]

The Securities and Exchange Commission suspended James T. McCurdy for one year after finding that he recklessly departed from generally accepted auditing standards ("GAAS") in his audit of a mutual fund's 1998 financial statements. The Commission charged McCurdy with improper professional conduct in violation of Rule 102(e) of the Commission's Rules of Practice, citing his failure to obtain sufficient competent evidence to support his conclusion regarding the receivable, his failure to render an accurate report, and his lack of professional skepticism and due professional care.

The relevant facts of the case can be summed up as follows:

- John W. Bagwell founded JWB Aggressive Growth Fund and registered it with the Commission in 1995. Bagwell served as the fund's chief executive officer and was a member of its board of trustees. JWB Investment Advisory & Research, Inc., Bagwell's sole proprietorship, was the investment advisor of the fund, its only client.
- When the fund began operations in 1996, Bagwell voluntarily agreed to waive any management fees and to reimburse the fund for its expenses exceeding 2.35% of the fund's assets. In the years that followed, the fund paid the expenses when incurred and Bagwell reimbursed it at the end of the year for the amount reported in the fund's "Due from Advisor" account. The arrangement was terminable at will, with advance notice to the board of trustees. Until the year ending December 31, 1998, Bagwell covered all such expenses. At the end of 1997, the unpaid balance in the "Due from Advisor" account was $3783.
- During 1998, the fund's expenses grew to approximately $100,000. By year end, the "Due from Advisor" account had an outstanding balance of about $80,000, after an approximately $20,000 offset for organizational expenses due to Bagwell.
- On November 20, 1998, Bagwell sent a letter to the board, outlining a proposed repayment plan, with monthly payments of at least $5,000 a month, beginning that month and continuing until the receivable was repaid.

[2]James Thomas McCurdy v. SEC, US Court of Appeals for the District of Columbia Circuit, No. 04-1047, Feb 8, 2005.

- At a meeting of the five-member board on December 3, 1998, Bagwell gave notice of his intention to withdraw from the reimbursement agreement. By this time, Bagwell had already missed his proposed first payment. He informed the board that it would be "extremely difficult" for him to pay off the receivable by year's end. The four other board members reviewed Bagwell's income statement and balance sheet, which he had provided at the meeting. Satisfied of his ability to pay, they agreed to allow him until June 1999 to repay the $80,000 balance on the payment terms he had proposed.
- At the same meeting, the board followed Bagwell's recommendation and retained a new auditor, McCurdy & Associates CPAs, Inc., an accounting firm specializing in mutual funds. The firm's founder, James Thomas McCurdy, had been a certified public accountant licensed to practice in Ohio since 1980.
- McCurdy completed his fieldwork on the audit in January 1999, and submitted a report dated January 25. By that time, Bagwell had missed his first two payments under the board- approved schedule and was at least $10,000 in arrears.
- McCurdy's report accompanied the fund's filings with the Commission on March 8, 1999.
- The fund's audited financial statements showed $340,484 in assets, of which $83,399 represented the "Due from Advisor" receivable. In light of the fact that 25% of the fund's assets depended on the collectibility of this related-party account, McCurdy recognized that the receivable was material and would require special scrutiny.
- In analyzing the probability of collecting the receivable, he relied on the board's decision to allow Bagwell time to repay his obligation. He read the minutes of the meeting. He also spoke to the fund's attorney, who was present at the meeting. But he did not speak with any board member or with Bagwell (except to confirm that the receivable existed), and he neither examined nor tested the financial data Bagwell presented to the board.
- McCurdy also relied on the February 1999 renewal of the fund's bond by Gulf Insurance Company, although he took no steps to ascertain the basis for the company's decision. And he considered Bagwell's history of making timely payments in previous years, as well as the fact that the receivable could no longer continue to grow because the reimbursement arrangement had terminated. On the

basis of this information, McCurdy concluded that the receivable was probably collectible and that it properly could be treated as an asset under generally accepted accounting principles.

- McCurdy took no steps to obtain or consult any of these sources with regard to this receivable. The question then is whether, in view of the information upon which he did rely, the Commission was warranted in finding that he lacked sufficient information to form a reasoned judgment about the receivable's collectibility.
- The Commission found, for instance, that Gulf Insurance Company's renewal of the fund's bond in February 1999 could not support a reasonable judgment that the receivable was collectible. The bond covered "Uncollectible Items," with a limit of liability of $25,000. The record does not establish whether, at the time, Gulf was aware of the status of the receivable.
- The Commission believed that Gulf had only the fund's 1997 financial statements, apparently because the 1998 financial statements listing the receivable were not filed with the Commission until March.
- In any case, McCurdy could not have known whether Gulf investigated the receivable in deciding to renew the bond. He did not contact Gulf or otherwise attempt to ascertain the reason for Gulf's decision; his inference of support for the collectibility of the receivable amounted to pure speculation.
- McCurdy viewed $83,399 as not "inherently large." However, what matters under GAAS is that the receivable comprised a quarter of the fund's assets, which made it important for an independent auditor to examine carefully whether Bagwell could and would repay the balance on time.
- Neither the reliability of Bagwell's balance sheet nor its financial condition at the time can be gleaned from these statements. Collection of the debt depended on both. Yet, McCurdy took no steps to investigate. The Commission determined, with ample support in the record, that the evidence McCurdy had before him at the conclusion of his audit was insufficient to support his conclusion that the receivable was probably collectible.
- In defense of his complete failure to seek firsthand corroboration of Bagwell's financial situation, McCurdy alleged:

(i) that his actions fell within the bounds of auditor judgment as contemplated by GAAS
(ii) the Commission ignored this scienter requirement
(iii) that GAAS in fact prefer independent evidence to records in the control of the audited company
(iv) that because the Commission based its suspension solely on his past conduct, the order was ultra vires and should be set aside.

After reexamining all the records, the Circuit held the SEC suspension on the basis that (i) he failed to obtain sufficient competent evidence to support his conclusion regarding the receivable, (ii) he failed to render an accurate report, and his lack of professional skepticism and due professional care.

Practice

Question 1

The auditor can perform an agreed-upon procedure attest engagement provided that:

(a) The auditor is independent
(b) The auditor and the specified parties agree upon the procedures performed or to be performed by the practitioner
(c) The specific subject matter to which the procedures are to be applied is subject to reasonably consistent measurement
(d) The procedures to be applied to the specific subject matter are expected to result in reasonably consistent findings using the criteria.
(e) All of the above

Question 2

In an agreed-upon procedure, the auditor is responsible for all the below, except:

(a) To carry out the procedures and report the findings in accordance with the general, fieldwork, and reporting standards
(b) Assumes the risk that misapplication of the procedures may result in inappropriate findings being reported

(c) Assumes the risk that appropriate findings may not be reported or may be reported inaccurately
(d) Assumes the risk of any inappropriately use of his findings by the specified parties

Question 3

In agreed-upon procedure, the specified parties are responsible for all, except:

(a) Assume the risk that such procedures might be insufficient for their purposes
(b) Assume the risk that they might misunderstand or otherwise inappropriately use findings properly reported by the practitioner
(c) Are responsible for the sufficiency (nature, timing, and extent) of the agreed-upon procedures because they best understand their own needs
(d) Assume the risk that the auditor misapplication of the procedures may result in inappropriate findings being reported

Question 4

The following assertions are true, concerning the agreed-upon procedure engagement, except:

(a) The subject matter of an agreed-upon procedures engagement may take many different forms and may be at a point in time or covering a period of time
(b) The auditor should not agree to perform procedures that are overly subjective and thus possibly open to varying interpretations
(c) Matters that should be agreed upon include the nature, timing, and extent of the procedures
(d) The auditor should obtain evidential matter from applying the agreed-upon procedures to provide a reasonable basis for the finding or findings expressed in his or her report

CHAPTER 7

Professional Standards: Independence, Integrity, and Objectivity

7.1 General

It is of utmost importance to the profession that the general public maintains confidence in the independence of the independent auditor. The twofold independence is either real or apparent.

a. Independence of mind

The state of mind that permits the expression of a conclusion without being affected by influences that compromise professional judgment, thereby allowing an individual to act with integrity and exercise objectivity and professional skepticism.

b. Independence in appearance

The avoidance of facts and circumstances that are so significant that a reasonable and informed third party would be likely to conclude, weighing all the specific facts and circumstances, that a firm's, or a member of the audit team's, integrity, objectivity, or professional skepticism has been compromised.

F. I. Lessambo, *Auditing, Assurance Services, and Forensics*,
https://doi.org/10.1007/978-3-319-90521-1_7

7.2 Independence Impairment[1]

A member in public practice shall be independent in the performance of professional services as required by standards promulgated by bodies designated by Council. Independence shall be considered to be impaired if:

A. During the period of the professional engagement a covered member:

(1) Had or was committed to acquire any direct or material indirect financial interest in the client
(2) was a trustee of any trust or executor or administrator of any estate if such trust or estate had or was committed to acquire any direct or material indirect financial interest in the client and

  (i) The covered member (individually or with others) had the authority to make investment decisions for the trust or estate; or
  (ii) The trust or estate owned or was committed to acquire more than 10% of the client's outstanding equity securities or other ownership interests; or
  (iii) The value of the trust's or estate's holdings in the client exceeded 10% of the total assets of the trust or estate.

(3) Had a joint closely held investment that was material to the covered member,
(4) except as specifically permitted in interpretation 101-5 [ET Section 101.07], had any loan to or from the client, any officer or director of the client, or any individual owning 10% or more of the client's outstanding equity securities or other ownership interests.

B. During the period of the professional engagement, a partner or professional employee of the firm, his or her immediate family, or any group of such persons acting together owned more than 5% of a client's outstanding equity securities or other ownership interests.
C. During the period covered by the financial statements or during the period of the professional engagement, a firm, or partner or professional employee of the firm was simultaneously associated with the client as a(n).

[1] ET Section 100.

(1) Director, officer, or employee, or in any capacity equivalent to that of a member of management;
(2) Promoter, underwriter, or voting trustee; or
(3) Trustee for any pension or profit-sharing trust of the client.

7.2.1 Scope of the Independence

Rule 101 covers (i) members formerly employed by a client or otherwise associated with a client; (ii) covered member's immediate family; (iii) close relatives; (iv) grandfathered employment relationships; and (v) others.

7.2.1.1 Members Formerly Employed by a Client or Otherwise Associated with a Client

An individual who was formerly (i) employed by a client or (ii) associated with a client as a(n) officer, director, promoter, underwriter, voting trustee, or trustee for a pension or profit-sharing trust of the client would impair his or her firm's independence if the individual:

- Participated on the attest engagement team or was an individual in a position to influence the attest engagement for the client when the attest engagement covers any period that includes his or her former employment or association with that client; or
- Was otherwise a covered member with respect to the client unless the individual first dissociates from the client by:

  (a) Terminating any relationships with the client described in interpretation 101-1.C;
  (b) Disposing of any direct or material indirect financial interest in the client;
  (c) Collecting or repaying any loans to or from the client, except for loans specifically permitted or grandfathered under interpretation 101-5;
  (d) Ceasing to participate in all employee benefit plans sponsored by the client, unless the client is legally required to allow the individual to participate in the plan (e.g., COBRA) and the individual pays 100% of the cost of participation on a current basis; and

(e) Liquidating or transferring all vested benefits in the client's defined benefit plans, defined contribution plans, deferred compensation plans, and other similar arrangements at the earliest date permitted under the plan. However, liquidation or transfer is not required if a penalty significant to the benefits is imposed upon liquidation or transfer.

7.2.1.2 Covered Member's Immediate Family

A covered member's immediate family is subject to rule 101. However, there are several exceptions:

- an individual in a covered member's immediate family was employed by the client in a position other than a key position.
- in connection with his or her employment, an individual in the immediate family of one of the following covered members participated in a retirement, savings, compensation, or similar plan that is a client, is sponsored by a client, or that invests in a client (provided such plan is normally offered to all employees in similar positions):

    (a) A partner or manager who provides ten or more hours of non-attest services to the client; or
    (b) Any partner in the office in which the lead attest engagement partner primarily practices in connection with the attest engagement.

7.2.1.3 Independence Rules to Close Relatives

Independence would be considered to be impaired if:

1. an individual participating on the attest engagement team has a close relative who had a key position with the client, or a financial interest in the client that (i) was material to the close relative and of which the individual has knowledge; or (ii) enabled the close relative to exercise significant influence over the client.
2. an individual in a position to influence the attest engagement or any partner in the office in which the lead attest engagement partner primarily practices in connection with the attest engagement has a close relative who had a key position with the client; or a financial interest in the client that (i) was material to the close relative and of which the individual or partner has knowledge; and (ii) enabled the close relative to exercise significant influence over the client.

7.2.1.4 Grandfathered Employment Relationships

Employment relationships of a covered member's immediate family and close relatives with an existing attest client that impair independence under this interpretation and that existed as of November 2001, will not be deemed to impair independence provided such relationships were permitted under preexisting requirements of rule 101.

Likewise, a firm's independence will be considered to be impaired with respect to a client if a partner or professional employee leaves the firm and is subsequently employed by or associated with that client in a key position unless all the following conditions are met:

- Amounts due to the former partner or professional employee for his or her previous interest in the firm and for unfunded, vested retirement benefits are not material to the firm, and the underlying formula used to calculate the payments remains fixed during the payout period. Retirement benefits may also be adjusted for inflation and interest may be paid on amounts due.
- The former partner or professional employee is not in a position to influence the accounting firm's operations or financial policies.
- The former partner or professional employee does not participate or appear to participate in, and is not associated with the firm, whether or not compensated for such participation or association, once employment or association with the client begins. An appearance of participation or association results from such actions as:
    - the individual provides consultation to the firm.
    - the firm provides the individual with an office and related amenities (e.g., secretarial and telephone services).
    - the individual's name is included in the firm's office directory.
    - the individual's name is included as a member of the firm in other membership lists of business, professional, or civic organizations, unless the individual is clearly designated as retired.
- The ongoing attest engagement team considers the appropriateness or necessity of modifying the engagement procedures to adjust for the risk that, by virtue of the former partner or professional employee's prior knowledge of the audit plan, audit effectiveness could be reduced.

- The firm assesses whether existing attest engagement team members have the appropriate experience and stature to effectively deal with the former partner or professional employee and his or her work, when that person will have significant interaction with the attest engagement team.
- The subsequent attest engagement is reviewed to determine whether the engagement team members maintained the appropriate level of skepticism when evaluating the representations and work of the former partner or professional employee, when the person joins the client in a key position within one year of disassociating from the firm and has significant interaction with the attest engagement team. The review should be performed by a professional with appropriate stature, expertise, and objectivity and should be tailored based on the position that the person assumed at the client, the position he or she held at the firm, the nature of the services he or she provided to the client, and other relevant facts and circumstances. Appropriate actions, as deemed necessary, should be taken based on the results of the review.

Moreover, when a member of the attest engagement team or an individual in a position to influence the attest engagement intends to seek or discuss potential employment or association with an attest client, or is in receipt of a specific offer of employment from an attest client, independence will be impaired with respect to the client unless the person promptly reports such consideration or offer to an appropriate person in the firm, and removes himself or herself from the engagement until the employment offer is rejected or employment is no longer being sought. When a covered member becomes aware that a member of the attest engagement team or an individual in a position to influence the attest engagement is considering employment or association with a client, the covered member should notify an appropriate person in the firm. The appropriate person should consider what additional procedures may be necessary to provide reasonable assurance that any work performed for the client by that person was performed with objectivity and integrity as required under rule 102 [ET Section 102.01]. Additional procedures, such as re-performance of work already done, will depend on the nature of the engagement and the individual involved.

Furthermore, a member or his or her firm ("member") who performs an attest engagement for a client may also perform other non-attest services ("other services") for that client. Before a member performs other services for an attest client, he or she must evaluate the effect of such services on his or her independence. In particular, care should be taken not to perform management functions or make management decisions for the attest client, the responsibility for which remains with the client's board of directors and management. Before performing other services, the member should establish an understanding with the client regarding the objectives of the engagement, the services to be performed, management's responsibilities, the member's responsibilities, and the limitations of the engagement. It is preferable that this understanding be documented in an engagement letter. In addition, the member should be satisfied that the client is in a position to have an informed judgment on the results of the other services and that the client understands its responsibility to:

- designate a management-level individual or individuals to be responsible for overseeing the services being provided
- evaluate the adequacy of the services performed and any findings that result
- make management decisions, including accepting responsibility for the results of the other services
- establish and maintain internal controls, including monitoring ongoing activities

As a rule thumb, the following are some general activities that would be considered to impair a member's independence:

- authorizing, executing, or consummating a transaction, or otherwise exercising authority on behalf of a client or having the authority to do so;
- preparing source documents or originating data, in electronic or other form, evidencing the occurrence of a transaction (e.g., purchase orders, payroll time records, and customer orders);
- having custody of client assets;
- supervising client employees in the performance of their normal recurring activities;
- determining which recommendations of the member should be implemented;
- reporting to the board of directors on behalf of management;

- serving as a client's stock transfer or escrow agent, registrar, general counsel or its equivalent.

Finally, independence shall be considered to be impaired if a covered member has any loan to or from a client, any officer, or director of the client, or any individual owning 10% or more of the client's outstanding equity securities or other ownership interests. However, there are several exceptions grouped under (i) grandfathered loans; and (ii) permitted loans.

i. Grandfathered loans
   Unsecured loans that are not material to the covered member's net worth, home mortgages, and other secured loans are grandfathered if:

   - they were obtained from a financial institution under that institution's normal lending procedures, terms, and requirements,
   - after becoming a covered member they are kept current as to all terms at all times and those terms do not change in any manner not provided for in the original loan agreement, and
   - they were: (a) obtained from the financial institution prior to its becoming a client requiring independence; or (b) obtained from a financial institution for which independence was not required and were later sold to a client for which independence is required; or (c) obtained prior to February 5, 2001 and met the requirements of previous provisions of Interpretation 101-5 [ET Section 101.07] covering grandfathered loans; or (d) obtained between February 5, 2001 and May 31, 2002, and the covered member was in compliance with the applicable independence requirements of the SEC during that period; or (e) obtained after May 31, 2002 from a financial institution client requiring independence by a borrower prior to his or her becoming a covered member with respect to that client.

   For purposes of applying the grandfathered loans provision when the covered member is a partner in a partnership:

   - A loan to a limited partnership (or similar type of entity) or a general partnership would be ascribed to each covered member who is a partner in the partnership on the basis of their legal liability as a limited or general partner if: (i) the covered member's

interest in the limited partnership, either individually or combined with the interest of one or more covered members, exceeds 50% of the total limited partnership interest; or (ii) the covered member, either individually or together with one or more covered members, can control the general partnership.
- Even if no amount of a partnership loan is ascribed to the covered member(s) identified above, independence is considered to be impaired if the partnership renegotiates the loan or enters into a new loan that is not one of the permitted loans described below.

ii. Permitted loans

These loans must be obtained under the institution's normal lending procedures, terms, and requirements and must, at all times, be kept current as to all terms.

- Automobile loans and leases collateralized by the automobile.
- Loans fully collateralized by the cash surrender value of an insurance policy.
- Loans fully collateralized by cash deposits at the same financial institution (e.g. "passbook loans").
- Credit cards and cash advances where the aggregate outstanding balance on the current statement is reduced to $5000 or less by the payment due date.

In some circumstances, independence may be considered to be impaired as a result of litigation or the expressed intention to commence litigation.

7.2.2 *Effects of Impairment of Independence*

If the covered member believes that the circumstances would lead a reasonable person having knowledge of the facts to conclude that the actual or intended litigation poses an unacceptable threat to independence, the covered member should either (a) disengage himself or herself, or (b) disclaim an opinion because of lack of independence. Such disengagement may take the form of resignation or cessation of any attest engagement than in progress pending resolution of the issue between the parties.

7.2.3 *Termination of Impairment*

The conditions giving rise to a lack of independence are generally eliminated when a final resolution is reached and the matters at issue no longer affect the relationship between the covered member and client. The covered member should carefully review the conditions of such resolution to determine that all impairments to the covered member's objectivity have been removed.

7.2.4 *Independence and Cooperative Arrangements with Clients*

Independence will be considered to be impaired if, during the period of a professional engagement, a member or his or her firm had any cooperative arrangement with the client that was material to the member's firm or to the client. A cooperative arrangement exists when a member's firm and a client jointly participate in a business activity. The following are examples, which are not all inclusive, of cooperative arrangements:

- Prime/subcontractor arrangements to provide services or products to a third party
- Joint ventures to develop or market products or services
- Arrangements to combine one or more services or products of the firm with one or more services or products of the client and market the package with references to both parties
- Distribution or marketing arrangements under which the firm acts as a distributor or marketer of the client's products or services, or the client acts as the distributor or marketer of the products or services of the firm.

Nevertheless, joint participation with a client in a business activity does not ordinarily constitute a cooperative arrangement when all the following conditions are present: (a) the participation of the firm and the participation of the client are governed by separate agreements, arrangements, or understandings; (b) the firm assumes no responsibility for the activities or results of the client, and vice versa; and (c) neither party has the authority to act as the representative or agent of the other party.

7.2.5 *Extended Service Engagement*

A member or his or her firm ("member") may be asked by a client, for which the member performs an attest engagement, to perform extended audit services. These services may include assistance in the performance of the client's internal audit activities and/or an extension of the member's audit service beyond the requirements of generally accepted auditing standards (hereinafter referred to as "extended audit services"). In general, a member's performance of extended audit services would not be considered to impair independence with respect to a client for which the member also performs an attest engagement, provided that the member or his or her firm is not an employee of the client or does not act or appear to act in a capacity equivalent to a member of client management.

The responsibilities of the client, including its board of directors, audit committee, and management, and the responsibilities of the member, as described below, should be understood by both the member and the client. It is preferable that this understanding be documented in an engagement letter that indicates that the member may not perform management functions or make management decisions.

A member should be satisfied that the client understands its responsibility for establishing and maintaining internal control and directing the internal audit function, if any. As part of its responsibility to establish and maintain internal control, management monitors internal control to assess the quality of its performance over time. Monitoring can be accomplished through ongoing activities, separate evaluations or a combination of both.

Ongoing monitoring activities are the procedures designed to assess the quality of internal control performance over time and that are built into the normal recurring activities of an entity and include regular management and supervisory activities, comparisons, reconciliations, and other routine actions. Separate evaluations focus on the continued effectiveness of a client's internal control. A member's independence would not be impaired by the performance of separate evaluations of the effectiveness of a client's internal control, including separate evaluations of the client's ongoing monitoring activities.

7.3 Integrity and Objectivity[2]

In the performance of any professional service, a member shall maintain objectivity and integrity, shall be free of conflicts of interest, and shall not knowingly misrepresent facts or subordinate his or her judgment to others. Under rule 102 [ET Section 102.01], a member must maintain objectivity and integrity in the performance of a professional service. In dealing with his or her employer's external accountant, a member must be candid and not knowingly misrepresent facts or knowingly fail to disclose material facts. This would include, for example, responding to specific inquiries for which his or her employer's external accountant requests written representation.

A member shall be considered to have knowingly misrepresented facts in violation of rule 102 when he or she knowingly:

- makes, or permits or directs another to make, materially false and misleading entries in an entity's financial statements or records; or
- fails to correct an entity's financial statements or records that are materially false and misleading when he or she has the authority to record an entry; or
- signs, or permits or directs another to sign, a document containing materially false and misleading information.

A conflict of interest may occur if a member performs a professional service for a client or employer and the member or his or her firm has a relationship with another person, entity, product, or service that could, in the member's professional judgment, be viewed by the client, employer, or other appropriate parties as impairing the member's objectivity. If the member believes that the professional service can be performed with objectivity, and the relationship is disclosed to and consent is obtained from such client, employer, or other appropriate parties, the rule shall not operate to prohibit the performance of the professional service. When making the disclosure, the member should consider Rule 301, Confidential Client Information [ET Section 301.01].

[2] ET Section 102 Prohibits a Member from Knowingly Misrepresenting Facts or Subordinating His or Her Judgment When Performing Professional Services.

Rule 102 [ET Section 102.01] prohibits a member from knowingly misrepresenting facts or subordinating his or her judgment when performing professional services. Under this rule, if a member and his or her supervisor have a disagreement or dispute relating to the preparation of financial statements or the recording of transactions, the member should take the following steps to ensure that the situation does not constitute a subordination of judgment:

- the member should consider whether (a) the entry or the failure to record a transaction in the records, or (b) the financial statement presentation or the nature or omission of disclosure in the financial statements, as proposed by the supervisor, represents the use of an acceptable alternative and does not materially misrepresent the facts. If, after appropriate research or consultation, the member concludes that the matter has authoritative support and/or does not result in a material misrepresentation, the member need do nothing further.
- if the member concludes that the financial statements or records could be materially misstated, the member should make his or her concerns known to the appropriate higher level(s) of management within the organization (e.g.,the supervisor's immediate superior, senior management, the audit committee or equivalent, the board of directors, the company's owners). The member should consider documenting his or her understanding of the facts, the accounting principles involved, the application of those principles to the facts, and the parties with whom these matters were discussed.
- if, after discussing his or her concerns with the appropriate person(s) in the organization, the member concludes that appropriate action was not taken, he or she should consider his or her continuing relationship with the employer. The member also should consider any responsibility that may exist to communicate to third parties, such as regulatory authorities or the employer's (former employer's) external accountant. In this connection, the member may wish to consult with his or her legal counsel.
- the member should at all times be cognizant of his or her obligations under interpretation 102-3 [ET Section 102.04].

Educational services (e.g.,teaching full- or part-time at a university, teaching a continuing professional education course, or engaging in research and scholarship) are professional services as defined in ET Section 92.11, and are therefore subject to rule 102 [ET Section 102.01]. Rule 102 [ET Section 102.01] provides that the member shall maintain objectivity and integrity, shall be free of conflicts of interest, and shall not knowingly misrepresent facts or subordinate his or her judgment to others.

A member or a member's firm may be requested by a client:

- To perform tax or consulting services engagements that involve acting as an advocate for the client.
- To act as an advocate in support of the client's position on accounting or financial reporting issues, either within the firm or outside the firm with standard setters, regulators, or others.

Services provided or actions taken pursuant to such types of client requests are professional services [ET Section 92.11] governed by the Code of Professional Conduct and shall be performed in compliance with Rule 201, General Standards [ET Section 201.01], Rule 202, Compliance With Standards [ET Section 202.01], and Rule 203, Accounting Principles [ET Section 203.01], and interpretations thereof, as applicable. Furthermore, in the performance of any professional service, a member shall comply with rule 102 [ET Section 102.01], which requires maintaining objectivity and integrity and prohibits subordination of judgment to others. Moreover, there is a possibility that some requested professional services involving client advocacy may appear to stretch the bounds of performance standards, may go beyond sound and reasonable professional practice, or may compromise credibility, and thereby pose an unacceptable risk of impairing the reputation of the member and his or her firm with respect to independence, integrity, and objectivity. In such circumstances, the member and the member's firm should consider whether it is appropriate to perform the service.

Appendix

- Auditor Independence: Evidence on the Joint Effects of Auditor Tenure and Non-audit Fees, by Ferdinand A. Gul, Bikki L. Jaggi, and Gopal V. Krishnan; *AUDITING: A Journal of Practice & Theory*, November 2006, Vol. 25, No. 2, pp. 1–23.

Practice

Question 1

The following are the attributes of an independent auditor, except:

(a) To be independent an auditor must be without bias with respect to the client since otherwise, he would lack that impartiality necessary for the dependability of his findings
(b) Independence does not imply the attitude of a prosecutor but rather a judicial impartiality that recognizes an obligation for fairness not only to management and owners of a business but also to creditors and those who may otherwise rely (in part, at least) upon
(c) To be independent, the auditor must be intellectually honest; or be recognized as such
(d) To be independent, the auditor must have limited obligation or interest in the client, its management, or its owners

Question 2

Which of the following assertions is inaccurate may challenge the auditor's independence in fact or/and the perceived independence?

(a) An independent auditor auditing a company in which he was also a director may be biased
(b) An auditor with a substantial financial interest in a company may be biased in expressing his opinion on the financial statements of the company
(c) Independent auditors should only be independent in fact
(d) Independent auditors should avoid situations that may lead outsiders to doubt their independence

Question 3

When the covered member's former employer is one of the sponsors of a governmental public employee retirement system, the covered member may continue to participate in the same governmental plan if:

(a) The covered member neither participates on nor is in a position to influence the attest engagement team during the entire period he or she participates in the plan

(b) His or her current employer is also one of the sponsors of the same plan and participation is required or offered to all employees in comparable employment positions
(c) The covered member has managerial responsibilities in governmental agency under the supervision of the Securities and Exchange Commission
(d) The covered member has no influence of control over the investment strategy, benefits, or other management activities associated with the plan

Question 4

An immediate family member's employment by an attest client would impair independence, unless:

(a) The immediate family member does not have primary responsibility for significant accounting functions that support material components of the financial statements
(b) The immediate family member does not have responsibility for the preparation of the financial statements
(c) The immediate family member is not in a key position at the audit client
(d) The immediate family member has the ability to exercise significant influence over the content of the financial statements

Question 5

If a covered person is the beneficiary of a trust that has a financial interest in a restricted entity, the independence of a member firm ordinarily would be impaired if:

(a) The indirect financial interest in the restricted entity is material to the covered person
(b) The trust was created by the covered person who is named as beneficiary, or
(c) The beneficiary had direct control over the investment decisions or assets of the trust
(d) The beneficiary had indirect control over the investment decisions or assets of the trust
(e) All of the above

PART II

Audit Planning

CHAPTER 8

Audit Planning, Testing, and Materiality

8.1 General

The purpose and objective of planning the audit are the same whether the audit is an initial or recurring engagement. However, for an initial audit, the auditor may need to expand the planning activities because the auditor does not ordinarily have the previous experience with the entity that is considered when planning recurring engagements. For an initial audit engagement, additional matters the auditor may consider in establishing the overall audit strategy and audit plan include the following:

- Arrangements to be made with the predecessor auditor (e.g., to review the predecessor auditor's working papers,
- Any major issues (including the application of accounting principles or auditing and reporting standards) discussed with management in connection with the initial selection as auditor, the communication of these matters to those charged with governance, and how these matters affect the overall audit strategy and audit plan
- The audit procedures necessary to obtain sufficient appropriate audit evidence regarding opening balances. The auditor should obtain sufficient appropriate audit evidence about whether the opening balances contain misstatements that materially affect the current period's financial statements by:

F. I. Lessambo, *Auditing, Assurance Services, and Forensics*,
https://doi.org/10.1007/978-3-319-90521-1_8

(a) Determining whether the prior period's closing balances have been correctly brought forward to the current period or, when appropriate, have been restated;
(b) Determining whether the opening balances reflect the application of appropriate accounting policies; and
(c) Evaluating whether audit procedures performed in the current period provide evidence relevant to the opening balances and performing one or both of the following:

  (i) When the prior year financial statements were audited, reviewing the predecessor auditor's audit documentation to obtain evidence regarding the opening balances
  (ii) Performing specific audit procedures to obtain evidence regarding the opening balances

- Other procedures required by the firm's system of quality control for initial audit engagements (e.g., the firm's system of quality control may require the involvement of another partner or senior individual to review the overall audit strategy prior to commencing significant audit procedures or to review reports prior to their issuance).

Planning an audit involves establishing the overall audit strategy for the engagement and developing an audit plan. Adequate planning provides several advantages, including, among others:

- Identifying and devoting appropriate attention to important areas of the audit
- Identifying and resolving potential problems on a timely basis
- organizing and managing the audit engagement so that it is performed in an effective and efficient manner
- responding to anticipated risks and allocating team member responsibilities
- Assisting, when applicable, in the coordination of work done by auditors of components and specialists.

8.2 Preliminary Engagement Activities

At the beginning of the current audit engagement, the auditor team leader must: (i) conduct the quality Control for an Engagement; (ii) evaluating compliance with relevant ethical requirements; (iii) establish an understanding of the terms of the engagement as required by Section 210—Terms of Engagement. Performing these preliminary engagement activities enables the auditor to plan an audit engagement for which, for example: (i) maintains the necessary independence and ability to perform the engagement; (ii) determines issues with management integrity that may affect the auditor's willingness to continue the engagement; (iii) has no misunderstanding with the entity about the terms of the engagement.

The auditor should establish an overall audit strategy that sets the scope, timing, and direction of the audit and that guides the development of the audit plan. To that end, the auditor should:

- identify the characteristics of the engagement that define its scope;
- ascertain the reporting objectives of the engagement in order to plan the timing of the audit and the nature of the communications required;
- consider the factors that, in the auditor's professional judgment, are significant in directing the engagement team's efforts;
- consider the results of preliminary engagement activities and, when applicable, whether knowledge gained on other engagements performed by the engagement partner for the entity is relevant; and
- ascertain the nature, timing, and extent of resources necessary to perform the engagement.

Performing these preliminary engagement activities enables the auditor to plan an audit engagement for which, for example:

- The auditor maintains the necessary independence and ability to perform the engagement
- The auditor has no issues with management integrity that may affect the auditor's willingness to continue the engagement
- The auditor has no misunderstanding with the entity about the terms of the engagement

The auditor should develop an audit plan that includes a description of the following:

- The nature and extent of planned risk assessment procedures, as determined under Section 315,[1]
- The nature, timing, and extent of planned further audit procedures at the relevant assertion level, as determined under Section 330,[2]
- Other planned audit procedures that are required to be carried out so that the engagement complies with generally accepted auditing standards.

The overall audit strategy and audit plan, is subject to change and updates, as necessary, during the course of the audit. As a result of unexpected events, changes in conditions, or the audit evidence obtained from the results of audit procedures, the auditor may need to modify the overall audit strategy and audit plan and, thereby, the resulting planned nature, timing, and extent of further audit procedures, based on the revised consideration of assessed risks. This may be the case when information comes to the auditor's attention that differs significantly from the information available when the auditor planned the audit procedures. For example, audit evidence obtained through the performance of substantive procedures may contradict the audit evidence obtained through tests of controls. Likewise, the nature, timing, and extent of the direction and supervision of engagement team members and review of their work vary, depending on many factors, including the following:

- the size and complexity of the entity;
- the area of the audit;
- the assessed risks of material misstatement (for example, an increase in the assessed risk of material misstatement for a given area of the audit ordinarily requires a corresponding increase in the extent and timeliness of direction and supervision of engagement team members and a more detailed review of their work);
- the capabilities and competence of the individual team members performing the audit work.

[1] AU-C Section 315.

[2] AU-C Section 330.

8.3 Involvement of Professionals Possessing Specialized Skills

The auditor should consider whether specialized skills are needed in performing the audit. If specialized skills are needed, the auditor should seek the assistance of a professional possessing such skills, who either may be on the auditor's staff or an outside professional. In such circumstances, the auditor should have sufficient knowledge to communicate the objectives of the other professional's work; evaluate whether the specified audit procedures will meet the auditor's objectives; and evaluate the results of the audit procedures applied as they relate to the nature, timing, and extent of further planned audit procedures.

8.4 Documentation

The documentation of the overall audit strategy is a record of the key decisions considered necessary to properly plan the audit and communicate significant issues to the engagement team. For example, the auditor may summarize the overall audit strategy in the form of a memorandum that contains key decisions regarding the overall scope, timing, and conduct of the audit. The documentation of the audit plan is a record of the planned nature, timing, and extent of risk assessment procedures and further audit procedures at the relevant assertion level in response to the assessed risks. It also serves as a record of the proper planning of the audit procedures that can be reviewed and approved prior to their performance. The auditor may use standard audit programs or audit completion checklists, tailored as needed to reflect the particular engagement circumstances. A record of the significant changes to the overall audit strategy and the audit plan and resulting changes to the planned nature, timing, and extent of audit procedures explain why the significant changes were made and why the overall strategy and audit plan were finally adopted for the audit. It also reflects the appropriate response to the significant changes occurring during the audit.

The audit documentation shall include the following:

- The overall audit strategy;
- The audit plan;
- Any significant changes made during the audit engagement to the overall audit strategy or the audit plan and the reasons for such changes.

8.5 Planning Activities

The audit plan is more detailed than the overall audit strategy in that it includes the nature, timing, and extent of audit procedures to be performed by engagement team members. Planning for these audit procedures takes place over the course of the audit as the audit plan for the engagement develops. However, planning the nature, timing, and extent of specific further audit procedures depends on the outcome of those risk assessment procedures. In addition, the auditor may begin the execution of further audit procedures for some classes of transactions, account balances, and disclosures before planning all remaining further audit procedures.

The process of establishing the overall audit strategy assists the auditor to determine, subject to the completion of the auditor's risk assessment procedures, such matters as the following:

- The resources to deploy for specific audit areas, such as the use of appropriately experienced team members for high-risk areas or the involvement of specialists on complex matters
- The amount of resources to allocate to specific audit areas, such as the number of team members assigned to observe the inventory count at material locations, the extent of review of component auditors' work in the case of group audits, or the audit budget (in hours) to allocate to high-risk areas
- When these resources are to be deployed, such as whether at an interim audit stage or at key cutoff dates
- How such resources are managed, directed, and supervised, such as when team briefing and debriefing meetings are expected to be held, how the engagement partner and manager reviews are expected to take place (e.g., on site or off site), and whether
- to complete engagement quality control reviews.

8.6 The Role and Timing of Planning

The nature and extent of planning activities will vary according to the size and complexity of the entity, the key engagement team members' previous experience with the entity, and changes in circumstances that occur during the audit engagement. Planning is not a discrete phase of an audit but rather a continual and iterative process that often begins shortly after (or in connection with) the completion of the previous audit and continues until the completion of the current audit engagement. Planning, however, includes consideration of the timing of certain activities and audit procedures that need to be completed prior to the performance of further audit procedures. For example, planning includes the need to consider, prior to the auditor's identification and assessment of the risks of material misstatement, such matters as the following:

- The analytical procedures to be applied as risk assessment procedures
- A general understanding of the legal and regulatory framework applicable to the entity and how the entity is complying with that framework
- The determination of materiality
- The involvement of specialists
- The performance of other risk assessment procedures

The auditor may decide to discuss elements of planning with the entity's management to facilitate the conduct and management of the audit engagement (e.g., to coordinate some of the planned audit procedures with the work of the entity's personnel). Although these discussions often occur, the overall audit strategy and the audit plan remain the auditor's responsibility. When discussing matters included in the overall audit strategy or audit plan, care is required in order not to compromise the effectiveness of the audit. For example, discussing the nature and timing of detailed audit procedures with management may compromise the effectiveness of the audit by making the audit procedures too predictable.

8.7 Changes During the Course of the Audit

The auditor should modify the overall audit strategy and the audit plan as necessary if circumstances change significantly during the course of the audit, including changes due to a revised assessment of the risks of material misstatement or the discovery of a previously unidentified risk of material misstatement.

8.8 Supervision of Engagement Team Members

The engagement partner and, as applicable, other engagement team members performing supervisory activities, should:

a. Inform engagement team members of their responsibilities including:
   - The objectives of the procedures that they are to perform;
   - The nature, timing, and extent of procedures they are to perform; and
   - Matters that could affect the procedures to be performed or the evaluation of the results of those procedures, including relevant aspects of the company, its environment, and its internal control over financial reporting, and possible accounting and auditing issues.

b. Direct engagement team members to bring significant accounting and auditing issues arising during the audit to the attention of the engagement partner or other engagement team members performing supervisory activities so they can evaluate those issues and determine that appropriate actions are taken in accordance with PCAOB standards

c. Review the work of engagement team members to evaluate whether:
   - The work was performed and documented;
   - The objectives of the procedures were achieved; and
   - The results of the work support the conclusions reached.

To determine the extent of supervision necessary for engagement team members to perform their work as directed and form appropriate conclusions, the engagement partner and other engagement team members performing supervisory activities should take into account: (i) the nature of the company, including its size and complexity; (ii) the nature of the assigned work for each engagement team member; (iii) the risks of material misstatement; and (iv) the knowledge, skill, and ability of each engagement team member.

8.9 Consideration of Materiality in Planning and Performing an Audit[3]

To obtain reasonable assurance about whether the financial statements are free of material misstatement, the auditor should plan and perform audit procedures to detect misstatements that, individually or in combination with other misstatements, would result in material misstatement of the financial statements. This includes being alert while planning and performing audit procedures for misstatements that could be material due to quantitative or qualitative factors.

To plan the nature, timing, and extent of audit procedures, the auditor should establish a materiality level for the financial statements as a whole that is appropriate in light of the particular circumstances. This includes consideration of the company's earnings and other relevant factors. To determine the nature, timing, and extent of audit procedures, the materiality level for the financial statements as a whole needs to be expressed as a specified amount. If financial statements for the audit period are not available, the auditor may establish an initial materiality level based on the estimated or preliminary financial statement amounts. In those situations, the auditor should take into account the effects of known or expected changes in the company's financial statements, including significant transactions or adjustments that are expected to be reflected in the financial statements at the end of the period.

The auditor should evaluate whether, in light of the particular circumstances, there are certain accounts or disclosures for which there is a substantial likelihood that misstatements of lesser amounts than the materiality level established for the financial statements as a whole would influence the judgment of a reasonable investor. If so, the auditor should establish separate materiality levels for those accounts or disclosures to plan the nature, timing, and extent of audit procedures for those accounts or disclosures.

8.9.1 Determining Tolerable Misstatement

The auditor should determine the amount or amounts of tolerable misstatement for purposes of assessing risks of material misstatement and planning and performing audit procedures at the account or disclosure

[3]Auditing Standard No. 11.

level. The auditor should determine tolerable misstatement at an amount or amounts that reduce to an appropriately low level the probability that the total of uncorrected and undetected misstatements would result in material misstatement of the financial statements. In determining tolerable misstatement and planning and performing audit procedures, the auditor should take into account nature, cause (if known), and amount of misstatements that were accumulated in audits of the financial statements of prior periods.

8.9.2 Considerations for Multi-location Engagements

For purposes of the audit of the consolidated financial statements of a company with multiple locations or business units, the auditor should determine tolerable misstatement for the individual locations or business units at an amount that reduces to an appropriately low level the probability that the total of uncorrected and undetected misstatements would result in material misstatement of the consolidated financial statements.

8.9.3 Considerations as the Audit Progresses

The auditor should reevaluate the established materiality level or levels and tolerable misstatement when, because of changes in the particular circumstances or additional information that comes to the auditor's attention, there is a substantial likelihood that misstatements of amounts that differ significantly from the materiality level or levels that were established initially would influence the judgment of a reasonable investor. Situations in which changes in circumstances or additional information that comes to the auditor's attention would require such reevaluation include:

- The materiality level or levels and tolerable misstatement were established initially based on the estimated or preliminary financial statement amounts that differ significantly from actual amounts.
- Events or changes in conditions occurring after the materiality level or levels and tolerable misstatement were established initially are likely to affect investors' perceptions about the company's financial position, results of operations, or cash flows.

If the auditor's reevaluation results in a lower amount for the materiality level or levels or tolerable misstatement than initially established by the auditor, the auditor should (1) evaluate the effect, if any, of the lower amount or amounts on his or her risk assessments and audit procedures and (2) modify the nature, timing, and extent of audit procedures as necessary to obtain sufficient appropriate audit evidence.

8.9.4 Identifying and Assessing Risks of Material Misstatement[4]

The auditor must identify and appropriately assess the risk of material misstatement. To that end, the auditor should perform risk assessment procedures that are sufficient to provide a reasonable basis for identifying and assessing the risks of material misstatement, whether due to error or fraud, and designing further audit procedures. Risks of material misstatement can arise from a variety of sources, including external factors, such as conditions in the company's industry and environment, and company-specific factors, such as the nature of the company, its activities, and internal control over financial reporting. Thus, the audit procedures that are necessary to identify and appropriately assess the risks of material misstatement include consideration of both external factors and company-specific factors.

8.9.4.1 Obtaining an Understanding of the Company and Its Environment

The auditor should obtain an understanding of the company and its environment ("understanding of the company") to understand the events, conditions, and company activities that might reasonably be expected to have a significant effect on the risks of material misstatement. Obtaining an understanding of the company includes understanding:

a. Relevant industry, regulatory, and other external factors
   Obtaining an understanding of relevant industry, regulatory, and other external factors encompasses industry factors, including the competitive environment and technological developments; the regulatory environment, including the applicable financial reporting framework and the legal and political environment; and external factors, including general economic conditions.

[4] Auditing Standard No. 12.

b. Nature of the Company
Obtaining an understanding of the nature of the company includes understanding:

- The company's organizational structure and management personnel;
- The sources of funding of the company's operations and investment activities, including the company's capital structure, non-capital funding;
- The company's significant investments, including equity method investments, joint ventures, and variable interest entities;
- The company's operating characteristics, including its size and complexity;
- The sources of the company's earnings, including the relative profitability of key products and services; and
- Key supplier and customer relationships.

c. Selection and Application of Accounting Principles, Including Related Disclosures
The auditor should evaluate whether the company's selection and application of accounting principles are appropriate for its business and consistent with the applicable financial reporting framework and accounting principles used in the relevant industry. Also, to identify and assess risks of material misstatement related to omitted, incomplete, or inaccurate disclosures, the auditor should develop expectations about the disclosures that are necessary for the company's financial statements to be presented fairly in conformity with the applicable financial reporting framework.

d. Company Objectives, Strategies, and Related Business Risks
The purpose of obtaining an understanding of the company's objectives, strategies, and related business risks is to identify business risks that could reasonably be expected to result in material misstatement of the financial statements.

e. Company Performance Measures
The purpose of obtaining an understanding of the company's performance measures is to identify performance measures, whether external or internal, affect the risks of material misstatement.

8.9.4.2 Obtaining an Understanding of Internal Control Over Financial Reporting

Obtaining an understanding of internal control includes evaluating the design of controls that are relevant to the audit and determining whether the controls have been implemented. Walkthroughs procedures ordinarily are sufficient to evaluate design effectiveness. Internal control over financial reporting can be described as consisting of the following components:

- the control environment,
- the company's risk assessment process,
- information and communication,
- control activities, and
- monitoring of controls.

Obtaining an understanding of the control environment includes assessing: (i) Whether management's philosophy and operating style promote effective internal control over financial reporting; (ii) whether sound integrity and ethical values, particularly of top management, are developed and understood; and (iii) whether the board or audit committee understands and exercises oversight responsibility over financial reporting and internal control. The auditor must identify: (i) the Company's Risk Assessment Process; (ii) Information and Communication; (iii) Control Activities; and further.

8.10 The Auditor's Responses to the Risks of Material Misstatement

To meet the objective in the preceding paragraph, the auditor must design and implement audit responses that address the risks of material misstatement that are identified and assessed in accordance with Auditing Standard No. 12.[5] The auditor's response can (i) have an overall effect on how the audit is conducted ("overall responses"), or (ii) involve the nature, timing, and extent of the audit procedures to be performed.[6]

[5] Auditing Standard No. 12, Identifying and Assessing Risks of Material Misstatement.

[6] Auditing Standard No. 13—The Auditor's Responses to the Risks of Material Misstatement.

8.10.1 Overall Responses

The auditor should design and implement overall responses to address the assessed risks of material misstatement as follows:

a. Making appropriate assignments of significant engagement responsibilities. The knowledge, skill, and ability of engagement team members with significant engagement responsibilities should be commensurate with the assessed risks of material misstatement.
b. Providing the extent of supervision that is appropriate for the circumstances, including, in particular, the assessed risks of material misstatement.
c. Incorporating elements of unpredictability in the selection of audit procedures to be performed. As part of the auditor's response to the assessed risks of material misstatement, including the assessed risks of material misstatement due to fraud ("fraud risks"), the auditor should incorporate an element of unpredictability in the selection of auditing procedures to be performed from year to year. Examples of ways to incorporate an element of unpredictability include:

    (1) Performing audit procedures related to accounts, disclosures, and assertions that would not otherwise be tested based on their amount or the auditor's assessment of risk;
    (2) Varying the timing of the audit procedures;
    (3) Selecting items for testing that have lower amounts or are otherwise outside customary selection parameters;
    (4) Performing audit procedures on an unannounced basis; and
    (5) In multi-location audits, varying the location or the nature, timing, and extent of audit procedures at related locations or business units from year to year.

d. Evaluating the company's selection and application of significant accounting principles. The auditor should evaluate whether the company's selection and application of significant accounting principles, particularly those related to subjective measurements and complex transactions, are indicative of bias that could lead to material misstatement of the financial statements.

The auditor also should determine whether it is necessary to make pervasive changes to the nature, timing, or extent of audit procedures to adequately address the assessed risks of material misstatement. Examples of such pervasive changes include modifying the audit strategy to: (i) increase the substantive testing of the valuation of numerous significant accounts at year-end because of significantly deteriorating market conditions, and (ii) obtain more persuasive audit evidence from substantive procedures due to the identification of pervasive weaknesses in the company's control environment.

Due professional care requires the auditor to exercise professional skepticism. Professional skepticism is an attitude that includes a questioning mind and a critical assessment of the appropriateness and sufficiency of audit evidence. The auditor's responses to the assessed risks of material misstatement, particularly fraud risks, should involve the application of professional skepticism in gathering and evaluating audit evidence. Examples of the application of professional skepticism in response to the assessed fraud risks are (a) modifying the planned audit procedures to obtain more reliable evidence regarding relevant assertions and (b) obtaining sufficient appropriate evidence to corroborate management's explanations or representations concerning important matters, such as through third-party confirmation, use of a specialist engaged or employed by the auditor, or examination of documentation from independent sources.

8.10.2 Responses Involving the Nature, Timing, and Extent of Audit Procedures

The auditor should design and perform audit procedures in a manner that addresses the assessed risks of material misstatement for each relevant assertion of each significant account and disclosure. In designing the audit procedures to be performed, the auditor should:

- Obtain more persuasive audit evidence the higher the auditor's assessment of risk;
- Take into account the types of potential misstatements that could result from the identified risks and the likelihood and magnitude of potential misstatement;
- In an integrated audit, design the testing of controls to accomplish the objectives of both audits simultaneously:

(i) To obtain sufficient evidence to support the auditor's control risk assessments for purposes of the audit of financial statements; and
(ii) To obtain sufficient evidence to support the auditor's opinion on internal control over financial reporting as of year-end.

The audit procedures performed in response to the assessed risks of material misstatement can be classified into two categories: (1) tests of controls and (2) substantive procedures. For significant risks, the auditor should perform substantive procedures, including tests of details that are specifically responsive to the assessed risks. The audit procedures that are necessary to address the assessed fraud risks depend upon the types of risks and the relevant assertions that might be affected. If the auditor identifies deficiencies in controls that are intended to address assessed fraud risks, the auditor should take into account those deficiencies when designing his or her response to those fraud risks. In the audit of financial statements, the auditor should perform substantive procedures, including tests of details that are specifically responsive to the assessed fraud risks.

- Testing Controls in an Audit of Financial Statements

If the auditor plans to assess control risk at less than the maximum by relying on controls, and the nature, timing, and extent of planned substantive procedures are based on that lower assessment, the auditor must obtain evidence that the controls selected for testing are designed effectively and operated effectively during the entire period of reliance. However, the auditor is not required to assess control risk at less than the maximum for all relevant assertions and, for a variety of reasons, the auditor may choose not to do so. Also, tests of controls must be performed in the audit of financial statements for each relevant assertion for which substantive procedures alone cannot provide sufficient appropriate audit evidence and when necessary to support the auditor's reliance on the accuracy and completeness of financial information used in performing other audit procedures.

In designing and performing tests of controls for the audit of financial statements, the evidence necessary to support the auditor's control risk assessment depends on the degree of reliance the auditor plans to place on the effectiveness of a control. The auditor should obtain more persuasive audit evidence from tests of controls the greater the reliance the auditor places on the effectiveness of a control. The auditor also should obtain more persuasive evidence about the effectiveness of controls for each relevant assertion for which the audit approach consists primarily of tests of controls, including situations in which substantive procedures alone cannot provide sufficient appropriate audit evidence.

- Testing Design Effectiveness

The auditor should test the design effectiveness of the controls selected for testing by determining whether the company's controls, if they are operated as prescribed by persons possessing the necessary authority and competence to perform the control effectively, satisfy the company's control objectives and can effectively prevent or detect error or fraud that could result in material misstatements in the financial statements. Procedures the auditor performs to test design effectiveness include a mix of inquiry of appropriate personnel, observation of the company's operations, and inspection of relevant documentation. Walkthroughs that include these procedures ordinarily are sufficient to evaluate design effectiveness. The auditor should test the operating effectiveness of a control selected for testing by determining whether the control is operating as designed and whether the person performing the control possesses the necessary authority and competence to perform the control effectively.

- Testing Operating Effectiveness

The auditor should test the operating effectiveness of a control selected for testing by determining whether the control is operating as designed and whether the person performing the control possesses the necessary authority and competence to perform the control effectively. Procedures the auditor performs to test operating effectiveness include a mix of inquiry of appropriate personnel, observation of the company's operations, inspection of relevant documentation, and re-performance of the control.

- Obtaining Evidence from Tests of Controls

The evidence provided by the auditor's tests of the effectiveness of controls depends upon the mix of the nature, timing, and extent of the auditor's procedures. Further, for an individual control, different combinations of the nature, timing, and extent of testing might provide sufficient evidence in relation to the degree of reliance in an audit of financial statements. To obtain evidence about whether a control is effective, the control must be tested directly; the effectiveness of a control cannot be inferred from the absence of misstatements detected by substantive procedures.

- Nature of Test of Control

Some types of tests, by their nature, produce greater evidence of the effectiveness of controls than other tests. The following tests that the auditor might perform are presented in the order of the evidence that they ordinarily would produce, from least to most: inquiry, observation, inspection of relevant documentation, and re-performance of a control. Inquiry alone does not provide sufficient evidence to support a conclusion about the effectiveness of a control.

The nature of the tests of controls that will provide appropriate evidence depends, to a large degree, on the nature of the control to be tested, including whether the operation of the control results in documentary evidence of its operation. Documentary evidence of the operation of some controls, such as management's philosophy and operating style, might not exist.

- Extent of Tests of Controls

The more extensively a control is tested, the greater the evidence obtained from that test. Matters that could affect the necessary extent of testing of a control in relation to the degree of reliance on a control include the following:

- The frequency of the performance of the control by the company during the audit period;
- The length of time during the audit period that the auditor is relying on the operating effectiveness of the control;
- The expected rate of deviation from a control;
- The relevance and reliability of the audit evidence to be obtained regarding the operating effectiveness of the control;

- The extent to which audit evidence is obtained from tests of other controls related to the assertion;
- The nature of the control, including, in particular, whether it is a manual control or an automated control; and
- For an automated control, the effectiveness of relevant information technology general controls.

- Timing of Tests of Controls

The timing of tests of controls relates to when the evidence about the operating effectiveness of the controls is obtained and the period of time to which it applies. Paragraph 16 of this standard indicates that the auditor must obtain evidence that the controls selected for testing are designed effectively and operated effectively during the entire period of reliance. When the auditor obtains evidence about the operating effectiveness of controls as of or through an interim date, he or she should determine what additional evidence is necessary concerning the operation of the controls for the remaining period of reliance. The additional evidence that is necessary to update the results of testing from an interim date through the remaining period of reliance depends on the following factors:

- the possibility that there have been any significant changes in internal control over financial reporting subsequent to the interim date;
- the inherent risk associated with the related account(s) or assertion(s);
- the specific control tested prior to year-end, including the nature of the control and the risk that the control is no longer effective during the remaining period, and the results of the tests of the control;
- the planned degree of reliance on the control;
- the sufficiency of the evidence of effectiveness obtained at an interim date; and
- the length of the remaining period.

For audits of financial statements, the auditor should obtain evidence during the current year audit about the design and operating effectiveness of controls upon which the auditor relies. When controls on which the auditor plans to rely have been tested in past audits and the auditor plans to use evidence about the effectiveness of those controls that was obtained in prior years, the auditor should take into account the following factors to determine the evidence needed during the current year audit to support the auditor's control risk assessments:

- the nature and materiality of misstatements that the control is intended to prevent or detect;
- the inherent risk associated with the related account(s) or assertion(s);
- whether there have been changes in the volume or nature of transactions that might adversely affect control design or operating effectiveness;
- whether the account has a history of errors;
- the effectiveness of entity-level controls that the auditor has tested, especially controls that monitor other controls;
- the nature of the controls and the frequency with which they operate;
- the degree to which the control relies on the effectiveness of other controls (e.g., the control environment or information technology general controls);
- the competence of the personnel who perform the control or monitor its performance and whether there have been changes in key personnel who perform the control or monitor its performance;
- whether the control relies on performance by an individual or is automated (i.e., an automated control would generally be expected to be lower risk if relevant information technology general controls are effective);
- the complexity of the control and the significance of the judgments that must be made in connection with its operation;
- the planned degree of reliance on the control;
- the nature, timing, and extent of procedures performed in past audits;
- the results of the previous years' testing of the control;
- whether there have been changes in the control or the process in which it operates since the previous audit; and
- for integrated audits, the evidence regarding the effectiveness of the controls obtained during the audit of internal control.

- Assessing Control Risk

The auditor should assess control risk for relevant assertions by evaluating the evidence obtained from all sources, including the auditor's testing of controls for the audit of internal control and the audit of financial statements, misstatements detected during the financial statement audit, and any identified control deficiencies. Control risk should be assessed at the maximum level for relevant assertions (i) for which controls necessary to sufficiently address the assessed risk of material misstatement in those assertions are missing or ineffective or (ii) when the auditor has not obtained sufficient appropriate evidence to support a control risk assessment below the maximum level. When deficiencies affecting the controls on which the auditor intends to rely are detected, the auditor should evaluate the severity of the deficiencies and the effect on the auditor's control risk assessments. If the auditor plans to rely on controls relating to an assertion but the controls that the auditor tests are ineffective because of control deficiencies, the auditor should: (a) perform tests of other controls related to the same assertion as the ineffective controls, or (b) revise the control risk assessment and modify the planned substantive procedures as necessary in light of the increased assessment of risk.

- Testing Controls in an Audit of Internal Control

Auditing Standard No. 5 states that the objective of the tests of controls in an audit of internal control is to obtain evidence about the effectiveness of controls to support the auditor's opinion on the company's internal control over financial reporting. The auditor's opinion relates to the effectiveness of the company's internal control over financial reporting as of a point in time and taken as a whole.

- Substantive Procedures

The auditor should perform substantive procedures for each relevant assertion of each significant account and disclosure, regardless of the assessed level of control risk. As the assessed risk of material misstatement increases, the evidence from substantive procedures that the auditor should obtain also increases. The evidence provided by the auditor's substantive procedures depends upon the mix of the nature, timing, and extent of those procedures. Further, for an individual assertion, different combinations of the nature, timing, and extent of testing might provide sufficient appropriate evidence to respond to the assessed risk of material misstatement. Internal control over financial reporting has inherent limitations, which, in turn, can affect the evidence that is needed from substantive procedures. For example, more evidence from substantive procedures ordinarily is needed for relevant assertions that have a higher susceptibility to management override or to lapses in judgment or breakdowns resulting from human failures. Substantive procedures generally provide persuasive evidence when they are designed and performed to obtain evidence that is relevant and reliable. Also, some types of substantive procedures, by their nature, produce more persuasive evidence than others. Inquiry alone does not provide sufficient appropriate evidence to support a conclusion about a relevant assertion. The auditor's substantive procedures must include the following audit procedures related to the period-end financial reporting process: (a) reconciling the financial statements with the underlying accounting records; and (b) examining material adjustments made during the course of preparing the financial statements.

The more extensively a substantive procedure is performed, the greater the evidence obtained from the procedure. The necessary extent of a substantive audit procedure depends on the materiality of the account or disclosure, the assessed risk of material misstatement, and the necessary degree of assurance from the procedure. However, increasing the extent of an audit procedure cannot adequately address an assessed risk of material misstatement unless the evidence to be obtained from the procedure is reliable and relevant. In determining whether it is appropriate to perform substantive procedures at an interim date, the auditor should take into account the following:

- the assessed risk of material misstatement, including:
  - (1) The auditor's assessment of control risk;
  - (2) The existence of conditions or circumstances, if any, that create incentives or pressures on management to misstate the financial statements between the interim test date and the end of the period covered by the financial statements;
  - (3) The effects of known or expected changes in the company, its environment, or its internal control over financial reporting during the remaining period;
- the nature of the substantive procedures;
- the nature of the account or disclosure and relevant assertion; and
- the ability of the auditor to perform the necessary audit procedures to cover the remaining period.

When substantive procedures are performed at an interim date, the auditor should cover the remaining period by performing substantive procedures, or substantive procedures combined with tests of controls, that provide a reasonable basis for extending the audit conclusions from the interim date to the period end. Such procedures should include (a) comparing relevant information about the account balance at the interim date with comparable information at the end of the period to identify amounts that appear unusual and investigating such amounts and (b) performing audit procedures to test the remaining period. If the auditor obtains evidence that contradicts the evidence on which the original risk assessments were based, including evidence of misstatements that he or she did not expect, the auditor should revise the related risk assessments and modify the planned nature, timing, or extent of substantive procedures covering the remaining period as necessary.

- Dual-Purpose Tests

In some situations, the auditor might perform a substantive test of a transaction concurrently with a test of a control relevant to that transaction (a "dual-purpose test"). In those situations, the auditor should design the dual-purpose test to achieve the objectives of both the test of the control and the substantive test. Also, when performing a dual-purpose test, the auditor should evaluate the results of the test in forming conclusions about both the assertion and the effectiveness of the control being tested.

Appendix

- Factors Affecting Auditors' Assessments of Planning Materiality, by Hans Blokdijk, Fred Drieenhuizen, Dan A. Simunic, and Michael T. Stein; *AUDITING: A Journal of Practice & Theory*, March 2003, Vol. 22, No. 1, pp. 165–179.
- The Effect of Misstatements on Decisions of Financial Statement Users: An Experimental Investigation of Auditor Materiality Thresholds, by Brad Tuttle, Maribeth Coller, and R. David Plumlee; *AUDITING: A Journal of Practice & Theory*, September 2001, Vol. 20, No. 2, pp. 49–70.

Practice

Question 1

Which one of the following assertions is inaccurate concerning the auditor responsibility in obtaining sufficient appropriate audit evidence about whether the opening balances contain misstatements that materially affect the current period's financial statements?

(a) The auditor shall determine whether the prior period's closing balances have been correctly brought forward to the current period
(b) The auditor shall determine whether the opening balances reflect the application of appropriate accounting policies
(c) The auditor shall close the prior year and not consider any balance therefrom
(d) The auditor shall evaluate whether audit procedures performed in the current period provide evidence relevant to the opening balances

Question 2

Which of the following is accurate concerning the auditor responsibilities in the performance of preliminary engagement activities?

(a) The auditor team leader must conduct the quality control for an engagement
(b) The Auditor team leader must evaluate compliance with relevant ethical requirements
(c) The auditor team leader must establish an understanding of the terms of the engagement as required by Section 210—Terms of Engagement
(d) The auditor team leader must determine issues with management integrity that may affect the auditor's willingness to continue the engagement
(e) All of the above

Question 3

Which one of the below is not a component of the internal control over financial reporting?

(a) The management overrides
(b) The control environment
(c) The company's risk assessment process
(d) The monitoring of controls

Question4

Obtaining an understanding of the control environment includes assessing the following except?

(a) Whether management's philosophy and operating style promote effective internal control over financial reporting
(b) Whether sound integrity and ethical values, particularly of top management, are developed and understood
(c) Whether the board or audit committee understands and exercises oversight responsibility over financial reporting and internal control
(d) None

Question 5

Which is of the following is accurate concerning the engagement partner and, as applicable, other engagement team members performing supervisory activities?

(a) Inform engagement team members of their responsibilities
(b) Direct engagement team members to bring significant accounting and auditing issues arising during the audit to the attention of the engagement partner or other engagement team members performing supervisory activities
(c) Review the work of engagement team members to evaluate whether the work was performed and documented
(d) All of the above

PART III

Audit Evidence Processing

CHAPTER 9

Audit Evidence and Documentation

9.1 General

The objective of the auditor is to design and perform audit procedures that enable the auditor to obtain sufficient appropriate audit evidence to be able to draw reasonable conclusions on which to base the auditor's opinion. Audit evidence refers to Information used by the auditor in arriving at the conclusions on which the auditor's opinion is based. Audit evidence includes both information contained in the accounting records underlying the financial statements and other information. The quantity of the audit evidence needed is affected by the auditor's assessment of the risks of material misstatement and also by the quality of such audit evidence.

An auditor must exercise, not his "inclination," but his "professional judgment" and that judgment must be guided by sound auditing principles, among which are a thorough search for evidential matter.

Audit documentation is the written record of the basis for the auditor's conclusions that provides the support for the auditor's representations, whether those representations are contained in the auditor's report or otherwise. Audit documentation also facilitates the planning, performance, and supervision of the engagement, and is the basis for the review of the quality of the work because it provides the reviewer with written documentation of the evidence supporting the auditor's significant conclusions. Among other things, audit documentation includes records of the planning and performance of the work, the procedures

F. I. Lessambo, *Auditing, Assurance Services, and Forensics*,
https://doi.org/10.1007/978-3-319-90521-1_9

performed, evidence obtained, and conclusions reached by the auditor. Audit documentation also may be referred to as work papers or working papers.

9.2 Sources of Audit Evidence

Some audit evidence is obtained by performing audit procedures to test the accounting records (e.g., through analysis and review, by re-performing procedures followed in the financial reporting process, and by reconciling related types and applications of the same information). Through the performance of such audit procedures, the auditor may determine that the accounting records are internally consistent and agree to the financial statements. However, accounting records alone do not provide sufficient appropriate audit evidence on which to base an audit opinion on the financial statements. More assurance is ordinarily obtained from consistent audit evidence obtained from different sources or of a different nature than from items of audit evidence considered individually. For example, corroborating information obtained from a source independent of the entity may increase the assurance that the auditor obtains from audit evidence that is generated internally, such as evidence existing within the accounting records, minutes of meetings, or a management representation.

Information from sources independent of the entity that the auditor may use as audit evidence include confirmations from third parties, analysts' reports, and comparable data about competitors.

9.3 Relevance and Reliability

Although audit evidence is primarily obtained from audit procedures performed during the course of the audit, it also may include information obtained from other sources (e.g., previous audits, in certain circumstances, and a firm's quality control procedures for client acceptance and continuance). The quality of all audit evidence is affected by the relevance and reliability of the information upon which it is based.

9.3.1 Relevance

Relevance relates to the logical connection with, or bearing upon, the purpose of the audit procedure and, when appropriate, the assertion under consideration. The relevance of information to be used as audit evidence may be affected by the direction of testing. For example, if the purpose of an audit procedure is to test for overstatement in the existence or valuation of accounts payable, testing the recorded accounts payable may be a relevant audit procedure. On the other hand, when testing for understatement in the existence or valuation of accounts payable, testing the recorded accounts payable would not be relevant, but testing such information as subsequent disbursements, unpaid invoices, suppliers' statements, and unmatched receiving reports may be relevant. A given set of audit procedures may provide audit evidence that is relevant to certain assertions but not others. For example, inspection of documents related to the collection of receivables after the period-end may provide audit evidence regarding existence and valuation but not necessarily cutoff. Similarly, obtaining audit evidence regarding a particular assertion (e.g., the existence of inventory) is not a substitute for obtaining audit evidence regarding another assertion (e.g., the valuation of that inventory). On the other hand, audit evidence from different sources or of a different nature may often be relevant to the same assertion.

9.3.2 Reliability

The reliability of information to be used as audit evidence and, therefore, of the audit evidence itself is influenced by its source and nature and the circumstances under which it is obtained, including the controls over its preparation and maintenance, when relevant. Therefore, generalizations about the reliability of various kinds of audit evidence are subject to important exceptions. Even when information to be used as audit evidence is obtained from sources external to the entity, circumstances may exist that could affect its reliability. Information obtained from an independent external source may not be reliable, for example, if the source is not knowledgeable or a management specialist lacks objectivity. While recognizing that exceptions may exist, the following generalizations about the reliability of audit evidence may be useful:

- The reliability of audit evidence is increased when it is obtained from independent sources outside the entity.
- The reliability of audit evidence that is generated internally is increased when the related controls, including those over its preparation and maintenance, imposed by the entity are effective.

- Audit evidence obtained directly by the auditor (e.g., observation of the application of a control) is more reliable than audit evidence obtained indirectly or by inference (e.g., inquiry about the application of a control).
- Audit evidence in documentary form, whether paper, electronic, or other medium, is more reliable than evidence obtained orally (e.g., a contemporaneously written record of a meeting is more reliable than a subsequent oral representation of the matters discussed).
- Audit evidence provided by original documents is more reliable than audit evidence provided by photocopies, facsimiles, or documents that have been filmed, digitized, or otherwise transformed into electronic form, the reliability of which may depend on the controls over their preparation and maintenance.

9.4 Management Assertions Over Financial Statement

In representing that the financial statements are presented fairly in conformity with the applicable financial reporting framework, management implicitly or explicitly makes assertions regarding the recognition, measurement, presentation, and disclosure of the various elements of financial statements and related disclosures. Those assertions can be classified into the following categories:

- Existence or occurrence—Assets or liabilities of the company exist at a given date, and recorded transactions have occurred during a given period.
- Completeness—All transactions and accounts that should be presented in the financial statements are so included.
- Valuation or allocation—Asset, liability, equity, revenue, and expense components have been included in the financial statements at appropriate amounts.
- Rights and obligations—The Company holds or controls rights to the assets, and liabilities are obligations of the company at a given date.
- Presentation and disclosure—The components of the financial statements are properly classified, described, and disclosed.

The auditor may base his or her work on financial statement assertions that differ from those in this standard if the assertions are sufficient for the auditor to identify the types of potential misstatements and to respond appropriately to the risks of material misstatement in each significant account and disclosure that has a reasonable possibility of containing misstatements that would cause the financial statements to be materially misstated, individually or in combination with other misstatements.

9.5 Audit Procedures for Obtaining Audit Evidence

Audit evidence to draw reasonable conclusions on which to base the auditor's opinion is obtained by performing the following:

a. Risk assessment procedures which include:

   (1) Inspection: Inspection involves examining records or documents, whether internal or external, in paper form, electronic form, or other media or a physical examination of an asset. Inspection of records and documents provides audit evidence of varying degrees of reliability, depending on their nature and source and, in the case of internal records and documents, the effectiveness of the controls over their production. An example of inspection used as a test of controls is inspection of records for evidence of authorization. Some documents represent direct audit evidence of the existence of an asset (e.g., a document constituting a financial instrument such as a stock or bond). Inspection of such documents may not necessarily provide audit evidence about ownership or value. In addition, inspecting an executed contract may provide audit evidence relevant to the entity's application of accounting policies, such as revenue recognition. Inspection of tangible assets may provide reliable audit evidence with respect to their existence but not necessarily about the entity's rights and obligations or the valuation of the assets. Inspection of individual inventory items may accompany the observation of inventory counting. For example, when observing an inventory count, the auditor may inspect individual inventory items (such as opening containers included in the inventory count to determine whether they are full or empty) to verify their existence.

(2) Observation: Observation consists of looking at a process or procedure being performed by others (e.g., the auditor's observation of inventory counting by the entity's personnel or the performance of control activities). Observation provides audit evidence about the performance of a process or procedure but is limited to the point in time at which the observation takes place and by the fact that the act of being observed may affect how the process or procedure is performed.
(3) External Confirmation: An external confirmation represents audit evidence obtained by the auditor as a direct written response to the auditor from a third party (the confirming party) in paper form or by electronic or other medium. External confirmation procedures frequently are relevant when addressing assertions associated with certain account balances and their elements. However, external confirmations need not be restricted to account balances only. For example, the auditor may request confirmation of the terms of agreements or transactions an entity has with third parties; the confirmation request may be designed to ask if any modifications have been made to the agreement and, if so, their relevant details. External confirmation procedures also are used to obtain audit evidence about the absence of certain conditions (e.g., the absence of a side agreement that may influence revenue recognition).
(4) Recalculation: Recalculation consists of checking the mathematical accuracy of documents or records. Recalculation may be performed manually or electronically.
(5) Re-performance: Re-performance involves the independent execution of procedures or controls that were originally performed as part of the entity's internal control.
(6) Analytical Procedures: Analytical procedures consist of evaluations of financial information through analysis of plausible relationships among both financial and nonfinancial data. Analytical procedures also encompass such investigation as is necessary of identified fluctuations and relationships that are inconsistent with other relevant information or that differ from expected values by a significant amount. Scanning is a type of analytical procedure involving the auditor's exercise of professional judgment to review accounting data to identify significant or unusual items to test. This may include

the identification of unusual individual items within account balances or other data through the reading or analysis of, for example, entries in transaction listings, subsidiary ledgers, general ledger control accounts, adjusting entries, suspense accounts, reconciliations, and other detailed reports. Scanning may include searching for large or unusual items in the accounting records (e.g., nonstandard journal entries), as well as in transaction data (e.g., suspense accounts and adjusting journal entries) for indications of misstatements that have occurred. Electronic audit procedures may assist the auditor in identifying unusual items. When the auditor selects items for testing by scanning and those items are tested, the auditor obtains audit evidence about those items. The auditor's scanning also may provide some audit evidence about the items not selected for testing because the auditor has exercised professional judgment to determine that the items not selected are less likely to be misstated.

(7) Inquiry: Inquiry consists of seeking information of knowledgeable persons, both financial and nonfinancial, within the entity or outside the entity. Inquiry is used extensively throughout the audit, in addition to other audit procedures. Inquiries may range from formal written inquiries to informal oral inquiries. Evaluating responses to inquiries is an integral part of the inquiry process. Responses to inquiries may provide the auditor with information not previously possessed or with corroborative audit evidence. Alternatively, responses might provide information that differs significantly from other information that the auditor has obtained (e.g., information regarding the possibility of management override of controls). In some cases, responses to inquiries provide a basis for the auditor to modify or perform additional audit procedures. Although corroboration of evidence obtained through inquiry is often of particular importance, in the case of inquiries about management intent, the information available to support management's intent may be limited. In these cases, understanding management's past history of carrying out its stated intentions, management's stated reasons for choosing a particular course of action, and management's ability to pursue a specific course of action may provide relevant information to corroborate the evidence obtained through inquiry.

b. Further audit procedures, which comprise

   (i) Tests of controls
   Tests of controls are designed to evaluate the operating effectiveness of controls in preventing, or detecting and correcting, material misstatements at the assertion level. Designing tests of controls to obtain relevant audit evidence includes identifying conditions (characteristics or attributes) that indicate performance of a control and identifying deviation conditions that indicate departures from adequate performance. The presence or absence of those conditions can then be tested by the auditor.

   (ii) Substantive procedures
   Substantive procedures are designed to detect material misstatements at the assertion level. They comprise tests of details and substantive analytical procedures. Designing substantive procedures includes identifying conditions relevant to the purpose of the test that constitute a misstatement in the relevant assertion.

   (iii) Selecting items for testing to obtain audit evidence
   Designing substantive tests of details and tests of controls includes determining the means of selecting items for testing from among the items included in an account or the occurrences of a control. The auditor should determine the means of selecting items for testing to obtain evidence that, in combination with other relevant evidence, is sufficient to meet the objective of the audit procedure. The alternative means of selecting items for testing are:

   - Selecting all items
     Selecting all items (100% examination) refers to testing the entire population of items in an account or the entire population of occurrences of a control (or an entire stratum within one of those populations). The following are examples of situations in which 100% examination might be applied:

     - The population constitutes a small number of large value items;

- The audit procedure is designed to respond to a significant risk, and other means of selecting items for testing do not provide sufficient appropriate audit evidence; and
- The audit procedure can be automated effectively and applied to the entire population.
- Selecting specific items

Selecting specific items refers to testing all of the items in a population that have a specified characteristic, such as:

- Key items. The auditor may decide to select specific items within a population because they are important to accomplishing the objective of the audit procedure or exhibit some other characteristic, e.g., items that are suspicious, unusual, or particularly risk-prone or items that have a history of error.
- All items over a certain amount. The auditor may decide to examine items whose recorded values exceed a certain amount to verify a large proportion of the total amount of the items included in an account.

The auditor also might select specific items to obtain an understanding about matters such as the nature of the company or the nature of transactions. However, the application of audit procedures to items that are selected as described in paragraphs 25–26 of this standard does not constitute audit sampling,

- Audit sampling
  Audit sampling is the application of an audit procedure to less than 100% of the items within an account balance or class of transactions for the purpose of evaluating some characteristic of the balance or class.

9.6 Reliability of Information Produced by a Management's Specialist

When information to be used as audit evidence has been prepared using the work of a management's specialist, such an individual or organization may possess expertise in the application of models to estimate the fair value of securities for which no observable market exists. If the individual or organization applies that expertise in making an estimate which the entity uses in preparing its financial statements, the individual or organization is a management's specialist and paragraph .08 applies. If, on the other hand, that individual or organization merely provides price data regarding private transactions not otherwise available to the entity which the entity uses in its own estimation methods, such information, if used as audit evidence, is subject to paragraph .07, but it is not the use of a management's specialist by the entity.

Competence relates to the nature and level of expertise of the management's specialist. Capability relates to the ability of the management's specialist to exercise that competence in the circumstances. Factors that influence capability may include, for example, geographic location and the availability of time and resources. Objectivity relates to the possible effects that bias, conflict of interest, or the influence of others may have on the professional or business judgment of the management's specialist. The competence, capabilities, and objectivity of a management's specialist, and any controls within the entity over that specialist's work, are important factors with regard to the reliability of any information produced by a management's specialist.

When evaluating the objectivity of a specialist engaged by the entity, it may be relevant to discuss with management and that specialist any interests and relationships that may create threats to the specialist's objectivity and any applicable safeguards, including any professional requirements that apply to the specialist, and to evaluate whether the safeguards are adequate. Interests and relationships creating threats may include the following: financial interests; business and personal relationships; and provision of other services.

9.7 Audit Documentation

Audit documentation is reviewed by members of the engagement team performing the work and might be reviewed by others. Reviewers might include, for example:

- Auditors who are new to an engagement and review the prior year's documentation to understand the work performed as an aid in planning and performing the current engagement.

- Supervisory personnel who review documentation prepared by other members of the engagement team.
- Engagement supervisors and engagement quality reviewers who review documentation to understand how the engagement team reached significant conclusions and whether there is adequate evidential support for those conclusions.
- A successor auditor who reviews a predecessor auditor's audit documentation.
- Internal and external inspection teams that review documentation to assess audit quality and compliance with auditing and related professional practice standards; applicable laws, rules, and regulations; and the auditor's own quality control policies.
- Others, including advisors engaged by the audit committee or representatives of a party to an acquisition.

9.7.1 Audit Documentation Requirement

The auditor must prepare audit documentation in connection with each engagement conducted pursuant to the standards of the PCAOB. Audit documentation should be prepared in sufficient detail to provide a clear understanding of its purpose, source, and the conclusions reached. Also, the documentation should be appropriately organized to provide a clear link to the significant findings or issues. Examples of audit documentation include memoranda, confirmations, correspondence, schedules, audit programs, and letters of representation. Audit documentation may be in the form of paper, electronic files, or other media. Because audit documentation is the written record that provides the support for the representations in the auditor's report, it should:

- Demonstrate that the engagement complied with the standards of the PCAOB,
- Support the basis for the auditor's conclusions concerning every relevant financial statement assertion, and
- Demonstrate that the underlying accounting records agreed or reconciled with the financial statements.

The auditor must document the procedures performed, evidence obtained, and conclusions reached with respect to relevant financial statement assertions. Audit documentation must clearly demonstrate that the work was in fact performed. This documentation requirement applies to the work of all those who participate in the engagement as well as to the work of specialists the auditor uses as evidential matter in evaluating relevant financial statement assertions. Audit documentation must contain sufficient information to enable an experienced auditor, having no previous connection with the engagement:

- To understand the nature, timing, extent, and results of the procedures performed, evidence obtained, and conclusions reached, and
- To determine who performed the work and the date such work was completed as well as the person who reviewed the work and the date of such review.

In determining the nature and extent of the documentation for a financial statement assertion, the auditor should consider the following factors:

- Nature of the auditing procedure;
- Risk of material misstatement associated with the assertion;
- Extent of judgment required in performing the work and evaluating the results, for example, accounting estimates require greater judgment and commensurately more extensive documentation;
- Significance of the evidence obtained to the assertion being tested; and
- Responsibility to document a conclusion not readily determinable from the documentation of the procedures performed or evidence obtained.

Application of these factors determines whether the nature and extent of audit documentation is adequate.

In addition to the documentation necessary to support the auditor's final conclusions, audit documentation must include information the auditor has identified relating to significant findings or issues that is inconsistent with or contradicts the auditor's final conclusions. The relevant records to be retained include, but are not limited to, procedures performed in response to the information, and records documenting consultations on, or resolutions of, differences in professional judgment among members of the engagement team or between the engagement team and others consulted. If, after the documentation completion date (defined in paragraph 15), the auditor becomes aware, as a result of a lack of documentation or otherwise, that audit procedures may not have been performed, evidence may not have been obtained, or appropriate conclusions may not have been reached, the auditor must determine, and if so demonstrate, that sufficient procedures were performed, sufficient evidence was obtained, and appropriate conclusions were reached with respect to the relevant financial statement assertions. To accomplish this, the auditor must have persuasive other evidence. Oral explanation alone does not constitute persuasive other evidence, but it may be used to clarify other written evidence.

If the auditor determines and demonstrates that sufficient procedures were performed, sufficient evidence was obtained, and appropriate conclusions were reached, but that documentation thereof is not adequate, then the auditor should consider what additional documentation is needed. In preparing additional documentation, the auditor should refer to paragraph 16.

If the auditor cannot determine or demonstrate that sufficient procedures were performed, sufficient evidence was obtained, or appropriate conclusions were reached, the auditor should comply with the provisions of AU sec. 390, Consideration of Omitted Procedures after the Report Date.

Documentation of risk assessment procedures and responses to risks of misstatement should include (1) a summary of the identified risks of misstatement and the auditor's assessment of risks of material misstatement at the financial statement and assertion levels and (2) the auditor's responses to the risks of material misstatement, including linkage of the responses to those risks.

9.7.2 Documentation of Specific Matters

Documentation of auditing procedures that involve the inspection of documents or confirmation, including tests of details, tests of operating effectiveness of controls, and walkthroughs, should include identification of the items inspected. Documentation of auditing procedures related to the inspection of significant contracts or agreements should include abstracts or copies of the documents. The identification of the items inspected may be satisfied by indicating the source from which the items were selected and the specific selection criteria, for example:

- If an audit sample is selected from a population of documents, the documentation should include identifying characteristics (for example, the specific check numbers of the items included in the sample).
- If all items over a specific dollar amount are selected from a population of documents, the documentation need describe only the scope and the identification of the population (e.g., all checks over $10,000 from the October disbursements journal).
- If a systematic sample is selected from a population of documents, the documentation need only provide an identification of the source of the documents and an indication of the starting point and the sampling interval (e.g., a systematic sample of sales invoices was selected from the sales journal for the period from October 1 to December 31, starting with invoice number 452 and selecting every 40th invoice).

Certain matters, such as auditor independence, staff training and proficiency, and client acceptance and retention, may be documented in a central repository for the public accounting firm ("firm") or in the particular office participating in the engagement. If such matters are documented in a central repository, the audit documentation of the engagement should include a reference to the central repository. Documentation of matters specific to a particular engagement should be included in the audit documentation of the pertinent engagement.

The auditor must document significant findings or issues, actions taken to address them (including additional evidence obtained), and the basis for the conclusions reached in connection with each engagement. Significant findings or issues are substantive matters that are important to the procedures performed, evidence obtained, or conclusions reached, and include, but are not limited to, the following:

a. Significant matters involving the selection, application, and consistency of accounting principles, including related disclosures.
b. Results of auditing procedures that indicate a need for significant modification of planned auditing procedures, the existence of material misstatements (including omissions in the financial statements), the existence of significant deficiencies, or material weaknesses in internal control over financial reporting.
c. Accumulated misstatements and evaluation of uncorrected misstatements, including the quantitative and qualitative factors the auditor considered to be relevant to the evaluation.

d. Disagreements among members of the engagement team or with others consulted on the engagement about final conclusions reached on significant accounting or auditing matters, including the basis for the final resolution of those disagreements. If an engagement team member disagrees with the final conclusions reached, he or she should document that disagreement.
e. Circumstances that cause significant difficulty in applying auditing procedures.
f. Significant changes in the auditor's risk assessments, including risks that were not identified previously, and the modifications to audit procedures or additional audit procedures performed in response to those changes.
f-1. Risks of material misstatement that are determined to be significant risks and the results of the auditing procedures performed in response to those risks.
g. Any matters that could result in modification of the auditor's report.

The auditor must identify all significant findings or issues in an engagement completion document. This document may include either all information necessary to understand the significant findings, issues or cross-references, as appropriate, to other available supporting audit documentation. This document, along with any documents cross-referenced, should collectively be as specific as necessary in the circumstances for a reviewer to gain a thorough understanding of the significant findings or issues. When conducting an attestation engagement pursuant to Attestation Standard No. 1, Examination Engagements Regarding Compliance Reports of Brokers and Dealers, or Attestation Standard No. 2, Review Engagements Regarding Exemption Reports of Brokers and Dealers, the auditor may include the documentation of significant findings or issues related to the attestation engagement in the engagement completion document prepared in connection with the audit of the financial statements.

9.7.3 Retention of and Subsequent Changes to Audit Documentation

The auditor must retain audit documentation for seven years from the date the auditor grants permission to use the auditor's report in connection with the issuance of the company's financial statements (report release date), unless a longer period of time is required by law. If a report is not issued in connection with an engagement, then the audit documentation must be retained for seven years from the date that fieldwork was substantially completed. If the auditor was unable to complete the engagement, then the audit documentation must be retained for seven years from the date the engagement ceased.

Prior to the report release date, the auditor must have completed all necessary auditing procedures and obtained sufficient evidence to support the representations in the auditor's report. A complete and final set of audit documentation should be assembled for retention as of a date not more than 45 days after the report release date. If a report is not issued in connection with an engagement, then the documentation completion date should not be more than 45 days from the date that fieldwork was substantially completed. If the auditor was unable to complete the engagement, then the documentation completion date should not be more than 45 days from the date the engagement ceased. Circumstances may require additions to audit documentation after the report release date. Audit documentation must not be deleted or discarded after the documentation completion date, however, information may be added. Any documentation added must indicate the date the information was added, the name of the person who prepared the additional documentation, and the reason for adding it.

Other standards require the auditor to perform procedures subsequent to the report release date in certain circumstances. For example, in accordance with AU sec. 711, Filings under Federal Securities Statutes, auditors are required to perform certain procedures up to the effective date of a registration statement. The auditor must identify and document any additions to audit documentation as a result of these procedures consistent with the previous paragraph.

The office of the firm issuing the auditor's report is responsible for ensuring that all audit documentation sufficient to meet the requirements of paragraphs 4–13 of this standard is prepared and retained. Audit documentation supporting the work performed by other auditors (including auditors associated with other offices of the firm, affiliated firms, or nonaffiliated firms), must be retained by or be accessible to the office issuing the auditor's report.

In addition, the office issuing the auditor's report must obtain, review and retain, prior to the report release date, the following documentation related to the work performed by other auditors (including auditors associated with other offices of the firm, affiliated firms, or nonaffiliated firms):

A schedule of accumulated misstatements, including a description of the nature and cause of each accumulated misstatement, and an evaluation of uncorrected misstatements, including the quantitative and qualitative factors the auditor considered to be relevant to the evaluation.

9.7.4 Matters to Be Communicated to the Audit Committee

If the auditor decides to make reference in his or her report to the audit of the other auditor, however, the auditor issuing the report need not perform the procedures in this paragraph and, instead, should refer to AU sec. 543, Part of Audit Performed by Other Independent Auditors. The auditor also might be required to maintain documentation in addition to that required by this standard.

9.8 Evaluating the Audit Result[1]

The auditor shall evaluate the results of the audit evidence collected to determine whether the audit evidence obtained is sufficient and appropriate to support the opinion to be expressed in the auditor's report.

9.8.1 Evaluating the Results of the Audit of Internal Control Over Financial Reporting

Auditing Standard No. 5, An Audit of Internal Control Over Financial Reporting That Is Integrated with An Audit of Financial Statements, indicates that the auditor should form an opinion on the effectiveness of internal control over financial reporting by evaluating evidence obtained from all sources, including the auditor's testing of controls, misstatements detected during the financial statement audit, and any identified control deficiencies. Auditing Standard No. 5 describes the auditor's responsibilities regarding evaluating the results of the audit, including evaluating the identified control deficiencies.

[1]PCAOB—Auditing Standard no. 14 Evaluating Audit Results.

9.8.2 *Evaluating the Results of the Audit of Financial Statements*

In forming an opinion on whether the financial statements are presented fairly, in all material respects, in conformity with the applicable financial reporting framework, the auditor should take into account all relevant audit evidence, regardless of whether it appears to corroborate or to contradict the assertions in the financial statements. In the audit of financial statements, the auditor's evaluation of audit results should include evaluation of the following:

A. Performing Analytical Procedures in the Overall Review

In the overall review, the auditor should read the financial statements and disclosures and perform analytical procedures to (a) evaluate the auditor's conclusions formed regarding significant accounts and disclosures and (b) assist in forming an opinion on whether the financial statements as a whole are free of material misstatement. As part of the overall review, the auditor should evaluate whether: (a) the evidence gathered in response to unusual or unexpected transactions, events, amounts, or relationships previously identified during the audit is sufficient; and (b) unusual or unexpected transactions, events, amounts, or relationships indicate risks of material misstatement that were not identified previously, including, in particular, fraud risks. If the auditor discovers a previously unidentified risk of material misstatement or concludes that the evidence gathered is not adequate, he or she should modify his or her audit procedures or perform additional procedures as necessary in accordance with the auditor risk assessment.

The nature and extent of the analytical procedures performed during the overall review may be similar to the analytical procedures performed as risk assessment procedures. The auditor should perform analytical procedures relating to revenue through the end of the reporting period. The auditor should obtain corroboration for management's explanations regarding significant unusual or unexpected transactions, events, amounts, or relationships. If management's responses to the auditor's inquiries appear to be implausible, inconsistent with other audit evidence, imprecise, or not at a sufficient level of detail to be useful, the auditor should perform procedures to address the matter. Whether an unusual or unexpected transaction, event, amount, or relationship indicates a fraud risk, depends on the relevant facts and circumstances, including the nature of the account or relationship among the data used in the analytical procedures.

B. Accumulating and Evaluating Identified Misstatements

The auditor should accumulate misstatements identified during the audit, other than those that are clearly trivial. Matters that are clearly trivial will be of a smaller order of magnitude than the materiality level established in accordance with Auditing Standard No. 11, Consideration of Materiality in Planning and Performing an Audit, and will be inconsequential, whether taken individually or in aggregate and whether judged by any criteria of size, nature, or circumstances. When there is any uncertainty about whether one or more items is clearly trivial, the matter is not considered trivial. The auditor may designate an amount below which misstatements are clearly trivial and do not need to be accumulated. In such cases, the amount should be set so that any misstatements below that amount would not be material to the financial statements, individually or in combination with other misstatements, considering the possibility of undetected misstatement. The auditor's accumulation of misstatements should include the auditor's best estimate of the total misstatement in the accounts and disclosures that he or she has tested, not just the amount of misstatements specifically identified. If the auditor concludes that the amount of an accounting estimate included in the financial statements is unreasonable or was not determined in conformity with the relevant requirements of the applicable financial reporting framework, he or she should treat the difference between that estimate and a reasonable estimate determined in conformity with the applicable accounting principles as a misstatement. If a range of reasonable estimates is supported by sufficient appropriate audit evidence and the recorded estimate is outside of the range of reasonable estimates, the auditor should treat the difference between the recorded accounting estimate and the closest reasonable estimate as a misstatement. If an accounting estimate is determined in conformity with the relevant requirements of the applicable financial reporting framework and the amount of the estimate is reasonable, a difference between an estimated amount best supported by the audit evidence and the recorded amount of the accounting estimate ordinarily would not be considered to be a misstatement. The auditor should determine whether the overall audit strategy and audit plan need to be modified if: (a) the nature of accumulated misstatements and the circumstances of their occurrence indicate that other misstatements might exist that, in combination with accumulated misstatements, could be material; or (b) the aggregate of misstatements accumulated during the audit approaches the materiality level or levels used in planning and performing the audit.

The auditor should communicate accumulated misstatements to management on a timely basis to provide management with an opportunity to correct them. If management has examined an account or a disclosure in response to misstatements detected by the auditor and has made corrections to the account or disclosure, the auditor should evaluate management's work to determine whether the corrections have been recorded properly and whether uncorrected misstatements remain. The auditor should evaluate whether uncorrected misstatements are material, individually or in combination with other misstatements. In making this evaluation, the auditor should evaluate the misstatements in relation to the specific accounts and disclosures involved and to the financial statements as a whole, taking into account relevant quantitative and qualitative factors. If the reevaluation of the established materiality level or levels, as set forth in Auditing Standard No. 11, results in a lower amount for the materiality level or levels, the auditor should take into account that lower materiality level or levels in the evaluation of uncorrected misstatements. The auditor's evaluation of uncorrected misstatements should include evaluation of the effects of uncorrected misstatements detected in prior years and misstatements detected in the current year that relate to prior years. The auditor cannot assume that an instance of error or fraud is an isolated occurrence. Therefore, the auditor should evaluate the nature and effects of the individual misstatements accumulated during the audit on the assessed risks of material misstatement. This evaluation is important in determining whether the risk assessments remain appropriate. The auditor should evaluate whether identified misstatements might be indicative of fraud and, in turn, how they affect the auditor's evaluation of materiality and the related audit responses.

If the auditor believes that a misstatement is or might be intentional, and if the effect on the financial statements could be material or cannot be readily determined, the auditor should perform procedures to obtain additional audit evidence to determine whether fraud has occurred or is likely to have occurred and, if so, its effect on the financial statements and the auditor's report thereon. For misstatements that the auditor believes are or might be intentional, the auditor should evaluate the implications on the integrity of management or employees and the possible effect on other aspects of the audit. If the misstatement involves higher-level management, it might be indicative of a more pervasive problem, such as an issue with the integrity of management, even if the amount of the misstatement is small. In such circumstances, the auditor should reevaluate the assessment of fraud risk and the effect of that assessment on (a) the nature, timing, and extent of the necessary tests of accounts or disclosures and (b) the assessment of the effectiveness of controls. The auditor also should evaluate whether the circumstances or conditions indicate possible collusion involving employees, management, or external parties and, if so, the effect of the collusion on the reliability of evidence obtained. If the auditor becomes aware of information indicating that fraud or another illegal act has occurred or might have occurred, he or she also must determine his or her responsibilities.

C. Evaluating the Qualitative Aspects of the Company's Accounting Practices

When evaluating whether the financial statements as a whole are free of material misstatement, the auditor should evaluate the qualitative aspects of the company's accounting practices, including potential bias in management's judgments about the amounts and disclosures in the financial statements. If the auditor identifies bias in management's judgments about the amounts and disclosures in the financial statements, the auditor should evaluate whether the effect of that bias, together with the effect of uncorrected misstatements, results in material misstatement of the financial statements. Also, the auditor should evaluate whether the auditor's risk assessments, including, in particular, the assessment of fraud risks, and the related audit responses remain appropriate. The auditor should evaluate whether the difference between estimates best supported by the audit evidence and estimates included in the financial statements, which are individually reasonable, indicate a possible bias on the part of the company's management. If each accounting estimate included in the financial statements was individually reasonable but the effect of the difference between each estimate and the estimate best supported by the audit evidence was to increase earnings or loss, the auditor should evaluate whether these circumstances indicate potential management bias in the estimates. Bias also can result from the cumulative effect of changes in multiple accounting estimates. If the estimates in the financial statements are grouped at one end of the range of reasonable estimates in the prior year and are grouped at the other end of the range of reasonable estimates in the current year, the auditor should evaluate whether management is using swings in estimates to achieve an expected or desired outcome, e.g., to offset higher or lower than expected earnings.

The following are examples of forms of management bias:

- The selective correction of misstatements brought to management's attention during the audit (e.g., correcting misstatements that have the effect of increasing reported earnings but not correcting misstatements that have the effect of decreasing reported earnings).

To evaluate the potential effect of selective correction of misstatements, the auditor should obtain an understanding of the reasons that management decided not to correct misstatements communicated by the auditor.

- The identification by management of additional adjusting entries that offset misstatements accumulated by the auditor. If such adjusting entries are identified, the auditor should perform procedures to determine why the underlying misstatements were not identified previously and evaluate the implications on the integrity of management and the auditor's risk assessments, including fraud risk assessments. The auditor also should perform additional procedures as necessary to address the risk of further undetected misstatement.
- Bias in the selection and application of accounting principles.
- Bias in accounting estimates.

D. Evaluating Conditions Relating to the Assessment of Fraud Risks

The auditor should evaluate whether the accumulated results of auditing procedures and other observations affect the assessment of the fraud risks made throughout the audit and whether the audit procedures need to be modified to respond to those risks. The engagement partner should determine whether there has been appropriate communication with the other engagement team members throughout the audit regarding information or conditions that are indicative of fraud risks.

E. Evaluating the Presentation of the Financial Statements, Including the Disclosures

The auditor must evaluate whether the financial statements are presented fairly, in all material respects, in conformity with the applicable financial reporting framework. The auditor should evaluate whether the financial statements contain the information essential for a fair presentation of the financial statements in conformity with the applicable financial reporting framework. Evaluation of the information disclosed in the financial statements includes consideration of the form, arrangement, and content of the financial statements (including the accompanying notes), encompassing matters such as the terminology used, the amount of detail given, the classification of items in the statements, and the bases of amounts set forth. If the financial statements, including the accompanying notes, fail to disclose information that is required by the applicable financial reporting framework, the auditor should express a qualified or adverse opinion and should provide the information in the report, if practicable, unless its omission from the report is recognized as appropriate by a specific auditing standard.

F. Evaluating the Sufficiency and Appropriateness of Audit Evidence

As part of evaluating audit results, the auditor must conclude on whether sufficient appropriate audit evidence has been obtained to support his or her opinion on the financial statements. If the auditor has not obtained sufficient appropriate audit evidence about a relevant assertion or has substantial doubt about a relevant assertion, the auditor should perform procedures to obtain further audit evidence to address the matter. If the auditor is unable to obtain sufficient appropriate audit evidence to have a reasonable basis to conclude about whether the financial statements as a whole are free of material misstatement, AU sec. 508 indicates that the auditor should express a qualified opinion or a disclaimer of opinion. The auditor should evaluate whether the assessments of the risks of material misstatement at the assertion level remain appropriate and whether the audit procedures need to be modified or additional procedures need to be performed as a result of any changes in the risk assessments. For example, the reevaluation of the auditor's risk assessments could result in the identification of relevant assertions or significant risks that were not identified previously and for which the auditor should perform additional audit procedures.

Factors that are relevant to the conclusion on whether sufficient appropriate audit evidence has been obtained include the following:

- The significance of uncorrected misstatements and the likelihood of their having a material effect, individually or in combination, on the financial statements, considering the possibility of further undetected misstatement.
- The results of audit procedures performed in the audit of financial statements, including whether the evidence obtained supports or contradicts management's assertions and whether such audit procedures identified specific instances of fraud.
- The auditor's risk assessments.
- The results of audit procedures performed in the audit of internal control over financial reporting, if the audit is an integrated audit.
- The appropriateness (i.e., the relevance and reliability) of the audit evidence obtained.

9.9 The Use of Blockchain Technology in Auditing

Blockchain is an open, distributed ledger where transactions are recorded and verified by the parties involved. Its use is considered by many in the profession as providing an opportunity to increase audit performance. Due to the large number of transactions and the amount of financial information a company handles, audits never provide 100% coverage. Rather, the opinion relies on a selected sample tested or statistical probabilities. Blockchain,[2] the protocol technology that has allowed for

[2]Blockchain is a cryptographic technology. It is a cryptographic, encoded, ledger comprising a digital log of transactions shared across a public or private network. The blockchain network consists of nodes or distributed servers. All the nodes can accept and process the transaction.

the creation of peer-to-peer cryptocurrency transactions ("bitcoin") can provide a solution for a 100% audit coverage as it confirms, verifies and records all the financial transactions entered by the parties. Blockchain as a public ledger stores data that have been verified, authenticated and confirmed as accurate. Because the computer code in each universally time-stamped block builds on the previous one, it becomes virtually impossible for any corporation to go back and alter earlier blocks. A blockchain solution would provide for an automated third party verification by a distributed network to ensure that transactions are complete and accurate and cannot be reversed. Auditors would have access to the documents at all times. Put differently, Blockchain technology enables secure electronic transactions without a centralized ledger and without double spending. Instead of a centralized ledger, it makes a collective accounting by distributing a shared public ledger—a complete record of all past transactions on the network.[3]

The opportunities provided by blockchain cannot be ignored by auditing firms such as Deloitte, or Ernst & Young. Not only blockchain enables them to access numerical data entries, but also offer the possibilities to go back and look at paper trails, contracts that support transactions, and old paper invoices.[4] The benefits of blockchain technology as specified by Forbes[5] are:

- As a public ledger system, blockchain records and validates each and every transaction made, which makes it secure and reliable;
- All the transactions made are authorized by miners, which makes the transactions immutable and prevent it from the threat of hacking;
- Blockchain technology discards the need of any third party or central authority for peer-to-peer transactions;
- Decentralization of technology.

[3] Trevor I. Kiviat (2015): Beyond Bitcoin: Issues in Regulating Blockchain Transactions, *Duke Law Journal*, Volume 65, No. 569, p. 578.

[4] Ian Allison (2015): Deloitte, Libra, Accenture: The Work of Auditors in the Age of Bitcoin 2.0 Technology.

[5] George Howard (2015): Blockchain Technology Is Our Chance to Rebuild the Internet in a Way That Benefits Creators.

Appendix

- Analytical Procedures and Audit-Planning Decisions, by Steven M. Glover, James Jiambalvo, and Jane Kennedy; *AUDITING: A Journal of Practice & Theory*, March 2000, Vol. 19, No. 1, pp. 123–143.
- An Analysis of the Relative Power Characteristics of Analytical Procedures, by Yining Chen and Robert A. Leitch; *AUDITING: A Journal of Practice & Theory*, March 1999, Vol. 18, No. 1, pp. 117–123.
- Factors Affecting Internal Auditors' Consideration of Fraudulent Financial Reporting during Analytical Procedures, by Bryan K. Church, Jeffrey J. McMillan, and Arnold Schneider; *AUDITING: A Journal of Practice & Theory*, September 2000, Vol. 19, No. 2, pp. 27–45.

Practice

Question 1

Which of the following assertions is inaccurate concerning audit evidence?

(a) Audit evidence consists of all the information, whether obtained from audit procedures or other sources
(b) Audit evidence consists of information used by the auditor in arriving at the conclusions on which his opinion is based
(c) The relevance of audit evidence does not refer to its relationship to the assertion or to the objective of the control being tested
(d) Audit evidence consists of both information that supports and corroborates management's assertions regarding the financial statements or internal control over financial reporting and information that contradicts such assertions.

Question 2

Audit procedures can be classified into the following categories, except:

(a) Risk assessment procedures
(b) Tests of controls
(c) Substantive procedures
(d) Substantive analytical procedures
(e) Confirmation

Question 3

Which of the below assertions is inaccurate concerning analytical procedures?

(a) Analytical procedures involve evaluations of financial information through analysis of plausible relationships among both financial and nonfinancial data
(b) Analytical procedures include investigation of fluctuations and relationships that are inconsistent with other relevant information or that differ from expected values by a significant amount
(c) Analytical procedures may be used as substantive procedures either on their own or in conjunction with tests of details
(d) Analytical procedures cannot be used as substantive procedures either on their own or in conjunction with tests of details

Question 4

The main assertions in the financial statements relating to inventory, for which audit procedures should be designed and performed are:

(a) Existence
(b) Ownership
(c) Completeness
(d) Valuation

Question 5

When the auditor attends an inventory count as a part of the inspection procedure, the auditor is required to:

(a) Evaluate management's instructions and procedures for recording and controlling the results of the entity's physical inventory counting
(b) Observe the performance of management's count procedures

(c) Inspect the inventory
(d) Perform test counts
(e) Inquire about the choice of the inventory method selected by the management

CHAPTER 10

Audit Risks: Identification and Procedures

10.1 General

To form an appropriate basis for expressing an opinion on the financial statements, the auditor must plan and perform the audit to obtain reasonable assurance about whether the financial statements are free of material misstatement due to error or fraud. Reasonable assurance is obtained by reducing audit risk to an appropriately low level through applying due professional care, including obtaining sufficient appropriate audit evidence.

10.2 Characteristics of Fraud

The characteristics of fraud that are identified as making absolute assurance unattainable and that create a possibility that a properly planned and performed audit may not detect a material misstatement are described in as follows[1]:

> Characteristics of fraud include (a) concealment through collusion among management, employees, or third parties; (b) withheld, misrepresented, or falsified documentation; and (c) the ability of management to override or instruct others to override what otherwise appears to be effective controls. For example, auditing procedures may be ineffective for detecting

[1] AU Section 230.12.

F. I. Lessambo, *Auditing, Assurance Services, and Forensics*,
https://doi.org/10.1007/978-3-319-90521-1_10

an intentional misstatement that is concealed through collusion among personnel within the entity and third parties or among management or employees of the entity. Collusion may cause the auditor who has properly performed the audit to conclude that evidence provided is persuasive when it is, in fact, false. In addition, an audit conducted in accordance with generally accepted auditing standards rarely involves authentication of documentation, nor are auditors trained as or expected to be experts in such authentication. Furthermore, an auditor may not discover the existence of a modification of documentation through a side agreement that management or a third party has not disclosed. Finally, management has the ability to directly or indirectly manipulate accounting records and present fraudulent financial information by overriding controls in unpredictable ways.

10.3 Risk of Material Misstatement

In an audit of financial statements, audit risk is the risk that the auditor expresses an inappropriate audit opinion when the financial statements are materially misstated. Audit risk is a function of the risk of material misstatement and detection risk. The auditor should assess the risks of material misstatement at two levels: (1) at the financial statement level and (2) at the assertion level.

Risks of material misstatement at the financial statement level relate pervasively to the financial statements as a whole and potentially affect many assertions. Risks of material misstatement at the financial statement level may be especially relevant to the auditor's consideration of the risk of material misstatement due to fraud. Risk of material misstatement at the assertion level consists of the following components:

a. Inherent risk, which refers to the susceptibility of an assertion to a misstatement, due to error or fraud, that could be material, individually or in combination with other misstatements, before consideration of any related controls.
b. Control risk, which is the risk that a misstatement due to error or fraud that could occur in an assertion and that could be material, individually or in combination with other misstatements, will not be prevented or detected on a timely basis by the company's internal control. Control risk is a function of the effectiveness of the design and operation of internal control.

Inherent risk and control risk are related to the company, its environment, and its internal control, and the auditor assesses those risks based on evidence he or she obtains. The auditor assesses inherent risk using information obtained from performing risk assessment procedures and considering the characteristics of the accounts and disclosures in the financial statements. The auditor assesses control risk using evidence obtained from tests of controls (if the auditor plans to rely on those controls to assess control risk at less than maximum) and from other sources.

10.4 Detection Risk

Detection risk is the risk that the procedures performed by the auditor will not detect misstatement that exists and that could be material, individually or in combination with other misstatements. Detection risk is affected by (1) the effectiveness of the substantive procedures and (2) their application by the auditor. The auditor uses the assessed risk of material misstatement to determine the appropriate level of detection risk for a financial statement assertion. The higher the risk of material misstatement, the lower the level of detection risk needs to be in order to reduce audit risk to an appropriately low level. The auditor reduces the level of detection risk through the nature, timing, and extent of the substantive procedures performed. As the appropriate level of detection risk decreases, the evidence from substantive procedures that the auditor should obtain increases.

10.5 Performing Risk Assessment Procedures

The auditor should perform risk assessment procedures that are sufficient to provide a reasonable basis for identifying and assessing the risks of material misstatement, whether due to error or fraud, and designing further audit procedures. Risks of material misstatement can arise from a variety of sources, including external factors, such as conditions in the company's industry and environment, and company-specific factors, such as the nature of the company, its activities, and internal control over financial reporting. Also, risks of material misstatement may relate to personnel who lack the necessary financial reporting competencies, information systems that fail to accurately capture business transactions, or financial reporting processes that are not adequately aligned with the requirements in the applicable financial reporting framework. Thus, the audit procedures that are necessary to identify and appropriately assess the risks of material misstatement include consideration of both external factors and company-specific factors. In an integrated audit, the risks of material misstatement of the financial statements are the same for both the audit of internal control over financial reporting and the audit of financial statements. The auditor's risk assessment procedures should apply to both the audit of internal control over financial reporting and the audit of financial statements. The following are risk assessment procedures:

10.5.1 Obtaining an Understanding of the Company and Its Environment

The auditor should obtain an understanding of the company and its environment ("understanding of the company") to understand the events, conditions, and company activities that might reasonably be expected to have a significant effect on the risks of material misstatement. Obtaining an understanding of the company includes understanding:

- Relevant industry, regulatory, and other external factors
  Obtaining an understanding of relevant industry, regulatory, and other external factors encompasses industry factors, including the competitive environment, and technological developments; the regulatory environment, including the applicable financial reporting framework and the legal and political environment; and external factors, including general economic conditions.
- The nature of the company
  Obtaining an understanding of the nature of the company includes understanding:
  - the company's organizational structure and management personnel;
  - the sources of funding of the company's operations and investment activities, including the company's capital structure, noncapital funding (e.g., subordinated debt or dependencies on supplier financing), and other debt instruments;
  - the company's significant investments, including equity method investments, joint ventures, and variable interest entities;
  - the company's operating characteristics, including its size and complexity;

- the sources of the company's earnings, including the relative profitability of key products and services; and
- key supplier and customer relationships.

To assist in obtaining information for identifying and assessing risks of material misstatement of the financial statements associated with a company's financial relationships and transactions with its executive officers (e.g., executive compensation, including perquisites, and any other arrangements), the auditor should perform procedures to obtain an understanding of the company's financial relationships and transactions with its executive officers. The procedures should be designed to identify risks of material misstatement and should include, but not be limited to (1) reading the employment and compensation contracts between the company and its executive officers and (2) reading the proxy statements and other relevant company filings with the Securities and Exchange Commission and other regulatory agencies that relate to the company's financial relationships and transactions with its executive officers.

As part of obtaining an understanding of the company, the auditor should consider performing the following procedures and the extent to which the procedures should be performed:

- reading public information about the company relevant to the evaluation of the likelihood of material financial statement misstatements and, in an integrated audit, the effectiveness of the company's internal control over financial reporting,
- observing or reading transcripts of earnings calls and, to the extent publicly available, other meetings with investors or rating agencies;
- obtaining an understanding of compensation arrangements with senior management other than executive officers including incentive compensation arrangements, changes or adjustments to those arrangements, and special bonuses;
- obtaining information about trading activity in the company's securities and holdings in the company's securities by significant holders to identify potentially significant unusual;
- inquiring of the chair of the compensation committee, or the compensation committee's equivalent, and any compensation

consultants engaged by either the compensation committee or the company regarding the structuring of the company's compensation for executive officers; and
- obtaining an understanding of established policies and procedures regarding the authorization and approval of executive officer expense reimbursements.

- The company's selection and application of accounting principles, including related disclosures
The auditor should evaluate whether the company's selection and application of accounting principles are appropriate for its business and consistent with the applicable financial reporting framework and accounting principles used in the relevant industry. Also, to identify and assess risks of material misstatement related to omitted, incomplete, or inaccurate disclosures, the auditor should develop expectations about the disclosures that are necessary for the company's financial statements to be presented fairly in conformity with the applicable financial reporting framework. The following matters, if present, are relevant to the necessary understanding of the company's selection and application of accounting principles, including related disclosures:

  - significant changes in the company's accounting principles, financial reporting policies, or disclosures and the reasons for such changes;
  - the financial reporting competencies of personnel involved in selecting and applying significant new or complex accounting principles;
  - the accounts or disclosures for which judgment is used in the application of significant accounting principles, especially in determining management's estimates and assumptions;
  - the effect of significant accounting principles in controversial or emerging areas for which there is a lack of authoritative guidance or consensus;
  - the methods the company uses to account for significant transactions that are outside the normal course of business for the company or that otherwise appear to be unusual due to their timing, size, or nature ("significant unusual transactions"); and

- financial reporting standards and laws and regulations that are new to the company, including when and how the company will adopt such requirements.

- The company's objectives and strategies and those related business risks
The purpose of obtaining an understanding of the company's objectives, strategies, and related business risks is to identify business risks that could reasonably be expected to result in material misstatement of the financial statements.

The following are examples of situations in which business risks might result in material misstatement of the financial statements:

- Industry developments (a potential related business risk might be, e.g., that the company does not have the personnel or expertise to deal with the changes in the industry).
- New products and services (a potential related business risk might be, e.g., that the new product or service will not be successful).
- Use of information technology ("IT") (a potential related business risk might be, e.g., that systems and processes are incompatible).
- New accounting requirements (a potential related business risk might be, e.g., incomplete or improper implementation of a new accounting requirement).
- Expansion of the business (a potential related business risk might be, e.g., that the demand for the company's products or services has not been accurately estimated).
- The effects of implementing a strategy, particularly any effects that will lead to new accounting requirements (a potential related business risk might be, e.g., incomplete or improper implementation of the strategy).
- Current and prospective financing requirements (a potential related business risk might be, e.g., the loss of financing due to the company's inability to meet financing requirements).
- Regulatory requirements (a potential related business risk might be, e.g., that there is increased legal exposure).

- The company's measurement and analysis of its financial performance
  The purpose of obtaining an understanding of the company's performance measures is to identify performance measures, whether external or internal, that affect the risks of material misstatement.

The following are examples of performance measures that might affect the risks of material misstatement:
– Measures that form the basis for contractual commitments or incentive compensation arrangements; – Measures used by external parties, such as analysts and rating agencies, to review the company's performance; and – Measures the company uses to monitor its operations that highlight unexpected results or trends that prompt management to investigate their cause and take corrective action, including correction of misstatements.

10.5.2 Obtaining an Understanding of Internal Control Over Financial Reporting

The auditor should obtain a sufficient understanding of each component of internal control over financial reporting ("understanding of internal control") to (a) identify the types of potential misstatements, (b) assess the factors that affect the risks of material misstatement, and (c) design further audit procedures. The nature, timing, and extent of procedures that are necessary to obtain an understanding of internal control depend on the size and complexity of the company; the auditor's existing knowledge of the company's internal control over financial reporting; the nature of the company's controls, including the company's use of IT; the nature and extent of changes in systems and operations; and the nature of the company's documentation of its internal control over financial reporting. Internal control over financial reporting can be described as consisting of the following components:

- The control environment
  The auditor should obtain an understanding of the company's control environment, including the policies and actions of management, the board, and the audit committee concerning the company's control environment. Obtaining an understanding of the control environment includes assessing:
  - Whether management's philosophy and operating style promote effective internal control over financial reporting;
  - Whether sound integrity and ethical values, particularly of top management, are developed and understood; and
  - Whether the board or audit committee understands and exercises oversight responsibility over financial reporting and internal control.

  If the auditor identifies a control deficiency in the company's control environment, the auditor should evaluate the extent to which this control deficiency is indicative of a fraud risk factor.
- The company's risk assessment process
  The auditor should obtain an understanding of management's process for:
  (a) Identifying risks relevant to financial reporting objectives, including risks of material misstatement due to fraud ("fraud risks");
  (b) Assessing the likelihood and significance of misstatements resulting from those risks; and
  (c) Deciding about actions to address those risks.

  Obtaining an understanding of the company's risk assessment process includes obtaining an understanding of the risks of material misstatement identified and assessed by management and the actions taken to address those risks.
- Information and communication
  The auditor should obtain an understanding of the information system, including the related business processes, relevant to financial reporting, including:
  (a) The classes of transactions in the company's operations that are significant to the financial statements;

(b) The procedures, within both automated and manual systems, by which those transactions are initiated, authorized, processed, recorded, and reported;
(c) The related accounting records, supporting information, and specific accounts in the financial statements that are used to initiate, authorize, process, and record transactions;
(d) how the information system captures events and conditions, other than transactions, 16/that are significant to the financial statements; and
(e) The period-end financial reporting process.

A company's business processes are the activities designed to:

(a) Develop, purchase, produce, sell and distribute a company's products or services;
(b) Record information, including accounting and financial reporting information; and
(c) Ensure compliance with laws and regulations relevant to the financial statements.

Obtaining an understanding of the company's business processes assists the auditor in obtaining an understanding of how transactions are initiated, authorized, processed, and recorded. A company's period-end financial reporting process, includes the following:

- procedures used to enter transaction totals into the general ledger;
- procedures related to the selection and application of accounting principles;
- procedures used to initiate, authorize, record, and process journal entries in the general ledger;
- procedures used to record recurring and nonrecurring adjustments to the annual financial statements (and quarterly financial statements, if applicable); and
- procedures for preparing annual financial statements and related disclosures (and quarterly financial statements, if applicable).

The auditor should obtain an understanding of how the company communicates financial reporting roles and responsibilities and significant matters relating to financial reporting to relevant company personnel and others, including: (i) communications between management, the audit committee, and the board of directors; and (ii) communications to external parties, including regulatory authorities and shareholders.

- Control activities
  The auditor should obtain an understanding of control activities that is sufficient to assess the factors that affect the risks of material misstatement and to design further audit procedures. As the auditor obtains an understanding of the other components of internal control over financial reporting, he or she is also likely to obtain knowledge about some control activities. The auditor should use his or her knowledge about the presence or absence of control activities obtained from the understanding of the other components of internal control over financial reporting in determining the extent to which it is necessary to devote additional attention to obtaining an understanding of control activities to assess the factors that affect the risks of material misstatement and to design further audit procedures.
- Monitoring of controls
  The auditor should obtain an understanding of the major types of activities that the company uses to monitor the effectiveness of its internal control over financial reporting and how the company initiates corrective actions related to its controls. An understanding of the company's monitoring activities includes understanding the source of the information used in the monitoring activities.

10.5.3 Considering Information from the Client Acceptance and Retention Evaluation, Audit Planning Activities, Past Audits, and Other Engagements Performed for the Company

The auditor should evaluate whether information obtained from the client acceptance and retention evaluation process or audit planning activities is relevant to identifying risks of material misstatement. Risks of material misstatement identified during those activities should be assessed. In subsequent years, the auditor should incorporate knowledge obtained during past audits into the auditor's process for identifying risks of material misstatement, including when identifying significant ongoing matters that affect the risks of material misstatement or determining how changes in the company or its environment affect the risks of material misstatement. If the auditor plans to limit the nature, timing, or extent of his or her risk assessment procedures by relying on information from past audits, the auditor should evaluate whether the prior years' information remains relevant and reliable. When the auditor has performed a review of interim financial information in accordance with AU sec. 722,[2] the auditor should evaluate whether information obtained during the review is relevant to identifying risks of material misstatement in the year-end audit. The auditor should obtain an understanding of the nature of the services that have been performed for the company by the auditor or affiliates of the firm and should take into account relevant information obtained from those engagements in identifying risks of material misstatement.

10.5.4 Performing Analytical Procedures

The auditor should perform analytical procedures that are designed to: (i) enhance the auditor's understanding of the client's business and the significant transactions and events that have occurred since the prior year end; and (ii) identify areas that might represent specific risks relevant to the audit, including the existence of unusual transactions and events, and amounts, ratios, and trends that warrant investigation.

10.5.5 Conducting a Discussion Among Engagement Team Members Regarding the Risks of Material Misstatement

The key engagement team members should discuss (i) the company's selection and application of accounting principles, including related disclosure requirements, and (ii) the susceptibility of the company's financial statements to material misstatement due to error or fraud.

The manner in which the discussion is conducted depends on the individuals involved and the circumstances of the engagement. The engagement partner or other key engagement team members should communicate the important matters from the discussion to engagement team members who are not involved in the discussion. Communication among the engagement team members about significant matters affecting the risks of material misstatement should continue throughout the audit, including when conditions change.

[2] Interim Financial Information.

10.5.6 Inquiring of the Audit Committee, Management, and Others Within the Company About the Risks of Material Misstatement

The auditor should inquire of the audit committee, or equivalent (or its chair), management, the internal audit function, and others within the company who might reasonably be expected to have information that is important to the identification and assessment of risks of material misstatement. The auditor's inquiries about risks of material misstatement should include inquiries regarding fraud risks. The auditor should use his or her knowledge of the company and its environment, as well as information from other risk assessment procedures, to determine the nature of the inquiries about risks of material misstatement.

The auditor's inquiries regarding fraud risks should include the following:

a. Inquiries of management regarding:

   (i) Whether management has knowledge of fraud, alleged fraud, or suspected fraud affecting the company;
   (ii) Management's process for identifying and responding to fraud risks in the company, including any specific fraud risks the company has identified or account balances or disclosures for which a fraud risk is likely to exist, and the nature, extent, and frequency of management's fraud risk assessment process;
   (iii) Controls that the company has established to address fraud risks the company has identified, or that otherwise help to prevent and detect fraud, including how management monitors those controls;
   (iv) For a company with multiple locations (a) the nature and extent of monitoring of operating locations or business segments and (b) whether there are particular operating locations or business segments for which a fraud risk might be more likely to exist;
   (v) Whether and how management communicates to employees its views on business practices and ethical behavior;
   (vi) Whether management has received tips or complaints regarding the company's financial reporting (including those received through the audit committee's internal

whistleblower program, if such program exists) and, if so, management's responses to such tips and complaints;

(vii) Whether management has reported to the audit committee on how the company's internal control serves to prevent and detect material misstatements due to fraud; and

(viii) Whether the company has entered into any significant unusual transactions and, if so, the nature, terms, and business purpose (or the lack thereof) of those transactions and whether such transactions involved related parties.

b. Inquiries of the audit committee, or equivalent, or its chair regarding:

(i) The audit committee's views about fraud risks in the company;

(ii) Whether the audit committee has knowledge of fraud, alleged fraud, or suspected fraud affecting the company;

(iii) Whether the audit committee is aware of tips or complaints regarding the company's financial reporting (including those received through the audit committee's internal whistleblower program, if such program exists) and, if so, the audit committee's responses to such tips and complaints;

(iv) How the audit committee exercises oversight of the company's assessment of fraud risks and the establishment of controls to address fraud risks; and

(v) Whether the company has entered into any significant unusual transactions.

c. If the company has an internal audit function, inquiries of appropriate internal audit personnel regarding:

(i) The internal auditors' views about fraud risks in the company;

(ii) Whether the internal auditors have knowledge of fraud, alleged fraud, or suspected fraud affecting the company;

(iii) Whether internal auditors have performed procedures to identify or detect fraud during the year, and whether management has satisfactorily responded to the findings resulting from those procedures;

(iv) Whether internal auditors are aware of instances of management override of controls and the nature and circumstances of such overrides; and

(v) Whether the company has entered into any significant unusual transactions.

The auditor should inquire of others within the company about their views regarding fraud risks, including, in particular, whether they have knowledge of fraud, alleged fraud, or suspected fraud. The auditor should identify other individuals within the company to whom inquiries should be directed and determine the extent of such inquiries by considering whether others in the company might have additional knowledge about fraud, alleged fraud, or suspected fraud or might be able to corroborate fraud risks identified in discussions with management or the audit committee.

Examples of other individuals within the company to whom inquiries might be directed include:

- Employees with varying levels of authority within the company, including, e.g., company personnel with whom the auditor comes into contact during the course of the audit (a) in obtaining an understanding of internal control, (b) in observing inventory or performing cutoff procedures, or (c) in obtaining explanations for significant differences identified when performing analytical procedures;
- Operating personnel not directly involved in the financial reporting process;
- Employees involved in initiating, recording, or processing complex or unusual transactions, e.g., a sales transaction with multiple elements, a significant unusual transaction, or a significant related party transaction; and
- In-house legal counsel.

When evaluating management's responses to inquiries about fraud risks and determining when it is necessary to corroborate management's responses, the auditor should take into account the fact that management is often in the best position to commit fraud. Also, the auditor should obtain evidence to address inconsistencies in responses to the inquiries.

10.6 Identifying and Assessing the Risks of Material Misstatement

The auditor should identify and assess the risks of material misstatement at the financial statement level and the assertion level. In identifying and assessing risks of material misstatement, the auditor should:

a. Identify risks of misstatement using information obtained from performing risk assessment procedures and considering the characteristics of the accounts and disclosures in the financial statements.
b. Evaluate whether the identified risks relate pervasively to the financial statements as a whole and potentially affect many assertions.
c. Evaluate the types of potential misstatements that could result from the identified risks and the accounts, disclosures, and assertions that could be affected. In identifying and assessing risks at the assertion level, the auditor should evaluate how risks at the financial statement level could affect risks of misstatement at the assertion level.
d. Assess the likelihood of misstatement, including the possibility of multiple misstatements, and the magnitude of potential misstatement to assess the possibility that the risk could result in material misstatement of the financial statements. In assessing the likelihood and magnitude of potential misstatement, the auditor may take into account the planned degree of reliance on controls selected to test.
e. Identify significant accounts and disclosures and their relevant assertions. The determination of whether an account or disclosure is significant or whether an assertion is a relevant assertion is based on inherent risk, without regard to the effect of controls.
f. Determine whether any of the identified and assessed risks of material misstatement are significant risks.

10.6.1 Identifying Significant Accounts and Disclosures and Their Relevant Assertions

To identify significant accounts and disclosures and their relevant assertions, the auditor should evaluate the qualitative and quantitative risk factors related to the financial statement line items and disclosures. Risk factors relevant to the identification of significant accounts and disclosures and their relevant assertions include:

- Size and composition of the account;
- Susceptibility to misstatement due to error or fraud;
- Volume of activity, complexity, and homogeneity of the individual transactions processed through the account or reflected in the disclosure;
- Nature of the account or disclosure;
- Accounting and reporting complexities associated with the account or disclosure;
- Exposure to losses in the account;
- Possibility of significant contingent liabilities arising from the activities reflected in the account or disclosure;
- Existence of related party transactions in the account; and
- Changes from the prior period in account and disclosure characteristics.

The auditor also should determine the likely sources of potential misstatements that would cause the financial statements to be materially misstated. The auditor might determine the likely sources of potential misstatements by asking himself or herself "what could go wrong?" within a given significant account or disclosure. The risk factors that the auditor should evaluate in the identification of significant accounts and disclosures and their relevant assertions are the same in the audit of internal control over financial reporting as in the audit of the financial statements; accordingly, significant accounts and disclosures and their relevant assertions are the same for both audits. In the financial statement audit, the auditor might perform substantive auditing procedures on financial statement accounts, disclosures, and assertions that are not determined to be significant accounts and disclosures and relevant assertions. The components of a potential significant account or disclosure might be subject to significantly differing risks. When a company has multiple locations or business units, the auditor should identify significant accounts and disclosures and their relevant assertions based on the consolidated financial statements.

10.6.2 Factors Relevant to Identifying Fraud Risks

The auditor should evaluate whether the information gathered from the risk assessment procedures indicates that one or more fraud risk factors are present and should be taken into account in identifying and assessing fraud risks. Fraud risk factors are events or conditions that indicate (i) an incentive or pressure to perpetrate fraud, (ii) an opportunity to carry out the fraud, or (iii) an attitude or rationalization that justifies the fraudulent action. Fraud risk factors do not necessarily indicate the existence of fraud; however, they often are present in circumstances in which fraud exists. The auditor's evaluation of fraud risk factors in accordance should include evaluation of how fraud could be perpetrated or concealed by presenting incomplete or inaccurate disclosures or by omitting disclosures that are necessary for the financial statements to be presented fairly in conformity with the applicable financial reporting framework. The auditor's identification of fraud risks should include the risk of management override of controls.

10.6.3 Factors Relevant to Identifying Significant Risks

To determine whether an identified and assessed risk is a significant risk, the auditor should evaluate whether the risk requires special audit consideration because of the nature of the risk or the likelihood and potential magnitude of misstatement related to the risk. The determination of whether a risk of material misstatement is a significant risk is based on inherent risk, without regard to the effect of controls.

Factors that should be evaluated in determining which risks are significant risks include:

(a) the effect of the quantitative and qualitative risk factors;
(b) whether the risk is a fraud risk;
(c) whether the risk is related to recent significant economic, accounting, or other developments;
(d) the complexity of transactions;
(e) whether the risk involves significant transactions with related parties;
(f) the degree of complexity or judgment in the recognition or measurement of financial information related to the risk, especially those measurements involving a wide range of measurement uncertainty; and
(g) Whether the risk involves significant unusual transactions.

10.6.4 *Further Consideration of Controls*

When the auditor has determined that a significant risk, including a fraud risk, exists, the auditor should evaluate the design of the company's controls that are intended to address fraud risks and other significant risks and determine whether those controls have been implemented, if the auditor has not already done so when obtaining an understanding of internal control. Controls that address fraud risks include (a) specific controls designed to mitigate specific risks of fraud, e.g., controls to address risks of intentional misstatement of specific accounts and (b) controls designed to prevent, deter, and detect fraud, e.g., controls to promote a culture of honesty and ethical behavior. Such controls also include those that address the risk of management override of other controls.

Practice

Question 1

Which of the following assertion is accurate concerning audit risk?

(a) Audit risk refers to the risk that the auditor expresses an inappropriate audit opinion
(b) Audit risk is a function of the risk of material misstatement and detection risk
(c) Audit risk includes risk of material misstatement
(d) Audit risk include detection risk
(e) All of the above

Question 2

Which of the following assertion is inaccurate concerning the risks of material misstatement?

(a) Risks of material misstatement can arise from a variety of sources, including external factors
(b) Risks of material misstatement never occur from the nature or the activities of a company
(c) Risks of material misstatement may relate to personnel who lack the necessary financial reporting competencies
(d) Risks of material misstatement may result from information systems that fail to accurately capture business transactions.

Question 3

Which of the following Assertion is inaccurate concerning the auditor's inquiry regarding fraud?

(a) Inquiries of management concerning its knowledge of fraud, alleged fraud, or suspected fraud affecting the company
(b) Inquiries of the audit committee, or its equivalent as to the fraud risks facing the company
(c) Inquiries of appropriate internal audit personnel regarding its knowledge of fraud
(d) Inquiries of the management structure

Question 4

Which one of the following is not included in fraud risk factors?

(a) An incentive or pressure to perpetrate fraud
(b) An opportunity to carry out the fraud
(c) An attitude or rationalization that justifies the fraudulent action.
(d) A commingling of the function of the CEO and Chairman of the board of directors

Question 5

Which one of the below assertions is incorrect concerning fraud risk factors?

(a) Fraud risk factors do not necessarily indicate the existence of fraud
(b) Fraud risk factors often are present in circumstances in which fraud exists
(c) Fraud risk factors may be unintentional
(d) The auditor's identification of fraud risks should include the risk of management override of controls

CHAPTER 11

Audit Sampling

11.1 General

Sampling technique was due to the voluminous transactions involved in the conduct of business by large corporations operating in widespread locations. It is no longer practical nor feasible for auditors to review and verify all the transactions performed during the period audited.[1] Audit sampling is the application of an audit procedure to less than 100% of the items within an account balance or class of transactions for the purpose of evaluating some characteristic of the balance or class.[2] There are two general approaches to audit sampling: nonstatistical and statistical. Both approaches require that the auditor use professional judgment in planning, performing, and evaluating a sample and in relating the audit evidence produced by the sample to other audit evidence when forming a conclusion about the related account balance or class of transactions. The size of a sample necessary to provide sufficient audit evidence depends on both the objectives and the efficiency of the sample.

[1] LEE Teck-Heang, Azham Md. Ali (2008): The Evolution of Auditing: An Analysis of the Historical Development, *Journal of Modern Auditing and Accounting*, Volume 4, No. 12, p. 4.

[2] AU Section 350.

F. I. Lessambo, *Auditing, Assurance Services, and Forensics*,
https://doi.org/10.1007/978-3-319-90521-1_11

11.2 Sampling and Non-sampling Risks

Sampling risk arises from the possibility that, when a test of controls or a substantive test is restricted to a sample, the auditor's conclusions may be different from the conclusions he would reach if the test were applied in the same way to all items in the account balance or class of transactions. That is, a particular sample may contain proportionately more or less monetary misstatements or deviations from prescribed controls than exist in the balance or class as a whole. For a sample of a specific design, sampling risk varies inversely with sample size: the smaller the sample size, the greater the sampling risk. Conversely, non-sampling risk includes all the aspects of audit risk that are not due to sampling. An auditor may apply a procedure to all transactions or balances and still fail to detect a material misstatement. Non-sampling risk includes the possibility of selecting audit procedures that are not appropriate to achieve the specific objective. For example, confirming recorded receivables cannot be relied on to reveal unrecorded receivables. Non-sampling risk also arises because the auditor may fail to recognize misstatements included in documents that he examines, which would make that procedure ineffective even if he were to examine all items.

11.2.1 Sampling Risk

The auditor should apply professional judgment in assessing sampling risk. In performing substantive tests of details the auditor is concerned with two aspects of sampling risk:

- The risk of incorrect acceptance is the risk that the sample supports the conclusion that the recorded account balance is not materially misstated when it is materially misstated.
- The risk of incorrect rejection is the risk that the sample supports the conclusion that the recorded account balance is materially misstated when it is not materially misstated.

The auditor is also concerned with two aspects of sampling risk in performing tests of controls when sampling is used:

- The risk of assessing control risk too low is the risk that the assessed level of control risk based on the sample is less than the true operating effectiveness of the control.

- The risk of assessing control risk too high is the risk that the assessed level of control risk based on the sample is greater than the true operating effectiveness of the control.

The risk of incorrect rejection and the risk of assessing control risk too high relate to the efficiency of the audit. For example, if the auditor's evaluation of an audit sample leads him to the initial erroneous conclusion that a balance is materially misstated when it is not, the application of additional audit procedures and consideration of other audit evidence would ordinarily lead the auditor to the correct conclusion. Similarly, if the auditor's evaluation of a sample leads him to unnecessarily assess control risk too high for an assertion, he would ordinarily increase the scope of substantive tests to compensate for the perceived ineffectiveness of the controls. Although the audit may be less efficient in these circumstances, the audit is, nevertheless, effective. The risk of incorrect acceptance and the risk of assessing control risk too low relate to the effectiveness of an audit in detecting an existing material misstatement.

11.3 Sampling in Substantive Tests of Details

The auditor needs to plan, select, perform and evaluate the sampling.

11.3.1 Planning the Sample

Planning involves developing a strategy for conducting an audit of financial statements. When planning a particular sample for a substantive test of details, the auditor should consider:

- The relationship of the sample to the relevant audit objective.
- Preliminary judgments about materiality levels.
- The auditor's allowable risk of incorrect acceptance.
- Characteristics of the population, that is, the items comprising the account balance or class of transactions of interest.

When planning a particular sample, the auditor should consider the specific audit objective to be achieved and should determine that the audit procedure, or combination of procedures, to be applied will achieve that objective. The auditor should determine that the population from which he draws the sample is appropriate for the specific audit objective.

For example, an auditor would not be able to detect understatements of an account due to omitted items by sampling the recorded items. An appropriate sampling plan for detecting such understatements would involve selecting from a source in which the omitted items are included. When planning a sample for a test of details, the auditor should consider how much monetary misstatement in the related account balance or class of transactions may exist when combined with misstatements that may be found in other tests without causing the financial statements to be materially misstated. This maximum monetary misstatement that the auditor is willing to accept for the balance or class is called tolerable misstatement for the sample. Tolerable misstatement is a planning concept and is related to the auditor's determination of materiality for planning the financial statement audit in such a way that tolerable misstatement, combined for all of the tests in the entire audit, does not exceed materiality for the financial statements. This means that auditors should normally set tolerable misstatement for a specific audit procedure at less than financial statement materiality so that when the results of the audit procedures are aggregated, the required overall assurance is attained.

The auditor may be able to reduce the required sample size by separating items subject to sampling into relatively homogeneous groups on the basis of some characteristic related to the specific audit objective. For example, common bases for such groupings are the recorded or book value of the items, the nature of controls related to processing the items, and special considerations associated with certain items. An appropriate number of items is then selected from each group.

To determine the number of items to be selected in a sample for a particular test of details, the auditor should consider the tolerable misstatement and the expected misstatement, the audit risk, the characteristics of the population, the assessed risk of material misstatement (inherent risk and control risk), and the assessed risk for other substantive procedures related to the same assertion.

11.3.2 Sample Selection

Sample items should be selected in such a way that the sample can be expected to be representative of the population. Therefore, all items in the population should have an opportunity to be selected. For example, haphazard and random-based selection of items represents two means of obtaining such samples.

11.3.3 Performance and Evaluation

Audit procedures that are appropriate to the particular audit objective should be applied to each sample item. In some circumstances the auditor may not be able to apply the planned audit procedures to selected sample items because, for example, the entity might not be able to locate supporting documentation. The auditor's treatment of unexamined items will depend on their effect on his or her evaluation of the sample. If the auditor's evaluation of the sample results would not be altered by considering those unexamined items to be misstated, it is not necessary to examine the items. However, if considering those unexamined items to be misstated would lead to a conclusion that the balance or class contains material misstatement, the auditor should consider alternative audit procedures that would provide sufficient appropriate audit evidence to form a conclusion. The auditor should also consider whether the reasons for his or her inability to examine the items have implications in relation to assessing risks of material misstatement due to fraud, the assessed level of control risk that he or she expects to be supported, or the degree of reliance on management representations. The auditor should project the misstatement results of the sample to the items from which the sample was elected. There are several acceptable ways to project misstatements from a sample. For example, an auditor may have selected a sample of every twentieth item (50 items) from a population containing one thousand items. If he discovered overstatements of $3000 in that sample, the auditor could project a $60,000 overstatement by dividing the amount of misstatement in the sample by the fraction of total items from the population included in the sample. The auditor should add that projection to the misstatements discovered in any items examined 100%. This total projected misstatement should be compared with the tolerable misstatement for the account balance or class of transactions, and appropriate consideration should be given to sampling risk. If the total projected misstatement is less than tolerable misstatement for the account balance or class of transactions, the auditor should consider the risk that such a result might be obtained even though the true monetary misstatement for the population exceeds tolerable misstatement.

In addition to the evaluation of the frequency and amounts of monetary misstatements, consideration should be given to the qualitative aspects of the misstatements. These include (a) the nature and cause of misstatements, such as whether they are differences in principle or in application, are errors or are caused by fraud, or are due to misunderstanding of instructions or to carelessness, and (b) the possible relationship of the misstatements to other phases of the audit. The discovery of fraud ordinarily requires a broader consideration of possible implications than does the discovery of an error. If the sample results suggest that the auditor's planning assumptions were incorrect, he should take appropriate action. For example, if monetary misstatements are discovered in a substantive test of details in amounts or frequency that is greater than is consistent with the assessed levels of inherent and control risk, the auditor should alter his risk assessments. The auditor should also consider whether to modify the other audit tests that were designed based upon the inherent and control risk assessments. For example, a large number of misstatements discovered in confirmation of receivables may indicate the need to reconsider the control risk assessment related to the assertions that impacted the design of substantive tests of sales or cash receipts. The auditor should relate the evaluation of the sample to other relevant audit evidence when forming a conclusion about the related account balance or class of transactions.

11.4 Sampling in Tests of Controls

Like in the substantive tests of details, the sampling in tests of control requires (i) planning, (ii) selecting; (iii) performing and evaluating.

11.4.1 Planning Samples

Planning involves developing a strategy for conducting an audit of financial statements. When planning a particular audit sample for a test of controls, the auditor should consider:

- The relationship of the sample to the objective of the test of controls.
- The maximum rate of deviations from prescribed controls that would support his planned assessed level of control risk.
- The auditor's allowable risk of assessing control risk too low.
- Characteristics of the population, that is, the items comprising the account balance or class of transactions of interest.

Sampling applies when the auditor needs to decide whether the rate of deviation from a prescribed procedure is no greater than a tolerable rate, for example in testing a matching process or an approval process. However, risk assessment procedures performed to obtain an understanding of internal control do not involve sampling. Sampling concepts also do not apply for some tests of controls. Tests of automated application controls are generally tested only once or a few times when effective (IT) general controls are present, and thus do not rely on the concepts of risk and tolerable deviation as applied in other sampling procedures. Sampling generally is not applicable to analyses of controls for determining the appropriate segregation of duties or other analyses that do not examine documentary evidence of performance. In addition, sampling may not apply to tests of certain documented controls or to analyses of the effectiveness of security and access controls. Sampling also may not apply to some tests directed toward obtaining audit evidence about the operation of the control environment or the accounting system, for example, inquiry or observation of explanation of variances from budgets when the auditor does not desire to estimate the rate of deviation from the prescribed control, or when examining the actions of those charged with governance. The auditor's overall assessment of control risk for a particular assertion involves combining judgments about the prescribed controls, the deviations from prescribed controls, and the degree of assurance provided by the sample and other tests of controls.

The auditor should determine the maximum rate of deviations from the prescribed control that he would be willing to accept without altering his planned assessed level of control risk. This is the tolerable rate. In determining the tolerable rate, the auditor should consider (a) the planned assessed level of control risk, and (b) the degree of assurance desired by the audit evidence in the sample. For example, if the auditor plans to assess control risk at a low level, and he desires a high degree of assurance from the audit evidence provided by the sample for tests of controls (i.e., not perform other tests of controls for the assertion), he might decide that a tolerable rate of 5% or possibly less would be reasonable. If the auditor either plans to assess control risk at a higher level, or he desires assurance from other tests of controls along with that provided by the sample (such as inquiries of appropriate entity personnel or observation of the application of the policy or procedure), the auditor might decide that a tolerable rate of 10% or more is reasonable. In assessing the tolerable rate of deviations, the auditor should consider that, while deviations from pertinent controls increase the risk of material misstatements in the accounting records, such deviations do not necessarily result in misstatements. When the degree of assurance desired by the audit evidence in the sample is high, the auditor should allow for a low level of sampling risk (that is, the risk of assessing control risk too low). To determine the number of items to be selected for a particular sample for a test of controls, the auditor should consider the tolerable rate of deviation from the controls being tested, the likely rate of deviations, and the allowable risk of assessing control risk too low.

11.4.2 Sample Selection

Sample items should be selected in such a way that the sample can be expected to be representative of the population. Therefore, all items in the population should have an opportunity to be selected. Random-based selection of items represents one means of obtaining such samples. Ideally, the auditor should use a selection method that has the potential for selecting items from the entire period under audit.

11.4.3 Performance and Evaluation

Auditing procedures that are appropriate to achieve the objective of the test of controls should be applied to each sample item. If the auditor is not able to apply the planned audit procedures or appropriate alternative procedures to selected items, he should consider the reasons for this limitation, and he should ordinarily consider those selected items to be deviations from the prescribed policy or procedure for the purpose of evaluating the sample. The deviation rate in the sample is the auditor's best estimate of the deviation rate in the population from which it was selected. If the estimated deviation rate is less than the tolerable rate for the population, the auditor should consider the risk that such a result might be obtained even though the true deviation rate for the population exceeds the tolerable rate for the population. In addition to the evaluation of the frequency of deviations from pertinent procedures, consideration should be given to the qualitative aspects of the deviations. These include (a) the nature and cause of the deviations, such as whether they are due to error or fraud, and (b) the possible relationship of the deviations to other phases of the audit. The discovery of fraud ordinarily requires a broader consideration of possible implications than does the discovery of an error.

If the auditor concludes that the sample results do not support the planned assessed level of control risk for an assertion, he should reevaluate the nature, timing, and extent of substantive procedures based on a revised consideration of the assessed level of control risk for the relevant financial statement assertions.

11.5 Dual-Purpose Samples

In some circumstances the auditor may design a sample that will be used for dual purposes: testing the operating effectiveness of an identified control and testing whether the recorded monetary amount of transactions is correct. In general, an auditor planning to use a dual-purpose sample would have made a preliminary assessment that there is an acceptably low risk that the rate of deviations from the prescribed control in the population exceeds the tolerable rate. For example, an auditor designing a test of control over en- tries in the voucher register may plan a related substantive procedure at a risk level that anticipates a particular assessed level of control risk. The size of a sample designed for dual purposes should be the larger of the samples that would otherwise have been designed for the two separate purposes. In evaluating such tests, deviations from the prescribed control and monetary misstatements should be evaluated separately using the risk levels applicable for the respective purposes. The absence of monetary misstatements detected in a sample does not necessarily imply that related controls are effective; however, misstatements that the auditor detects by performing substantive procedures should be considered by the auditor as a possible indication of a control failure when assessing the operating effectiveness of related controls. Statistical sampling helps the auditor (a) to design an efficient sample, (b) to measure the sufficiency of the audit evidence obtained, and (c) to evaluate the sample results. By using statistical theory, the auditor can quantify sampling risk to assist himself in limiting it to a level he considers acceptable. However, statistical sampling involves additional costs of training auditors, designing individual samples to meet the statistical requirements, and selecting the items to be examined. Because either non-statistical or statistical sampling can provide sufficient audit evidence, the auditor chooses between them after considering their relative cost and effectiveness in the circumstances.

11.6 Use of IT in Sampling

Auditors face increasing challenges concerning their expected duties, with very often tightening budgets from their clients. To keep up with the demand, audit firms can integrate technologies such as TeamMate Analytics tools. Data analytics enable auditors to reduce risk by auditing 100% of a population rather than a small sample.[3] TeamMate Analytics is based in Microsoft Excel. Further, the TemMate Analytics library includes 200 audit tests which provide needed analytics. It includes 10 pre-built modules designed to audit areas such as: expenses, general ledger journals, payables, receivables, HR and payroll, fixed assets, inventories.[4]

Appendix

- Selecting Audit Samples Using Benford's Law, by Carlos Gomes da Silva and Pedro M. R. Carreira; *AUDITING: A Journal of Practice & Theory*, February 2013, Vol. 32, No. 1, pp. 203–219

Practice

<u>Question 1</u>

Which of the below assertions concerning audit sampling is inaccurate?

(a) Audit sampling is the application of an audit procedure to less than 100% of the items within an account balance or class of transactions
(b) In order to have statistical relevance, a sampling approach should be determined either using a random selection method or probability theory to evaluate a sample result
(c) The objective of the auditor, when using audit sampling, is to provide a reasonable basis for the auditor to draw conclusions about the population from which the sample is selected

[3] TeaMate Analytics—Kluwer Wolters @ http://www.teammatesolutions.com/analytics/summary-of-tools.aspx.

[4] TeaMate Analytics—Kluwer Wolters @ http://www.teammatesolutions.com/analytics/summary-of-tools.aspx.

(d) Sample size is always a valid criterion to use in deciding between statistical and non-statistical approaches
(e) In a dual purposes sampling, the auditor uses the same sample to perform both tests of controls and tests of details

Question 2

Which of the following assertions is inaccurate concerning sampling risk?

(a) The auditor's conclusion based on a sample may be different from the conclusion if the entire population were subjected to the same audit procedure
(b) Sampling risk includes drawing an incorrect inference from the sample results
(c) Dividing the population into relatively homogeneous groups in order to reduce sample size (a.k.a stratification) leads to better sampling result
(d) Haphazard and random-based selection of items should not be used in sampling

Question 3

Which of the following assertions is true when determining sampling size in attribute sampling?

(a) The Population size is not a major factor
(b) A failure rate is not to be expected
(c) The sampling risk is often too high
(d) Tolerable failure rate is predetermined

Question 4

Non-sampling risk occurs in the following situations, except:

(a) The auditor has chosen the right sample but has applied the wrong audit procedure
(b) The auditor has applied the appropriate procedure but he did not properly understand the evidence
(c) The auditor sampling method was faulty
(d) The auditor has applied the appropriate procedure, identified the misstatement but failed to recognize it

Question 5

Which one of the below assertions is inaccurate concerning statistical sampling?

(a) Statistical sampling involves additional costs of training auditors
(b) Statistical sampling requires designing individual samples to meet the statistical requirements, and selecting the items to be examined
(c) Statistical sampling requires selecting the items to be examined
(d) Statistical sampling must be preferred over non-statistical sampling

CHAPTER 12

Auditing Accounting Estimates, Including Fair Value Accounting Estimates

12.1 General

Some financial statement items cannot be measured precisely but can only be estimated. The nature and reliability of information available to management to support the making of an accounting estimate varies widely, which thereby affects the degree of estimation uncertainty associated with accounting estimates. The measurement objective of accounting estimates can vary, depending on the applicable financial reporting framework and the financial item being reported. However, a difference between the outcome of an accounting estimate and the amount originally recognized or disclosed in the financial statements does not necessarily represent a misstatement of the financial statements; rather, it could be an outcome of estimation uncertainty.

12.2 Auditing Accounting Estimates

The auditor should review the outcome of accounting estimates included in the prior period financial statements or, when applicable, their subsequent re-estimation for the purpose of the current period. The nature and extent of the auditor's review takes account of the nature of the accounting estimates and whether the information obtained from the review would be relevant to identifying and assessing risks of material misstatement of accounting estimates made in the current period financial statements. However, the review is not intended to call into question

F. I. Lessambo, *Auditing, Assurance Services, and Forensics*,
https://doi.org/10.1007/978-3-319-90521-1_12

the auditor's professional judgments made in the prior periods that were based on information available at the time.

In responding to the assessed risks of material misstatement, as required by section 330, the auditor should undertake one or more of the following, taking into account the nature of the accounting estimate:

a. Determine whether events occurring up to the date of the auditor's report provide audit evidence regarding the accounting estimate
b. Test how management made the accounting estimate and the data on which it is based. In doing so, the auditor should evaluate whether:

   (i) The method of measurement used is appropriate in the circumstances,
   (ii) The assumptions used by management are reasonable in light of the measurement objectives of the applicable financial reporting framework, and
   (iii) The data on which the estimate is based is sufficiently re- liable for the auditor's purposes.

c. Test the operating effectiveness of the controls over how management made the accounting estimate, together with appropriate substantive procedures
d. Develop a point estimate or range to evaluate management's point estimate:

   (i) if the auditor uses assumptions or methods that differ from management's, the auditor should obtain an understanding of management's assumptions or methods sufficient to establish that the auditor's point estimate or range takes into account relevant variables and to evaluate any significant differences from management's point estimate
   (ii) if the auditor concludes that it is appropriate to use a range, the auditor should narrow the range, based on audit evidence available, until all outcomes within the range are considered reasonable.

12.2.1 Estimation Uncertainty

For accounting estimates that give rise to significant risks, the auditor should evaluate the following:

a. How management has considered alternative assumptions or outcomes and why it has rejected them or how management has otherwise addressed estimation uncertainty in making the accounting estimate
b. Whether the significant assumptions used by management are reasonable
c. When relevant to the reasonableness of the significant assumptions used by management or the appropriate application of the applicable financial reporting framework, management's intent to carry out specific courses of action and its ability to do so.

If, in the auditor's professional judgment, management has not addressed adequately the effects of estimation uncertainty on the accounting estimates that give rise to significant risks, the auditor should, if considered necessary, develop a range with which to evaluate the reasonableness of the accounting estimate.

12.2.2 Recognition and Measurement Criteria

For accounting estimates that give rise to significant risks, the auditor should obtain sufficient appropriate audit evidence about whether: (a) management's decision to recognize or not recognize the accounting estimates in the financial statements and (b) the selected measurement basis for the accounting estimates are in accordance with the requirements of the applicable financial reporting framework. The auditor should evaluate, based on the audit evidence, whether the accounting estimates in the financial statements are either reasonable in the context of the applicable financial reporting framework or are misstated. The auditor should obtain sufficient appropriate audit evidence about whether the disclosures in the financial statements related to accounting estimates are in accordance with the requirements of the applicable financial reporting framework. For accounting estimates that give rise to significant risks, the auditor also should evaluate the adequacy of the disclosure of estimation uncertainty in the financial statements in the context of the applicable financial reporting framework. The auditor should review the judgments and decisions made by management in the making of accounting estimates to identify whether indicators of possible management bias exist. Indicators of possible management bias do not, themselves, constitute misstatements for the purposes of drawing conclusions on the reasonableness of individual accounting estimates.

In evaluating the reasonableness of an estimate, the auditor normally concentrates on key factors and assumptions that are:

- significant to the accounting estimate
- sensitive to variations
- deviations from historical patterns
- subjective and susceptible to misstatement and bias.

The auditor normally should consider the historical experience of the entity in making past estimates as well as the auditor's experience in the industry. However, changes in facts, circumstances, or entity's procedures may cause factors different from those considered in the past to become significant to the accounting estimate. In evaluating reasonableness, the auditor should obtain an understanding of how management developed the estimate. Based on that understanding, the auditor should use one or a combination of the following approaches: (a) review and test the process used by management to develop the estimate; (b) develop an independent expectation of the estimate to corroborate the reasonableness of management's estimate, and (c) review subsequent events or transactions occurring prior to the date of the auditor's report. In many situations, the auditor assesses the reasonableness of an accounting estimate by performing procedures to test the process used by management to make the estimate. The following are procedures the auditor may consider performing when using this approach:

- identify whether there are controls over the preparation of accounting estimates and supporting data that may be useful in the evaluation
- identify the sources of data and factors that management used in forming the assumptions, and consider whether such data and factors are relevant, reliable, and sufficient for the purpose based on information gathered in other audit tests
- consider whether there are additional key factors or alternative assumptions about the factors
- evaluate whether the assumptions are consistent with each other, the supporting data, relevant historical data, and industry data
- analyze historical data used in developing the assumptions to assess whether the data is comparable and consistent with data of the

period under audit, and consider whether such data is sufficiently reliable for the purpose
- consider whether changes in the business or industry may cause other factors to become significant to the assumptions
- review available documentation of the assumptions used in developing the accounting estimates and inquire about any other plans, goals, and objectives of the entity, as well as consider their relationship to the assumptions
- consider using the work of a specialist regarding certain assumptions[1]
- test the calculations used by management to translate the assumptions and key factors into the accounting estimate.

Events or transactions sometimes occur subsequent to the date of the balance sheet, but prior to the date of the auditor's report, that are important in identifying and evaluating the reasonableness of accounting estimates or key factors or assumptions used in the preparation of the estimate. In such circumstances, an evaluation of the estimate or of a key factor or assumption may be minimized or unnecessary as the event or transaction can be used by the auditor in evaluating their reasonableness.

12.3 Auditing Fair Value Estimates

Both Auditing Standard No. 12,[2] and Auditing Standard No. 14[3] provide specific procedures relevant to auditing accounting estimates and fair value measurements. These standards share common approaches for substantively testing accounting estimates and fair value measurements and certain common concepts under each approach. In general, there are three approaches common to both standards, as discussed below. When performing an audit, the auditor selects one or a combination of these approaches.

[1] Section 336—Using the Work of a Specialist.

[2] Paragraph 13, Auditing standard No. 12.

[3] Paragraph 13, Auditing standard No. 12.

12.3.1 *Testing Management's Process*

Management is responsible for establishing an accounting and financial reporting process for determining fair value measurements. In some cases, the measurement of fair value and therefore the process set up by management to determine fair value may be simple and reliable. For example, management may be able to refer to published price quotations in an active market to determine fair value for marketable securities held by the entity. Some fair value measurements, however, are inherently more complex than others and involve uncertainty about the occurrence of future events or their outcome, and therefore assumptions that may involve the use of judgment need to be made as part of the measurement process.

- The auditor generally evaluates significant assumptions used by management for reasonableness and tests the data used, including evaluating whether the data is complete, accurate and relevant.
- The auditor also evaluates the consistency of assumptions used by management.

When obtaining an understanding of the entity's process for determining fair value measurements and disclosures, the auditor considers, for example:

- controls over the process used to determine fair value measurements, including, for example, controls over data and the segregation of duties between those committing the entity to the underlying transactions and those responsible for undertaking the valuations.
- the expertise and experience of those persons determining the fair value measurements.
- the role that information technology has in the process.
- the types of accounts or transactions requiring fair value measurements or disclosures (i.e., whether the accounts arise from the recording of routine and recurring transactions or whether they arise from nonroutine or unusual transactions).
- the extent to which the entity's process relies on a service organization to provide fair value measurements or the data that supports the measurement.

- the extent to which the entity engages or employs specialists in determining fair value measurements and disclosures.
- the significant management assumptions used in determining fair value.
- the documentation supporting management's assumptions.
- the process used to develop and apply management assumptions, including whether management used available market information to develop the assumptions.
- the process used to monitor changes in management's assumptions.
- the integrity of change controls and security procedures for valuation models and relevant information systems, including approval processes.
- The controls over the consistency, timeliness, and reliability of the data used in valuation models.
- Developing an independent estimate.

– The auditor can use management's or alternative assumptions to develop an independent estimate or an expectation as to the estimate.

12.3.2 Reviewing Subsequent Events or Transactions

The auditor should evaluate whether the fair value measurements and disclosures in the financial statements are in conformity with GAAP. The auditor's understanding of the requirements of GAAP and knowledge of the business and industry, together with the results of other audit procedures, are used to evaluate the accounting for assets or liabilities requiring fair value measurements, and the disclosures about the basis for the fair value measurements and significant uncertainties related thereto.

The evaluation of the entity's fair value measurements and of the audit evidence depends, in part, on the auditor's knowledge of the nature of the business. This is particularly true where the asset or liability or the valuation method is highly complex. For example, derivative financial instruments may be highly complex, with a risk that differing assumptions used in determining fair values will result in different conclusions. The measurement of the fair value of some items, for example "in process research and development" or intangible assets acquired in a business combination, may involve special considerations that are affected by the nature of the entity and its operations. Also, the auditor's knowledge of the business, together with the results of other audit procedures, may help identify assets for which management should assess the need to recognize an impairment loss under applicable GAAP.

The auditor should evaluate management's intent to carry out specific courses of action where intent is relevant to the use of fair value measurements, the related requirements involving presentation and disclosures, and how changes in fair values are reported in financial statements. The auditor also should evaluate management's ability to carry out those courses of action. Management often documents plans and intentions relevant to specific assets or liabilities and GAAP may require it to do so. While the extent of evidence to be obtained about management's intent and ability is a matter of professional judgment, the auditor's procedures ordinarily include inquiries of management, with appropriate corroboration of responses, for example, by: (i) considering management's past history of carrying out its stated intentions with respect to assets or liabilities; (ii) reviewing written plans and other documentation, including, where applicable, budgets, minutes, and other such items (iii) considering management's stated reasons for choosing a particular course of action, and (iv) considering management's ability to carry out a particular course of action given the entity's economic circumstances, including the implications of its contractual commitments.

When there are no observable market prices and the entity estimates fair value using a valuation method, the auditor should evaluate whether the entity's method of measurement is appropriate in the circumstances. That evaluation requires the use of professional judgment. It also involves obtaining an understanding of management's rationale for selecting a particular method by discussing with management its reasons for selecting the valuation method. The auditor considers whether:

a. management has sufficiently evaluated and appropriately applied the criteria, if any, provided by GAAP to support the selected method
b. the valuation method is appropriate in the circumstances given the nature of the item being valued
c. the valuation method is appropriate in relation to the business, industry, and environment in which the entity operates.

The auditor should evaluate whether the entity's method for determining fair value measurements is applied consistently and if so, whether the consistency is appropriate considering possible changes in the environment or circumstances affecting the entity, or changes in accounting principles. If management has changed the method for determining fair value, the auditor considers whether management can adequately demonstrate that the method to which it has changed provides a more appropriate basis of measurement or whether the change is supported by a change in the GAAP requirements or a change in circumstances. For example, the introduction of an active market for an equity security may indicate that the use of the discounted cash flows method to estimate the fair value of the security is no longer appropriate.

12.3.3 Engaging a Specialist

The auditor should consider whether to engage a specialist and use the work of that specialist as evidential matter in performing substantive tests to evaluate material financial statement assertions. The auditor may have the necessary skill and knowledge to plan and perform audit procedures related to fair values or may decide to use the work of a specialist. When planning to use the work of a specialist in auditing fair value measurements, the auditor considers whether the specialist's understanding of the definition of fair value and the method that the specialist will use to determine fair value are consistent with those of management and with GAAP. For example, the method used by a specialist for estimating the fair value of real estate or a complex derivative may not be consistent with the measurement principles specified in GAAP. Accordingly, the auditor considers such matters, often through discussions with the specialist or by reading the report of the specialist.

12.4 Assessment of Fair Value Levels

The fair value hierarchy prioritizes the inputs used to measure fair value into three Levels (Levels 1, 2, and 3), moving from quoted prices in active markets in Level 1 to unobservable inputs in Level 3.

- **Level 1 inputs**—observable, quoted prices for identical assets or liabilities in active markets.

- **Level 2 inputs**—quoted prices for similar assets or liabilities in active markets; quoted prices for identical or similar assets in markets that are not active; and inputs other than quoted prices, e.g., interest rates and yield curves.
- **Level 3 inputs**—unobservable inputs for the asset or liability. These should be based on the best information available. The company should utilize all reasonably available information, but need not incur excessive cost or effort to do so.

Note 4: Fair Value Measurements

Assets and Liabilities Measured at Fair Value on a Recurring Basis (in millions):

		Fair Value Measurements at Reporting Date Using		
	Balance at Sep 28, 2014	Quoted Prices in Active Markets for Identical Assets (Level 1)	Significant Other Observable Inputs (Level 2)	Significant Unobservable Inputs (Level 3)
Assets:				
Cash and cash equivalents	$ 1,708.4	$ 1,708.4	$ —	$ —
Short-term investments:				
Available-for-sale securities				
Corporate debt securities	4.9	—	4.9	—
Foreign government obligations	33.7	—	33.7	—
US government treasury securities	10.9	10.9	—	—
State and local government obligations	12.7	—	12.7	—
Certificates of deposit	1.0	—	1.0	—
Total available-for-sale securities	63.2	10.9	52.3	—
Trading securities	72.2	72.2	—	—
Total short-term investments	135.4	83.1	52.3	—
Prepaid expenses and other current assets:				
Derivative assets	28.7	0.9	27.8	—
Long-term investments:				
Available-for-sale securities				
Agency obligations	8.9	—	8.9	—
Corporate debt securities	130.9	—	130.9	—
Auction rate securities	13.8	—	—	13.8
Foreign government obligations	17.4	—	17.4	—
US government treasury securities	94.8	94.8	—	—
State and local government obligations	6.7	—	6.7	—
Mortgage and asset-backed securities	45.9	—	45.9	—
Total long-term investments	318.4	94.8	209.8	13.8
Other assets:				
Derivative assets	18.0	—	18.0	—
Total	$ 2,208.9	$ 1,887.2	$ 307.9	$ 13.8
Liabilities:				
Accrued liabilities:				
Derivative liabilities	$ 2.4	$ 0.4	$ 2.0	$ —

Starbucks Corporation 2014 Form 10-K 63

Fig. 12.1 Securities and Exchange Commission: Starbucks fair value measurement of assets and liabilities (2014)

	Balance at Sep 29, 2013	Fair Value Measurements at Reporting Date Using: Quoted Prices in Active Markets for Identical Assets (Level 1)	Significant Other Observable Inputs (Level 2)	Significant Unobservable Inputs (Level 3)
Assets:				
Cash and cash equivalents	$ 2,575.7	$ 2,575.7	$ —	$ —
Short-term investments:				
Available-for-sale securities				
Agency obligations	20.0	—	20.0	—
Commercial paper	127.0	—	127.0	—
Corporate debt securities	57.5	—	57.5	—
US government treasury securities	352.9	352.9	—	—
Certificates of deposit	34.1	—	34.1	—
Total available-for-sale securities	591.5	352.9	238.6	—
Trading securities	66.6	66.6	—	—
Total short-term investments	658.1	419.5	238.6	—
Prepaid expenses and other current assets:				
Derivative assets	12.5	—	12.5	—
Long-term investments:				
Available-for-sale securities				
Agency obligations	8.1	—	8.1	—
Corporate debt securities	36.8	—	36.8	—
Auction rate securities	13.4	—	—	13.4
Total long-term investments	58.3	—	44.9	13.4
Other assets:				
Derivative assets	11.4	—	11.4	—
Total	$ 3,316.0	$ 2,995.2	$ 307.4	$ 13.4
Liabilities:				
Accrued liabilities:				
Derivative liabilities	$ 3.5	$ —	$ 3.5	$ —
Other long-term liabilities:				
Derivative liabilities	0.5	—	0.5	—
Total	$ 4.0	$ —	$ 4.0	$ —

Fig. 12.2 Securities and Exchange Commission: Starbucks fair value measurement of assets and liabilities (2013)

From the FY 2013, and 2014, SBX assets and liabilities reported at fair value included: (i) securities available for sale, (ii) trading securities, and (iii) derivative assets and liabilities. Securities available for sale are always Level 1. As to its trading securities, SBX, in 2013 used quoted prices in active markets for identical assets to determine their fair values, and measured them at level 1. However, for its derivative assets and liabilities, SBX used quoted prices in active market for identical derivative assets and liabilities that were traded on exchanges. SBX measured them at Level 2, using industry-standard valuation models. Finally, the only financial instruments measured at Level 3 were the auction rate securities (ARS).

During FY 2014, SBX revised the classification of coffee and diary futures from Level 2 to Level 1, using quoted prices in active markets for identical assets to determine fair value. During FY 2013, 2014, there were no material fair value adjustment (Figs. 12.1 and 12.2).

Appendix

- The Effect of Accounting Uncertainty and Auditor Reputation on Auditor Objectivity, by Brian W. Mayhew, Jeffrey W. Schatzberg, and Galen R. Sevcik; *AUDITING: A Journal of Practice & Theory*, March 2001, Vol. 20, No. 1, pp. 65–80.
- Extreme Estimation Uncertainty in Fair Value Estimates: Implications for Audit Assurance, by Brant E. Christensen, Steven M. Glover, and David A. Wood; *AUDITING: A Journal of Practice & Theory*, November 2011, Vol. 30, No. 4, pp. 149–171.

Practice

Question 1

When evaluating the reasonableness of the accounting estimates as provided by the management of the client, the auditor shall perform the following except:

(a) The auditor should evaluate, based on the audit evidence, whether the accounting estimates in the financial statements are either reasonable in the context of the applicable financial reporting framework or are misstated
(b) The auditor should obtain sufficient appropriate audit evidence about whether the disclosures in the financial statements related to accounting estimates are in accordance with the requirements of the applicable financial reporting framework
(c) The auditor should consider that the management has better understanding of the financial statement than anyone
(d) The auditor should evaluate the adequacy of the disclosure of estimation uncertainty in the financial statements in the context of the applicable financial reporting framework
(e) The auditor should review the judgments and decisions made by management in the making of accounting estimates to identify whether indicators of possible management bias exist

Question 2

- Daxa Company is a US North-East regional firm in the business of selling red widgets
- Daxa Company has historically experienced a warranty expense of 0.2% of sales
- In FY 2017, it sold $500,000 of red widgets, and recorded a debit of $10,000 to the warranty expense account and $10,000 to the warranty liability account
- By December 2017, Daxa Company received a warranty claim to replace red widgets
- The cost of this claim is $4000, which Daxa Compnay recorded as a debit to the warranty liability account and a credit to the inventory account

What amount should Daxa Company report under the Warranty expense account in FY 2017?

(a) $10,000
(b) $4000
(c) $14,000
(d) $6000

Question 3

In which of the following situations the auditor is likely to audit accounting estimates:

(a) Allowance for doubtful accounts
(b) Reserve for obsolete inventory
(c) Changes in the useful life of depreciable assets
(d) Changes in the salvage values of depreciable assets
(e) All the above

Question 4

In evaluating the reasonableness of an estimate, the auditor normally concentrates on the following key factors and assumptions, with the exceptions of:

(a) Significant to the accounting estimate
(b) Sensitive to variations
(c) Management skills
(d) Deviations from historical patterns
(e) Subjective and susceptible to misstatement and bias

Question 5

The following are procedures the auditor may consider when assessing the reasonableness of an accounting estimate, except:

(a) Identify the sources of data and factors that management used in forming the assumptions, and consider whether such data and factors are relevant, reliable, and sufficient for the purpose based on information gathered in other audit tests
(b) Consider whether there are additional key factors or alternative assumptions about the factors
(c) Evaluate whether the assumptions are consistent with each other, the supporting data, relevant historical data, and industry data
(d) Analyze historical data used in developing the assumptions to assess whether the data is comparable and consistent with data of the period under audit, and consider whether such data is sufficiently reliable for the purpose
(e) All of the above

CHAPTER 13

Related Party Transactions

13.1 General

Because it is not possible to give each transaction the fullest scrutiny, professional auditing standards have come to recognize, through decades of experience, particular factors that arouse suspicion and call for focused investigation. These factors are the so-called "red flags" for which all auditors are trained to remain alert. Among transactions calling for close inspection are related—party transactions, including transactions between a company and its officers or directors. Such dealings are viewed with extreme skepticism in all areas of finance. The reason for this is apparent: Although in an ordinary arms-length transaction, one may assume that parties will act in their own economic self-interest, this assumption breaks down when the parties are related. Accordingly, GAAS explicitly recognize the need for particular care in the auditor's examination of material related party transactions.

The economic substance of a related party transaction may differ materially from its form. Thus, the objective of the auditor is to obtain sufficient appropriate audit evidence to determine whether related parties and relationships and transactions with related parties have been properly identified, accounted for, and disclosed in the financial statements. Such transactions potentially provide more of an opportunity for management

Auditing Standard No. 18, Related Parties (the "standard").

F. I. Lessambo, *Auditing, Assurance Services, and Forensics*,
https://doi.org/10.1007/978-3-319-90521-1_13

to act in its own interests, rather than in the interests of the company and its investors. Moreover, in some instances, related party transactions have been used to engage in fraudulent financial reporting and to conceal misappropriation of assets—types of misstatements that are relevant to the auditor's consideration of fraud. The importance to investors of auditing related party transactions is reflected in Section 10A of the Securities Exchange Act of 1934 (the "Exchange Act"), which requires each audit of financial statements of an issuer to include procedures designed to identify related party transactions that are material to the financial statements or otherwise require disclosure therein.[1] The need for heightened scrutiny of related party transactions has been highlighted by SEC enforcement actions. For example, in a 2012 opinion issued by the SEC involving a company's transactions with its executive officers, the SEC stated "although in an ordinary arms-length transaction, one may assume that parties will act in their own economic interest, this assumption breaks down when the parties are related."[2]

13.2 Examples of Transactions with Related Parties Include, Among Others

- Buying or selling goods or services at prices that differ significantly from prevailing market prices;
- Sales transactions with unusual terms, including unusual rights of return or extended payment terms generally not offered;
- "Bill and hold" type transactions;
- Borrowing or lending on an interest-free basis or with no fixed repayment terms;
- Occupying premises or receiving other assets or rendering or receiving management services when no consideration is exchanged;
- Engaging in a nonmonetary transaction that lacks commercial substance;
- Sales without economic substance (e.g., funding the other party to the transaction to facilitate collection of the sales price, or entering

[1] See Section 10A(a)(2) of the Exchange Act, 15 U.S.C. §78j-1(a)(2), which was added to the Exchange Act by the Private Securities Litigation Reform Act, enacted by Congress in 1995.

[2] SEC, In the Matter of the Application of Wendy McNeeley, CPA, AAER No. 3427, at 15 (December 13, 2012), http://www.sec.gov/litigation/opinions/2012/34-68431.pdf.

into a transaction shortly prior to period end and unwinding that transaction shortly after period end);

- Loans to parties that, at the time of the loan transaction, do not have the ability to repay and possess insufficient or no collateral;
- Loans made without prior consideration of the ability of the party to repay;
- A subsequent repurchase of goods that indicates that at the time of sale an implicit obligation to repurchase may have existed that would have precluded revenue recognition or sales treatment;
- Advancing company funds that are used directly or indirectly to pay what would otherwise be an uncollectible loan or receivable;
- Sales at below market rates to an intermediary whose involvement serves no apparent business purpose and who, in turn, sells to the ultimate customer at a higher price, with the intermediary (and ultimately its principals) retaining the difference;
- Guarantees and guarantor relationships outside the normal course of business; or
- Transactions between two or more entities in which each party provides and receives the same or similar amounts of consideration (e.g., round-trip transactions).

13.3 Audit Procedures

The auditor should perform procedures to obtain an understanding of the company's relationships and transactions with its related parties that might reasonably be expected to affect the risks of material misstatement of the financial statements in conjunction with performing risk assessment procedures in accordance with Auditing Standard No. 12, Identifying and Assessing Risks of Material Misstatement. The procedures performed to obtain an understanding of the company's relationships and transactions with its related parties include: (i) Obtaining an understanding of the company's process; (ii) Performing inquiries; and (iii) Communicating with the audit engagement team and other auditors.

13.3.1 Obtaining an Understanding of the Company's Process

Understanding the nature and business purpose (or the lack thereof) of a company's relationships and transactions with its related parties is important for the auditor's evaluation of the company's accounting for and disclosure of related party transactions because a company's relationships and transactions with its related parties could pose increased risks of material misstatement. For example, to improve the appearance of its financial condition, a company and a related party could attempt to "dress up" the appearance of the company's balance sheet at period end by agreeing to have the company temporarily pay down its related party debt prior to the balance sheet date while having an undisclosed side agreement to subsequently borrow the same or a comparable amount shortly after period end.

In conjunction with obtaining an understanding of internal control over financial reporting, the auditor should obtain an understanding of the company's process for:

- Identifying related parties and relationships and transactions with related parties;
- Authorizing and approving transactions with related parties; and
- Accounting for and disclosing relationships and transactions with related parties in the financial statements.

13.3.2 Performing Inquiries

The auditor should inquire of management regarding:

- The names of the company's related parties during the period under audit, including changes from the prior period;
- Background information concerning the related parties (for example, physical location, industry, size, and extent of operations);
- The nature of any relationships, including ownership structure, between the company and its related parties;
- The transactions entered into, modified, or terminated, with its related parties during the period under audit and the terms and business purposes (or the lack thereof) of such transactions;
- The business purpose for entering into a transaction with a related party versus an unrelated party;
- Any related party transactions that have not been authorized and approved in accordance with the company's established policies or procedures regarding the authorization and approval of transactions with related parties; and

- Any related party transactions for which exceptions to the company's established policies or procedures were granted and the reasons for granting those exceptions.

The auditor should inquire of others within the company regarding their knowledge of the matters. The auditor should identify others within the company to whom inquiries should be directed, and determine the extent of such inquires, by considering whether such individuals are likely to have knowledge regarding:

- The company's related parties or relationships or transactions with related parties;
- The company's controls over relationships or transactions with related parties; and
- The existence of related parties or relationships or transactions with related parties previously undisclosed to the auditor.

Examples of other procedures that might be appropriate for the auditor to perform, depending on the nature of the transaction and the risks of material misstatement of the financial statements, include:

- Inquiring directly of the related party regarding the business purpose of the transaction;
- Inspecting information in the possession of the related party or other parties to the transaction, if available;
- Reading public information regarding the related party and the transaction, if any;
- Reading the financial statements or other relevant financial information obtained from the related party, if available, to understand how the related party accounted for the transaction;
- Confirming the terms of the transaction with other parties with knowledge of the transaction (e.g., banks, guarantors, agents, or attorneys), if any;
- Determining whether there are any side agreements or other arrangements (either written or oral) with the related party, including confirming that none exist, if appropriate;
- Evaluating the transferability and value of collateral provided by the related party, if any; and
- Performing procedures at the related party, if possible.

The auditor should inquire of the audit committee, or its chair, regarding: (i) the audit committee's understanding of the company's relationships and transactions with related parties that are significant to the company; and (ii) whether any member of the audit committee has concerns regarding relationships or transactions with related parties and, if so, the substance of those concerns.

13.3.3 Communicating with the Audit Engagement Team and Other Auditors

The auditor should communicate to engagement team members relevant information about related parties, including the names of the related parties and the nature of the company's relationships and transactions with those related parties.

If the auditor is using the work of another auditor, the auditor should communicate to the other auditor relevant information about related parties, including the names of the company's related parties and the nature of the company's relationships and transactions with those related parties. The auditor also should inquire of the other auditor regarding the other auditor's knowledge of any related parties or relationships or transactions with related parties that were not included in the auditor's communications.

The auditor should identify and assess the risks of material misstatement at the financial statement level and the assertion level. This includes identifying and assessing the risks of material misstatement associated with related parties and relationships and transactions with related parties, including whether the company has properly identified, accounted for, and disclosed its related parties and relationships and transactions with related parties.

13.3.4 Assessing the Risks of Material Misstatement

The auditor must design and implement audit responses that address the identified and assessed risks of material misstatement. This includes designing and performing audit procedures in a manner that addresses the risks of material misstatement associated with related parties and relationships and transactions with related parties.

For each related party transaction that is either required to be disclosed in the financial statements or determined to be a significant risk, the auditor should:

- Read the underlying documentation and evaluate whether the terms and other information about the transaction are consistent with explanations from inquiries and other audit evidence about the business purpose (or the lack thereof) of the transaction;
- Determine whether the transaction has been authorized and approved in accordance with the company's established policies and procedures regarding the authorization and approval of transactions with related parties;
- Determine whether any exceptions to the company's established policies or procedures were granted;
- Evaluate the financial capability of the related parties with respect to significant uncollected balances, loan commitments, supply arrangements, guarantees, and other obligations, if any; and
- Perform other procedures as necessary to address the identified and assessed risks of material misstatement.

The auditor should perform procedures on intercompany account balances as of concurrent dates, even if fiscal years of the respective companies differ.

13.4 Evaluating Whether the Company Has Properly Identified Its Related Parties and Relationships and Transactions with Related Parties

The auditor should evaluate whether the company has properly identified its related parties and relationships and transactions with related parties. Evaluating whether a company has properly identified its related parties and relationships and transactions with related parties involves more than assessing the process used by the company. This evaluation requires the auditor to perform procedures to test the accuracy and completeness of the related parties and relationships and transactions with related parties identified by the company, taking into account the information gathered during the audit. As part of this evaluation, the auditor should read minutes of the meetings of stockholders, directors, and committees of directors, or summaries of actions of recent meetings for which minutes have not yet been prepared.

If the auditor identifies information that indicates that related parties or relationships or transactions with related parties previously undisclosed to the auditor might exist, the auditor should perform the procedures necessary to determine whether previously undisclosed relationships or transactions with related parties, in fact, exist.

If the auditor determines that a related party or relationship or transaction with a related party previously undisclosed to the auditor exists, the auditor should:

- Inquire of management regarding the existence of the related party or relationship or transaction with a related party previously undisclosed to the auditor and the possible existence of other transactions with the related party previously undisclosed to the auditor;
- Evaluate why the related party or relationship or transaction with a related party was previously undisclosed to the auditor;
- Promptly communicate to appropriate members of the engagement team and other auditors participating in the audit engagement relevant information about the related party or relationship or transaction with the related party;
- Assess the need to perform additional procedures to identify other relationships or transactions with the related party previously undisclosed to the auditor;
- Perform the procedures required by paragraph 12 of this standard for each related party transaction previously undisclosed to the auditor that is required to be disclosed in the financial statements or determined to be a significant risk; and
- Perform the following procedures, taking into account the information gathered from performing the procedures in a. through e. above:

  (i) Evaluate the implications on the auditor's assessment of internal control over financial reporting, if applicable;
  (ii) Reassess the risk of material misstatement and perform additional procedures as necessary if such reassessment results in a higher risk; and
  (iii) Evaluate the implications for the audit if management's nondisclosure to the auditor of a related party or relationship or transaction with a related party indicates that fraud or an illegal act may have occurred. If the auditor becomes aware of information indicating that fraud or another illegal act has occurred or might have occurred, the auditor must determine

his or her responsibilities under AU secs. 316.79-.82, AU sec. 317, Illegal Acts by Clients, and Section 10A of the Securities Exchange Act of 1934, 15 U.S.C. §78j-1.

If the financial statements include a statement by management that transactions with related parties were conducted on terms equivalent to those prevailing in an arm's- length transaction, the auditor should determine whether the evidence obtained supports or contradicts management's assertion. If the auditor is unable to obtain sufficient appropriate audit evidence to substantiate management's assertion, and if management does not agree to modify the disclosure, the auditor should express a qualified or adverse opinion.

13.5 Communications with the Audit Committee

The auditor should communicate to the audit committee the auditor's evaluation of the company's identification of, accounting for, and disclosure of its relationships and transactions with related parties. The auditor also should communicate other significant matters arising from the audit regarding the company's relationships and transactions with related parties including, but not limited to:

a. The identification of related parties or relationships or transactions with related parties that were previously undisclosed to the auditor;
b. The identification of significant related party transactions that have not been authorized or approved in accordance with the company's established policies or procedures;
c. The identification of significant related party transactions for which exceptions to the company's established policies or procedures were granted;
d. The inclusion of a statement in the financial statements that a transaction with a related party was conducted on terms equivalent to those prevailing in an arm's-length transaction and the evidence obtained by the auditor to support or contradict such an assertion; and
e. The identification of significant related party transactions that appear to the auditor to lack a business purpose.

Practice

Question 1

Which of the following statement(s) is/are accurate:

(a) Related party transactions should be assessed in the context of the company's overall governance structure
(b) The definition of related parties varies across regulatory bodies.
(c) Related party transactions are very often significant indicator of fraud, when fraud does exist
(d) Related party transactions have no impact on the corporate governance of a firm

Question 2

Which of the following is not required under Auditing Standard 18 (related Party transaction)?

(a) Management is expected to be the initial source of the auditor's information identifying related parties and transactions
(b) Management is expected to be the initial source of the auditor's information as to the business purpose for engaging in transactions with related
(c) Specific audit procedures are required if the auditor identifies a previously undisclosed related party relationship or transaction
(d) The results of the auditor's evaluation must be communicated to the audit committee, including transactions with the related parties that were not authorized in accordance with
(e) Management alone must determine the impact of the related transactions

CHAPTER 14

Significant Unusual Transactions

14.1 General

Significant unusual transactions as significant transactions that are outside the normal course of business for the company or that otherwise appear to be unusual due to their timing, size, or nature.[1] A significant unusual transaction does not necessarily need to occur infrequently. Whether a transaction constitutes a significant unusual transaction should be based upon the specific facts and circumstances. The timing or frequency of transactions is only one element to be considered in determining whether a transaction is a significant unusual transaction.

A company's significant unusual transactions can create complex accounting and financial statement disclosure issues that could pose increased risks of material misstatement. Among other things, the amendments regarding significant unusual transactions:

- Require the auditor to perform procedures to identify significant unusual transactions;
- Require the auditor to perform procedures to obtain an understanding of, and evaluate, the business purpose (or the lack thereof) of identified significant unusual transactions; and

[1]AU Section 316.66.

AU Section 316.

F. I. Lessambo, *Auditing, Assurance Services, and Forensics*,
https://doi.org/10.1007/978-3-319-90521-1_14

- Add factors for the auditor to consider in evaluating whether significant unusual transactions may have been entered into to engage in fraudulent financial reporting or conceal misappropriation of assets.

14.2 Auditor Requirements

AU Section 316.66 requires that, if the auditor becomes aware of significant unusual transactions during the course of an audit, the auditor should gain an understanding of the business rationale of such transactions and whether that rationale (or the lack thereof) suggests that such transactions may have been entered into to engage in fraudulent financial reporting or to conceal the misappropriation of assets.

The auditor should conduct basic procedures for obtaining information for evaluating significant unusual transactions. The basic procedures include:

i. reading the underlying documentation relating to significant unusual transactions and evaluating whether the terms and other information about the transaction are consistent with explanations from inquiries and other audit evidence about the business purpose (or the lack thereof) of the transaction;
ii. determining whether the transaction has been authorized and approved in accordance with the company's established policies and procedures;
iii. evaluating the financial capability of the other parties to the transaction with respect to significant uncollected balances, guarantees, and other obligations; and
iv. Performing other procedures as necessary depending on the identified and assessed risks of material misstatement

The basic procedures are designed to assist the auditor in identifying red flags that indicate potential risks of material misstatement. Additionally, the standard requires more in-depth procedures that are designed to be scalable and commensurate with the facts and circumstances of the audit.

The auditor should evaluate whether the business purpose (or the lack thereof) indicates that the significant unusual transaction may have been entered into to engage in fraudulent financial reporting or conceal misappropriation of assets. In making that evaluation, the auditor should evaluate whether[2]:

- The form of the transaction is overly complex (e.g., the transaction involves multiple entities within a consolidated group or unrelated third parties);
- The transaction involves unconsolidated related parties, including variable interest entities;
- The transaction involves related parties or relationships or transactions with related parties previously undisclosed to the auditor;
- The transaction involves other parties that do not appear to have the financial capability to support the transaction without assistance from the company, or any related party of the company;
- The transaction lacks commercial or economic substance, or is part of a larger series of connected, linked, or otherwise interdependent arrangements that lack commercial or economic substance individually or in the aggregate (e.g., the transaction is entered into shortly prior to period end and is unwound shortly after period end);
- The transaction occurs with a party that falls outside the definition of a related party (as defined by the accounting principles applicable to that company), with either party able to negotiate terms that may not be available for other, more clearly independent, parties on an arm's-length basis;
- The transaction enables the company to achieve certain financial targets;
- Management is placing more emphasis on the need for a particular accounting treatment than on the underlying economic substance of the transaction (e.g., accounting-motivated structured transaction); and
- Management has discussed the nature of and accounting for the transaction with the audit committee or another committee of the board of directors or the entire board.

The auditor must evaluate whether significant unusual transactions that the auditor has identified have been properly accounted for and disclosed in the financial statements. This includes evaluating whether the financial

[2] AU Section 316.67.

statements contain the information regarding significant unusual transactions essential for a fair presentation of the financial statements in conformity with the applicable financial reporting framework.

14.3 Identifying Significant Unusual Transactions

Concerning the identification of the significant unusual transactions, the amended Standard requires the auditor to:

- inquire of management and internal audit personnel (if any) as to whether the company has entered into any significant unusual transactions, and, if so, the nature, terms and business purpose (or lack thereof) of those transactions and whether such transactions involved related parties; and
- inquire of others within the company—including employees involved in initiating, recording, or processing complex or unusual transactions—about their views regarding fraud risk.

14.4 Audit Risk Procedures

The auditor design and perform audit procedures in a manner that addresses the assessed risks of material misstatement for each relevant assertion of each significant account and disclosure. Procedures that might be appropriate, depends on the nature of the significant unusual transaction and the risks of material misstatement of the financial statements, include:

- Inquiring directly of the other party regarding the business purpose of the transaction;
- Reading public information regarding the transaction and the parties to the transaction, if available;
- Reading the financial statements or other relevant financial information obtained from other parties involved in the transaction, if available, to understand how the other party accounted for the transaction;
- Evaluating the transferability and value of collateral provided by the other party, if any;
- Confirming the terms of the transaction with other parties with knowledge of the transaction (e.g., banks, guarantors, agents, or attorneys), if any; and

– Confirming whether there are any side agreements or other arrangements (either written or oral) with the other party.

14.5 Management and Audit Committee Responsibilities

Company management teams are required to co-labor with the auditor in its newly expanded inquiry relative to unusual significant transactions. To that end, management may consider taking the following actions helpful in light of these developments:

- review the company's internal controls and procedures on an ongoing basis to ensure that the company is adequately identifying, accounting for and disclosing transactions and relationships with related parties and significant unusual transactions;
- ensure that related party transactions and significant unusual transactions have been authorized or approved in accordance with the company's established policies and procedures and that adequate substantiation exists for departures from these procedures;
- prepare adequate evidence to support any statements in the financial statements that a transaction with a related party was conducted on terms equivalent to those prevailing in an arm's-length transaction;
- ensure that adequate documentation and other evidence is available to substantiate the business purpose(s) for entering into related party transactions or significant unusual transactions.

Practice

Question 1

Which of the following assertions is inaccurate concerning significant unusual transactions?

(a) Significant unusual transactions can create complex accounting and financial statement disclosure issues that could pose increased risks of material misstatement
(b) A significant unusual transaction does necessarily need to occur infrequently

(c) The timing or frequency of transactions is only one element to be considered in determining whether a transaction is a significant unusual transaction
(d) Significant unusual transactions are often entered into to engage in fraudulent financial reporting or to conceal the misappropriation of assets

Question 2

The basic procedures in auditing significant unusual transactions include:

(a) Reading the underlying documentation relating to significant unusual transactions and evaluating whether the terms and other information about the transaction are consistent with explanations from inquiries and other audit evidence about the business purpose (or the lack thereof) of the transaction
(b) Determining whether the transaction has been authorized and approved in accordance with the company's established policies and procedures
(c) Evaluating the financial capability of the other parties to the transaction with respect to significant uncollected balances, guarantees, and other obligations
(d) Performing other procedures as necessary depending on the identified and assessed risks of material misstatement
(e) All of the above

Question 3

Appropriate audit procedures applicable to significant unusual transactions and the risks of material misstatement of the financial statements, include:

(a) Inquiring directly of the other party regarding the business purpose of the transaction
(b) Reading public information regarding the transaction and the parties to the transaction
(c) Reading the financial statements or other relevant financial information obtained from other parties involved in the transaction, if available, to understand how the other party accounted for the transaction

(d) Confirming the terms of the transaction with other parties with knowledge of the transaction (e.g., banks, guarantors, agents, or attorneys)
(e) All of the above

CHAPTER 15

Subsequent Events; and Going Concern

15.1 General

These are events or transactions that occur subsequent to the balance-sheet date, but prior to the issuance of the financial statements that have a material effect on the financial statements and therefore require adjustment or disclosure in the statements. Two types of subsequent events require consideration by management and evaluation by the independent auditor.

The auditor has a responsibility to evaluate whether there is substantial doubt about the entity's ability to continue as a going concern for a reasonable period of time, not to exceed one year beyond the date of the financial statements being audited (hereinafter referred to as a reasonable period of time). The auditor's evaluation is based on his or her knowledge of relevant conditions and events that exist at or have occurred prior to the date of the auditor's report. Information about such conditions or events is obtained from the application of auditing procedures planned and performed to achieve audit objectives that are related

AU Section 560.
AU Section 341.

F. I. Lessambo, *Auditing, Assurance Services, and Forensics*,
https://doi.org/10.1007/978-3-319-90521-1_15

to management's assertions embodied in the financial statements being audited.[1]

15.2 Types of Subsequent Events

Two types of subsequent events require consideration by management and evaluation by the independent auditor.

15.2.1 Events that Provide Additional Evidence with Respect to Pre-existed Elements

The first type consists of those events that provide additional evidence with respect to conditions that existed at the date of the balance sheet and affect the estimates inherent in the process of preparing financial statements. All information that becomes available prior to the issuance of the financial statements should be used by management in its evaluation of the conditions on which the estimates were based. The financial statements should be adjusted for any changes in estimates resulting from the use of such evidence.

Identifying events that require adjustment of the financial statements under the criteria stated above calls for the exercise of judgment and knowledge of the facts and circumstances. For example, a loss on an uncollectible trade account receivable as a result of a customer's deteriorating financial condition leading to bankruptcy subsequent to the balance-sheet date would be indicative of conditions existing at the balance-sheet date, thereby calling for adjustment of the financial statements before their issuance. On the other hand, a similar loss resulting from a customer's major casualty such as a fire or flood subsequent to the balance-sheet date would not be indicative of conditions existing at the balance-sheet date and adjustment of the financial statements would not be appropriate. The settlement of litigation for an amount different from the liability recorded in the accounts would require adjustment of the financial statements if the events, such as personal injury or patent infringement that gave rise to the litigation had taken place prior to the balance-sheet date.

[1] Auditing Standard No. 15, Audit Evidence.

15.2.2 *Events that Provide Additional Evidence with Respect to Non-existed Elements*

The second type consists of those events that provide evidence with respect to conditions that did not exist at the date of the balance sheet being reported on but arose subsequent to that date. These events should not result in adjustment of the financial statements. However, some of these events may be of such a nature that disclosure of them is required to keep the financial statements from being misleading. Occasionally such an event may be so significant that disclosure can best be made by supplementing the historical financial statements with pro forma financial data giving effect to the event as if it had occurred on the date of the balance sheet.

Examples of events of the second type that require disclosure to the financial statements (but should not result in adjustment) are:

- Sale of a bond or capital stock issue;
- Purchase of a business;
- Settlement of litigation when the event giving rise to the claim took place subsequent to the balance-sheet date;
- Loss of plant or inventories as a result of fire or flood;
- Losses on receivables resulting from conditions (such as a customer's major casualty) arising subsequent to the balance-sheet date.

Occasionally, a subsequent event of the second type has such a material impact on the entity that the auditor may wish to include in his report an explanatory paragraph directing the reader's attention to the event and its effects.

15.3 Re-issuance of Financial Statements

When financial statements are reissued, for example, in reports filed with the Securities and Exchange Commission or other regulatory agencies, events that require disclosure in the reissued financial statements to keep them from being misleading may have occurred subsequent to the original issuance of the financial statements. Events occurring between the time of original issuance and re-issuance of financial statements should not result in adjustment of the financial statements unless the adjustment meets the criteria for the correction of an error or the criteria for prior period adjustments set forth in Opinions of the Accounting Principles Board. Similarly, financial statements reissued in comparative form with financial statements of subsequent periods should not be adjusted for events occurring subsequent to the original issuance unless the adjustment meets the criteria stated above.

15.4 Audit Procedures for Subsequent Events

There is a period after the balance-sheet date with which the auditor must be concerned in completing various phases of his audit. This period is known as the "subsequent period" and is considered to extend to the date of the auditor's report. Its duration will depend upon the practical requirements of each audit and may vary from a relatively short period to one of several months. Also, all auditing procedures are not carried out at the same time and some phases of an audit will be performed during the subsequent period, whereas other phases will be substantially completed on or before the balance-sheet date. As an audit approaches completion, the auditor will be concentrating on the unresolved auditing and reporting matters and he is not expected to be conducting a continuing review of those matters to which he has previously applied auditing procedures and reached satisfaction.

Certain specific procedures are applied to transactions occurring after the balance-sheet date such as (a) the examination of data to assure that proper cutoffs have been made, and (b) the examination of data which provide information to aid the auditor in his evaluation of the assets and liabilities as of the balance-sheet date. In addition, the independent auditor should perform other auditing procedures with respect to the period after the balance-sheet date for the purpose of ascertaining the occurrence of subsequent events that may require adjustment or disclosure essential to a fair presentation of the financial statements in conformity with generally accepted accounting principles. These procedures should be performed at or near the date of the auditor's report. The auditor generally should:

a. Read the latest available interim financial statements; compare them with the financial statements being reported upon; and make any other comparisons considered appropriate in the circumstances. In order to make these procedures as meaningful as possible for the purpose expressed above, the auditor should inquire of officers and other executives having responsibility for financial and accounting matters as to whether the interim statements have been prepared on the same basis as that used for the statements under audit.

b. Inquire of and discuss with officers and other executives having responsibility for financial and accounting matters (limited where appropriate to major locations) as to:

    (i) Whether any substantial contingent liabilities or commitments existed at the date of the balance sheet being reported on or at the date of inquiry.
    (ii) Whether there was any significant change in the capital stock, long-term debt, or working capital to the date of inquiry.
    (iii) The current status of items, in the financial statements being reported on, that were accounted for on the basis of tentative, preliminary, or inconclusive data.
    (iv) Whether any unusual adjustments had been made during the period from the balance-sheet date to the date of inquiry.
    (v) Whether there have been any changes in the company's related parties.
    (vi) Whether there have been any significant new related party transactions.
    (vii) Whether the company has entered into any significant unusual transactions.

c. Read the available minutes of meetings of stockholders, directors, and appropriate committees; as to meetings for which minutes are not available, inquire about matters dealt with at such meetings.
d. Inquire of client's legal counsel concerning litigation, claims, and assessments.
e. Obtain a letter of representations, dated as of the date of the auditor's report, from appropriate officials, generally the chief executive officer, chief financial officer, or others with equivalent positions in the entity, as to whether any events occurred subsequent to the date of the financial statements being reported on by the independent auditor that in the officer's opinion would require adjustment or disclosure in these statements. The auditor may elect to have the client include representations as to significant matters disclosed to the auditor in his performance of these procedures.
f. Make such additional inquiries or perform such procedures as he considers necessary and appropriate to dispose of questions that arise in carrying out the foregoing procedures, inquiries, and discussions.

15.5 Going Concern

The auditor should evaluate whether there is substantial doubt about the entity's ability to continue as a going concern for a reasonable period of time in the following manner:

a. The auditor considers whether the results of his procedures performed in planning, gathering evidential matter relative to the various audit objectives, and completing the audit identify conditions and events that, when considered in the aggregate, indicate there could be substantial doubt about the entity's ability to continue as a going concern for a reasonable period of time. It may be necessary to obtain additional information about such conditions and events, as well as the appropriate evidential matter to support information that mitigates the auditor's doubt.
b. If the auditor believes there is substantial doubt about the entity's ability to continue as a going concern for a reasonable period of time, he should (1) obtain information about management's plans that are intended to mitigate the effect of such conditions or events, and (2) assess the likelihood that such plans can be effectively implemented.
c. After the auditor has evaluated management's plans, he concludes whether he has substantial doubt about the entity's ability to continue as a going concern for a reasonable period of time. If the auditor concludes there is substantial doubt, he should (1) consider the adequacy of disclosure about the entity's possible inability to continue as a going concern for a reasonable period of time, and (2) include an explanatory paragraph (following the opinion paragraph) in his audit report to reflect his conclusion. If the auditor concludes that substantial doubt does not exist, he should consider the need for disclosure.

The auditor is not responsible for predicting future conditions or events. The fact that the entity may cease to exist as a going concern subsequent to receiving a report from the auditor that does not refer to substantial doubt, even within one year following the date of the financial statements, does not, in itself, indicate inadequate performance by the auditor. Accordingly, the absence of reference to substantial doubt in an auditor's report should not be viewed as providing assurance as to an entity's ability to continue as a going concern.

15.5.1 *Going Concern: Audit Procedures*

It is not necessary to design audit procedures solely to identify conditions and events that, when considered in the aggregate, indicate there could be substantial doubt about the entity's ability to continue as a going concern for a reasonable period of time. The results of auditing procedures designed and performed to achieve other audit objectives should be sufficient for that purpose. The following are examples of procedures that may identify such conditions and events:

- Analytical procedures
- Review of subsequent events
- Review of compliance with the terms of debt and loan agreements
- Reading of minutes of meetings of stockholders, board of directors, and important committees of the board
- Inquiry of an entity's legal counsel about litigation, claims, and assessments
- Confirmation with related and third parties of the details of arrangements to provide or maintain financial support.

15.5.2 *Consideration of Conditions and Events*

In performing the aforementioned audit procedures, the auditor may identify information about certain conditions or events that, when considered in the aggregate, indicate there could be substantial doubt about the entity's ability to continue as a going concern for a reasonable period of time. The significance of such conditions and events will depend on the circumstances, and some may have significance only when viewed in conjunction with others. The following are examples of such conditions and events:

Negative trends: recurring operating losses, working capital deficiencies, negative cash flows from operating activities, adverse key financial ratios.

Other indications of possible financial difficulties: default on loan or similar agreements, arrearages in dividends, denial of usual trade credit from suppliers, restructuring of debt, noncompliance with statutory capital requirements, need to seek new sources or methods of financing or to dispose of substantial assets.

Internal matters: work stoppages or other labor difficulties, substantial dependence on the success of a particular project, uneconomic long-term commitments, need to significantly revise operations. External matters that have occurred—for example, legal proceedings, legislation, or similar matters that might jeopardize an entity's ability to operate; loss of a key franchise, license, or patent; loss of a principal customer or supplier; uninsured or underinsured catastrophe such as a drought, earthquake, or flood.

15.5.3 Consideration of Management's Plans

When evaluating management's plans, the auditor should identify those elements that are particularly significant to overcome the adverse effects of the conditions and events and should plan and perform auditing procedures to obtain evidential matter about them. For example, the auditor should consider the adequacy of support regarding the ability to obtain additional financing or the planned disposal of assets. When prospective financial information is particularly significant to management's plans, the auditor should request management to provide that information and should consider the adequacy of support for significant assumptions underlying that information. The auditor should give particular attention to assumptions that are: (i) material to the prospective financial information; (ii) especially sensitive or susceptible to change; and (iii) inconsistent with historical trends.

If, after considering the identified conditions and events in the aggregate, the auditor believes there is substantial doubt about the ability of the entity to continue as a going concern for a reasonable period of time, he should consider management's plans for dealing with the adverse effects of the conditions and events. The auditor should obtain information about the plans and consider whether it is likely the adverse effects will be mitigated for a reasonable period of time and that such plans can be effectively implemented. The auditor's considerations relating to management plans may include the following:

- *Plans to dispose of assets*
  - Restrictions on disposal of assets, such as covenants limiting such transactions in loan or similar agreements or encumbrances against assets
  - Apparent marketability of assets that management plans to sell
  - Possible direct or indirect effects of disposal of assets

- *Plans to borrow money or restructure debt*
  - Availability of debt financing, including existing or committed credit arrangements, such as lines of credit or arrangements for factoring receivables or sale-leaseback of assets
  - Existing or committed arrangements to restructure or subordinate debt or to guarantee loans to the entity
  - Possible effects on management's borrowing plans of existing restrictions on additional borrowing or the sufficiency of available collateral
- *Plans to reduce or delay expenditures*
  - Apparent feasibility of plans to reduce overhead or administrative expenditures, to postpone maintenance or research and development projects, or to lease rather than purchase assets
  - Possible direct or indirect effects of reduced or delayed expenditures
- *Plans to increase ownership equity*
  - Apparent feasibility of plans to increase ownership equity, including existing or committed arrangements to raise additional capital
  - Existing or committed arrangements to reduce current dividend requirements or to accelerate cash distributions from affiliates or other investors

The auditor's consideration should be based on knowledge of the entity, its business, and its management and should include (a) reading of the prospective financial information and the underlying assumptions, and (b) comparing prospective financial information in prior periods with actual results and comparing prospective information for the current period with results achieved to date. If the auditor becomes aware of factors, the effects of which are not reflected in such prospective financial information, he should discuss those factors with management and, if necessary, request revision of the prospective financial information.

15.5.4 Consideration of Financial Statement Effects

When, after considering management's plans, the auditor concludes there is substantial doubt about the entity's ability to continue as a going concern for a reasonable period of time, the auditor should consider the possible effects on the financial statements and the adequacy of the related disclosure. Some of the information that might be disclosed includes:

- Pertinent conditions and events giving rise to the assessment of substantial doubt about the entity's ability to continue as a going concern for a reasonable period of time.
- The possible effects of such conditions and events.
- Management's evaluation of the significance of those conditions and events and any mitigating factors.
- Possible discontinuance of operations.
- Management's plans (including relevant prospective financial information).
- Information about the recoverability or classification of recorded asset amounts or the amounts or classification of liabilities.

When, primarily because of the auditor's consideration of management's plans, he concludes that substantial doubt about the entity's ability to continue as a going concern for a reasonable period of time is alleviated, he should consider the need for disclosure of the principal conditions and events that initially caused him to believe there was substantial doubt. The auditor's consideration of disclosure should include the possible effects of such conditions and events, and any mitigating factors, including management's plans.

15.5.5 Consideration of the Effects on the Auditor's Report

If, after considering identified conditions and events and management's plans, the auditor concludes that substantial doubt about the entity's ability to continue as a going concern for a reasonable period of time remains, the audit report should include an explanatory paragraph (following the opinion paragraph) to reflect that conclusion. The auditor's conclusion about the entity's ability to continue as a going concern should be expressed through the use of the phrase "substantial doubt about its (the entity's) ability to continue as a going concern." If the auditor concludes that the entity's disclosures with respect to the entity's ability to continue as a going concern for a reasonable period of time are inadequate, a departure from generally accepted accounting principles exists. This may result in either a qualified (except for) or an adverse opinion. Substantial doubt about the entity's ability to continue as a going concern for a reasonable period of time that arose in the current period does not imply that a basis for such doubt existed in the prior period and, therefore, should not affect the auditor's report on the financial statements of the prior period that are presented on a comparative basis. When financial statements of one or more prior periods are presented on a comparative basis with financial statements of the current period, reporting guidance is provided in section 508.

If substantial doubt about the entity's ability to continue as a going concern for a reasonable period of time existed at the date of prior period financial statements that are presented on a comparative basis, and that doubt has been removed in the current period, the explanatory paragraph included in the auditor's report (following the opinion paragraph) on the financial statements of the prior period should not be repeated.

15.5.6 Documentation

The auditor has to consider whether the results of the auditing procedures performed in planning, gathering evidential matter relative to the various audit objectives, and completing the audit identify conditions and events that, when considered in the aggregate, indicate there could be substantial doubt about the entity's ability to continue as a going concern for a reasonable period of time. If, after considering the identified conditions and events in the aggregate, the auditor believes there is substantial doubt about the ability of the entity to continue as a going concern for a reasonable period of time, the auditor should document all of the following:

a. The conditions or events that led him or her to believe that there is substantial doubt about the entity's ability to continue as a going concern for a reasonable period of time.
b. The elements of management's plans that the auditor considered to be particularly significant to overcoming the adverse effects of the conditions or events.
c. The auditing procedures performed and evidence obtained to evaluate the significant elements of management's plans.

d. The auditor's conclusion as to whether substantial doubt about the entity's ability to continue as a going concern for a reasonable period of time remains or is alleviated. If substantial doubt remains, the auditor also should document the possible effects of the conditions or events on the financial statements and the adequacy of the related disclosures. If substantial doubt is alleviated, the auditor also should document the conclusion as to the need for disclosure of the principal conditions and events that initially caused him or her to believe there was substantial doubt.
e. The auditor's conclusion as to whether he or she should include an explanatory paragraph in the audit report. If disclosures with respect to an entity's ability to continue as a going concern are inadequate, the auditor also should document the conclusion as to whether to express a qualified or adverse opinion for the resultant departure from generally accepted accounting principles.

Practice

Question 1

All the following assertions are correct concerning the auditing of subsequent events, except:

(a) The auditor should perform audit procedures designed to obtain sufficient appropriate audit evidence that all subsequent events that require adjustment of, or disclosure in, the financial statements have been identified
(b) The auditor should perform additional audit procedures on matters to which previously applied audit procedures have provided satisfactory conclusions
(c) The auditor is not required to perform any audit procedures regarding the financial statements after the date of the auditor's report
(d) The auditor must discuss any subsequent event brought to his attention before the signing of the opinion with management and, when appropriate, those charged with governance

Question 2

Which one of the below assertions is accurate concerning subsequent period?

(a) The subsequent period is considered to extend to the date of the auditor's report
(b) The subsequent period must be approved by the firm management
(c) Its duration depends upon the practical requirements of each audit and may vary from a relatively short period to one of several months
(d) Some phases of an audit will be performed during the subsequent period

CHAPTER 16

Reporting on Condensed Financial Statements, Selected Financial Data, and Supplemental Information

16.1 General

An auditor may be engaged to report on condensed financial statements that are derived from audited financial statements. Because condensed financial statements do not constitute a fair presentation of financial position, results of operations, and cash flows in conformity with generally accepted accounting principles, an auditor should not report on condensed financial statements in the same manner as he reported on the complete financial statements from which they are derived.

Selected financial data are not a required part of the basic financial statements, and the entity's management is responsible for determining the specific selected financial data to be presented. However, an auditor can be engaged to report on the selected financial data. In that case, his report should be limited to data that are derived from audited financial statements (which may include data that are calculated from amounts presented in the financial statements, such as working capital). Finally, an auditor can be engaged to perform audit procedures and report on supplemental information that accompanies financial statements.

F. I. Lessambo, *Auditing, Assurance Services, and Forensics*,
https://doi.org/10.1007/978-3-319-90521-1_16

16.2 Condensed Financial Statements[1]

Condensed financial statements are presented in considerably less detail than complete financial statements that are intended to present financial position, results of operations, and cash flows in conformity with generally accepted accounting principles. Condensed financial statements should be read in conjunction with the entity's most recent complete financial statements that include all the disclosures required by generally accepted accounting principles.

Because condensed financial statements do not constitute a fair presentation of financial position, results of operations, and cash flows in conformity with generally accepted accounting principles, an auditor should not report on condensed financial statements in the same manner as he reported on the complete financial statements from which they are derived. To do so might lead users to assume, erroneously, that the condensed financial statements include all the disclosures necessary for complete financial statements.

The auditor's report on condensed financial statements that are derived from financial statements that he has audited should indicate:

a. that the auditor has audited and expressed an opinion on the complete financial statements,
b. the date of the auditor's report on the complete financial statements,
c. the type of opinion expressed, and
d. whether, in the auditor's opinion, the information set forth in the condensed financial statements is fairly stated in all material respects in relation to the complete financial statements from which it has been derived.

A client might make a statement in a client-prepared document that names the auditor and also states that condensed financial statements have been derived from audited financial statements. Such a statement does not, in itself, require the auditor to report on the condensed financial statements, provided that they are included in a document that contains audited financial statements (or that incorporates such statements by reference to information filed with a regulatory agency). However,

[1] AU Section 552.

if such a statement is made in a client-prepared document of a public entity that is required to file, at least annually, complete audited financial statements with a regulatory agency and that document does not include audited financial statements (or does not incorporate such statements by reference to information filed with a regulatory agency), the auditor should request that the client either (a) not include the auditor's name in the document or (b), include the auditor's report on the condensed financial statements. If the client does neither delete the reference to the auditor nor allow the appropriate report to be included, the auditor must advise the client that he does not consent to either the use of his name or the reference to him, and he should consider what other actions might be appropriate.

Condensed financial statements derived from audited financial statements of a public entity may be presented on a comparative basis with interim financial information as of a subsequent date that is accompanied by the auditor's review report. In that case, the auditor should report on the condensed financial statements of each period in a manner appropriate for the type of service provided for each period.

Example

We have reviewed the condensed consolidated balance sheet of ABC Company and subsidiaries as of March 31, 19X1, and the related condensed consolidated statements of income and cash flows for the three-month periods ended March 31, 19X1 and 19X0. These financial statements are the responsibility of the company's management.

We conducted our review in accordance with standards established by the American Institute of Certified Public Accountants. A review of interim financial information consists principally of applying analytical procedures to financial data and making inquiries of persons responsible for financial and accounting matters. It is substantially less in scope than an audit conducted in accordance with generally accepted auditing standards, the objective of which is the expression of an opinion regarding the financial statements taken as a whole. Accordingly, we do not express such an opinion.

Based on our review, we are not aware of any material modifications that should be made to the condensed consolidated financial

> statements referred to above for them to be in conformity with generally accepted accounting principles.
>
> We have previously audited, in accordance with auditing standards generally accepted in the United States of America, the consolidated balance sheet as of December 31, 20X0, and the related consolidated statements of income, retained earnings, and cash flows for the year then ended (not presented herein); and in our report dated February 15, 20X1, we expressed an unqualified opinion on those consolidated financial statements. In our opinion, the information set forth in the accompanying condensed consolidated balance sheet as of December 31, 2017, is fairly stated, in all material respects, in relation to the consolidated balance sheet from which it has been derived.

16.3 Selected Financial Data[2]

An auditor may be engaged to report on selected financial data that are included in a client-prepared document that contains audited financial statements (or, with respect to a public entity, that incorporates such statements by reference to information filed with a regulatory agency). Selected financial data are not a required part of the basic financial statements, and the entity's management is responsible for determining the specific selected financial data to be presented. If the auditor is engaged to report on the selected financial data, his report must be limited to data that are derived from audited financial statements (which may include data that are calculated from amounts presented in the financial statements, such as working capital). If the selected financial data that management presents include both data derived from audited financial statements and other information (i.e., number of employees or square footage of facilities), the auditor's report should specifically identify the data on which he is reporting. The report should indicate

- that the auditor has audited and expressed an opinion on the complete financial statements,
- the type of opinion expressed, and

[2] AU Section 552.

- whether, in the auditor's opinion, the information set forth in the selected financial data is fairly stated in all material respects in relation to the complete financial statements from which it has been derived. If the selected financial data for any of the years presented are derived from financial statements that were audited by another independent auditor, the report on the selected financial data should state that fact, and the auditor should not express an opinion on that data.

Independent Auditor's Report

We have audited the consolidated balance sheets of ABC Company and subsidiaries as of December 31, 19X5 and 19X4, and the related consolidated statements of income, retained earnings, and cash flows for each of the three years in the period ended December 31, 19X5. These financial statements are the responsibility of the Company's management. Our responsibility is to express an opinion on these financial statements based on our audit.

We conducted our audits in accordance with auditing standards generally accepted in the United States of America. Those standards require that we plan and perform the audit to obtain reasonable assurance about whether the financial statements are free of material misstatement. An audit includes examining, on a test basis, evidence supporting the amounts and disclosures in the financial statements. An audit also includes assessing the accounting principles used and significant estimates made by management, as well as evaluating the overall financial statement presentation. We believe that our audits provided a reasonable basis for our opinion.

In our opinion, the consolidated financial statements referred to above present fairly, in all material respects, the financial position of the ABC Company and subsidiaries as of December 31, 20X5 and 20X4, and the results of their operations and their cash flows for each of the three years in the period ended December 31, 20X5, in conformity with accounting principles generally accepted in the United States of America.

We have also previously audited, in accordance with auditing standards generally accepted in the United States of America, the consolidated balance sheets as of December 31, 20X3, 20X2, and 20X1, and the related statements of income, retained earnings, and cash flows for the years ended December 31, 20X2, and 20X1 (none of which are presented herein); and we expressed unqualified opinions on those consolidated financial statements. In our opinion, the information set forth in the selected financial data for each of the five years in the period ended December 31, 20X5, appearing on page xx, is fairly stated, in all material respects, in relation to the consolidated financial statements from which it has been derived.

In introductory material regarding the selected financial data included in a client-prepared document, an entity might name the independent auditor and state that the data are derived from financial statements that he audited. Such a statement does not, in itself, require the auditor to report on the selected financial data, provided that the selected financial data are presented in a document that contains audited financial statements (or, with respect to a public entity, that incorporates such statements by reference to information filed with a regulatory agency). If such a statement is made in a document that does not include (or incorporate by reference) audited financial statements, the auditor should request that neither his name nor reference to him be associated with the information, or he should disclaim an opinion on the selected financial data and request that the disclaimer be included in the document. If the client does not comply, the auditor should advise the client that he does not consent to either the use of his name or the reference to him, and he should consider what other actions might be appropriate.

16.3.1 Auditing Supplemental Information Accompanying Audited Financial Statements[3]

In developing Auditing Standard No. 17, the Board sought to develop a new auditing standard that takes into account the SEC's requirements for supplemental information in SEC Rule 17a-5. More, the PCAOB sought to adopt a standard that is tailored to the circumstances under

[3] Auditing Standard no. 17.

which supplemental information is required in SEC filings of brokers and dealers and covered 11-K filers.

Supplemental information is often in the form of schedules accompanying the financial statements. Supplemental information is required by regulators, including the Securities and Exchange Commission ("SEC" or "Commission"), who have determined the information is important in carrying out their regulatory oversight.

A number of developments led the Board to re-examine its requirements regarding supplemental information. Primarily, Section 982 of the Dodd-Frank Wall Street Reform and Consumer Protection Act (the "Dodd-Frank Act") gave the Board oversight of audits of brokers and dealers registered with the SEC. Under SEC Rule 17a-5, brokers and dealers are required to submit to the SEC financial reports containing certain schedules, including supporting schedules regarding (i) the computation of net capital; (ii) the computation for determination of reserve requirements; and (iii) information related to the broker's or dealer's possession or control of its clients' assets.

In the Board's view, Auditing Standard No. 17 promotes investor protection because of the importance of supplemental information in meeting regulatory objectives regarding audits of financial statements of brokers, dealers, and others. Because such information is often critical to the effectiveness of regulatory oversight, Auditing Standard No. 17 requires the performance of audit procedures to test the supplemental information to support the auditor's report on the supplemental information. The standard also requires the auditor to evaluate whether the supplemental information complies with applicable regulatory requirements, which should help facilitate consistent compliance with regulatory requirements and give regulators greater confidence about the reliability of the supplemental information provided for regulatory oversight activities that are important to investor protection.

Auditing Standard No. 17 also requires the auditor to coordinate the auditor's work with the financial statement audit. To the extent that the supplemental information relates to information in the financial statements, the enhanced audit attention to the supplemental information could enhance the confidence of regulators and other users in the reliability of the financial statements and supplemental information.

The standard applies when the auditor of the company's financial statements is engaged to perform audit procedures and report on supplemental information that accompanies financial statements audited pursuant to PCAOB standards.[4]

The objective of the auditor of the financial statements, when engaged to perform audit procedures and report on supplemental information that accompanies audited financial statements, is to obtain sufficient appropriate audit evidence to express an opinion on whether the supplemental information is fairly stated, in all material respects, in relation to the financial statements as a whole.

16.3.2 Performing Audit Procedures

The auditor should perform audit procedures to obtain appropriate audit evidence that is sufficient to support the auditor's opinion regarding whether the supplemental information is fairly stated, in all material respects, in relation to the financial statements as a whole. The nature, timing, and extent of audit procedures necessary to obtain sufficient appropriate audit evidence and to report on the supplemental information depend on, among other things:

a. The risk of material misstatement of the supplemental information;
b. The materiality considerations relevant to the information presented;
c. The evidence obtained from the audit of the financial statements and, if applicable, other engagements by the auditor or affiliates of the firm, for the period presented; and
d. Whether a qualified opinion, an adverse opinion, or a disclaimer of opinion was issued on the financial statements.

[4] Such supplemental information includes:

- Supporting schedules that brokers and dealers are required to file pursuant to SEC Rule 17a-5;
- Supplemental information (i) required to be presented pursuant to the rules and regulations of a regulatory authority and (ii) covered by an independent public accountant's report on that information in relation to financial statements that are audited in accordance with PCAOB standards; or
- Information that is (i) ancillary to the audited financial statements, (ii) derived from the company's accounting books and records, and (iii) covered by an independent public accountant's report on that information in relation to the financial statements that are audited in accordance with PCAOB standards.

In performing the audit procedures on supplemental information, the auditor should:

(a) Obtain an understanding of the purpose of the supplemental information and the criteria management used to prepare the supplemental information, including relevant regulatory requirements;
(b) Obtain an understanding of the methods of preparing the supplemental information, evaluate the appropriateness of those methods, and determine whether those methods have changed from the methods used in the prior period and, if the methods have changed, determine the reasons for and evaluate the appropriateness of such changes;
(c) Inquire of management about any significant assumptions or interpretations underlying the measurement or presentation of the supplemental information;
(d) Determine that the supplemental information reconciles to the underlying accounting and other records or to the financial statements, as applicable;
(e) Perform procedures to test the completeness and accuracy of the information presented in the supplemental information to the extent that it was not tested as part of the audit of financial statements; and
(f) Evaluate whether the supplemental information, including its form and content, complies with relevant regulatory requirements or other applicable criteria, if any.

16.3.3 Performance and Reporting Requirements

The standard establishes procedural and reporting responsibilities for the auditor regarding supplemental information accompanying financial statements. The standard establishes:

Requirements that the auditor perform audit procedures to test the supplemental information;

- Requirements that the auditor evaluate the supplemental information, which include evaluating (1) whether the supplemental information, including its form and content, is fairly stated, in all material respects, in relation to the financial statements as a whole, and (2) whether the supplemental information is presented in conformity, in all material respects, with the relevant regulatory requirements or other applicable criteria;

- Requirements that promote enhanced coordination between the work performed on the supplemental information with work performed on the financial statement audit and, if applicable, other engagements, such as a compliance attestation engagement for brokers and dealers; and
- Reporting requirements that clearly articulate the auditor's responsibilities when reporting on supplemental information.

Two principal alternatives were considered in developing the new standard:

- A stand-alone audit of the supplemental information
- An "in relation to" approach

Auditing Standard No. 17 requires that the audit procedures on the supplemental information be "planned and performed" "in conjunction with" the auditor's work on the financial statement audit and, if applicable, other engagements.

Practice

Question 1

Which of the below assertion is accurate concerning the auditor's report on condensed financial statements?

(a) The auditor report must indicate that the auditor has audited and expressed an opinion on the complete financial statements
(b) The auditor report must indicate the date of the auditor's report on the complete financial statements
(c) The auditor report must indicate the type of opinion expressed
(d) The auditor report must indicate whether, in the auditor's opinion, the information set forth in the condensed financial statements is fairly stated in all material respects in relation to the complete financial statements from which it has been derived
(e) All of the above

Question 2

In performing the audit procedures on supplemental information, the auditor should consider the below, except:

(a) Obtain an understanding of the purpose of the supplemental information and the criteria management used to prepare the supplemental information, including relevant regulatory requirements
(b) Abstain from evaluating whether the supplemental information complies with relevant regulatory requirements
(c) Inquire of management about any significant assumptions or interpretations underlying the measurement or presentation of the supplemental information
(d) Determine that the supplemental information reconciles to the underlying accounting and other records or to the financial statements, as applicable

Question 3

Which of the following is accurate concerning the objective of the auditor of the financial statements, when engaged to perform audit procedures and report on supplemental information that accompanies audited financial statements,

(a) To obtain sufficient appropriate audit evidence to express an opinion on whether the supplemental information is fairly stated, in all material respects, in relation to the financial statements as a whole
(b) Inquire of management about any significant assumptions or interpretations underlying the measurement or presentation of the supplemental information
(c) Determine that the supplemental information reconciles to the underlying accounting and other records or to the financial statements, as applicable
(d) Obtain an understanding of the purpose of the supplemental information and the criteria management used to prepare the supplemental information
(e) All of the above

CHAPTER 17

Consideration of Fraud and of Internal Control Over Financial Reporting Audit

17.1 General

The auditor has a responsibility to plan and perform the audit to obtain reasonable assurance about whether the financial statements are free of material misstatement, whether caused by error or fraud. However, it is management's responsibility to design and implement programs and controls to prevent, deter, and detect fraud. Fraud is defined as an intentional act that results in a material misstatement in financial statements that are the subject of an audit. The primary factor that distinguishes fraud from error is whether the underlying action that results in the misstatement of the financial statements is intentional or unintentional.

Effective internal control over financial reporting ("internal control") helps assure that companies produce reliable published financial statements that investors can use in making investment decisions.

17.2 Types of Misstatements

Two types of misstatements are relevant to the auditor's consideration of fraud: misstatements arising from fraudulent financial reporting and misstatements arising from misappropriation of assets. Fraudulent financial reporting may be accomplished by the following:

F. I. Lessambo, *Auditing, Assurance Services, and Forensics*,
https://doi.org/10.1007/978-3-319-90521-1_17

- Manipulation, falsification, or alteration of accounting records or supporting documents from which financial statements are prepared;
- Misrepresentation in or intentional omission from the financial statements of events, transactions, or other significant information;
- Intentional misapplication of accounting principles relating to amounts, classification, manner of presentation, or disclosure.

Misstatements arising from misappropriation of assets (sometimes referred to as theft or defalcation) involve the theft of an entity's assets where the effect of the theft causes the financial statements not to be presented, in all material respects, in conformity with GAAP. Misappropriation of assets can be accomplished in various ways, including embezzling receipts, stealing assets, or causing an entity to pay for goods or services that have not been received.

Three conditions generally are present when fraud occurs. First, management or other employees have an incentive or are under pressure, which provides a reason to commit fraud. Second, circumstances exist—for example, the absence of controls, ineffective controls, or the ability of management to override controls—that provide an opportunity for a fraud to be perpetrated. Third, those involved are able to rationalize committing a fraudulent act. Some individuals possess an attitude, character, or set of ethical values that allow them to knowingly and intentionally commit a dishonest act. However, even otherwise honest individuals can commit fraud in an environment that imposes sufficient pressure on them. The greater the incentive or pressure, the more likely an individual will be able to rationalize the acceptability of committing fraud.

17.3 Exercising Professional Skepticism

Due professional care requires the auditor to exercise professional skepticism. Professional skepticism is an attitude that includes a questioning mind and a critical assessment of audit evidence. The auditor should conduct the engagement with a mindset that recognizes the possibility that a material misstatement due to fraud could be present, regardless of any past experience with the entity and regardless of the auditor's belief about management's honesty and integrity. Furthermore, professional skepticism requires an ongoing questioning of whether the information and evidence obtained suggests that a material misstatement due to fraud has occurred. In exercising professional skepticism in gathering and evaluating evidence, the auditor should not be satisfied with less-than-persuasive evidence because of a belief that management is honest.

17.4 Identifying the Risks of Material Misstatement Due to Fraud

In identifying risks of material misstatement due to fraud, it is helpful for the auditor to consider the information that has been gathered in the context of the three conditions present when a material misstatement due to fraud occurs—that is, incentives/pressures opportunities, and attitudes/rationalizations. However, the auditor should not assume that all three conditions must be observed or evident before concluding that there are identified risks. The auditor's identification of fraud risks also may be influenced by characteristics such as the size, complexity, and ownership attributes of the entity. For example, in the case of a larger entity, the auditor ordinarily considers factors that generally constrain improper conduct by management, such as the effectiveness of the audit committee and the internal audit function, and the existence and enforcement of a formal code of conduct. The risks of material misstatement due to fraud may vary among operating locations or business segments of an entity, requiring an identification of the risks related to specific geographic areas or business segments, as well as for the entity as a whole. The auditor should evaluate whether identified risks of material misstatement due to fraud can be related to specific financial statement account balances or classes of transactions and related assertions, or whether they relate more pervasively to the financial statements as a whole.

The identification of a risk of material misstatement due to fraud involves the application of professional judgment and includes the consideration of the attributes of the risk, including:

- The type of risk that may exist, that is, whether it involves fraudulent financial reporting or misappropriation of assets;
- The significance of the risk, that is, whether it is of a magnitude that could lead to result in a possible material misstatement of the financial statements;

- The likelihood of the risk, that is, the likelihood that it will result in a material misstatement in the financial statements;
- The pervasiveness of the risk, that is, whether the potential risk is pervasive to the financial statements as a whole or specifically related to a particular assertion, account, or class of transactions.

The auditor should perform the following procedures to obtain information that identify the risks of material misstatement due to fraud.

- Make inquiries of management and others within the entity to obtain their views about the risks of fraud and how they are addressed.
- Consider any unusual or unexpected relationships that have been identified in performing analytical procedures in planning the audit.
- Consider whether one or more fraud risk factors exist
- Consider other information that may be helpful in the identification of risks of material misstatement due to fraud.

17.5 Evaluating Audit Evidence

The auditor's assessment of the risks of material misstatement due to fraud should be ongoing throughout the audit. Conditions may be identified during fieldwork that change or support a judgment regarding the assessment of the risks, such as the following:

- Discrepancies in the accounting records, including:
  - Transactions that are not recorded in a complete or timely manner or are improperly recorded as to amount, accounting period, classification, or entity policy;
  - Unsupported or unauthorized balances or transactions;
  - Last-minute adjustments that significantly affect financial results;
  - Evidence of employees' access to systems and records inconsistent with that necessary to perform their authorized duties;
  - Tips or complaints to the auditor about alleged fraud.
- Conflicting or missing audit evidence, including:
  - Missing documents;
  - Documents that appear to have been altered;

  - Significant unexplained items on reconciliations;
  - Inconsistent, vague, or implausible responses from management or employees arising from inquiries or analytical procedures;
  - Unusual discrepancies between the entity's records and confirmation replies;
  - Missing inventory or physical assets of significant magnitude;
  - Unavailable or missing electronic evidence, inconsistent with the entity's record retention practices or policies;
  - Inability to produce evidence of key systems development and program change testing and implementation activities for current year system changes and deployments.

- Problematic or unusual relationships between the auditor and management, including:

  - Denial of access to records, facilities, certain employees, customers, vendors, or others from whom audit evidence might be sought;
  - Undue time pressures imposed by management to resolve complex or contentious issues;
  - Complaints by management about the conduct of the audit or management intimidation of audit team members, particularly in connection with the auditor's critical assessment of audit evidence or in the resolution of potential disagreements with management;
  - Unusual delays by the entity in providing requested information;
  - Unwillingness to facilitate auditor access to key electronic files for testing through the use of computer-assisted audit techniques
  - Denial of access to key IT operations staff and facilities, including security, operations, and systems development personnel
  - An unwillingness to add or revise disclosures in the financial statements to make them more complete and transparent.

17.6 Communicating to Management, Those Charged with Governance, and Others

Whenever the auditor has determined that there is evidence that fraud may exist, that matter should be brought to the attention of an appropriate level of management. This is appropriate even if the matter might be considered inconsequential, such as a minor defalcation by an employee at a low level in the entity's organization. Fraud involving senior management and fraud (whether caused by senior management or other employees) that causes a material misstatement of the financial statements should be reported directly to those charged with governance. In addition, the auditor should reach an understanding with those charged with governance regarding the nature and extent of communications with them about misappropriations perpetrated by lower-level employees.

If the auditor, as a result of the assessment of the risks of material misstatement, has identified risks of material misstatement due to fraud that have continuing control implications (whether or not transactions or adjustments that could be the result of fraud have been detected), the auditor should consider whether these risks represent significant deficiencies or material weaknesses in the entity's internal control that should be communicated to management and those charged with governance. The auditor also may wish to communicate other risks of fraud identified as a result of the assessment of the risks of material misstatements due to fraud. Such a communication may be a part of an overall communication with those charged with governance of business and financial statement risks affecting the entity and/or in conjunction with the auditor communication about the quality of the entity's accounting principles.

The disclosure of possible fraud to parties other than the client's senior management and those charged with governance ordinarily is not part of the auditor's responsibility and ordinarily would be precluded by the auditor's ethical or legal obligations of confidentiality unless the matter is reflected in the auditor's report. The auditor should recognize, however, that in the following circumstances a duty to disclose to parties outside the entity may exist:

- To comply with certain legal and regulatory requirements;
- To a successor auditor when the successor makes inquiries in accordance with section 315.[1]
- In response to a subpoena
- To a funding agency or other specified agency in accordance with requirements for the audits of entities that receive governmental financial assistance

[1]AU Section 315—Communications between Predecessor and Successor Auditors.

17.7 Audits of Internal Control Over Financial Reporting

Since the 1970s, federal laws have required public companies to maintain sufficient internal accounting controls. The Sarbanes-Oxley Act of 2002, as amended, ("Act") requires company management to annually assess and report on the effectiveness of the company's internal control. For larger companies, the Act also requires independent auditors to attest to management's assessment of the effectiveness of the company's internal control. Deficiencies in audits of internal control also can affect the audit of the financial statements. Significant auditing deficiencies in audits of internal control that have been frequently cited in PCAOB inspection reports include failures to:

- Identify and sufficiently test controls that are intended to address the risks of material misstatement;
- Sufficiently test the design and operating effectiveness of management review controls that are used to monitor the results of operations;
- Obtain sufficient evidence to update the results of testing of controls from an interim date to the company's year end
- Sufficiently test controls over the system-generated data and reports that support important controls
- Sufficiently perform procedures regarding the use of the work of others; and
- Sufficiently evaluate identified control deficiencies.

17.7.1 Risk Assessment and the Audit of Internal Control

One of the potential root causes for the deficiencies in audits of internal control, is improper application of the top-down approach set forth in PCAOB standards. The risk assessment procedures required by Auditing Standard No. 12 include, among other things, obtaining an understanding of the company and its environment and obtaining an understanding of internal control. The auditing standard also sets forth a process for assessing identified risks, which includes determining the likely sources of potential misstatement and evaluating the types of misstatements that could result from the risks; the accounts, disclosures, and assertions that could be affected; and the likelihood and magnitude of potential misstatements. In an audit of internal control, a thorough understanding of the company's internal control is important because it enables the auditor to appropriately plan and perform the necessary tests of controls. Auditing Standard No. 12 requires the auditor to obtain a sufficient understanding of each component of internal control to (1) identify the types of potential misstatements, (2) assess the factors that affect the risks of material misstatement, and (3) design tests of controls and substantive procedures. Understanding internal control includes understanding the information system, including the related business processes, relevant to financial reporting, which comprise the following:

- The classes of transactions in the company's operations that are significant to the financial statements;
- The procedures, within both automated and manual systems, by which those transactions are initiated, authorized, processed, recorded, and reported;
- The related accounting records, supporting information, and specific accounts in the financial statements that are used to initiate, authorize, process, and record transactions;
- How the information system captures events and conditions, other than transactions, that are significant to the financial statements; and
- The period-end financial reporting process.

In assessing risks of material misstatement and selecting controls to test, it is important for auditors to be aware that the components of a potential significant account or disclosure might be subject to significantly different risks. Also, different risks of material misstatement affecting the same assertion of an account or disclosure might arise at different points within the company's processes. If risks differ among components, the auditor might need to select and test different controls to support a conclusion that the controls adequately address the risks to the account or disclosure.

In multi-location engagements, PCAOB standards require the auditor to assess the risks of material misstatement to the consolidated financial statements associated with the location or business unit and correlate the amount of auditing attention devoted to the location or business unit with the degree of risk. In testing controls at locations or business units other than controls that address specific risks, the auditor should reassess the audit strategy if the auditor obtains information that is contrary to the premises under which the audit strategy was developed.

17.7.2 Selecting Controls to Test

In the audit of internal control, PCAOB standards require the auditor to test:

a. Entity-level controls that are important to the auditor's conclusion about whether the company has effective internal control over financial reporting, including evaluating the control environment and period-end financial reporting process; and
b. Controls that are important to the auditor's conclusion about whether the company's controls sufficiently address the assessed risk of misstatement to each relevant assertion (which may be entity-level controls or other controls).

The procedures performed to obtain an understanding of internal control pursuant to Auditing Standard No. 12 can provide a basis for the auditor to determine whether the selected controls cover the identified risks. Another important consideration in selecting controls to test is whether the controls, individually or in combination, are capable of addressing the risks of material misstatement to the relevant assertion. Internal control is not limited to frequent processes and normal recurring transactions. It also applies to infrequent processes, such as an analysis of whether long-term assets are impaired, and to nonrecurring transactions outside the normal course of business, such as a material business combination. When a company has infrequent processes or enters into nonrecurring transactions that present a reasonable possibility of material misstatement of the financial statements, the auditor should test the controls over those processes or transactions. Performing substantive audit procedures to determine whether the accounts or transactions are accounted for properly is important for the financial statement audit but, by itself, does not provide sufficient appropriate evidence to support a conclusion that the controls over those transactions or analyses are designed and operating effectively. An auditor cannot merely infer that a control is effective because no misstatements were detected by substantive procedures. In some cases, auditors are able to design and perform procedures that test controls over nonrecurring transactions concurrently with substantive tests of those transactions, thereby obtaining sufficient appropriate evidence to fulfill the related objectives for the financial statement audit and the audit of internal control.

17.7.3 Testing Management Review Controls

Auditors often select and test management review controls in audits of internal control. Such management reviews might be performed to monitor the results of operations, such as (1) monthly comparisons of actual results to forecasted revenues or budgeted expenses; (2) comparisons of other metrics, such as gross profit margins and expenses as a percentage of sales; and (3) quarterly balance sheet reviews. These reviews typically involve comparing recorded financial statement amounts to expected amounts and investigating significant differences from expectations. The auditor should perform procedures to obtain evidence about how a management review control is designed and operates to prevent or detect misstatements. The main consideration in assessing the level of precision is whether the control is designed and operating to prevent or detect on timely basis misstatements that could cause the financial statements to be materially misstated. Factors that can affect the level of precision of an entity-level control include the following:

- Objective of the review: A procedure that functions to prevent or detect misstatements generally is more precise than a procedure that merely identifies and explains differences.
- Level of aggregation: A control that is performed at a more granular level generally is more precise than one performed at a higher level. For example, an analysis of revenue by location or product line normally is more precise than an analysis of total company revenue.
- Consistency of performance: A control that is performed routinely and consistently generally is more precise than one performed sporadically.
- Correlation to relevant assertions: A control that is indirectly related to an assertion normally is less likely to prevent or detect misstatements in the assertion than a control that is directly related to an assertion. For example, a control designed to detect errors in the recorded amounts of accounts receivable might not operate with a

sufficient level of precision to detect errors in the valuation of delinquent receivables.

- Predictability of expectations: Some entity-level controls are designed to detect misstatements by using key performance indicators or other information to develop expectations about reported amounts ("detective controls"). The precision of those controls depends on the ability to develop sufficiently precise expectations to highlight potentially material misstatements.
- Criteria for investigation: For detective controls, the threshold for investigating deviations or differences from expectations relative to materiality is an indication of a control's precision. For example, a control that investigates items that are near the threshold for financial statement materiality has less precision and a greater risk of failing to prevent or detect misstatements that could be material than a control with a lower threshold for investigation.

17.7.4 Testing Design Effectiveness

Evaluating whether a management review control is capable of preventing or detecting potential material misstatements generally involves obtaining an understanding of and evaluating the following:

a. Whether the control satisfies the corresponding control objective, including whether it addresses the risks of material misstatement to the relevant assertion of the significant account or disclosure;
b. The factors affecting the precision of the review, including the objective of the review and the appropriateness of the expectations, level of aggregation, and criteria for investigation for identifying potentially material misstatements;
c. The steps involved in identifying, investigating, and resolving significant differences from expectations;
d. The person(s) who performs the control, including the competence and authority of the person(s);
e. The frequency of performance of the control, that is, whether the review occurs often enough to prevent or detect misstatements before they have a material effect on the financial statements; and
f. The information used in the review, for example, whether the review uses system-generated data or reports, as discussed later in this alert.

17.7.5 Testing Operating Effectiveness

Testing the operating effectiveness of a management review control involves performing procedures to evaluate whether the control is working as designed to prevent or detect potentially material misstatements. Testing typically involves, for selected operations of the control, obtaining and evaluating evidence about:

a. The steps performed to identify and investigate significant differences; and
b. The conclusions reached in the reviewer's investigation, including whether potential misstatements were appropriately investigated and whether corrective actions were taken as needed.

17.7.6 Information Technology Considerations, Including System-Generated Data and Reports

A company's use of IT can significantly affect a company's internal control. The following are examples of IT-related matters that can affect the auditor's evaluation of internal control:

- Risks of material misstatement resulting from the company's IT processes or systems;
- Important controls that depend on the effectiveness of IT controls ("IT-dependent controls"), for example, because they use system-generated data or reports; and
- Important IT controls, such as, automated controls that address risks of material misstatement to one or more assertions, along with the IT controls that support the effectiveness of the automated controls.

PCAOB standards require the auditor to obtain an understanding of the company's information system relevant to financial reporting and take into account IT considerations in assessing the risks of material misstatement. This includes obtaining an understanding of the extent of manual controls and automated controls used by the company, including the ITGCs that are important to the effective operation of the automated controls. The auditor also should obtain an understanding of specific risks to a company's internal control resulting from IT. In an audit of internal control, if the auditor selects an IT-dependent control for testing, the auditor should test the IT-dependent controls and the IT controls on which the selected control relies to support a conclusion about whether those controls address the risks of material misstatement. PCAOB standards require evaluation of the severity of identified control deficiencies. This includes deficiencies in IT controls. However, the nature of IT systems, processes, and controls can affect how deficiencies in IT controls should be evaluated.

17.7.7 Roll-Forward of Controls Tested at an Interim Date

Although the auditor expresses an opinion on internal control as of the end of the year, auditors may decide to test some important controls at an earlier date. When auditors test controls at an interim date, PCAOB standards require auditors to perform "roll-forward" procedures to update the results of interim testing to year end. The amount of evidence needed from the roll-forward procedures depends on the following factors:

- The specific control tested at an interim date, including the risks associated with the control and the nature of the control, and the results of those tests;
- The sufficiency of the evidence of effectiveness obtained at an interim date;
- The length of the roll-forward period; and
- The possibility that there have been any significant changes in internal control over financial reporting subsequent to the interim date.

17.7.8 Using the Work of Others

When the auditor uses the work of others, the auditor also should test and evaluate that work, including evaluating the quality and effectiveness of the others' work. The necessary extent of testing of that work depends on the risk associated with the control and the competence and objectivity of the others. More extensive testing of the others' work is needed as the risk increases or the others' level of competence or objectivity decreases. When using the work of others that provide direct assistance, the auditor should supervise that work, including reviewing the work, as well as testing and evaluating it.

PCAOB standards allow the auditor to use the work of others as evidence of the effectiveness of selected controls, and Auditing Standard No. 5 requires auditors to determine the extent to which the work of others will be used. PCAOB standards provide that the extent to which the work of others can be used depends on the following factors:

- The risk associated with the control being tested; and
- The competence and objectivity of the persons whose work the auditor plans to use. For example, persons who test controls are less objective if they report to those responsible for the operation of the controls being tested.

17.7.9 Evaluating Identified Control Deficiencies

PCAOB standards require auditors to evaluate the severity of each control deficiency that comes to his or her attention to determine whether the deficiencies, individually or in combination, are material weaknesses. The severity of a deficiency does not depend on whether a misstatement actually has occurred but rather on whether there is a reasonable possibility that the company's controls will fail to prevent or detect a misstatement. In forming a conclusion about whether a control deficiency or combination of deficiencies is a material weakness, the auditor should evaluate the effect of compensating controls, if any. This includes testing the compensating controls to determine whether they operate at a level of precision that would prevent or detect a misstatement that could be material. This includes evaluating whether the control addresses the risk of material misstatement to the relevant assertion intended to be addressed by the deficient control. If the compensating control is a management review control, the previously discussed considerations for testing management review controls apply to the compensating control. Evaluating whether a control deficiency, or a combination of control deficiencies, results in a material weakness requires professional skepticism and a careful analysis of all the evidence obtained.

Appendix

- Internal Control Reporting and Audit Report Lags: Further Evidence, by Vishal Munsif, K. Raghunandan, Dasaratha V. Rama; *AUDITING: A Journal of Practice & Theory*, May 2012, Vol. 31, No. 2, pp. 167–188.

- Management Reporting on Internal Control and Accruals Quality: Insights from a "Comply-or-Explain" Internal Control Regime, by Katrien Van de Poel and Ann Vanstraelen; *AUDITING: A Journal of Practice & Theory*, May 2011, Vol. 30, No. 2, pp. 19–50.

Practice

Question 1

Which of the following assertions is incorrect concerning fraud?

(a) Fraud is a broad legal concept
(b) Auditors do make legal determinations of whether fraud has occurred
(c) The auditor's interest relates to acts that result in a material misstatement of the financial statements
(d) The primary factor that distinguishes fraud from error is whether the underlying action that results in the misstatement of the financial statements is intentional or unintentional
(e) Fraud may be concealed by withholding evidence or misrepresenting information in response to inquiries or by falsifying documentation

Question 2

Which of the following assertions concerning fraudulent financial reporting is inaccurate?

(a) The two types of misstatements relevant to the auditor's consideration of fraud are (i) misstatements arising from fraudulent financial reporting and (ii) misstatements arising from misappropriation of assets
(b) Misstatements arising from fraudulent financial reporting are intentional misstatements or omissions of amounts or disclosures in financial statements
(c) Fraudulent financial reporting may be accomplished through manipulation, falsification, or alteration of accounting records
(d) Fraudulent financial reporting need not be the result of a grand plan or conspiracy

Question 3

Which of the following assertions concerning misappropriation of asset is inaccurate?

(a) Misstatements arising from misappropriation of assets involve the theft of an entity's assets
(b) Misappropriation of assets can be accomplished in various ways, including embezzling receipts, stealing assets, or causing an entity to pay for goods or services that have not been received
(c) Misappropriation of assets may be accompanied by false or misleading records or documents, possibly created by circumventing controls
(d) Misstatements arising from misappropriation of assets always involve the theft of an entity's assets

Question 4

Which of the following assertion is inaccurate concerning management override of control?

(a) Management is in a better position to perpetrate fraud because of its ability to directly or indirectly manipulate accounting records and prepare fraudulent financial statements
(b) Management can easily override established controls that otherwise appear to be operating effectively
(c) Management override of controls can occur in unpredictable ways
(d) Management can override cumbersome controls though effective by their very nature

CHAPTER 18

Financial Statements' Audit

18.1 General

A financial statement audit is the examination of an entity's financial statements and accompanying disclosures by an independent auditor. The result of this examination is a report by the auditor, attesting to the fairness of presentation of the financial statements and related disclosures. The auditor's report must accompany the financial statements when they are issued to the intended recipients. In so doing, the external auditor adds or provides credibility to the reported financial position and performance of a business.

18.2 Financial Statement Assertions

In representing that the financial statements are presented fairly in conformity with the applicable financial reporting framework, management implicitly or explicitly makes assertions regarding the recognition, measurement, presentation, and disclosure of the various elements of financial statements and related disclosures. Those assertions can be classified into the following categories:

- Existence or occurrence: assets or liabilities of the company exist at a given date, and recorded transactions have occurred during a given period.

F. I. Lessambo, *Auditing, Assurance Services, and Forensics*,
https://doi.org/10.1007/978-3-319-90521-1_18

- Completeness: all transactions and accounts that should be presented in the financial statements are so included.
- Valuation or allocation: asset, liability, equity, revenue, and expense components have been included in the financial statements at appropriate amounts.
- Rights and obligations: the company holds or controls rights to the assets, and liabilities are obligations of the company at a given date.
- Presentation and disclosure: the components of the financial statements are properly classified, described, and disclosed.

The auditor may base his or her work on financial statement assertions that differ from those in this standard if the assertions are sufficient for the auditor to identify the types of potential misstatements and to respond appropriately to the risks of material misstatement in each significant account and disclosure that has a reasonable possibility of containing misstatements that would cause the financial statements to be materially misstated, individually, or in combination with other misstatements.

18.3 Cash and Cash Equivalent

Cash balances include un-deposited receipts at hands, cash in the bank in unrestricted accounts, and imprest accounts (i.e., petty cash and payroll bank accounts), and cash equivalents.

18.3.1 Cash and Cash Equivalent-Related Accounts

Cash and Cash Equivalents is an asset that appears on the statement of financial position of a business and includes currency (coins and bank notes) held by a business (in hand and in bank accounts) and cash equivalents. Cash is a medium of exchange, a store of value and a unit of account and a business needs to have sufficient cash in order to be able to pay its liabilities. Higher cash ratio (ratio of cash and cash equivalents to current liabilities) suggests that the business is liquid (i.e., it is expected not to face any difficulty in paying its very short-term liabilities).

A business generates cash from sale of products and services, sale of assets, borrowings from banks and other creditors, and from capital contributions by its owners. It uses cash to pay for its operating and capital expenditure, its liabilities, and in paying dividends to its owners. Information about sources and uses of cash are presented in the statement of cash flows. Businesses keep a small amount of cash (called petty cash) for day to day cash expenses and keep a larger percentage of cash at its bank. Control over cash is vital for efficient and profitable operations of a business that is why businesses prepare their cash and bank reconciliations periodically.

Cash equivalents are not precisely coins and banknotes but are marketable securities of very short-term maturity (typically always less than three months) which are not expected to deteriorate significantly in value till maturity. They are treated as equivalent to cash under IAS 7 Statements of Cash Flows.

The five transaction cycles which relate directly to general cash balances are (i) revenue, (ii) expenditure, (iii) financing, (iv) investing, and (v) personnel services. Some misstatements can normally be discovered through the test on bank reconciliation. These include:

- Failure to include a check that has not cleared the bank, even though it has been recorded in the cash disbursements journal
- Cash received by the client subsequent to the balance sheet date but recorded as cash receipts in the current year
- Deposits recorded as cash receipts near the end of the year, deposited in the bank in the same month, and included in the bank reconciliation as a deposit in transit
- Payments on notes payable debited directly to the bank balance by the bank but not entered in the client's records

Other misstatements may not be discovered as a part of the audit of the bank reconciliation. These include:

- Failure to bill a customer
- An embezzlement of cash by interception of cash receipts from customers before they are recorded, with the account charged off as a bad debt
- Duplicate payment of a vendor's invoice
- Improper payments of officers' personal expenditures
- Payment for raw materials that were not received

- Payment to an employee for more hours worked
- Payment of interest to a related party for an amount in excess of the going rate

18.3.2 Audit Procedures

The auditor must conduct audit procedures in the audit of year-end cash to determine the possibility of a material fraud. The auditor should design and perform audit test concerning cash account in several phases: (i) identify client business risks that affects cash and cash equivalents; (ii) design and perform tests of controls and substantive tests; and (iii) design and perform analytical procedures for cash in bank.

18.4 Receivables or Revenue Cycle

Receivables include all amounts due from third parties. Receivable is a general term which refers to all monetary obligations owed to the business by its customers or debtors. Receivables can be broadly classified as trade-receivables and non-trade receivables.

Trade receivables are those receivables which originate from sales of goods and services by a business to its customers in the ordinary course of business. There are two main accounts used for trade receivables which are accounts receivable and notes receivable. When the customers orally promise to pay, the receivables are recorded as accounts receivable. However, if the customers' promise is written one, the receivables are recorded as notes receivable. Notes receivable usually require the debtor to pay interest. Both accounts receivable and notes receivable may be current and noncurrent.

Non-trade-receivables are the amounts due from third parties for transactions outside its normal course of business of selling goods and services. Example of non-trade receivables are loans to employees, tax refunds owed to the business by tax authorities, etc.

As long as a business expects to recover the money from the debtors, it records its receivables as assets in its balance sheet because it expects to derive future benefits (i.e., cash) from them. It does not matter whether they are due in the current period or not.

18.4.1 Audit Objectives

The auditor shall determine whether:

- All sales, receivables, cash balances are recorded
- All receivables, sales, cash of period are presented in financial statements
- Entity has property rights to cash, accounts receivable
- Entity has recorded items in correct amounts, accounts, and time periods
- Recorded transactions, balances properly classified, described, disclosed

Revenue cycle can be traced through several documents, including: (i) customer purchase order; (ii) sales order; (iii) bill of lading; (iv) invoice; (v) control listing; and (vi) credit memo.

18.4.2 Control Environment

The purpose of accounts receivable internal controls is to ensure that sales invoices are properly recorded and that customers pay promptly in accordance with the agreed terms of the contract. An internal control system shall focus on the separation of duties, processing controls, document controls, safeguard controls, and system controls.

18.4.3 Audit Procedures

In applying analytical procedures as risk assessment procedures, the auditor should perform analytical procedures relating to revenue with the objective of identifying unusual or unexpected relationships involving revenue accounts that might indicate a material misstatement, including material misstatement due to fraud. Also, when the auditor has performed a review of interim financial information in accordance with AU sec. 722,[1] he or she should take into account the analytical procedures applied in that review when designing and applying analytical procedures as risk assessment procedures. The auditor should presume that there is a fraud risk involving improper revenue recognition and evaluate which types of revenue, revenue transactions, or assertions may give rise to such risks.

[1]AU Section 722—Interim Financial Information.

Confirmation of accounts receivable is a generally accepted auditing procedure. It is generally presumed that evidence obtained from third parties will provide the auditor with higher-quality audit evidence than is typically available from within the entity. Thus, there is a presumption that the auditor will request the confirmation of accounts receivable during an audit unless one of the following is true:

- Accounts receivable are immaterial to the financial statements
- The use of confirmations would be ineffective
- the auditor's combined assessed level of inherent and control risk is low, and the assessed level, in conjunction with the evidence expected to be provided by analytical procedures or other substantive tests of details, is sufficient to reduce audit risk to an acceptably low level for the applicable financial statement assertions. In many situations, both confirmation of accounts receivable and other substantive tests of details are necessary to reduce audit risk to an acceptably low level for the applicable financial statement assertions.

18.5 Inventories[2]

Inventory includes the raw materials, work-in-process, and finished goods that a company has on hand for its own production processes or for sale to customers. Inventory is considered an asset, so the accountant must consistently use a valid method for assigning costs to inventory in order to record it as an asset. The primary basis of accounting for inventories is cost, which is the price paid or consideration given to acquire an asset. Although principles for the determination of inventory costs may be easily stated, their application, particularly to such inventory items as work in process and finished goods, is difficult because of the variety of considerations in the allocation of costs and charges. In certain cases, a departure from the cost basis of pricing the inventory is required when the utility of the goods is no longer as great as their cost. That is, where there is evidence that the utility of goods, in their disposal in the ordinary course of business, will be less than cost, whether due to physical deterioration, obsolescence, changes in price levels, or other causes, the difference shall be recognized as a loss of the current period. This is

[2]AU Section 331.

generally accomplished by stating such goods at a lower level commonly designated as a market.

There are two main types of inventory systems: the perpetual inventory system and the periodic inventory system.

- The Perpetual inventory system

The perpetual inventory method is one in which inventory data is updated continuously. When an order is placed or received, that data immediately is entered into the system to update the quantity and inventory availability right away. Thus, a perpetual inventory system has the advantages of both providing up-to-date inventory balance information and requiring a reduced level of physical inventory counts. The system works best when coupled with a computer database of inventory quantities and bin locations, which is updated in real time by the warehouse staff using wireless bar code scanners, or by sales clerks using point of sale terminals. It is least effective when changes are recorded on inventory cards, since there is a significant chance that entries will not be made, will be made incorrectly, or will not be made in a timely manner. Thus, technology makes keeping this type of inventory control system even easier to use.

The Perpetual Inventory system debits the purchases of inventory and related cost directly to the account "inventory," and credits the sales or thefts of inventories to the same inventory account.

- The Periodic Inventory System

The periodic inventory system only updates the ending inventory balance in the general ledger when a physical inventory count is conducted. In the meantime, the inventory account in the accounting system continues to show the cost of the inventory that was recorded as of the last physical inventory count. Under the periodic inventory system, all purchases made between physical inventory counts are recorded in a purchases account. When a physical inventory count is done, then the balance in the purchases account is shifted into the inventory account, which in turn is adjusted to match the cost of the ending inventory.

18.5.1 *Audit Objectives*

The objectives of the inventory audit are to determine that:

- Inventories included in the balance sheet physically exist
- Inventories represent items held for sale or use in the normal course of business.
- Inventory quantities include all products, materials, and supplies on hand
- Inventory quantities include all products, materials, and supplies owned by the company that are in transit or stored at outside locations.
- Inventory listings are accurately compiled and the totals are properly included in the inventory accounts.
- The entity has legal title or similar rights of ownership to the inventories.
- Inventories exclude items billed to customers or owned by others.
- Inventories are properly stated at cost (except when market is lower).
- Slow-moving, excess, defective, and obsolete items included in inventories are properly identified.
- Inventories are reduced, when appropriate, to replacement cost or net realizable value.
- Inventories are properly classified in the balance sheet as current assets. The major categories of inventories and their bases of valuation are adequately disclosed in the financial statements.
- The pledge or assignment of any inventories is appropriately disclosed.

18.5.2 *Control Environment*

The auditors need to be reassured that the client control system is strong to track all the movement of the inventories. To obtain assurance that management's procedures are adequately implemented, the auditor observes employees' procedures and performs test counts. When inventory is material, the auditor is required to obtain sufficient appropriate audit evidence regarding its existence and condition by attendance at a physical inventory count unless it is impractical.

18.5.3 Audit Procedures

When inventory quantities are determined solely by means of a physical count, and all counts are made as of the balance-sheet date or as of a single date within a reasonable time before or after the balance-sheet date, it is ordinarily necessary for the independent auditor to be present at the time of count and, by suitable observation, tests, and inquiries, satisfy himself respecting the effectiveness of the methods of inventory-taking and the measure of reliance which may be placed upon the client's representations about the quantities and physical condition of the inventories.

When the well-kept perpetual inventory records are checked by the client periodically by comparisons with physical counts, the auditor's observation procedures usually can be performed either during or after the end of the period under audit. For companies that have developed inventory controls or methods of determining inventories, including statistical sampling, the independent auditor must satisfy himself that the client's procedures or methods are sufficiently reliable to produce results substantially the same as those which would be obtained by a count of all items each year. The auditor must be present to observe such counts as he deems necessary and must satisfy himself as to the effectiveness of the counting procedures used. If statistical sampling methods are used by the client in the taking of the physical inventory, the auditor must be satisfied that the sampling plan is reasonable and statistically valid, that it has been properly applied, and that the results are reasonable in the circumstances. It will always be necessary for the auditor to make, or observe, some physical counts of the inventory and apply appropriate tests of intervening transactions. This should be coupled with inspection of the records of any client's counts and procedures relating to the physical inventory on which the balance-sheet inventory is based.

The independent auditor may be asked to audit financial statements covering the current period and one or more periods for which he had not observed or made some physical counts of prior inventories. He may, nevertheless, be able to become satisfied as to such prior inventories through appropriate procedures, such as tests of prior transactions, reviews of the records of prior counts, and the application of gross profit tests, provided that he has been able to become satisfied as to the current inventory.

Inventories Held in Public Warehouses

If inventories are in the hands of public warehouses or other outside custodians, the auditor ordinarily would obtain direct confirmation in writing from the custodian. If such inventories represent a significant proportion of current or total assets, to obtain reasonable assurance with respect to their existence, the auditor should apply one or more of the following procedures as he considers necessary in the circumstances.

a. Test the owner's procedures for investigating the warehouseman and evaluating the warehouseman's performance.
b. Obtain an independent accountant's report on the warehouseman's control procedures relevant to custody of goods and, if applicable, pledging of receipts, or apply alternative procedures at the warehouse to gain reasonable assurance that information received from the warehouseman is reliable.
c. Observe physical counts of the goods, if practicable and reasonable.
d. If warehouse receipts have been pledged as collateral, confirm with lenders pertinent details of the pledged receipts (on a test basis, if appropriate).

- Substantive tests of the inventories include:
  - Observing physical inventory counts
  - Obtaining confirmation of inventories at locations outside the entity
  - Testing of inventory transactions between a preliminary physical inventory date and the balance sheet date.
  - Reviewing perpetual inventory records, production records, and purchasing records for indications of current activity.
  - Comparing inventories with a current sales catalog and subsequent sales and delivery reports.
  - Using the work of specialists to corroborate the nature of specialized products.
  - Analytically comparing the relationship of inventory balances to recent purchasing, production, and sales activities
  - Testing shipping and receiving cutoff procedures
  - Testing the clerical accuracy of inventory listings
  - Reconciling physical counts to perpetual records and general ledger balances and investigating significant fluctuations

- Examining paid vendors' invoices, consignment agreements, and contracts
- Examining paid vendors' invoices, consignment agreements, and contracts.
- Inquiring of production and sales personnel concerning possible excess or obsolete inventory items
- Obtaining confirmation of inventories pledged under loan agreements.

Further, analytical procedures such the computation of ratios for inventory turnover and detailed gross margin, and comparison to previous periods are often performed.

18.6 Plant, Property, and Equipment

Capital expenditures are significant for many companies. For example, at Jet Blue Airways, plant assets are 69% of its total assets. For Walmart Stores, Inc., it's 53%. Conversely, Microsoft's percentage is just 3%. Thus, not only do companies have to be careful in planning the proper amount of capital expenditures, but also users must understand the impact of these expenditures on measures of financial performance.

18.6.1 Audit Objectives

The objectives of PPE audit aim to:

- Determine whether the acquisition costs are recorded properly, including costs assigned to internally constructed fixed assets;
- Inspect property and equipment to gather evidence for the existence assertion and to identify any unrecorded equipment (completeness assertion);
- Determine whether any repairs of assets meet the improvement or betterment rule and should be capitalized;
- Analyze repairs and maintenance, supplies, small tools, and other related accounts to determine capitalization limits have been met;
- Review the management's depreciation methods and rates;
- Identify any idle equipment, fully depreciated equipment, or property related to discontinued operations for separate accounting and reporting;

- Read any available lease agreements for proper classification either as a capitalized lease or rental expense;
- Analyze the rental income and expense for the existence of other leases and subleases;
- Review the calculations of gain or loss on any disposals of property and equipment.

18.6.2 *Control Environment*

A proper environment control would (i) include a system that maintains records of all purchases, retirements, and dispositions of property or equipment, (ii) require appropriate authorization for their use, (iii) require a periodic verification of the record by physical confirmation, and (iv) require a proper segregation of duties.

18.6.3 *Risk Assessment*

The auditor shall consider the risk PPE misstatement due to misapplication of accounting principles, given that the accounting principles in this area are challenging and complex. For instance, the classification of the lease contract as capital or expense may not always be obvious.[3] Likewise, the auditor consider whether the client has an appropriate internal control over its PPE

18.6.4 *Audit Procedures*

A combination of controls testing and substantive testing is usually adopted when obtaining audit assurance on PPE. The auditor may reduce the planned level of substantive assurance, if the internal controls are found to be strong. The auditor may, as well, be interested in entities impairment review documentation to determine whether an item of property, plant, and equipment is impaired. The auditor shall also perform some analytical procedures in order to detect misclassified additions, unrecorded retirements and miscalculation of depreciation expense. For instance, the auditor may choose to compare property,

[3]Accounting Standard Update (ASU) N0. 2016-02, Leases (Topic 842), effective as of 2019 requires the lessee to recognize assets/liabilities on their balance sheet for leases with lease terms of more than 12 months.

plant, and equipment balances and depreciation expense with previously reported amounts and budgets.

Key areas when testing tangible noncurrent assets include:

- confirmation of ownership,
- inspection of noncurrent assets,
- valuation by third parties,
- adequacy of depreciation rates,
- potential impairment.

18.7 Account and Notes Payables

Accounts payable, listed under current liabilities on the balance sheet represent payments a company has promised or is committed to pay. A/P is a promise of short-term debt obligations and is generally used when dealing with suppliers and creditors. Notes payable are payments or liabilities due for payment within one year, or the operating cycle, whichever is longer. Notes payable represent obligations or short-term liabilities in the form of written notes (e.g., promissory notes). Notes payable are often used instead of accounts payable because they give the lender written documentation of the obligation in case legal remedies are needed to collect the debt. Notes payable usually require the borrower to pay interest and frequently are issued to meet short-term financing needs.

18.7.1 Audit Objectives

The auditors' objectives in auditing both the account and note payables can be summarized as follow:

- determine the existence of recorded accounts and note payable and the occurrence of purchase transactions
- establish the completeness of accounts and note payable and purchase transactions
- determine whether the client is legally obliged to pay the recorded accounts and note payable
- determine the appropriate valuation of accounts payable
- determine whether the presentation and disclosure of accounts and note payable and purchases are appropriate.

18.7.2 *Control Environment*

The environment control can be performed through:

- Segregation of duties to minimize the risk of frauds: ensure that payment documents are processed correctly by different people involved in the payment process. Best practice is to have different people: (i) approve purchases; (ii) receive ordered materials; (iii) approve invoices for payment; and (iv) review and reconcile financial records.
- Accountability, authorization, and approval: ensure that the firms have authorize, review, and approve invoices for payment based on the signed agreements, contract terms, and purchase orders.
- Secure the received materials in a safe location
- Review and reconciliation: perform monthly ledger reconciliations to catch improper charges and validate transactions.

18.7.3 *Risk Assessment*

A proper internal control environment would mitigate the risk of material misstatement. Otherwise, the auditor would need to pursue an audit trail of payables or purchasing related activities. The inherent risk factors the auditor shall consider include: (i) the number of principal suppliers, (ii) supplier billing practices, and (iii) the clients' purchasing methods and the principal types of goods or services purchased. Further consideration such as, management's attitude to control and factors that predispose management to condone misrepresentations should also be covered.

18.7.4 *Audit Procedures*

Similar to the account receivables, the auditors shall perform substantive procedures such as confirmation requests to valuable suppliers of the client during the audited period. Additionally, analytical procedures, such as comparison of expenses, budgets, and level of activity in the current period with similar information from previous periods can provide evidence for recorded expense and liability balances.

18.8 Equity Capital

A firm can finance its activities either through debt or equity instruments. Each option has its drawbacks in terms of control of the firm, earnings, and various financial ratios. The choice between equity and debt depends on a firm's individual circumstances one firm may prefer issuing equity, while another may prefer the debt financing. The traditional distinction between equity and debt is blurred through the use of instruments with characteristics of both. These hybrid instruments raise the question of whether they should be recorded as a liability or equity for the issuing firm. The GAAP treatment of convertible debt depends on the specific terms involved. Traditional convertible debt is classified entirely as a liability and upon conversion the carrying amount of the liability is reclassified as equity. Stockholders' equity has three common components: paid-in capital, treasury stock, and retained earnings.

18.8.1 Audit Objectives

The objectives of the auditor in auditing the shareholders' equity accounts can be summarized as follow:

- To determine, where appropriate, that transactions have been entered in accordance with resolutions of the board of directors;
- To determine whether the owners' equity account transactions are complete and properly recorded;
- To determine whether the owners' equity balances are properly presented and disclosed;
- To determine whether the retained earnings account is accurately disclosed accurately in the financial statements;
- To determine whether the internal control over the shareholders' equity accounts is adequate.

These objectives are accomplished by proving detail records to controls, accounting for stock certificates, reviewing transfers, verifying capital changes, verifying entries, and tracing authority for the entries to the minutes of the board of directors, and by reviewing the system of internal control.

18.8.2 Control Environment

Though equity transactions are few, in principle, the firm must provide a clear segregation of duties to avoid fraud. The auditor has to ensure that such an internal control does exist. For instance, the employee responsible for issuing, transferring, and cancelling securities certificates must bear not accounting responsibilities.

18.8.3 Risk Assessment

The auditor shall obtain an understanding of internal control over capital stock transactions. The better the internal control the lesser would be the risk of material misstatement.

18.8.4 Audit Procedures

The auditor shall perform both substantive and analytical procedure related to the three segments of the shareholders' equity accounts. To that end, he shall:

- perform analytical procedures to test the reasonableness of owners' equity accounts (including dividends);
- confirm shares outstanding with the independent registrar and the stock transfer agent;
- examine the stock certificate records and test any changes;
- trace receipts from stock issues from cash receipts journal to bank statement to deposit slips to board minutes;
- trace payments related to dividends and treasury stock from cash payments journal to bank statement to cancelled checks to board minutes;
- recalculate dividend distribution to common and preferred shareholders;
- inspect treasury stock; recalculate treasury stock transactions;
- analyze all changes in retained earnings.

18.9 Long-Term Debt

Long-term debts are arrangements that require full repayment within twelve months after issuance or greater than the normal operating cycle of the company, if longer. Firms must disclose all their long-term debts, including repayment terms, conversion features, interest rates, restrictions on assets and activities, debt covenants, and other matters important to users of the financial statements. Types of long-term debt arrangements include borrowing under notes payable, bonds payable, debentures, term loans, and other contractual obligations for payment.

18.9.1 Audit Objectives

In auditing long-term debts, the auditor's objectives are as follow:

- determine whether all debts, loans are properly recorded;
- determine whether proper authorization for issues of notes or bonds;
- determine whether adequate controls over payment of interest and principal;
- determine whether the firm (client) has periodic independent verification system.

18.9.2 Control Environment

The auditor needs to establish the client inherent risk based upon the number, size of existing long term debts, such as bond debentures, leases, and more. The risk will often be low if the client has an adequate internal control system, such custodial procedures for unused notes and bonds.

18.9.3 Risk Assessment

The audit risk assessment considers whether the client has contracted the loan in accordance with its set up policy, with proper authorization form the Board of the Financing Committee of the Board. Also, the auditor need to determine whether the client has a reliable internal control and performs within the blueprints of its rules or policies.

18.9.4 Audit Procedures

The auditor shall perform analytical procedures to test the reasonableness of long-term liabilities and interest expense. The auditor conducts some substantive procedures, along the line with confirmation. The form of confirmation is similar to that which is used for accounts payable. For instance, the auditor would seek confirmation of the issuance contract with the trustee to assess the amount of the loan debenture, the interest rate and terms and interest paid and accrued. The auditor shall enquire the management regarding the existence, if any, of restrictions upon assets. Analytical procedures such balance sheets comparisons between the audited period and the previously reported year is often performed.

Practice

Question 1

In auditing the account receivables, the auditor will request the confirmation of accounts receivable during an audit unless one of the following is true:

(a) Accounts receivable are immaterial to the financial statements
(b) The use of confirmations would be ineffective
(c) The auditor's combined assessed level of inherent and control risk is low
(d) All of the above

Question 2

The objectives of the inventory audit include the below, except:

(a) Inventories included in the balance sheet physically exist
(b) Inventories represent items held for sale or use in the normal course of business
(c) Inventory quantities include all products, materials, and supplies on hand
(d) Inventory listings are accurately compiled and the totals are properly included in the inventory accounts
(e) None

Question 3

Key areas when testing tangible noncurrent assets include the following, except:

(a) Confirmation of ownership
(b) Inspection of noncurrent assets

(c) Valuation by the firm management
(d) Potential impairment.

Question 4

In auditing long-term debts, the auditor's objectives include the below, except:

(a) Determine whether all debts, loans are properly recorded
(b) Determine whether proper authorization for issues of notes or bonds
(c) Determine whether adequate controls over payment of interest and principal
(d) Determine whether the firm (client) has a periodic independent verification system
(e) None

Question 5

The objectives of the auditor in auditing the shareholders' equity accounts include the below, except:

(a) To determine, where appropriate, that transactions have been entered in accordance with resolutions of the board of directors
(b) To determine whether the owners' equity account transactions are complete and properly recorded
(c) To determine whether the owners' equity balances are properly presented and disclosed
(d) To determine whether the retained earnings account is accurately disclosed accurately in the financial statements
(e) None

CHAPTER 19

The Integrated Audit Process

19.1 General

Section 404 of the Sarbanes-Oxley Act requires that the management ensure that a permanent and adequate system of internal control of processing and reporting financial statements exists within the entity. The PCAOB goes on to require that the external auditor performs two distinct audits for publicly traded companies: (i) the audit of internal control over financial reporting, and (ii) the audit of financial statements. In these audits, the auditor may either issue separate reports on financial statements and internal control over financial statements (ICFR) or issue a combined report.

19.2 Audit of Internal Control Over Financial Reporting (ICFR)

The auditor's objective in an audit of internal control over financial reporting is to express an opinion on the effectiveness of the company's internal control over financial reporting. That is, the auditor has to opine whether the financial statements of any given entity submitted to his review were prepared in accordance with the required financial

PCAOB Standard No. 5.

F. I. Lessambo, *Auditing, Assurance Services, and Forensics*,
https://doi.org/10.1007/978-3-319-90521-1_19

framework. In the United States, it is generally the GAAP for publicly held corporations.[1] The PCAOB requires that, the auditor plan and perform the audit to obtain appropriate evidence that is sufficient to obtain reasonable assurance about whether material weaknesses exist as of the date specified in management's assessment. A material weakness in internal control over financial reporting may exist even when financial statements are not materially misstated. As for the audit of financial statements, the PCAOB also requires that the audit of ICFR be conducted by an independent auditor with due care and professional skepticism.

The auditor should use the same suitable, recognized control framework to perform his or her audit of internal control over financial reporting as management uses for its annual evaluation of the effectiveness of the company's internal control over financial reporting. In an integrated audit of internal control over financial reporting and the financial statements, the auditor should design his or her testing of controls to accomplish the objectives of both audits simultaneously.

- To obtain sufficient evidence to support the auditor's opinion on internal control over financial reporting as of year-end, and
- To obtain sufficient evidence to support the auditor's control risk assessments for purposes of the audit of financial statements.

If the auditor decides it is appropriate to serve as the principal auditor of the financial statements, then that auditor also should be the principal auditor of the company's internal control over financial reporting. This relationship results from the requirement that an audit of the financial statements must be performed to audit internal control over financial reporting. That is, only the principal auditor of the financial statements can be the principal auditor of internal control over financial reporting. In this circumstance, the principal auditor of the financial statements must participate sufficiently in the audit of internal control over financial reporting to provide a basis for serving as the principal auditor of internal control over financial reporting.

[1] The GAAP do not apply to local, state, or federal government entities.

19.2.1 Planning the Audit

The auditor should properly plan the audit of internal control over financial reporting and properly supervise the engagement team members. When planning an integrated audit, the auditor should evaluate whether the following matters are important to the company's financial statements and internal control over financial reporting and, if so, how they will affect the auditor's procedures:

- Knowledge of the company's internal control over financial reporting obtained during other engagements performed by the auditor;
- Matters affecting the industry in which the company operates, such as financial reporting practices, economic conditions, laws and regulations, and technological changes;
- Matters relating to the company's business, including its organization, operating characteristics, and capital structure;
- The extent of recent changes, if any, in the company, its operations, or its internal control over financial reporting;
- The auditor's preliminary judgments about materiality, risk, and other factors relating to the determination of material weaknesses;
- Control deficiencies previously communicated to the audit committee or management;
- Legal or regulatory matters of which the company is aware;
- The type and extent of available evidence related to the effectiveness of the company's internal control over financial reporting;
- Preliminary judgments about the effectiveness of internal control over financial reporting;
- Public information about the company relevant to the evaluation of the likelihood of material financial statement misstatements and the effectiveness of the company's internal control over financial reporting;
- Knowledge about risks related to the company evaluated as part of the auditor's client acceptance and retention evaluation; and
- The relative complexity of the company's operations.

In planning an audit of the ICFR, the auditor shall consider: (i) the role of risk assessment, (ii) addressing the risk of fraud, and (iii) using the work of others.

19.2.1.1 Role of Risk Assessment

Risk assessment underlies the entire audit process of the ICFR, including the determination of significant accounts and disclosures and relevant assertions, the selection of controls to test, and the determination of the evidence necessary for a given control. The complexity of the organization, business unit, or process, plays an important role in the auditor's risk assessment and the determination of the necessary procedures. A direct relationship exists between the degree of risk that a material weakness could exist in a particular area of the company's internal control over financial reporting and the amount of audit attention that should be devoted to that area. The auditor should focus more of his or her attention on the areas of highest risk. On the other hand, it is not necessary to test controls that, even if deficient, would not present a reasonable possibility of material misstatement to the financial statements.

The size and complexity of the company also might affect the risks of misstatement and the controls necessary to address those risks.

19.2.1.2 Addressing the Risk of Fraud

When planning and performing the audit of internal control over financial reporting, the auditor takes into account the results of his or her fraud risk assessment. As part of identifying and testing entity-level controls, and selecting other controls to test, the auditor evaluates whether the company's controls sufficiently address identified risks of material misstatement due to fraud and controls intended to address the risk of management override of other controls. Controls that might address these risks include:

- Controls over significant, unusual transactions, particularly those that result in late or unusual journal entries;
- Controls over journal entries and adjustments made in the period-end financial reporting process;
- Controls over related party transactions;
- Controls related to significant management estimates; and
- Controls that mitigate incentives for, and pressures on, management to falsify or inappropriately manage financial results.

19.2.1.3 Using the Work of Others

For purposes of the audit of internal control, however, the auditor may use the work performed by, or receive direct assistance from, internal auditors, company personnel (in addition to internal auditors), and third parties working under the direction of management or the audit committee that provides evidence about the effectiveness of internal control over financial reporting. The auditor should evaluate the extent to which he or she will use the work of others to reduce the work the auditor might otherwise perform himself or herself. The auditor should assess the competence and objectivity of the persons whose work the auditor plans to use to determine the extent to which the auditor may use their work. The higher the degree of competence[2] and objectivity,[3] the greater use the auditor may make of the work.

The extent to which the auditor may use the work of others in an audit of internal control also depends on the risk associated with the control being tested. As the risk associated with a control increases, the need for the auditor to perform his or her own work on the control increases.

In planning the audit of internal control over financial reporting, the auditor should use the same materiality considerations he or she would use in planning the audit of the company's annual financial statements.

19.2.2 The Auditor's Approach

The auditor should use a top-down approach, which begins at the financial statement level and with the auditor's understanding of the overall risks to internal control over financial reporting. Put differently, the auditor focuses on entity-level controls and works down to significant accounts and disclosures and their relevant assertions, understands the likely source of misstatements, selects controls tests.

[2]Competence means the attainment and maintenance of a level of understanding and knowledge that enables that person to perform ably the tasks assigned to them. To assess competence, the auditor should evaluate factors about the person's qualifications and ability to perform the work the auditor plans to use.

[3]Objectivity means the ability to perform those tasks impartially and with intellectual honesty. To assess objectivity, the auditor should evaluate whether factors are present that either inhibit or promote a person's ability to perform with the necessary degree of objectivity the work the auditor plans to use.

19.2.2.1 Identifying Entity-Level Controls

The auditor must test those entity-level controls that are important to the auditor's conclusion about whether the company has effective internal control over financial reporting. The auditor's evaluation of entity-level controls can result in increasing or decreasing the testing that the auditor otherwise would have performed on other controls. Entity-level controls include:

- Controls related to the control environment;
- Controls over management override;
- The company's risk assessment process;
- Centralized processing and controls, including shared service environments;
- Controls to monitor results of operations;
- Controls to monitor other controls, including activities of the internal audit function, the audit committee, and self-assessment programs;
- Controls over the period-end financial reporting process; and
- Policies that address significant business control and risk management practices.

The seven control environment factors include:

1. Integrity and Ethical Values
2. Commitment to Competence
3. Management's Philosophy and Operating Style
4. Organizational Structure
5. Assignment of Authority and Responsibility
6. Financial Reporting Competencies
7. Human Resource Policies and Practices

The entity-level control consists of (i) control environment and (ii) period-end financial reporting process.

i. Control Environment

   The auditor must evaluate the control environment at the company. As part of evaluating the control environment, the auditor should assess:

- Whether management's philosophy and operating style promote effective internal control over financial reporting;
- Whether sound integrity and ethical values, particularly of top management, are developed and understood; and
- Whether the Board or audit committee understands and exercises oversight responsibility over financial reporting and internal control.

ii. Period-end Financial Reporting Process

The auditor must evaluate the period-end financial reporting process.[4] The period-end financial reporting process includes the following:

- Procedures used to enter transaction totals into the general ledger;
- Procedures related to the selection and application of accounting policies;
- Procedures used to initiate, authorize, record, and process journal entries in the general ledger;
- Procedures used to record recurring and nonrecurring adjustments to the annual and quarterly financial statements; and
- Procedures for preparing annual and quarterly financial statements and related disclosures.
- The nature and extent of the oversight of the process by management, the board of directors, and the audit committee.

19.2.2.2 Identifying Significant Accounts and Disclosures and Their Relevant Assertions

The auditor should identify significant accounts and disclosures and their relevant assertions. Relevant assertions are those financial statement assertions that have a reasonable possibility of containing a misstatement

[4] As part of evaluating the period-end financial reporting process, the auditor should assess:

- Inputs, procedures performed, and outputs of the processes the company uses to produce its annual and quarterly financial statements;
- The extent of information technology ("IT") involvement in the period-end financial reporting process;
- Who participates in management;
- The locations involved in the period-end financial reporting process;
- The types of adjusting and consolidating entries; and

that would cause the financial statements to be materially misstated. To identify significant accounts and disclosures and their relevant assertions, the auditor should evaluate the qualitative and quantitative risk factors[5] related to the financial statement line items and disclosures.

As part of identifying significant accounts and disclosures and their relevant assertions, the auditor also should determine the likely sources of potential misstatements that would cause the financial statements to be materially misstated. The auditor might determine the likely sources of potential misstatements by asking himself or herself "what could go wrong?" within a given significant account or disclosure.

When a company has multiple locations or business units, the auditor should identify significant accounts and disclosures and their relevant assertions based on the consolidated financial statements. Having made those determinations, the auditor should then comply with proper guidelines under PCAOB No. 5.

19.2.2.3 Understanding Likely Sources of Misstatement

At this stage, the auditor should achieve the following objectives:

- Understand the flow of transactions related to the relevant assertions, including how these transactions are initiated, authorized, processed, and recorded;
- Verify that the auditor has identified the points within the company's processes at which a misstatement—including a misstatement

[5] Risk factors relevant to the identification of significant accounts and disclosures and their relevant assertions include:

- Size and composition of the account;
- Susceptibility to misstatement due to errors or fraud;
- Volume of activity, complexity, and homogeneity of the individual transactions processed through the account or reflected in the disclosure;
- Nature of the account or disclosure;
- Accounting and reporting complexities associated with the account or disclosure;
- Exposure to losses in the account;
- Possibility of significant contingent liabilities arising from the activities reflected in the account or disclosure;
- Existence of related party transactions in the account; and
- Changes from the prior period in account or disclosure characteristics.

due to fraud—could arise that, individually or in combination with other misstatements, would be material;

- Identify the controls that management has implemented to address these potential misstatements; and
- Identify the controls that management has implemented over the prevention or timely detection of unauthorized acquisition, use, or disposition of the company's assets that could result in a material misstatement of the financial statements.

Most of the times, the auditor would perform walkthroughs' procedures. In performing a walkthrough, the auditor follows a transaction from origination through the company's processes, including information systems, until it is reflected in the company's financial records, using the same documents and information technology that company personnel use. Walkthrough procedures usually include a combination of inquiry, observation, inspection of relevant documentation, and re-performance of controls. The auditor then questions the company's personnel about their understanding of what is required by the company's prescribed procedures and controls. These probing questions, combined with the other walkthrough procedures, allow the auditor to gain a sufficient understanding of the process and to be able to identify important points at which a necessary control is missing or not designed effectively. Additionally, probing questions that go beyond a narrow focus on the single transaction used as the basis for the walkthrough allow the auditor to gain an understanding of the different types of significant transactions handled by the process.

19.2.2.4 Selecting Controls to Test

The auditor should test those controls that are important to the auditor's conclusion about whether the company's controls sufficiently address the assessed risk of misstatement to each relevant assertion.

The decision as to whether a control should be selected for testing depends on which controls, individually or in combination, sufficiently address the assessed risk of misstatement to a given relevant assertion rather than on how the control is labeled (e.g., entity-level control, transaction-level control, control activity, monitoring control, preventive control, detective control).

Once the first step is complete, the auditor would proceed with testing controls.

19.2.3 Testing Controls

Testing controls include both (i) testing of the design effectiveness, (ii) testing of operating effectiveness, and (iii) the relationship of risk to evidence to be obtained.

(i) Testing Design Effectiveness
The auditor should test the design effectiveness of controls by determining whether the company's controls, if they are operated as prescribed by persons possessing the necessary authority and competence to perform the control effectively, satisfy the company's control objectives and can effectively prevent or detect errors or fraud that could result in material misstatements in the financial statements.
Procedures the auditor performs to test design effectiveness include a mix of inquiry of appropriate personnel, observation of the company's operations, and inspection of relevant documentation. Walkthroughs that include these procedures ordinarily are sufficient to evaluate design effectiveness.

(ii) Testing Operating Effectiveness
The auditor should test the operating effectiveness of a control by determining whether the control is operating as designed and whether the person performing the control possesses the necessary authority and competence to perform the control effectively.
Procedures the auditor performs to test operating effectiveness include a mix of inquiry of appropriate personnel, observation of the company's operations, inspection of relevant documentation, and re-performance of the control.

(iii) Relationship of Risk to the Evidence to be obtained
For each control selected for testing, the evidence necessary to persuade the auditor that the control is effective depends upon the risk associated with the control. The risk associated with a control consists of the risk that the control might not be effective and, if not effective, the risk that a material weakness would result. As the risk associated with the control being tested increases, the evidence that the auditor should obtain also increases.

Factors that affect the risk associated with a control include:

- The nature and materiality of misstatements that the control is intended to prevent or detect;
- The inherent risk associated with the related account(s) and assertion(s);
- Whether there have been changes in the volume or nature of transactions that might adversely affect control design or operating effectiveness;
- Whether the account has a history of errors;
- The effectiveness of entity-level controls especially controls that monitor other controls;
- The nature of the control and the frequency with which it operates;
- The degree to which the control relies on the effectiveness of other controls (e.g., the control environment or information technology general controls);
- The competence of the personnel who perform the control or monitor its performance and whether there have been changes in key personnel who perform the control or monitor its performance;
- Whether the control relies on performance by an individual or is automated (i.e., an automated control would generally be expected to be lower risk if relevant information technology general controls are effective); and
- The complexity of the control and the significance of the judgments that must be made in connection with its operation.

19.2.3.1 Nature of Tests of Controls

Some types of tests, by their nature, produce greater evidence of the effectiveness of controls than other tests. The following tests that the auditor might perform are presented in order of the evidence that they ordinarily would produce, from least to most: inquiry, observation, inspection of relevant documentation, and re-performance of a control. The nature of the tests of effectiveness that will provide appropriate evidence depends, to a large degree, on the nature of the control to be tested, including whether the operation of the control results in documentary evidence of its operation. Documentary evidence of the operation of some controls, such as management's philosophy and operating style, might not exist.

(i) Timing of Tests of Controls
Testing controls over a greater period of time provides more evidence of the effectiveness of controls than testing over a shorter period of time. Further, testing performed closer to the date of management's assessment provides more evidence than testing performed earlier in the year. The auditor should balance performing the tests of controls closer to the as-of date with the need to test controls over a sufficient period of time to obtain sufficient evidence of operating effectiveness. If the auditor determines that the new controls achieve the related objectives of the control criteria and have been in effect for a sufficient period to permit the auditor to assess their design and operating effectiveness by performing tests of controls, he or she will not need to test the design and operating effectiveness of the superseded controls for purposes of expressing an opinion on internal control over financial reporting

(ii) Extent of Tests of Controls
The more extensively a control is tested, the greater the evidence obtained from that test.

(iii) Subsequent Years' Audits
In subsequent years' audits, the auditor should incorporate knowledge obtained during past audits he or she performed of the company's internal control over financial reporting into the decision-making process for determining the nature, timing, and extent of testing necessary.
Factors that affect the risk associated with a control in subsequent years' audits include the following:

- The nature, timing, and extent of procedures performed in previous audits,
- The results of the previous years' testing of the control, and
- Whether there have been changes in the control or the process in which it operates since the previous audit.

In addition, the auditor should vary the nature, timing, and extent of testing of controls from year to year to introduce unpredictability into the testing and respond to changes in circumstances. For this reason, each year the auditor might test controls at a different interim period, increase or reduce the number and types of tests performed, or change the combination of procedures used.

19.2.3.2 Evaluating Identified Deficiencies

The auditor must evaluate the severity of each control deficiency that comes to his or her attention to determine whether the deficiencies, individually or in combination, are material weaknesses as of the date of management's assessment. The severity of a deficiency does not depend on whether a misstatement actually has occurred but rather on whether there is a reasonable possibility that the company's controls will fail to prevent or detect a misstatement.

The severity of a deficiency depends on:

- Whether there is a reasonable possibility that the company's controls will fail to prevent or detect a misstatement of an account balance or disclosure; and
- The magnitude of the potential misstatement resulting from the deficiency or deficiencies.

When evaluating the severity of a deficiency, or combination of deficiencies, the auditor also should determine the level of detail and degree of assurance that would satisfy prudent officials in the conduct of their own affairs that they have reasonable assurance that transactions are recorded as necessary to permit the preparation of financial statements in conformity with generally accepted accounting principles. If the auditor determines that a deficiency, or combination of deficiencies, might prevent prudent officials in the conduct of their own affairs from concluding that they have reasonable assurance that transactions are recorded as necessary to permit the preparation of financial statements in conformity with generally accepted accounting principles, then the auditor should treat the deficiency, or combination of deficiencies, as an indicator of a material weakness.

The severity of a deficiency does not depend on whether a misstatement actually has occurred but rather on whether there is a reasonable possibility that the company's controls will fail to prevent or detect a misstatement.

i. Reasonable Possibility
   Risk factors affect whether there is a reasonable possibility that a deficiency, or a combination of deficiencies, will result in a misstatement of an account balance or disclosure. The factors include, but are not limited to, the following:

   - The nature of the financial statement accounts, disclosures, and assertions involved;
   - The susceptibility of the related asset or liability to loss or fraud;
   - The subjectivity, complexity, or extent of judgment required to determine the amount involved;
   - The interaction or relationship of the control with other controls, including whether they are interdependent or redundant;
   - The interaction of the deficiencies; and
   - The possible future consequences of the deficiency.

The evaluation of whether a control deficiency presents a reasonable possibility of misstatement can be made without quantifying the probability of occurrence as a specific percentage or range.

Multiple control deficiencies that affect the same financial statement account balance or disclosure increase the likelihood of misstatement and may, in combination, constitute a material weakness, even though such deficiencies may individually be less severe. Therefore, the auditor should determine whether individual control deficiencies that affect the same significant account or disclosure, relevant assertion, or component of internal control collectively result in a material weakness.

ii. Magnitude
   In evaluating the magnitude of the potential misstatement, the maximum amount that an account balance or total of transactions can be overstated is generally the recorded amount, while understatements could be larger. Also, in many cases, the probability of a small misstatement will be greater than the probability of a large misstatement. Factors that affect the magnitude of the misstatement that might result from a deficiency or deficiencies in controls include, but are not limited to, the following:

   - The financial statement amounts or total of transactions exposed to the deficiency; and

- The volume of activity in the account balance or class of transactions exposed to the deficiency that has occurred in the current period or that is expected in future periods.

The auditor should evaluate the effect of compensating controls when determining whether a control deficiency or combination of deficiencies is a material weakness. To have a mitigating effect, the compensating control should operate at a level of precision that would prevent or detect a misstatement that could be material.

Indicators of material weaknesses in internal control over financial reporting include:

- Identification of fraud, whether or not material, on the part of senior management;
- Restatement of previously issued financial statements to reflect the correction of a material misstatement;
- Identification by the auditor of a material misstatement of financial statements in the current period in circumstances that indicate that the misstatement would not have been detected by the company's internal control over financial reporting; and
- Ineffective oversight of the company's external financial reporting and internal control over financial reporting by the company's audit committee.

19.2.4 Wrapping-Up

At this point at time, the auditor is about to deliver his opinion, but to do so, he needs to obtain written representations from the entity's management and communicates certain matters to the management.

i. Forming an Opinion
The auditor should form an opinion on the effectiveness of internal control over financial reporting by evaluating evidence obtained from all sources, including the auditor's testing of controls, misstatements detected during the financial statement audit, and any identified control deficiencies.
After forming an opinion on the effectiveness of the company's internal control over financial reporting, the auditor should evaluate the presentation of the elements that management is required,

under the SEC's rules, to present in its annual report on internal control over financial reporting.
If the auditor determines that any required elements of management's annual report on internal control over financial reporting are incomplete or improperly presented.
The auditor may form an opinion on the effectiveness of internal control over financial reporting only when there have been no restrictions on the scope of the auditor's work. A scope limitation requires the auditor to disclaim an opinion or withdraw from the engagement.

ii. Obtaining Written Representations
In an audit of internal control over financial reporting, the auditor should obtain written representations from management:

(a) Acknowledging management's responsibility for establishing and maintaining effective internal control over financial reporting;
(b) Stating that management has performed an evaluation and made an assessment of the effectiveness of the company's internal control over financial reporting and specifying the control criteria;
(c) Stating that management did not use the auditor's procedures performed during the audits of internal control over financial reporting or the financial statements as part of the basis for management's assessment of the effectiveness of internal control over financial reporting;
(d) Stating management's conclusion, as set forth in its assessment, about the effectiveness of the company's internal control over financial reporting based on the control criteria as of a specified date;
(e) Stating that management has disclosed to the auditor all deficiencies in the design or operation of internal control over financial reporting identified as part of management's evaluation, including separately disclosing to the auditor all such deficiencies that it believes to be significant deficiencies or material weaknesses in internal control over financial reporting;
(f) Describing any fraud resulting in a material misstatement to the company's financial statements and any other fraud that

does not result in a material misstatement to the company's financial statements but involves senior management or management or other employees who have a significant role in the company's internal control over financial reporting;

(g) Stating whether control deficiencies identified and communicated to the audit committee during previous engagements have been resolved, and specifically identifying any that have not; and

(h) Stating whether there were, subsequent to the date being reported on, any changes in internal control over financial reporting or other factors that might significantly affect internal control over financial reporting, including any corrective actions taken by management with regard to significant deficiencies and material weaknesses.

The failure to obtain written representations from management, including management's refusal to furnish them, constitutes a limitation on the scope of the audit. Further, the auditor should evaluate the effects of management's refusal on his or her ability to rely on other representations, including those obtained in the audit of the company's financial statements.

iii. Communicating Certain Matters

The auditor must communicate, in writing, to management and the audit committee all material weaknesses identified during the audit. The written communication should be made prior to the issuance of the auditor's report on internal control over financial reporting. If the auditor concludes that the oversight of the company's external financial reporting and internal control over financial reporting by the company's audit committee is ineffective, the auditor must communicate that conclusion in writing to the board of directors. The auditor also should consider whether there are any deficiencies, or combinations of deficiencies, that have been identified during the audit that are significant deficiencies and must communicate such deficiencies, in writing, to the audit committee. The auditor also should communicate to management, in writing, all deficiencies in internal control over financial reporting (i.e., those deficiencies in internal control over financial reporting that are of a lesser magnitude than material weaknesses) identified during the audit and inform the audit committee when such a communication has been made. When making this communication, it is not necessary for the auditor to repeat information about such deficiencies that had been included in previously issued written communications, whether those communications were made by the auditor, internal auditors, or others within the organization. When auditing internal control over financial reporting, the auditor may become aware of fraud or possible illegal acts.

19.2.5 Reporting on Internal Control

After the completion of the audit, the auditor has the option to deliver a separate or combined opinion. The auditor's report on the audit of internal control over financial reporting must include the following elements:

a. A title that includes the word independent;
b. A statement that management is responsible for maintaining effective internal control over financial reporting and for assessing the effectiveness of internal control over financial reporting;
c. An identification of management's report on internal control;
d. A statement that the auditor's responsibility is to express an opinion on the company's internal control over financial reporting based on his or her audit;
e. A definition of internal control over financial;
f. A statement that the audit was conducted in accordance with the standards of the Public Company Accounting Oversight Board (United States);
g. A statement that the standards of the Public Company Accounting Oversight Board require that the auditor plan and perform the audit to obtain reasonable assurance about whether effective internal control over financial reporting was maintained in all material respects;
h. A statement that an audit includes obtaining an understanding of internal control over financial reporting, assessing the risk that a material weakness exists, testing and evaluating the design and operating effectiveness of internal control based on the assessed risk, and performing such other procedures as the auditor considered necessary in the circumstances;

i. A statement that the auditor believes the audit provides a reasonable basis for his or her opinion;
j. A paragraph stating that, because of inherent limitations, internal control over financial reporting may not prevent or detect misstatements and that projections of any evaluation of effectiveness to future periods are subject to the risk that controls may become inadequate because of changes in conditions, or that the degree of compliance with the policies or procedures may deteriorate;
k. The auditor's opinion on whether the company maintained, in all material respects, effective internal control over financial reporting as of the specified date, based on the control criteria;
l. The manual or printed signature of the auditor's firm;
m. The city and state (or city and country, in the case of non-US auditors) from which the auditor's report has been issued; and
n. The date of the audit report.

19.3 Audit of Financial Statements

The purpose of the audit of a company's financial documents is to determine whether the financial statements are recorded and reported in accordance with the applicable financial reporting framework. In the United States, the framework is ordinarily GAAP. The applicable framework corresponds to the "suitable criteria" of an attest engagement.

The auditor would then provide assurance that the financial statements, and assertions provided by company management, are complete and accurate. In the United States, the Securities and Exchange Commission (SEC) requires all companies with publicly traded stock to hire a third party to complete financial audits at least annually. Generally, a financial statement audit is completed in several steps: planning phase, sample testing, controls and transaction testing, disclosure testing, final reporting, and delivery of the auditor's opinion.

19.3.1 Planning

The auditor is required to plan the audit so that the audit can be conducted effectively. The nature and extent of planning activities that are necessary depend on the size and complexity of the company, the auditor's previous experience with the company, and changes in circumstances that occur during the audit. The auditor should develop and document an audit plan that includes a description of:

- The planned nature, timing, and extent of the risk assessment procedures;
- The planned nature, timing, and extent of tests of controls and substantive procedures; and
- Other planned audit procedures required to be performed so that the engagement complies with PCAOB standards.

The engagement partner is responsible for planning the audit and may seek assistance from appropriate engagement team members in fulfilling this responsibility. Engagement team members who assist the engagement partner with audit planning also should comply with the relevant requirements in this standard.

Planning an audit includes establishing the overall audit strategy for the engagement and developing an audit plan, which includes, in particular, planned risk assessment procedures and planned responses to the risks of material misstatement. At the inception of the engagement, the auditor should perform certain preliminary activities:

- Perform procedures regarding the continuance of the client relationship and the specific audit engagement,
- Determine compliance with independence and ethics requirements, and
- Establish an understanding with the client regarding the services to be performed on the engagement.

The auditor should establish an overall audit strategy that sets the scope, timing, and direction of the audit and guides the development of the audit plan. In establishing the overall audit strategy, the auditor should take into account:

- The reporting objectives of the engagement and the nature of the communications required by PCAOB standards,
- The factors that are significant in directing the activities of the engagement team,

- The results of preliminary engagement activities and the auditor's evaluation of the important matters in accordance with paragraph 7 of this standard, and
- The nature, timing, and extent of resources necessary to perform the engagement.

The auditor shall be able to modify the overall audit strategy and the audit plan if necessary based upon the circumstances. Finally, at the planning, the auditor would have to assess whether there is a need for person(s) with specialized skills (i.e., Lawyer, tax expert).

19.3.2 Sample Testing

The auditor never reviews the full transactions that occurred during the Fiscal Year under audit. He often or always reviews and tests a small sample of the company's financial transactions and reporting procedures. The aim is to determine areas of audit risks. Audit risk includes both uncertainties due to sampling and uncertainties due to factors other than sampling. If the auditor finds insufficient controls in place when reviewing policies and procedures, this also creates audit risk. The financial statement audit consists of testing of a large portion of financial transactions in the controls and testing phase. This step makes up the bulk of the financial statement audit. The auditor places special emphasis on those transactions that created audit risk during the sample testing phase. The auditor reviews all documentation, as well as authorization and approval of the financial transactions.

Audit sampling is the application of an audit procedure to less than 100% of the items within an account balance or class of transactions for the purpose of evaluating some characteristic of the balance or class. The auditor often is aware of account balances and transactions that may be more likely to contain misstatements. There are two general approaches to audit sampling: (i) non-statistical and (ii) statistical.

Statistical sampling helps the auditor (a) to design an efficient sample, (b) to measure the sufficiency of the audit evidence obtained, and (c) to evaluate the sample results. By using statistical theory, the auditor can quantify sampling risk to assist himself in limiting it to a level he considers acceptable. However, statistical sampling involves additional costs of training auditors, designing individual samples to meet the statistical requirements, and selecting the items to be examined. As neither non-statistical nor statistical sampling can provide sufficient audit evidence, the auditor chooses between them after considering their relative cost and effectiveness in the circumstances In both approaches the auditor must use his (her) professional judgment in planning, performing, and evaluating a sample and in relating the audit evidence produced by the sample to other audit evidence when forming a conclusion about the related account balance or class of transactions. Sample items should be selected in such a way that the sample can be expected to be representative of the population. That is, all items in the population should have an opportunity to be selected.

The sufficiency of audit evidence is related to the design and size of an audit sample, among other factors. The size of a sample necessary to provide sufficient audit evidence depends on both the objectives and the efficiency of the sample. Stricto-sensu, the sample evaluation relates only to the likelihood that existing monetary misstatements or deviations from prescribed controls are proportionately included in the sample, not to the auditor's treatment of such items. Given the fact that less than 100% of the entity audited transactions/accounts are audited, there remains some risk referred to as "sampling risk" when the audit procedures—substantive tests of details, and/or tests of controls are applied to the sample, or for both (dual-purpose sample).

19.3.2.1 Sample Risk in Substantive Tests of Details

With respect to substantive tests of details the auditor shall be concerned with two aspects of sampling risk:

- The risk of incorrect acceptance. The risk that the sample supports the conclusion that the recorded account balance is not materially misstated when, in fact, it is materially misstated.
- The risk of incorrect rejection. The risk that the sample supports the conclusion that the recorded account balance is materially misstated while this is not the case.

When planning a particular sample for a substantive test of details, the auditor should consider:

- The relationship of the sample to the relevant audit;
- Preliminary judgments about materiality levels;

- The auditor's allowable risk of incorrect acceptance;
- Characteristics of the population, that is, the items comprising the account balance or class of transactions of interest.

Moreover, the auditor should consider the specific audit objective to be achieved and should determine that the audit procedure, or combination of procedures, to be applied will achieve that objective. Evaluation in monetary terms of the results of a sample for a test of details contributes directly to the auditor's purpose since such an evaluation can be related to the auditor's judgment of the monetary amount of misstatements that would be material for the test. When planning a sample for a test of details, the auditor should consider how much monetary misstatement in the related account balance or class of transactions may exist when combined with misstatements that may be found in other tests without causing the financial statements to be materially misstated. This maximum monetary misstatement that the auditor is willing to accept for the balance or class is called tolerable misstatement. The auditor uses his judgment to determine which items, if any, in an account balance or class of transactions should be individually examined and which items, if any, should be subject to sampling. The auditor should examine those items for which, in his judgment, acceptance of some sampling risk is not justified. He may be able to reduce the required sample size by separating items subject to sampling into relatively homogeneous groups on the basis of some characteristic related to the specific audit objective.

The auditor's treatment of unexamined items will depend on their effect on his or her evaluation of the sample. If the auditor's evaluation of the sample results would not be altered by considering those unexamined items to be misstated, it is not necessary to examine the items. However, if considering those unexamined items to be misstated would lead to a conclusion that the balance or class contains material misstatement, the auditor should consider alternative audit procedures that would provide sufficient appropriate audit evidence to form a conclusion. Then, the auditor projects the misstatement results of the sample to the items from which the sample was selected. There are several acceptable ways to project misstatements from a sample. For example, an auditor may have selected a sample of every twentieth item (50 items) from a population containing one thousand items. If he discovered overstatements of \$3000 in that sample, the auditor could project a \$60,000 overstatement by dividing the amount of misstatement in the sample by the fraction of total items from the population included in the sample. The auditor should add that projection to the misstatements discovered in any items examined 100%. The total projected misstatement should be compared with the tolerable misstatement for the account balance or class of transactions, and appropriate consideration should be given to sampling risk.

19.3.2.2 Sample Risk in Tests of Controls

The auditor shall also be concerned with two aspects of sampling risk in performing tests of controls when sampling is used:

- The risk of assessing control risk too low is the risk that the assessed level of control risk based on the sample is less than the true operating effectiveness of the control.
- The risk of assessing control risk too high is the risk that the assessed level of control risk based on the sample is greater than the true operating effectiveness of the control.

It should be noted that sampling, generally, is not applicable to analyses of controls for determining the appropriate segregation of duties or other analyses that do not examine documentary evidence of performance. In addition, sampling may not apply to tests of certain documented controls or to analyses of the effectiveness of security and access controls. Sampling also may not apply to some tests directed toward obtaining audit evidence about the operation of the control environment or the accounting system, for example, inquiry or observation of explanation of variances from budgets when the auditor does not desire to estimate the rate of deviation from the prescribed control, or when examining the actions of those charged with governance11 for assessing their effectiveness. However, when sampling does apply for tests of controls, the auditor shall consider:

- The relationship of the sample to the objective of the test of controls;
- The maximum rate of deviations from prescribed controls that would support his planned assessed level of control risk;
- The auditor's allowable risk of assessing control risk too low;
- Characteristics of the population, that is, the items comprising the account balance or class of transactions of interest.

When designing samples for tests of controls the auditor ordinarily should plan to evaluate operating effectiveness in terms of deviations from prescribed controls, as to either the rate of such deviations or the monetary amount of the related transactions.

The auditor should determine the maximum rate of deviations from the prescribed control that he would be willing to accept without altering his planned assessed level of control risk. This is the tolerable rate. In determining the tolerable rate, the auditor should consider (a) the planned assessed level of control risk, and (b) the degree of assurance desired by the audit evidence in the sample. In assessing the tolerable rate of deviations, the auditor should consider that, while deviations from pertinent controls increase the risk of material misstatements in the accounting records, such deviations do not necessarily result in misstatements.

In order to determine the number of items to be selected for a particular sample for a test of controls, the auditor should consider the tolerable rate of deviation from the controls being tested, the likely rate of deviations, and the allowable risk of assessing control risk too low. The deviation rate in the sample is the auditor's best estimate of the deviation rate in the population from which it was selected. If the estimated deviation rate is less than the tolerable rate for the population, the auditor should consider the risk that such a result might be obtained even though the true deviation rate for the population exceeds the tolerable rate for the population. If the auditor is not able to apply the planned audit procedures or appropriate alternative procedures to selected items, he should consider the reasons for this limitation, and he should ordinarily consider those selected items to be deviations from the prescribed policy or procedure for the purpose of evaluating the sample.

19.3.2.3 Dual-Purpose Sample

An auditor planning to use a dual-purpose sample would have made a preliminary assessment that there is an acceptably low risk that the rate of deviations from the prescribed control in the population exceeds the tolerable rate. For example, an auditor designing a test of control over entries in the voucher register may plan a related substantive procedure at a risk level that anticipates a particular assessed level of control risk. The size of a sample designed for dual purposes should be the larger of the samples that would otherwise have been designed for the two separate purposes. In evaluating such tests, deviations from the prescribed control and monetary misstatements should be evaluated separately using the risk levels applicable for the respective purposes.

19.3.3 Controls and Transactions Testing

Auditors also review the company's segregation of duties during this phase. Segregation of duties helps create a system of checks and balances within the company. For example, is the person submitting an invoice for payment the same person who approves the invoice and sends out the payment?

It is also the auditor's responsibility to review company management's disclosures in financial statements. Testing is required to support the financial assertions in their disclosures. The auditor reviews the documentation supplied by the company to support any claims made in the financial statement.

19.3.4 Disclosure of Testing

Once the testing and review phases are complete, the auditor can finalize the financial statement audit. The auditor summarizes the findings in a written report that is delivered to company management.

19.3.5 Issuance of the Audit Report

Finally, the auditor issues an opinion based on its final report. By and large, four types of opinions are issued:

19.3.5.1 An Unqualified Opinion

An unqualified opinion signifies that the financial statements conform to the entity financial framework (i.e., GAAP). Since 2012, the auditor can insert additional information within an unqualified opinion referred to as (i) emphasis of matter or (ii) other emphasis.

- Emphasis-of-Matter Paragraph

  The auditor would add an emphasis of matter to draw user's attention to a matter or matters presented or disclosed in the financial statements that are of such importance that they are fundamental to user's understanding of the financial statements (emphasis-of-matter paragraph). Circumstances when the auditor may consider it necessary to include an emphasis-of-matter paragraph include, inter alia:

- An uncertainty relating to the future outcome of unusually important litigation or regulatory action;
- A major catastrophe that has had, or continues to have, a significant effect on the entity's financial position;
- Significant transactions with related parties;
- Unusually important subsequent events.

- Other-Matter Paragraph

  The auditor would add in its unqualified opinion a paragraph referred to as "other-matter" to draw user's attention to any matter or matters other than those presented or disclosed in the financial statements that are relevant to user's understanding of the audit, the auditor's responsibilities, or the auditor's report (other-matter paragraph).[6]
  In the rare circumstance when the auditor is unable to withdraw from an engagement even though the possible effect of an inability to obtain sufficient appropriate audit evidence due to a limitation on the scope of the audit imposed by management is pervasive, the auditor may consider it necessary to include any other-matter paragraph in the auditor's report to explain why it is not possible for the auditor to withdraw from the engagement.

19.3.5.2 A Qualified Opinion

An auditor can issue a qualified opinion if there has been some limitation on the scope of the audit, or if during the audit, he finds a deviation from the financial framework. The limitation though significant was not so significant to overshadow an overall opinion on the financial statements.[7]

[6] SAS no. 122. Effective for audits of financial statements for periods ending on or after December 15, 2012.

[7] Ray Whittington (2012): *Principles of Auditing & Other Assurances Services*, McGraw Hill, 18 Edition, p. 47.

19.3.5.3 An Adverse Opinion

An adverse opinion may be issued if the auditor finds material misstatements, or if procedures do not follow GAAP standards. Put differently, the auditor finds that the financial statements are not fairly presented. The opinion is usually published with the company's financial numbers in its annual reports.

19.3.5.4 A Disclaimer of Opinion

If the auditor cannot issue a financial statement audit opinion it may issue a disclaimer. This disclaimer will explain why an opinion could not be delivered. Reasons for this can include that the scope of the audit was limited, or that a material conflict of interest exists. The disclaimer may also state that the auditor questions the company's financial strength and ability to continue to do business.

19.4 The Ongoing Concern Report[8]

Continuation of an entity as a going concern is assumed in financial reporting in the absence of significant information to the contrary.[9] The auditor has a responsibility to evaluate whether there is substantial doubt about the entity's ability to continue as a going concern for a reasonable period of time, not to exceed one year beyond the date of the financial statements being audited. The auditor's evaluation is based on his or her knowledge of relevant conditions and events that exist at or have occurred prior to the date of the auditor's report. Usually, the auditor comes across these conditions or events while performing auditing procedures over financial statements submitted to him by the management of the firm. It is not necessary to design audit procedures solely to identify conditions and events that, when considered in the aggregate, indicate there could be substantial doubt about the entity's ability to continue as a going concern for a reasonable period of time. The results of auditing procedures designed and performed to achieve other audit objectives should be sufficient for that purpose. It should also be noted that substantial doubt about the entity's ability to continue as a going concern

[8]Source: SAS no. 59; SAS no. 64; SAS no. 77; SAS no. 96; SAS no. 113; SAS no. 114.

[9]AU Section 341 does not apply to an audit of financial statements based on the assumption of liquidation.

for a reasonable period of time that arose in the current period does not imply that a basis for such doubt existed in the prior period and, therefore, should not affect the auditor's report on the financial statements of the prior period that are presented on a comparative basis. The auditor evaluates whether there is substantial doubt about the entity's ability to continue as a going concern for a reasonable period of time.

If the results of his procedures performed in planning, gathering audit evidence relative to the various audit objectives, the auditor identify conditions and events that, when considered in the aggregate, indicate a substantial doubt about the entity's ability to continue as a going concern for a reasonable period of time, the auditor shall (1) require and obtain information about management's plans that are intended to mitigate the effect of such conditions or events, and (2) assess the likelihood that such plans can be effectively implemented.

The auditor's considerations relating to management plans may include the following:

- Plans to dispose of assets
  - Restrictions on disposal of assets, such as covenants limiting such transactions in loan or similar agreements or encumbrances against assets.
  - Apparent marketability of assets that management plans to sell.
  - Possible direct or indirect effects of disposal of assets.
- Plans to borrow money or restructure debt
  - Availability of debt financing, including existing or committed credit arrangements, such as lines of credit or arrangements for factoring receivables or sale-leaseback of assets.
  - Existing or committed arrangements to restructure or subordinate debt or to guarantee loans to the entity.
  - Possible effects on management's borrowing plans of existing restrictions on additional borrowing or the sufficiency of available collateral.
- Plans to reduce or delay expenditures
  - Apparent feasibility of plans to reduce overhead or administrative expenditures, to postpone maintenance or research and development projects, or to lease rather than purchase assets.

  - Possible direct or indirect effects of reduced or delayed expenditures.
- Plans to increase ownership equity
  - Apparent feasibility of plans to increase ownership equity, including existing or committed arrangements to raise additional capital.
  - Existing or committed arrangements to reduce current dividend requirements or to accelerate cash distributions from affiliates or other investors.

When, after considering management's plans, the auditor concludes there is substantial doubt about the entity's ability to continue as a going concern for a reasonable period of time, the auditor should consider the possible effects on the financial statements and the adequacy of the related disclosure. Some of the information that might be disclosed includes:

- Pertinent conditions and events giving rise to the assessment of substantial doubt about the entity's ability to continue as a going concern for a reasonable period of time.
- The possible effects of such conditions and events.
- Management's evaluation of the significance of those conditions and events and any mitigating factors.
- Possible discontinuance of operations.
- Management's plans (including relevant prospective financial information).
- Information about the recoverability or classification of recorded asset amounts or the amounts or classification of liabilities.

Practice

Question 1

Frazier LLC is an audit firm. In 2017, Frazier audited the financial statements of Charlie Corp. (FY 2017). At the closing of the audit, two issues remained pending: (i) Charlie Corp. has changed its inventory method in the midst of the fiscal year, and (ii) the management of Charlie Corp. refused to disclose the method used to value their financial investments. Under these circumstances, what type of audit opinion shall Frazier LLC express?

(a) A qualified opinion with an Emphasis of Matter paragraph
(b) An unqualified opinion
(c) A disclaimer
(d) An unqualified opinion with an Emphasis of Matter paragraph
Answer

Question 2

Soriano LLP is an audit firm based in Connecticut. Soriano has been hired to perform external audit for Rigolo Inc. At the closing of the audit, Soriano LLP found that there is a material inconsistency in the MD&A attached to the audited financial statements. The financial statements do not contain any mistake or misstatement. If the auditor concludes that the financial statements do not require revision, but requires that Rigolo Inc. eliminate the inconsistent paragraph in the MD&A. Rigolo Inc. refused do so. Under these circumstances, the auditor may:

(a) Issue a qualified opinion after discussing the matter with the board of directors of Rigolo Inc.
(b) Issue an unqualified opinion since the other information is not part of the audited financial statements
(c) Revise the auditor's report to include an emphasis of matter paragraph
(d) Issue an unqualified opinion

Question 3

When the auditor includes an emphasis-of-matter paragraph in the auditor's report, the auditor should do the following, except:

(a) Include it immediately after the opinion paragraph in the auditor's report
(b) Use the heading "Emphasis of Matter" or other appropriate heading
(c) Include in the paragraph a clear reference to the matter being emphasized and to where relevant disclosures that fully describe the matter can be found in the financial statements

(d) Indicate that the auditor's opinion is not modified with respect to the matter emphasized
(e) Add it as a footnote to its core opinion

Question 4

(a) The auditor can only add an "Emphasis of Matter Paragraph" if:
(b) The matter has been appropriately presented or disclosed in the financial statements
(c) In the auditor's professional judgment, the matter is fundamental to users' understanding of the financial statements
(d) The auditor has obtained sufficient appropriate audit evidence that the matter is not materially misstated in the financial statements
(e) The matter has not been appropriately presented or disclosed in the financial statements

Question 5

The following are circumstances when the auditor may consider it necessary to include an emphasis-of-matter paragraph, except:

(a) An uncertainty relating to the future outcome of unusually important litigation or regulatory action
(b) A major catastrophe that has had, or continues to have, a significant effect on the entity's financial position
(c) Significant transactions with related parties
(d) Unusually important subsequent events
(e) None

Question 6

If the auditor considers it necessary to communicate a matter other than those that are presented or disclosed in the financial statements, the auditor should:

(a) The auditor should do so in a paragraph in his/her report with the heading "Other Matter" or other appropriate heading
(b) The auditor should include this paragraph immediately after the opinion paragraph and any emphasis-of-matter paragraph

(c) The auditor should include this paragraph elsewhere in the auditor's report if the content of the other-matter paragraph is relevant to the "Other Reporting Responsibilities" section
(d) The auditor should include it in the management report of audit

Question 7

The content of the other-matter paragraph does not include the following information, except:

(a) Information required to be presented and disclosed in the financial statements
(b) Information that the auditor is prohibited from providing by law, regulation, or other professional standards
(c) Confidential information received through the audit process
(d) Information required to be provided by management

Question 8

The auditor's evaluation about the entity's ability to continue as a going concern for a reasonable period of time, not to exceed one year beyond the date of the financial statements being audited is based on:

(a) The auditor's knowledge of relevant conditions and events that exist at or have occurred prior to the date of the auditor's report
(b) The auditor information obtained from the application of auditing procedures planned and performed to achieve audit objectives that are related to management's assertions embodied in the financial statements being audited
(c) The management assertions concerning its ability to maintain the firm for a foreseeable period of time
(d) The auditor conclusion after assessing the management assertions that there is a substantial doubt about the entity's ability to continue as a going concern for a reasonable period of time

Question 9

The following are factors that an auditor should consider in reaching the conclusion as to the ability of an entity to continue as a going concern, except:

(a) Negative trends
(b) Default on loan or similar agreements
(c) Substantial dependence on the success of a particular project
(d) Legal proceedings, legislation, or similar matters that might jeopardize an entity's ability to operate
(e) None

CHAPTER 20

Audits of Group Financial Statements

20.1 General

Audit of Group Financial Statements includes the financial information of more than one component. A component is defined as an entity or business activity for which group or component management prepares financial information that is required by the applicable financial reporting framework to be included in the group financial statements. The concept of component includes a subsidiary, a division, an account balance or an investment accounted for under the equity method of accounting.

Components are classified as either not significant, or significant. A component is deemed significant due to either its individual financial significance to the group, or because it is likely to include significant risks of material misstatement of the group financial statements due to its specific nature or circumstances.

A component auditor may be required by law or regulation or may have been engaged by component management for another reason to express an audit opinion on the financial statements of a component. The group engagement partner is responsible for the direction, supervision, and performance of the group audit engagement. To that end, the group engagement partner is required to be satisfied that those performing the group audit engagement, including component auditors,

AU-C Section 600.

F. I. Lessambo, *Auditing, Assurance Services, and Forensics*,
https://doi.org/10.1007/978-3-319-90521-1_20

collectively possess the appropriate competence and capabilities.[1] The group engagement partner is responsible for deciding, individually for each component, to either:

- assume responsibility for, and thus be required to be involved in, the work of a component auditor, insofar as that work relates to the expression of an opinion on the group financial statements, or
- not assume responsibility for, and accordingly make reference to, the audit of a component auditor in the auditor's report on the group financial statements.

20.2 Audit Strategy and Audit Plan

The group engagement team should establish an overall group audit strategy and develop a group audit plan. In developing the group audit plan, the group engagement team should assess the extent to which the group engagement team will use the work of component auditors and whether the auditor's report on the group financial statements will make reference to the audit of a component auditor. The group engagement partner should review and approve the overall group audit strategy and group audit plan. In a group audit, detection risk includes the risk that a component auditor may not detect a misstatement in the financial information of a component that could cause a material misstatement of the group financial statements and the risk that the group engagement team may not detect this misstatement. The group engagement partner should determine whether sufficient appropriate audit evidence can reasonably be expected to be obtained regarding the consolidation process and the financial information of the components on which to base the group audit opinion. To that end, the group engagement team should obtain an understanding of the group, its components, and their environments that is sufficient to identify components that are likely to be significant components. The group engagement partner should evaluate whether the group engagement team will be able to obtain sufficient appropriate audit evidence through the group engagement team's work or use of the work of component auditors to act as the auditor of the group financial statements and report as such on the group financial statements.

[1] Section 220, Quality, Control for an Engagement Conducted in Accordance with the Generally Accepted Auditing Standards.

In some circumstances, the group engagement partner may conclude that it will not be possible, due to restrictions imposed by group management, for the group engagement team to obtain sufficient appropriate audit evidence.

The group engagement team should:

a. Enhance its understanding of the group, its components, and their environments, including group-wide controls, obtained during the acceptance or continuance stage;
b. Obtain an understanding of the consolidation process, including the instructions issued by group management to components.

20.2.1 The Group Engagement Team Assuming Responsibility

In the case of an audit of the financial information of a component in which the auditor of the group financial statements is assuming responsibility for the component auditor's work, the group engagement team should evaluate the appropriateness of performance materiality at the component level. The group engagement team should determine the type of work to be performed by the group engagement team or by component auditors on its behalf on the financial information of the components. The group engagement team also should determine the nature, timing, and extent of its involvement in the work of component auditors. For a component that is significant due to its individual financial significance to the group, the group engagement team, or a component auditor on its behalf, should perform an audit of the financial information of the component, adapted as necessary to meet the needs of the group engagement team, using component materiality. For a component that is significant, not due to its individual financial significance but because it is likely to include significant risks of material misstatement of the group financial statements due to its specific nature or circumstances, the group engagement team, or a component auditor on its behalf, should perform one or more of the following:

a. An audit, adapted as necessary to meet the needs of the group engagement team, of the financial information of the component, using component materiality;
b. An audit, adapted as necessary to meet the needs of the group engagement team, of one or more account balances, classes of

transactions, or disclosures relating to the likely significant risks of material misstatement of the group financial;

c. Specified audit procedures relating to the likely significant risks of material misstatement of the group financial statements.

When the auditor of the group financial statements is assuming responsibility for the work of a component auditor, the communication requested from the component auditor, should include the following:

a. Whether the component auditor has complied with the group engagement team's requirements.
b. Information on instances of noncompliance with laws or regulations at the component or group level that could give rise to a material misstatement of the group financial statements.
c. Significant risks of material misstatement of the group financial statements, due to fraud or error, identified by the component auditor in the component and the component auditor's responses to such risks. The group engagement team should request the component auditor to communicate such significant risks on a timely basis.
d. A list of corrected and uncorrected misstatements of the financial information of the component (the list need not include misstatements that are below the threshold for clearly trivial misstatements communicated by the group engagement team).
e. Indicators of possible management bias regarding accounting estimates and the application of accounting principles.
f. Description of any identified material weaknesses and significant deficiencies in internal control at the component level.
g. Other significant findings and issues that the component auditor communicated or expects to communicate to those charged with governance of the component, including fraud or suspected fraud involving component management, employees who have significant roles in internal control at the component level, or others that resulted in a material misstatement of the financial information of the component.
h. Any other matters that may be relevant to the group audit or that the component auditor wishes to draw to the attention of the group engagement team, including exceptions noted in the written

representations that the component auditor requested from component management.

20.2.2 The Group Engagement Team Not Assuming Responsibility

When he/she chooses not to assume responsibility, the engagement team leader must rather make reference to the audit conducted by the component auditor in his audit's report on the group financial statements. The standard permits reference to the report of a component auditor when the component's financial statements are prepared using a different financial reporting framework than that of the group financial statements, as long as the group auditor audits the component's conversion adjustments. However, the standard does not permit reference unless the component auditor has performed an audit in accordance with GAAS in the United States and has issued an unrestricted auditor's report on those financial statements.

20.3 Independence and Competence of the Component Auditor

When performing work on the financial information of a component for a group audit, the component auditor is subject to ethical requirements that are relevant to the group audit. Such requirements may be different or in addition to those applying to the component auditor when performing an audit in the component auditor's jurisdiction. The group engagement team, therefore, obtains an understanding about the component auditor's understanding of, and compliance with, the ethical requirements that are relevant to the group audit and whether that is sufficient to fulfill the component auditor's responsibilities in the group audit. When the component auditor is not subject to the AICPA Code of Professional Conduct, compliance by the component auditor with the ethics and independence requirements set forth in the International Federation of Accountants Code of Ethics for Professional Accountants is sufficient to fulfill the component auditor's ethical responsibilities in the group audit. Besides ethical requirements, the component auditor must also be professionally competent in order to participate in the group engagement. The group engagement team must assess the component auditor's professional competence. To that end, the group engagement team may inquire whether the component auditor:

- Possesses an understanding of the auditing and other standards applicable to the group audit, such as U.S. GAAS, that is sufficient to fulfill the component auditor's responsibilities.
- Possesses the special skills (for example, industry-specific knowledge or knowledge of relevant financial reporting requirements for statements and schedules to be filed with regulatory agencies) necessary to perform the work on the financial information of the particular component.
- When relevant, possesses an understanding of the applicable financial reporting framework that is sufficient to fulfill the component auditor's responsibilities in the group audit (instructions issued by group management to components often describe the characteristics of the applicable financial reporting framework.

Regardless of whether reference will be made in the auditor's report on the group financial statements to the audit of a component auditor, the group engagement team should obtain an understanding of the following:

- Whether a component auditor understands and will comply with the ethical requirements that are relevant to the group audit and, in particular, is independent;
- A component auditor's professional competence;
- The extent, if any, to which the group engagement team will be able to be involved in the work of the component auditor;
- Whether the group engagement team will be able to obtain information affecting the consolidation process from a component auditor;
- Whether a component auditor operates in a regulatory environment that actively oversees auditors.

When a component auditor does not meet the independence requirements that are relevant to the group audit or the group engagement team has serious concerns about the other matters, the group engagement team should obtain sufficient appropriate audit evidence relating to the financial information of the component without making reference to the audit of that component auditor in the auditor's report on the group financial statements or otherwise using the work of that component auditor.

20.4 Assessment of Materiality in Group Audit

The group auditor should assess materiality, including performance materiality, for the group financial statements as a whole when establishing the overall group audit strategy. Component materiality should be determined taking into account all components, regardless of whether reference is made in the auditor's report on the group financial statements to the audit of a component auditor. To reduce the risk that the aggregate of uncorrected and undetected misstatements in the group financial statements exceeds the materiality for the group financial statements as a whole, component materiality should be lower than the materiality for the group financial statements as a whole, and component performance materiality should be lower than performance materiality for the group financial statements as a whole. The auditor is required to design and implement appropriate responses to address the assessed risks of material misstatement of the financial statements. If the nature, timing, and extent of the work to be performed on the consolidation process or the financial information of the components is based on an expectation that group-wide controls are operating effectively or when substantive procedures alone cannot provide sufficient appropriate audit evidence at the assertion level, the group engagement team should test, or have a component auditor test on the group engagement team's behalf, the operating effectiveness of those controls.

The group engagement team designs and performs further audit procedures on the consolidation process to respond to the assessed risks of material misstatement of the group financial statements arising from the consolidation process. This includes evaluating whether all components have been included in the group financial statements. The group engagement team should evaluate the appropriateness, completeness, and accuracy of consolidation adjustments and reclassifications and should evaluate whether any fraud risk factors or indicators of possible management bias exist.

20.4.1 Assessment of the Component Financial Framework

If the financial information of a component has not been prepared in accordance with the same accounting policies applied to the group financial statements, the group engagement team should evaluate whether the financial information of that component has been appropriately adjusted for purposes of the preparation and fair presentation of the group financial statements in accordance with the applicable financial reporting framework. The group engagement team should determine whether the financial information identified in a component auditor's communication is the financial information that is incorporated into the group financial statements. If the group financial statements include the financial statements of a component with a financial reporting period-end that differs from that of the group, the group engagement team should evaluate whether appropriate adjustments have been made to those financial statements in accordance with the applicable financial reporting framework.

20.4.2 Communication with a Component Auditor

AU-C 600 provides a two-way communication between the group engagement team and all the components. The group engagement team should communicate its requirements to a component auditor on a timely basis. This communication includes the following:

a. A request that the component auditor, knowing the context in which the group engagement team will use the work of the component auditor, confirm that the component auditor will cooperate with the group engagement team.
b. The ethical requirements that are relevant to the group audit and, in particular, the independence requirements.
c. A list of related parties prepared by group management and any other related parties of which the group engagement team is aware. The group engagement team should request the component auditor to communicate on a timely basis related parties not previously identified by group management or the group engagement team. The group engagement team should identify such additional related parties to other component auditors.

d. Identified significant risks of material misstatement of the group financial statements, due to fraud or error, that are relevant to the work of the component auditor.

The group engagement team should request a component auditor to communicate matters relevant to the group engagement team's conclusion, with regard to the group audit. Such communication should include the following:

a. Whether the component auditor has complied with ethical requirements relevant to the group audit, including independence and professional competence;
b. Identification of the financial information of the component on which the component auditor is reporting;
c. The component auditor's overall findings, conclusions, or opinion.

20.5 Audit Test Related to Group Audit

The audit test to perform depends on whether the Component deemed significant or not significant.

20.5.1 Audit Test for Not-significant Components

For components that are not significant components, the group engagement team should perform analytical procedures at the group level. In some circumstances, the group engagement team may determine that sufficient appropriate audit evidence on which to base the group audit opinion will not be obtained from the following:

a. The work performed on the financial information of significant components;
b. The work performed on group-wide controls and the consolidation process;
c. The analytical procedures performed at group level.

In such circumstances, the group engagement team should select additional components that are not significant components and should perform or request a component auditor to perform one or more of the following on the financial information of the individual components selected:

- An audit, adapted as necessary to meet the needs of the group engagement team, of the financial information of the component, using component materiality;
- An audit, adapted as necessary to meet the needs of the group engagement team, of one or more account balances, classes of transactions, or disclosures;
- A review of the financial information of the component, adapted as necessary to meet the needs of the group engagement team, using component materiality;
- Specified audit procedures.

It should be noted that the group engagement team should vary the selection of such individual components over a period of time.

20.5.2 *Audit Tests for Significant Components*

When a component auditor performs an audit or other specified audit procedures of the financial information of a significant component for which the auditor of the group financial statements is assuming responsibility for the component auditor's work, the group engagement team should be involved in the risk assessment of the component to identify significant risks of material misstatement of the group financial statements. The nature, timing, and extent of this involvement are affected by the group engagement team's understanding of the component auditor but, at a minimum, should include the following:

a. Discussing with the component auditor or component management the component's business activities of significance to the group;
b. Discussing with the component auditor the susceptibility of the component to material misstatement of the financial information due to fraud or error;
c. Reviewing the component auditor's documentation of identified significant risks of material misstatement of the group financial statements. Such documentation may take the form of a memorandum that reflects the component auditor's conclusion with regard to the identified significant risks.

20.6 The Evaluation of the Sufficiency and Appropriateness of Audit Evidence

The group engagement team should evaluate a component auditor's communication. The group engagement team should discuss significant findings and issues arising from that evaluation with the component auditor, component management, or group management, as appropriate. The group engagement team should evaluate whether sufficient appropriate audit evidence on which to base the group audit opinion has been obtained from the audit procedures performed on the consolidation process and the work performed by the group engagement team and the component auditors on the financial information of the components. Likewise, the group engagement partner should evaluate the effect on the group audit opinion of any uncorrected misstatements (either identified by the group engagement team or communicated by component auditors) and any instances in which there has been an inability to obtain sufficient appropriate audit evidence.

20.7 Communication Between the Lead Auditor and the Group

The lead auditor shall communicate with both the group management and the governance people.

20.7.1 Communication Between the Lead Auditor and the Group Management

The group engagement team should communicate to group management and those charged with governance of the group material weaknesses and significant deficiencies in internal control that are relevant to the group (either identified by the group engagement team or brought to its attention by a component auditor) during the audit.

If fraud has been identified by the group engagement team or brought to its attention by a component auditor or information indicates that a fraud may exist, the group engagement team should communicate this on a timely basis to the appropriate level of group management in order to inform those with primary responsibility for the prevention and detection of fraud of matters relevant to their responsibilities.

When a component auditor has been engaged to express an audit opinion on the financial statements of a component, the group engagement team should request group management to inform component management of any matter of which the group engagement team becomes aware that may be significant to the financial statements of the component, but of which component management may be unaware. If group management refuses to communicate the matter to component management, the group engagement team should discuss the matter with those charged with governance of the group. If the matter remains unresolved, the group engagement team, subject to legal and professional confidentiality considerations, should consider whether to advise the component auditor not to issue the auditor's report on the financial statements of the component until the matter is resolved and whether to withdraw from the engagement.

20.7.2 Communication Between the Lead Auditor and the Governance Team

The group engagement team should communicate the following matters with those charged with governance of the group:

a. An overview of the type of work to be performed on the financial information of the components, including the basis for the decision to make reference to the audit of a component auditor in the auditor's report on the group financial statements;
b. An overview of the nature of the group engagement team's planned involvement in the work to be performed by the component auditors on the financial information of significant components;
c. Instances in which the group engagement team's evaluation of the work of a component auditor gave rise to a concern about the quality of that auditor's work
d. Any limitations on the group audit;
e. Fraud or suspected fraud involving group management, component management, employees who have significant roles in group-wide controls, or others in which a material misstatement of the group financial statements has or may have resulted from fraud.

20.8 Documenting a Group Audit

The group engagement team should include in the audit documentation the following:

a. An analysis of components indicating those that are significant and the type of work performed on the financial information of the components;
b. Those components for which reference to the reports of component auditors is made in the auditor's report on the group financial statements;
c. Written communications between the group engagement team and the component auditors about the group engagement team's requirements;
d. For those components for which reference is made in the auditor's report on the group financial statements to the audit of a component auditor, the financial statements of the component and the report of the component auditor thereon.

20.9 The Consolidation Process

International Standard on Auditing 600—Consolidation Adjustments and Reclassifications[2] provides specific details concerning the consolidation process within an international group. The consolidation process may require adjustments to amounts reported in the group financial statements that do not pass through the usual transaction processing systems and may not be subject to the same internal controls to which other financial information is subject. The group engagement team's evaluation of the appropriateness, completeness, and accuracy of the adjustments may include:

- Evaluating whether significant adjustments appropriately reflect the events and transactions underlying them;

[2] International Standard on Auditing 600 Special Considerations—Audits of Group Financial Statements (Including the Work of Component Auditors) (Effective for audits of group financial statements for periods beginning on or after December 15, 2009), par. 56.

- Determining whether significant adjustments have been correctly calculated, processed and authorized by group management and, where applicable, by component management;
- Determining whether significant adjustments are properly supported and sufficiently documented; and
- Checking the reconciliation and elimination of intra-group transactions and unrealized profits, and intra-group account balances.

20.10 Conclusion

The provisions of the new standard, AU-C 600 provide clear guidelines as to the Audits of Group Financial Statements. The new standard allows the group audit team to make reference to the report of the component auditor even in circumstances when the component auditor provides financial statements in another financial framework different from the US GAAP, so long as the group audit team can properly audit the component's conversion adjustments. However, the new standard departs a bit from the International Standard Audit in that it still allows the group auditor not to assume responsibility for components auditors' work while making reference to the component auditor's report.

Practice

Question 1

In the group audit, the group engagement team should obtain an understanding of the following, except:

(a) Whether all component auditors understand and are committed to comply with the ethical requirements that are relevant to the group audit and, in particular, are independent
(b) All component auditors are professionally competent
(c) The extent, if any, to which the group engagement team will be able to be involved in the work of the component auditor
(d) Whether the group engagement team will be able to obtain information affecting the consolidation process from a component auditor
(e) None

Question 2

In a group audit, when the group engagement partner decides to make reference to the audit of a component auditor in the auditor's report on the group financial statements, the report on the group financial statements should clearly indicate the following, except:

(a) That the component was not audited by the auditor of the group financial statements but was audited by the component auditor
(b) The magnitude of the portion of the financial statements audited by the component auditor
(c) The financial reporting framework when the component's financial statements are prepared using a different financial reporting framework from that used for the group financial statements
(d) The auditor of the group financial statements is not responsible for evaluating the appropriateness of the adjustments to convert the component's financial statements to the financial reporting framework used by the group

Question 3

In assessing materiality, the group engagement team should determine the following, except:

(a) The performance materiality for the group financial statements as a whole when establishing the overall group audit strategy
(b) Determine the materiality to be applied to particular classes of transactions, account balances, or disclosures in the group financial statements
(c) The threshold above which misstatements cannot be regarded as clearly trivial to the group financial statements.
(d) Recognize the materiality as assessed by each component auditor

Question 4

The following factors may affect the group engagement team's involvement in the work of a component auditor, except:

(a) The significance of the component
(b) The identified significant risks of material misstatement of the group financial statements

(c) The seniority of the group engagement team relative to the component auditor
(d) The group engagement team's understanding of the component auditor

Question 5

The involvement of the group engagement partner in the work of a component auditor can take different forms, except:

(a) Meeting with the component auditor to obtain an understanding of the component and its environment
(b) Reviewing the component auditor's overall audit strategy and audit plan
(c) Performing risk assessment procedures to identify and assess the risks of material misstatement at the component level
(d) Designing and performing further audit procedures. These may be designed and performed with the component auditor or by the group engagement team
(e) Re-performing the all audit procedures of the component auditor

CHAPTER 21

Communications with Audit Committees

21.1 General

The auditor shall establish an understanding of the terms of the audit engagement with the audit committee and to record that understanding in an engagement letter. The communication requirements of this standard do not modify or replace communications to the audit committee required by such other PCAOB rules and standards, and other laws or regulations. Nothing in this standard precludes the auditor from communicating other matters to the audit committee. The auditor should discuss with the audit committee any significant issues that the auditor discussed with management in connection with the appointment or retention of the auditor, including significant discussions regarding the application of accounting principles and auditing standards. The communication required is meant to encourage effective two-way communication between the auditor and the audit committee throughout the audit to assist in understanding matters relevant to the audit.

21.2 Objectives

The objectives of the auditor are to:

- communicate to the audit committee the responsibilities of the auditor in relation to the audit and establish an understanding of the terms of the audit engagement with the audit committee;

F. I. Lessambo, *Auditing, Assurance Services, and Forensics*,
https://doi.org/10.1007/978-3-319-90521-1_21

- obtain information from the audit committee relevant to the audit;
- communicate to the audit committee an overview of the overall audit strategy and timing of the audit; and
- provide the audit committee with timely observations arising from the audit that are significant to the financial reporting process.

21.3 The Scope of the Communication

The scope of the communication between the auditor and the audit committee covers a series of matters including the following:

- Appointment and Retention
  The auditor should discuss with the audit committee any significant issues that the auditor discussed with management in connection with the appointment or retention of the auditor, including significant discussions regarding the application of accounting principles and auditing standards.

- Understanding of the Terms of the Audit
  The auditor should establish an understanding of the terms of the audit engagement with the audit committee. This understanding includes communicating to the audit committee the following: (i) the objective of the audit; (ii) the responsibilities of the auditor; and (iii) the responsibilities of management.
  The auditor should record the understanding of the terms of the audit engagement in an engagement letter and provide the engagement letter to the audit committee annually. The auditor should have the engagement letter executed by the appropriate party or parties on behalf of the company. If the appropriate party or parties are other than the audit committee, or its chair on behalf of the audit committee, the auditor should determine that the audit committee has acknowledged and agreed to the terms of the engagement. An auditor who cannot establish an understanding of the terms of the audit engagement with the audit committee, the auditor should decline to accept, continue, or perform the engagement.

- Obtaining Information and Communicating the Audit Strategy
  The auditor should inquire of the audit committee about whether it is aware of matters relevant to the audit, including, but not limited to, violations or possible violations of laws or regulations. The

auditor should communicate to the audit committee an overview of the overall audit strategy, including the timing of the audit, and discuss with the audit committee the significant risks identified during the auditor's risk assessment procedures. As part of communicating the overall audit strategy, the auditor should communicate the following matters to the audit committee, if applicable:

(a) The nature and extent of specialized skill or knowledge needed to perform the planned audit procedures or evaluate the audit results related to significant risks;
(b) The extent to which the auditor plans to use the work of the company's internal auditors in an audit of financial statements;
(c) The extent to which the auditor plans to use the work of internal auditors, company personnel (in addition to internal auditors), and third parties working under the direction of management or the audit committee when performing an audit of internal control over financial reporting;
(d) The names, locations, and planned responsibilities of other independent public accounting firms or other persons, who are not employed by the auditor, that perform audit procedures in the current period audit; and
(e) The basis for the auditor's determination that the auditor can serve as principal auditor, if significant parts of the audit are to be performed by other auditors.

The auditor should communicate to the audit committee significant changes to the planned audit strategy or the significant risks initially identified and the reasons for such changes.

- Results of the Audit

  The auditor should communicate to the audit committee the following matters:

  (a) Significant accounting policies and practices.

    (1) Management's initial selection of, or changes in, significant accounting policies or the application of such policies in the current period; and
    (2) The effect on financial statements or disclosures of significant accounting policies in (i) controversial areas or (ii) areas for which there is a lack of authoritative guidance or consensus, or diversity in practice.

(b) Critical accounting policies and practices. All critical accounting policies and practices to be used, including:

  (1) The reasons certain policies and practices are considered critical; and
  (2) How current and anticipated future events might affect the determination of whether certain policies and practices are considered critical.

(c) Critical accounting estimates.

  (1) A description of the process management used to develop critical accounting estimates;
  (2) Management's significant assumptions used in critical accounting estimates that have a high degree of subjectivity; and
  (3) Any significant changes management made to the processes used to develop critical accounting estimates or significant assumptions, a description of management's reasons for the changes, and the effects of the changes on the financial statements.

(d) Significant unusual transactions.

  (1) Significant transactions that are outside the normal course of business for the company or that otherwise appear to be unusual due to their timing, size, or nature; and
  (2) The policies and practices management used to account for significant unusual transactions.

Management might communicate some or all of the matters in paragraph 12. If management communicates any of these matters, the auditor does not need to communicate them at the same level of detail as management, as long as the auditor (1) participated in management's discussion with the audit committee, (2) affirmatively confirmed to the audit committee that management has adequately communicated these matters, and (3) with respect to critical accounting policies and practices, identified for the audit committee those accounting policies and practices that the auditor considers critical. The auditor should communicate any omitted or inadequately described matters to the audit committee.

- Evaluation of the Quality of the Company's Financial Reporting
  The auditor should communicate to the audit committee the following matters:
  (a) Qualitative aspects of significant accounting policies and practices.
    (1) The results of the auditor's evaluation of, and conclusions about, the qualitative aspects of the company's significant accounting policies and practices, including situations in which the auditor identified bias in management's judgments about the amounts and disclosures in the financial statements; and
    (2) The results of the auditor's evaluation of the differences between (i) estimates best supported by the audit evidence and (ii) estimates included in the financial statements, which are individually reasonable, that indicate a possible bias on the part of the company's management.
  (b) Assessment of critical accounting policies and practices. The auditor's assessment of management's disclosures related to the critical accounting policies and practices, along with any significant modifications to the disclosure of those policies and practices proposed by the auditor that management did not make.
  (c) Conclusions regarding critical accounting estimates. The basis for the auditor's conclusions regarding the reasonableness of the critical accounting estimates.
  (d) Significant unusual transactions. The auditor's understanding of the business purpose (or the lack thereof) of significant unusual transactions.
  (e) Financial statement presentation. The results of the auditor's evaluation of whether the presentation of the financial statements and the related disclosures are in conformity with the applicable financial reporting framework, including the auditor's consideration of the form, arrangement, and content of the financial statements (including the accompanying notes), encompassing matters such as the terminology used, the amount of detail given, the classification of items, and the bases of amounts set forth.
  (f) New accounting pronouncements. Situations in which, as a result of the auditor's procedures, the auditor identified a

concern regarding management's anticipated application of accounting pronouncements that have been issued but are not yet effective and might have a significant effect on future financial reporting.

(g) Alternative accounting treatments. All alternative treatments permissible under the applicable financial reporting framework for policies and practices related to material items that have been discussed with management, including the ramifications of the use of such alternative disclosures and treatments and the treatment preferred by the auditor.

- Contentious Matters for which the Auditor Consulted
  The auditor should communicate to the audit committee matters that are difficult or contentious for which the auditor consulted outside the engagement team and that the auditor reasonably determined are relevant to the audit committee's oversight of the financial reporting process.

- Management Consultation with Other Accountants
  When the auditor is aware that management consulted with other accountants about significant auditing or accounting matters and the auditor has identified a concern regarding such matters, the auditor should communicate to the audit committee his or her views about such matters that were the subject of such consultation.

- Going Concern
  The auditor should communicate to the audit committee, when applicable, the following matters relating to the auditor's evaluation of the company's ability to continue as a going concern:

  (a) If the auditor believes there is substantial doubt about the company's ability to continue as a going concern for a reasonable period of time, the conditions and events that the auditor identified that, when considered in the aggregate, indicate that there is substantial doubt;
  (b) If the auditor concludes, after consideration of management's plans, that substantial doubt about the company's ability to continue as a going concern is alleviated, the basis for the auditor's conclusion, including elements the auditor identified within management's plans that are significant to overcoming the adverse effects of the conditions and events;

(c) If the auditor concludes, after consideration of management's plans, that substantial doubt about the company's ability to continue as a going concern for a reasonable period of time remains: (i) the effects, if any, on the financial statements and the adequacy of the related disclosure; and (ii) the effects on the auditor's report.

- Uncorrected and Corrected Misstatements
The auditor should provide the audit committee with the schedule of uncorrected misstatements related to accounts and disclosures that the auditor presented to management. The auditor should discuss with the audit committee, or determine that management has adequately discussed with the audit committee, the basis for the determination that the uncorrected misstatements were immaterial, including the qualitative factors considered. The auditor also should communicate that uncorrected misstatements or matters underlying those uncorrected misstatements could potentially cause future period financial statements to be materially misstated, even if the auditor has concluded that the uncorrected misstatements are immaterial to the financial statements under audit. The auditor should communicate to the audit committee those corrected misstatements, other than those that are clearly trivial related to accounts and disclosures that might not have been detected except through the auditing procedures performed, and discuss with the audit committee the implications that such corrected misstatements might have on the company's financial reporting process.

- Material Written Communications
The auditor should communicate to the audit committee other material written communications between the auditor and management.

- Departure from the Auditor's Standard Report
The auditor should communicate to the audit committee the following matters related to the auditor's report: (i) when the auditor expects to modify the opinion in the auditor's report, the reasons for the modification, and the wording of the report; and (ii) when the auditor expects to include explanatory language or an explanatory paragraph in the auditor's report, the reasons for the explanatory language or paragraph, and the wording of the explanatory language or paragraph.

- Disagreements with Management
  The auditor should communicate to the audit committee any disagreements with management about matters, whether or not satisfactorily resolved, that individually or in the aggregate could be significant to the company's financial statements or the auditor's report. Disagreements with management do not include differences of opinion based on incomplete facts or preliminary information that are later resolved by the auditor obtaining additional relevant facts or information prior to the issuance of the auditor's report.

- Difficulties Encountered in Performing the Audit
  Difficulties encountered by the auditor during the audit could represent a scope limitation, which may result in the auditor modifying the auditor's opinion or withdrawing from the engagement. The auditor should communicate to the audit committee any significant difficulties encountered during the audit. Significant difficulties encountered during the audit include, but are not limited to:

  (a) Significant delays by management, the unavailability of company personnel, or an unwillingness by management to provide information needed for the auditor to perform his or her audit procedures;
  (b) An unreasonably brief time within which to complete the audit;
  (c) Unexpected extensive effort required by the auditor to obtain sufficient appropriate audit evidence;
  (d) Unreasonable management restrictions encountered by the auditor on the conduct of the audit; and
  (e) Management's unwillingness to make or extend its assessment of the company's ability to continue as a going concern when requested by the auditor.

- Other Matters
  The auditor should communicate to the audit committee other matters arising from the audit that are significant to the oversight of the company's financial reporting process. This communication includes, among other matters, complaints or concerns regarding accounting or auditing matters that have come to the auditor's attention during the audit and the results of the auditor's procedures regarding such matters.

21.4 Form and Documentation of Communications

The auditor should communicate to the audit committee the matters in this standard, either orally or in writing, unless otherwise specified in this standard. The auditor must document the communications in the work papers, whether such communications took place orally or in writing. If, as part of its communications to the audit committee, management communicated some or all of the matters such as its initial selection or changes in significant accounting policies or areas lacking authoritative guidance, the auditor must include a copy of or a summary of management's communications provided to the audit committee in the audit documentation.

21.5 Timing

All audit committee communications required by this standard should be made in a timely manner and prior to the issuance of the auditor's report. The appropriate timing of a particular communication to the audit committee depends on factors such as the significance of the matters to be communicated and corrective or follow-up action needed, unless other timing requirements are specified by PCAOB rules or standards or the securities laws. An auditor may communicate to only the audit committee chair if done in order to communicate matters in a timely manner during the audit. The auditor, however, should communicate such matters to the audit committee prior to the issuance of the auditor's report.

Practice

Question 1

Which of the below is included in the auditor's objectives in his communication with the audit committee:

(a) Communicate to the audit committee the responsibilities of the auditor in relation to the audit and establish an understanding of the terms of the audit engagement with the audit committee
(b) Obtain information from the audit committee relevant to the audit
(c) Communicate to the audit committee an overview of the overall audit strategy and timing of the audit

(d) Provide the audit committee with timely observations arising from the audit that are significant to the financial reporting process
(e) All of the above

Question 2

The scope of the communication between the auditor and the audit committee includes:

(a) Appointment and retention
(b) Understanding the terms of the audit
(c) Obtaining information
(d) Communicating the audit strategy
(e) All of the above

Question 3

In communication the result of the audit to the audit committee, the auditor shall cover the following matters with the exception of:

(a) Significant accounting policies and practices
(b) Critical accounting policies and practices
(c) Critical accounting estimates
(d) The overall audit expenses
(e) Significant unusual transactions

Question 4

Which of the below assertion is inaccurate concerning the auditor attitude when facing disagreement with the management:

(a) The auditor shall communicate the issues to the audit committee whether the disagreement has been resolved or not
(b) The auditor shall communicate the issues to the audit committee only when the disagreement has not been resolved
(c) Disagreement with management does not include differences of opinion based on incomplete facts
(d) Disagreement with management does not include preliminary information that has been resolved through additional facts provided

Question 5

Which of the below assertion is inaccurate concerning the form and documentation of communications:

(a) Unless otherwise stated, the auditor communication to the audit committee can either be oral or in writing
(b) The auditor communication to the audit committee must always be in writing
(c) The auditor must document the communications in the work papers. Whether such communication took place orally or in writing
(d) None

CHAPTER 22

Audit Tools: Financial Ratios Analysis

22.1 General

Ratio analysis is a diagnostic tool that helps to identify problem areas and opportunities within a company. There several ratios that the auditor can consider while performing analytical procedures. Among the dozens of financial ratios available, we've chosen the most relevant to and organized them into eight main categories as per the following list:

22.2 Liquidity Measurement Ratios

Liquidity ratios analyze the ability of a company to pay off both its current liabilities as they become due as well as their long-term liabilities as they become current. In other words, these ratios show the cash levels of a company and the ability to turn other assets into cash to pay off liabilities and other current obligations.

Liquidity is not only a measure of how much cash a business has. It is also a measure of how easy it will be for the company to raise enough cash or convert assets into cash. Assets like accounts receivable, trading securities, and inventory are relatively easy for many companies to convert into cash in the short term. Thus, all of these assets go into the liquidity calculation of a company.

Here are the most common liquidity ratios

F. I. Lessambo, *Auditing, Assurance Services, and Forensics*,
https://doi.org/10.1007/978-3-319-90521-1_22

- Current Ratio

The current ratio is a liquidity and efficiency ratio that measures a firm's ability to pay off its short-term liabilities with its current assets. The current ratio is an important measure of liquidity because short-term liabilities are due within the next year.

This means that a company has a limited amount of time in order to raise the funds to pay for these liabilities. Current assets like cash, cash equivalents, and marketable securities can easily be converted into cash in the short term. This means that companies with larger amounts of current assets will more easily be able to pay off current liabilities when they become due without having to sell off long-term, revenue-generating assets.

Formula = Current assets/Current liabilities

The current ratio is calculated by dividing current assets by current liabilities.

- Quick Ratio

The quick ratio or acid test ratio is a liquidity ratio that measures the ability of a company to pay its current liabilities when they come due with only quick assets. Quick assets are current assets that can be converted to cash within 90 days or in the short-term. Cash, cash equivalents, short-term investments or marketable securities, and current accounts receivable are considered quick assets.

Short-term investments or marketable securities include trading securities and available for sale securities that can easily be converted into cash within the next 90 days. Marketable securities are traded on an open market with a known price and readily available buyers. Any stock on the New York Stock Exchange would be considered a marketable security because they can easily be sold to any investor when the market is open.

The quick ratio is often called the acid test ratio in reference to the historical use of acid to test metals for gold by the early miners. If the metal passed the acid test, it was pure gold. If metal failed the acid test by corroding from the acid, it was a base metal and of no value.

The acid test of finance shows how well a company can quickly convert its assets into cash in order to pay off its current liabilities. It also shows the level of quick assets to current liabilities.

Formula = Cash + Cash equivalents + Short term investment + Current receivables/Current liabilities

The quick ratio is calculated by adding cash, cash equivalents, short-term investments, and current receivables together then dividing them by current liabilities.

- Cash Ratio

The cash ratio or cash coverage ratio is a liquidity ratio that measures a firm's ability to pay off its current liabilities with only cash and cash equivalents. The cash ratio is much more restrictive than the current ratio or quick ratio because no other current assets can be used to pay off current debt–only cash.

This is why many creditors look at the cash ratio. They want to see if a company maintains adequate cash balances to pay off all of their current debts as they come due. Creditors also like the fact that inventory and accounts receivable are left out of the equation because both of these accounts are not guaranteed to be available for debt servicing. Inventory could take months or years to sell and receivables could take weeks to collect. Cash is guaranteed to be available for creditors.

Formula = Cash + Cash equivalents/Total current liabilities

The cash coverage ratio is calculated by adding cash and cash equivalents and dividing by the total current liabilities of a company.

- Cash Conversion Cycle

The cash conversion cycle is a cash flow calculation that attempts to measure the time it takes a company to convert its investment in inventory and other resource inputs into cash. In other words, the cash conversion cycle calculation measures how long cash is tied up in inventory before the inventory is sold and cash is collected from customers. The cash cycle has three distinct parts. The *first stage* of the cycle represents the current inventory level and how long it will take the company to sell this inventory. This stage is calculated by using the days inventory outstanding calculation. The *second stage* of the cash cycle represents the current sales and the amount of time it takes to collect the cash from these sales. This is calculated by using the days sales outstanding calculation. The *third stage* represents the current outstanding payables. In other words, this represents how much a company owes its current vendors for inventory and goods purchases and when the company will have to pay off its vendors. This is calculated by using the days payables outstanding calculation.

Formula = Days of inventory outstanding − Days payable outstanding

The cash conversion cycle is calculated by adding the days inventory outstanding to the days sales outstanding and subtracting the days payable outstanding.

- Working Capital Ratio

The working capital ratio, also called the current ratio, is a liquidity ratio that measures a firm's ability to pay off its current liabilities with current assets. The working capital ratio is important to creditors because it shows the liquidity of the company. Current liabilities are best paid with current assets like cash, cash equivalents, and marketable securities because these assets can be converted into cash much quicker than fixed assets. The faster the assets can be converted into cash, the more likely the company will have the cash in time to pay its debts.

The reason this ratio is called the working capital ratio comes from the working capital calculation. When current assets exceed current liabilities, the firm has enough capital to run its day-to-day operations. In other words, it has even capital to work. The working capital ratio transforms the working capital calculation into a comparison between current assets and current liabilities.

Formula = Currents assets/Current liabilities

The working capital ratio is calculated by dividing current assets by current liabilities.

- Times Interest Earned Ratio

The times interest earned ratio, sometimes called the interest coverage ratio, is a coverage ratio that measures the proportionate amount of income that can be used to cover interest expenses in the future. In some respects the times interest ratio is considered a solvency ratio because it measures a firm's ability to make interest and debt service payments. Since these interest payments are usually made on a long-term basis, they are often treated as an ongoing, fixed expense. As with most fixed expenses, if the company can't make the payments, it could go bankrupt and cease to exist. Thus, this ratio could be considered a solvency ratio as well.

Formula = Income before interest and income taxes/Interest expense

The times interest earned ratio is calculated by dividing income before interest and income taxes by the interest expense.

22.3 Solvency Ratios

Solvency ratios, also called leverage ratios, measure a company's ability to sustain operations indefinitely by comparing debt levels with equity, assets, and earnings. In other words, solvency ratios identify going concern issues and a firm's ability to pay its bills in the long term. Many people confuse solvency ratios with liquidity ratios. Although they both measure the ability of a company to pay off its obligations, solvency ratios focus more on the long-term sustainability of a company instead of the current liability payments. Solvency ratios show a company's ability to make payments and pay off its long-term obligations to creditors, bondholders, and banks. Put differently, solvency ratios indicate a more creditworthy and financially sound company in the long-term.

The most common solvency ratios include:

- Debt to Equity Ratio

The debt to equity ratio is a financial, liquidity ratio that compares a company's total debt to total equity. The debt to equity ratio shows the percentage of company financing that comes from creditors and investors. A higher debt to equity ratio indicates that more creditor financing (bank loans) is used than investor financing (shareholders).

Formula = Total liability/Total equity

The debt to equity ratio is calculated by dividing total liabilities by total equity. The debt to equity ratio is considered a balance sheet ratio because all of the elements are reported on the balance sheet.

- Equity Ratio

The equity ratio is an investment leverage or solvency ratio that measures the amount of assets that are financed by owners' investments by comparing the total equity in the company to the total assets. The equity ratio highlights two important financial concepts of a solvent and sustainable business. The first component shows how much of the total company assets are owned outright by the investors. In other words, after all of the liabilities are paid off, the investors will end up with the remaining assets.

The second component inversely shows how leveraged the company is with debt. The equity ratio measures how much of a firm's assets were financed by investors. In other words, this is the investors' stake in the company. This is what they are on the hook for. The inverse of this calculation shows the amount of assets that were financed by debt. Companies with higher equity ratios show new investors and creditors that investors believe in the company and are willing to finance it with their investments.

Formula = Total equity/Total assets

The equity ratio is calculated by dividing total equity by total assets. Both of these numbers truly include all of the accounts in that category. In other words, all of the assets and equity reported on the balance sheet are included in the equity ratio calculation.

- Debt Ratio

Debt ratio is a solvency ratio that measures a firm's total liabilities as a percentage of its total assets. In a sense, this ratio shows a company's ability to pay off its liabilities with its assets. In other words, this shows how many assets the company must sell in order to pay off all of its liabilities. Companies with higher levels of liabilities compared with assets are considered highly leveraged and more risky for lenders.

This helps investors and creditors analysis the overall debt burden on the company as well as the firm's ability to pay off the debt in future, uncertain economic times.

Formula = Total liabilities/Total assets

The debt ratio is calculated by dividing total liabilities by total assets. Both of these numbers can easily be found on the balance sheet. Here is the calculation:

22.4 Profitability Indicator Ratios

Profitability ratios compare income statement accounts and categories to show a company's ability to generate profits from its operations. Profitability ratios focus on a company's return on investment in inventory and other assets. These ratios basically show how well companies can achieve profits from their operations. Investors and creditors can use profitability ratios to judge a company's return on investment based on its relative level of resources and assets. In other words, profitability ratios can be used to judge whether companies are making enough operational profit from their assets. In this sense, profitability ratios relate to efficiency ratios because they show how well companies are using their assets to generate profits. Profitability is also important to the concept of solvency and going concern.

Here are some of the key ratios that investors and creditors consider when judging how profitable a company should be:

- Profit Margin Analysis

The profit margin ratio, also called the return on sales ratio or gross profit ratio, is a profitability ratio that measures the amount of net income earned with each dollar of sales generated by comparing the net income and net sales of a company. In other words, the profit margin ratio shows what percentage of sales are left over after all expenses are paid by the business.

Creditors and investors use this ratio to measure how effectively a company can convert sales into net income. Investors want to make sure profits are high enough to distribute dividends while creditors want to make sure the company has enough profits to pay back its loans. In other words, outside users want to know that the company is running efficiently. An extremely low-profit margin would indicate the expenses are too high and the management needs to budget and cut expenses.

The return on sales ratio is often used by internal management to set performance goals for the future.

$$\boxed{\text{Formula} = \text{Net income/Net sales}}$$

The profit margin ratio formula can be calculated by dividing net income by net sales.

- Effective Tax Rate

The effective tax rate is the average rate at which an individual is taxed on earned income, or the average rate at which a corporation is taxed on pre-tax profits.

The formulas for effective tax rate are as follows:

$$\boxed{\text{Individual : Total tax expense/Taxable income}}$$

Or

$$\boxed{\text{Corporation : Total tax expense/Earnings before taxes}}$$

Effective tax rates simplify comparisons among companies or taxpayers. This is especially true where a progressive, or tiered tax system is in place. Those subject to progressive taxes will see different levels of income taxed at different rates.

- Return on Assets

The return on assets ratio, often called the return on total assets, is a profitability ratio that measures the net income produced by total assets during a period by comparing net income to the average total assets. In other words, the return on assets ratio or ROA measures how efficiently a company can manage its assets to produce profits during a period. Since company assets' sole purpose is to generate revenues and produce profits, this ratio helps both management and investors see how well the company can convert its investments in assets into profits. Analysts look at ROA as a return on investment for the company since capital assets are often the biggest investment for most companies. In this case, the company invests money into capital assets and the return is measured in profits.

Formula = Net income/Average total assets

The return on assets ratio formula is calculated by dividing net income by average total assets.

- Return on Equity

The return on equity ratio or ROE is a profitability ratio that measures the ability of a firm to generate profits from its shareholders investments in the company. In other words, the return on equity ratio shows how much profit each dollar of common stockholders' equity generates. This is an important measurement for potential investors because they want to see how efficiently a company will use their money to generate net income. ROE is also an indicator of how effective management is at using equity financing to fund operations and grow the company.

Formula = Net income/Shareholder's equity

The return on equity ratio formula is calculated by dividing net income by shareholder's equity.

- Return on Capital Employed

Return on capital employed or ROCE is a profitability ratio that measures how efficiently a company can generate profits from its capital employed by comparing net operating profit to capital employed. In other words, return on capital employed tells investors how many dollars in profits each dollar of capital employed generates. ROCE is a long-term profitability ratio because it shows how effectively assets are performing while taking into consideration long-term financing. This is why ROCE is a more useful ratio than return on equity to evaluate the longevity of a company. This ratio is based on two important calculations: operating profit and capital employed. Net operating profit is often called EBIT or earnings before interest and taxes. EBIT is often reported on the income statement because it shows the company profits generated from operations. EBIT can be calculated by adding interest and taxes back into net income if need be. Capital employed is a fairly convoluted term because it can be used to refer to many different financial ratios. Most often capital employed refers to the total assets of a company less all current liabilities. This could also be looked at as stockholders' equity less long-term liabilities. Both equal the same figure.

Formula = Net operating profit/Employed capital

Return on capital employed formula is calculated by dividing net operating profit or EBIT by the employed capital.

22.5 Efficiency Ratios

Efficiency ratios also called *activity ratios* measure how well companies utilize their assets to generate income. Efficiency ratios often look at the time it takes companies to collect cash from customer or the time it takes companies to convert inventory into cash—in other words, make sales. These ratios are used by management to help improve the company as well as outside investors and creditors looking at the operations of profitability of the company.

Efficiency ratios go hand in hand with profitability ratios. Most often when companies are efficient with their resources, they become profitable. Wal-Mart is a good example. Wal-Mart is extremely good at selling low margin products at high volumes. In other words, they are efficient at turning their assets. Even though they don't make much profit per sale, they make a ton of sales.

Here are the most common efficiency Ratios include:

- Account Receivable Turnover Ratio

This is an efficiency ratio or activity ratio that measures how many times a business can turn its accounts receivable into cash during a period. In other words, the accounts receivable turnover ratio measures how many times a business can collect its average accounts receivable during the year. A turn refers to each time a company collects its average receivables. This ratio shows how efficient a company is at collecting its credit sales from customers. Some companies collect their receivables from customers in 90 days while other take up to 6 months to collect from customers.

In some ways the receivables turnover ratio can be viewed as a liquidity ratio as well. Companies are more liquid the faster they can convert their receivables into cash.

Formula = Net credit sales/Average account receivables

Accounts receivable turnover is calculated by dividing net credit sales by the average accounts receivable for that period.

- Working Capital Ratio

The working capital ratio, also called the current ratio, is a liquidity ratio that measures a firm's ability to pay off its current liabilities with current assets. The working capital ratio is important to creditors because it shows the liquidity of the company. Current liabilities are best paid with current assets like cash, cash equivalents, and marketable securities because these assets can be converted into cash much quicker than fixed assets. The faster the assets can be converted into cash, the more likely the company will have the cash in time to pay its debts.

The reason this ratio is called the working capital ratio comes from the working capital calculation. When current assets exceed current liabilities, the firm has enough capital to run its day-to-day operations. In other words, it has even capital to work. The working capital ratio transforms the working capital calculation into a comparison between current assets and current liabilities.

Formula = Current assets/Current liabilities

The working capital ratio is calculated by dividing current assets by current liabilities.

- Asset Turnover Ratio

The asset turnover ratio is an efficiency ratio that measures a company's ability to generate sales from its assets by comparing net sales with average total assets. In other words, this ratio shows how efficiently a company can use its assets to generate sales.

The total asset turnover ratio calculates net sales as a percentage of assets to show how many sales are generated from each dollar of company assets. For instance, a ratio of .5 means that each dollar of assets generates 50 cents of sales.

Formula = Net sales/Average total assets

The asset turnover ratio is calculated by dividing net sales by average total assets.

- Inventory Turnover Ratio

The inventory turnover ratio is an efficiency ratio that shows how effectively inventory is managed by comparing cost of goods sold with average inventory for a period. This measures how many times average inventory is "turned" or sold during a period. In other words, it measures how many times a company sold its total average inventory dollar amount during the year. This ratio is important because total turnover depends on two main components of performance. *The first component is stock purchasing*. If larger amounts of inventory are purchased during the year, the company will have to sell greater amounts of inventory to improve its turnover. If the company can't sell these greater amounts of inventory, it will incur storage costs and other holding costs. The *second component is sales.* Sales have to match inventory purchases otherwise the inventory will not turn effectively. That's why the purchasing and sales departments must be in tune with each other.

Formula = COGS/Average inventory

The inventory turnover ratio is calculated by dividing the cost of goods sold for a period by the average inventory for that period.

- Days' sale to Inventory

The days sales of inventory value measures a firm performance by telling readers of financial statements how long it takes a firm to turn its inventory (including goods that are a work in progress, if applicable) into sales. This ratio is important to creditors and investors as it measures value, liquidity, and cash flows. Investors and creditors are always interested in knowing the value of a trade partner's inventory.

$$\boxed{\text{Formula} = (\text{Inventory}/\text{Cost of sales}) \times 365}$$

22.6 Debt Ratios

- Debt Ratio

Debt ratio is a solvency ratio that measures a firm's total liabilities as a percentage of its total assets. In a sense, the debt ratio shows a company's ability to pay off its liabilities with its assets. In other words, this shows how many assets the company must sell in order to pay off all of its liabilities. This ratio measures the financial leverage of a company. Companies with higher levels of liabilities compared with assets are considered highly leveraged and more risky for lenders. This helps investors and creditors analysis the overall debt burden on the company as well as the firm's ability to pay off the debt in future, uncertain economic times.

$$\boxed{\text{Formula} = \text{Total liabilities}/\text{Total assets}}$$

The debt ratio is calculated by dividing total liabilities by total assets. Both of these numbers can easily be found the balance sheet. Here is the calculation.

- Debt-Equity Ratio

The debt to equity ratio is a measure of the relationship between the capital contributed by creditors and the capital contributed by shareholders. It also shows the extent to which shareholders' equity can fulfill a company's obligations to creditors in the event of a liquidation.

$$\boxed{\text{Formula} = \text{Total liabilities}/\text{Shareholder's equity}}$$

Both total liabilities and shareholders' equity figures in the above formula can be obtained from the balance sheet of a business. A variation of the above formula uses only the interest bearing long-term liabilities in the numerator.

- Capitalization Ratio

The capitalization ratio compares total debt to total capitalization (capital structure). The capitalization ratio reflects the extent to which a company is operating on its equity. Capitalization ratio is also known as the financial leverage ratio. It tells the investors about the extent to which the company is using its equity to support its operations and growth. This ratio helps in the assessment of risk. The companies with high capitalization ratio are considered to be risky because they are at a risk of insolvency if they fail to repay their debt on time. Companies with a high capitalization ratio may also find it difficult to get more loans in the future. A high capitalization ratio is not always bad, however, higher financial leverage can increase the return on a shareholder's investment because usually there are tax advantages associated with the borrowings.

The capitalization ratio is calculated by dividing the long-term debt by the total shareholder's equity and long-term debt. This can be expressed as:

Capitalization ratio = Long-term debt/(Long-term debt + Shareholder's Equity)

The capitalization ratio is a very meaningful debt ratio because it gives an important insight into the use of financial leverage by a company. It focuses on the relationship of long-term debt as a component of the company's total capital base. The total capital is the capital raised by the shareholders and the lenders. The company's capitalization (it should not be confused with the market capitalization) explains the make-up of the long-term capital of the company. Capitalization is also known as capital structure. A company's long-term capital consists of long-term borrowings and shareholder's equity.

- Interest Coverage Ratio

The interest coverage ratio (ICR) is a measure of a company's ability to meet its interest payments. The interest coverage ratio is a measure of the number of times a company could make the interest payments on its debt with its EBIT. It determines how easily a company can pay interest expenses on outstanding debt. Interest coverage ratio is equal to earnings before interest and taxes (EBIT) for a time period, often one year, divided by interest expenses for the same time period.

Formula = EBIT/Interest expenses

The interest coverage ratio is calculated by dividing a company's earnings before interest and taxes (EBIT) by the company's interest expenses for the same period.

The lower the interest coverage ratio, the higher the company's debt burden and the greater the possibility of bankruptcy or default. A lower ICR means less earnings are available to meet interest payments and that the business is more vulnerable to increases in interest rates. An interest coverage ratio below 1.0 indicates the business is having difficulties generating the cash necessary to pay its interest obligations (i.e. interest payments exceed its earnings (EBIT)).

A higher ratio indicates a better financial health as it means that the company is more capable to meet its interest obligations from operating earnings. On the other hand, a high ICR may suggest a company is "too safe" and is neglecting opportunities to magnify earnings through leverage.

- Cash Flow to Debt Ratio

This coverage ratio compares a company's operating cash flow to its total debt, which, for purposes of this ratio, is defined as the sum of short-term borrowings, the current portion of long-term debt and long-term debt. This ratio provides an indication of a company's ability to cover total debt with its yearly cash flow from operations. The higher the percentage ratio, the better the company's ability to carry its total debt.

Formula = Operating cash flow/Total debt

22.7 Operating Performance Ratios

Operating performance ratios measure how different aspects of a company's finances are performing. The fixed-asset turnover ratio, operating cycle ratio and revenue per employee ratio each provide a different look into how a company is bringing in revenue, if the business is spending its money well and how efficiently it is using its assets and resources. Analyzing these ratios provides deeper insight into the company's finances than simply studying accounting or other financial records.

- Fixed-Asset Turnover

The fixed-asset turnover ratio is a measure of whether the money a company spends on the equipment and buildings the company owns, often referred to as property, plant and equipment. The fixed-asset turnover ratio is obtained by dividing the company's net revenue by the current value of the fixed assets.

Formula = Net revenue/Current value of fixed assets

A high ratio generally indicates that the company is generating adequate revenue with its assets and that the fixed assets are a wise investment of the company's resources. However, companies that don't require much investment in PP&E, such as consulting firms or IT companies, often have lower fixed-asset turnover ratios than companies that rely more on equipment to make money, such as manufacturers. This means that you must analyze the fixed-assets turnover ratio within the norms of the industry. You also must compare the current fixed-assets turnover ratio to historical fixed-asset turnover ratio figures to determine if the ratio is increasing or decreasing. A declining ratio may indicate that the company has too much money tied up in its equipment or property. An increasing ratio often indicates that the company is making better use of its property and equipment or has upgraded effectively

- Sales/Revenue per Employee

The revenue per employee ratio indicates how much revenue each employee is producing for the company. To find the revenue per employee ratio, divide the annual revenue the company earns by the number of employees it has. This ratio is expressed as a dollar amount.

Formula = Annual revenue/Number of employees

A high revenue per employee ratio means that employees are generating adequate sales or revenue for the company, while a low ratio is often a sign of low productivity. This is especially true for labor-heavy industries, such as retail and manufacturing. However, businesses that do not rely as much on employee productivity, such as technology fields, may have lower revenue per employee ratios, even if the company's employees are producing adequate revenue. For this reason, you must compare the revenue per employee ratio to other companies in the same industry to get an accurate idea of what is normal.

- Operating Cycle

The operating cycle ratio shows if a company is managing its accounts payable, accounts receivable and inventory efficiently. The operating cycle ratio involves three aspects of the company's finances; the days inventory outstanding, the days sales outstanding and the days payable outstanding. These aspects all are calculated the same way. Divide the cost of processing the accounts payable, accounts receivable or inventory by 365, the number of days in a year, to get the daily cost. Add the beginning and ending balances of the accounts payable, accounts receivable or inventory account and divide the answer by two to get the average amount for each account. Divide the average amount by the cost per day to find the days inventory outstanding, days sales outstanding or days payable outstanding. Calculate the operating cycle ratio by adding the days inventory outstanding and the days sales outstanding, then subtracting the days payable outstanding. The resulting figure is expressed as a number of days.

Formula = Day's sale of inventory + Day's sales outstanding

A shorter operating cycle means that a company collects money from customers efficiently, has good payment terms with businesses and other entities to which it owes money and is moving inventory at a pace that keeps up with average production ability and customer demand. A longer operating cycle indicates that the business has too much money tied up in unsold inventory, uncollected payments, and unpaid operating expenses. To perform an accurate analysis, the operating cycle ratio should be compared against industry standards, competitor operating cycle data and the company's own historical operating cycle information.

22.8 Cash Flow Indicator Ratios

These ratios can give users another look at the financial health and performance of a company.

- Operating Cash Flow/Sales Ratio

This ratio, which is expressed as a percentage, compares a company's operating cash flow to its net sales or revenues, which gives investors an idea of the company's ability to turn sales into cash.

It would be worrisome to see a company's sales grow without a parallel growth in operating cash flow. Positive and negative changes in a company's terms of sale and/or the collection experience of its accounts receivable will show up in this indicator.

Formula = Operating cash flow/Net sales (revenue)

- Free Cash Flow/Operating Cash Ratio

The free cash flow/operating cash flow ratio measures the relationship between free cash flow and operating cash flow.

Free cash flow is most often defined as operating cash flow minus capital expenditures, which, in analytical terms, are considered to be an essential outflow of funds to maintain a company's competitiveness and efficiency.

The cash flow remaining after this deduction is considered "free" cash flow, which becomes available to a company to use for expansion, acquisitions, and/or financial stability to weather difficult market conditions. The higher the percentage of free cash flow embedded in a company's operating cash flow, the greater the financial strength of the company.

Formula = Free cash flow (Operating cash flow − Capital expenditures)/ Operating cash flow

- Cash Flow Coverage Ratio

This ratio measures the ability of the company's operating cash flow to meet its obligations - including its liabilities or ongoing concern costs.

The operating cash flow is simply the amount of cash generated by the company from its main operations, which are used to keep the business funded.

The larger the operating cash flow coverage for these items, the greater the company's ability to meet its obligations, along with giving the company more cash flow to expand its business, withstand hard times, and not be burdened by debt servicing and the restrictions typically included in credit agreements.

Formulas = Operating cash flow/Total debt

- Dividend Payout Ratio

This ratio identifies the percentage of earnings (net income) per common share allocated to paying cash dividends to shareholders. The dividend payout ratio is an indicator of how well earnings support the dividend payment.

Here's how dividends "start" and "end." During a fiscal year quarter, a company's board of directors declares a dividend. This event triggers the posting of a current liability for "dividends payable." At the end of the quarter, net income is credited to a company's retained earnings, and assuming there's sufficient cash on hand and/or from current operating cash flow, the dividend is paid out. This reduces cash, and the dividends payable liability is eliminated.

The payment of a cash dividend is recorded in the statement of cash flows under the "financing activities" section.

Formula = Dividends per common share/Earnings per share

22.9 Investment Valuation Ratios

- Price Earning Ratio

The price/earnings ratio (P/E) is the best known of the investment valuation indicators. The P/E ratio has its imperfections, but it is nevertheless the most widely reported and used valuation by investment professionals and the investing public. The financial reporting of both companies and investment research services use a basic earnings per share (EPS) figure divided into the current stock price to calculate the P/E multiple (i.e. how many times a stock is trading (its price) per each dollar of EPS).

Historically, the average P/E ratio for the broad market has been around 15, although it can fluctuate significantly depending on economic and market conditions. The ratio will also vary widely among different companies and industries.

Formula = Share price/EPS

- Price/Book Value Ratio

A valuation ratio used by investors which compares a stock's per-share price (market value) to its book value (shareholders' equity). The price-to-book value ratio, expressed as a multiple (i.e. how many times a company's stock is trading per share compared to the company's book value per share), is an indication of how much shareholders are paying for the net assets of a company.

The book value of a company is the value of a company's assets expressed on the balance sheet. It is the difference between the balance sheet assets and balance sheet liabilities and is an estimation of the value if it were to be liquidated.

The price/book value ratio, often expressed simply as "price-to-book", provides investors a way to compare the market value, or what they are paying for each share, to a conservative measure of the value of the firm.

Formula = Stock price per share/Shareholders equity per share

- Price/Earnings to Growth Ratio

The price/earnings to growth (PEG) ratio is used to determine a stock's value while taking the company's earnings growth into account, and is considered to provide a more complete picture than the P/E ratio. While a high P/E ratio may make a stock look like a good buy, factoring in the company's growth rate to get the stock's PEG ratio can tell a different story. The lower the PEG ratio, the more the stock may be undervalued given its earnings performance. The calculation is as follows:

Formula = P/E ratio ÷ Annual EPS growth

The ratio is based on projected earnings per share growth. Projections are not always accurate.

- Price/Sales Ratio

The price-to-sales ratio is an indicator of the value placed on each dollar of a company's sales or revenues. It can be calculated either by dividing the company's market capitalization by its total sales over a 12-month period, or on a per-share basis by dividing the stock price by sales per share for a 12-month period. Like all ratios, the price-to-sales ratio is most relevant when used to compare companies in the same sector. A low ratio may indicate possible undervaluation, while a ratio that is significantly above the average may suggest overvaluation. Abbreviated as the P/S ratio or PSR, this ratio is also known as a "sales multiple" or "revenue multiple."

Formula = Market value of equity/Total revenue

- Dividend Yield

Dividend yield is the ratio of dividend per share to current share price. It is a measure of what percentage an investor is earning in the form of dividends.

Formula = Dividend yield = Dividend per share/Current share price

Dividend yield is a measure of investor return. While dividend payout ratio judges the amount of dividend in relation to the company's earnings for the period, dividend yield ratio provides a comparison of amount of dividend in relation to investment needed to purchase its share.

- Enterprise Value Multiple

Enterprise value multiple is the comparison of enterprise value and earnings before interest, taxes, depreciation, and amortization. This is a very commonly used metric for estimating the business valuations. It compares the value of a company, inclusive of debt and other liabilities, to the actual cash earnings exclusive of the non-cash expenses.

This ratio is also known as "EV/EBITDA ratio" and "EBITDA multiple". Enterprise multiple can be used to compare the value of one company to the value of another company within the same industry. A lower enterprise multiple can be indicative of undervaluation of a company. Enterprise value multiple is calculated by dividing the enterprise value (EV) by the earnings before interest, taxes, depreciation, and amortization (EBITDA). This can be written as

Enterprise value multiple = Enterprise value/EBITDA

Enterprise value multiple is a better measure than the P/E ratio because it is not affected by the changes in the capital structure. Consider a scenario in which a company raises equity finance and uses these funds to repay the loans. This will usually result in lower earnings per share (EPS) and therefore a higher P/E ratio. But the Enterprise value multiple will not be affected by this change in capital structure. This means that Enterprise value multiple cannot be manipulated by the changes in capital structure. Another benefit of Enterprise value multiple is that it makes possible fair comparison of companies with different capital structures.

Another positive point about the Enterprise value multiple is that it removes the effects of non-cash expenses such as depreciation and amortization. These non-cash items are of less significance to the investors because they are ultimately interested in the cash flows. Enterprise value multiple is not usually appropriate for comparison of companies in different industries. Capital requirements of other industries are different. Therefore, Enterprise value multiple may not give reliable conclusions when comparing different industries.

22.10 Limitations

There is considerable subjectivity involved, as there is no correct number for the various ratios. Further, it is hard to reach a definite conclusion when some of the ratios are favorable and some are unfavorable. Still. Auditors must use ratios while conducting analytical procedures, keeping in mind that departures from industry average would not provide conclusive evidence of risk or fraudulent.

Practice

Question 1

Yin Company has gross fixed assets of $6,000,000 and accumulated depreciation of $2,000,000. Sales over the last 12 months totaled $12,000,000.

- Compute Yin Company fixed asset turnover ratio is:

(a) $4,000,000
(b) $6,000,000
(c) 3.0
(d) 6.0

Question 2

- At the end of FY 2018, Mignon Corporation financial statements show an ending inventory of $100,000.
- The COGS as reported in the Income Statement: $300,000

Task: compute Mignon Corporation Days' sale-to-inventory in FY 2018

(a) 3.0
(b) 122
(c) 212
(d) 0.3

Question 3

Wally, Inc. had $20,000 of average receivables during FY 2018 and collected $40,000 of receivables during the same fiscal year.

Task: Compute Wally Inc. account receivable turnover ratio in FY 2018

(a) 0.5
(b) 2
(c) $60,000
(d) $20,000

Question 4

Daxa Inc. has a net profit of $150,000 in 2018, and an average capital employed of $3,000,000.

Task: compute Daxa Inc. ROCE in FY 2018

(a) 20%
(b) 5%
(c) $2,850,000
(d) $3,150,000

Question 5

Allison LLC generates $400,000 of business each year and shows operating profit of $100,000 before any taxes or interest expenses are accounted for.

Task: Compute Allison LLC Return-on-Sales ratio

(a) $300,000
(b) 25%
(c) 2.5%
(d) 250%

CHAPTER 23

Corporate Governance, Accounting, and Auditing Scandals

23.1 General

The corporate governance sagas in the United States, the United Kingdom, Italy, Japan have stroke the essential belief our generation shares about corporation. Though a corporation is a social construct, we came to look and consider it as a person and expect it to comply with the societal tie or bondage without with no society or group can withstand. The chapter will cover the most known corporate scandals in the US, the EU, Asia-Pacific and South Africa. Most frauds could be prevented if preventive actions were taken to curve the well-known triangle of fraud.

23.2 The Triangle of Fraud

Three factors: (i) the pressure or incentive; (ii) the opportunity; and (iii) the rationalization of fraudulent behavior are of constant observance in any financial fraud.

Some authors who studied criminal sociology, such as Lumbroso, have also argued that propensity was the mean feature in the commission of any fraudulent or criminal act.[1] They argued that those who perpetrate fraudulent acts have pre-disposed propensity to cross the red line than their counterparts facing the same challenges or dilemmas. Whether

[1] Jean-Claude Lombois (1989): Droit Pénal et Sociologie Criminelle, LGDJ.

F. I. Lessambo, *Auditing, Assurance Services, and Forensics*,
https://doi.org/10.1007/978-3-319-90521-1_23

it propensity of or pressure the triggering elements of fraudulent behavior are well understood.

23.2.1 Pressure or Incentive

A management team facing the pressure to make the number or to defeat market expectations would be inclined to cook the books in order to achieve the short-term goal assigned to it. Usually when the real performance is good but below the threshold, management would be more likely to hide the "bad news" or to manipulate the financial statements in order to save their face, or create an appearance of justified bonuses despite the accounting realities. In the US, particularly when management compensation is tailored to the profit made or the "bottom-line", such incentive entices the managing team to engage in accounting massage.

23.2.2 Opportunity

Whenever the opportunity or perceived opportunity showed up, the management team would seize the occasion to falsify the accountings or override the internal control in place. The opportunity for fraud is often high in companies where the internal deterrence and detection mechanisms are lax. Often the scandal starts with mere adjustments, mere anticipation of income or recognition of expenses regarding the expected result. Then the habit persists to create a sort of addiction on the part of the management team.

23.2.3 Rationalization of Fraudulent Behavior

The rationalization of the financial offense or the need to justify the conduct would often exacerbate the magnitude of the financial misconduct. In the case of Enron, for instance, the management defended that all the "off-balance sheet transactions" were justify and there was no breach of any accounting rules. When the form of the transaction seems to align with the wording of the statute, such as with most IFRS, the management would hide behind the form to justify the substance. The ends justify the means (Fig. 23.1).

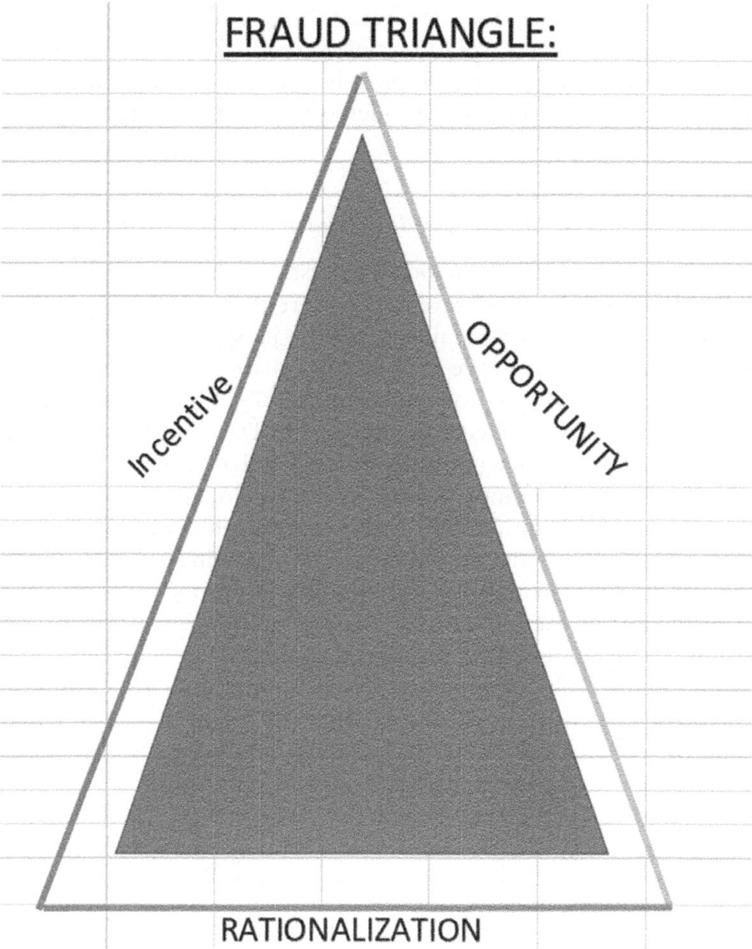

Fig. 23.1 Triangle of Fraud (*Source* The Author)

23.3 Scandals in the United States

Among developed countries, the US holds a palm record pursuant to corporate governance, accounting and auditing scandals. It is estimated that US organizations lost, on average, seven percent of their revenue to fraud.[2] A recent Deloitte Forensic Center Survey reveals that more financial statement fraud would be uncovered in 2010 and 2011 relative to the previous three years.[3] Despite the gloomy predictions, many US organizations still do not have risk deterrence and prevention systems to avoid its happening.

23.3.1 The Enron Scandal (Auditor: Arthur Andersen)

Enron Corporation was the nation's largest natural gas and electric marketer, with reported annual revenue of more than $150 billion. When it filed for bankruptcy on December 2, 2001, its stock price had dropped, in less than a year, from more than $80 per share to less than $1.[4] Enron was one of the ten largest companies in the US. The company operated in the field or business or energy trading. On December 2, 2001, Enron filed for Chapter 11 bankruptcy. Enron, which has come to identify infamous corporate governance scandal in the world, used and abused the Special Purpose Vehicle ("SPV") hid a considerable amount of its debt off-balance sheet in order to minimize the reporting of debt, hid some financial risks related to commodity trading in derivatives out of its balance sheet. Enron used several SPV out of its balance sheet to hide the extent of its liabilities. That is, Enron managed earnings very aggressively by prematurely recognizing revenue and hiding or shifting losses and liabilities to many non-consolidated SPV.[5] The financial statement Enron was enticing all but lacked fairness and accuracy. In fiscal year 2000, through accounting improprieties and fraudulent accounting estimates, Enron reported gross revenues of $101 billion. The balance sheet lacked transparency, the statement of income was overstated, and its cash flow statements inconsistent. The management was aware of the distress but chose to inflate the numbers through inside trading, wire fraud and

[2] Jean-Claude Lombois (1989): Droit Pénal et Sociologie Criminelle, LGDJ.

[3] Deloitte Financial-Advisory Services LLP (2010), http://www.deloitte.com/view/en_US/us/Services/7ba0852e4de38210VgnVCM200000bb42f00aRCDR.htm.

[4] See SEC Settles Civil Fraud Charges Filed Against Richard A. Causey, Former Enron Chief Accounting Officer; Causey Barred From Acting as an Officer or Director of a Public Company (U.S. Securities and Exchange Commission ("SEC" or "Commission") Litigation Release No. 19996, February 9, 2007).

[5] Cheol S. Eun and Bruce G. Resnik (2015): *International Financial Management*, McGraw Hill, 7th Edition, p. 102.

money laundering. On October 2, 2002, Andrew Fastow, former finance director was charged with, inter alia, conspiracy to inflate Enron's profit and self- enrichment to the expense or detriment of shareholders.

Meanwhile, Arthur Andersen, then, auditor collected in FY2000 solely from Enron $52 million ($25 million for auditing and another $27 million for consulting services). Though Enron had a code of corporate governance, its practice of corporate governance was inefficient in almost all respect:

- Non-executive directors lacked independence to perform their duties;
- Conflicts of interest involving members of the firm's internal audit committee. It was established that Wendy Gramm, the chairwoman of Enron's audit committee and her husband, Phil Gramm, a senator, received substantial political donation from Enron[6];
- Moreover, Lord Wakeham who sat on the audit committee had a consulting contract with Enron[7];
- Several top executive, particularly its chief executive officer (CEO) and the financial director had poor moral character.

23.3.2 *The Bristol-Myers Squibb Scandal (Auditor: PricewaterhouseCoopers)*

Bristol-Myers Squibb is a US-based pharmaceutical company, which received in 1999, the National Medal of technology, the nation highest recognition for technological achievement, "for extending and enhancing human life through innovative pharmaceutical research and development and for redefining the science of clinical study through groundbreaking and huge complex clinical trials recognized in the industry. In 2002, BMS was involved in an accounting scandal restatement of revenue from 1999 to 2001. BMS was improperly offering excess inventory to customers to create higher sales numbers. BMS settled with the SEC for $150 million while neither admitting nor denying any wrongdoing

[6] Jill Solomon (2010): *Corporate Governance and Accountability*, Wiley, 3rd Edition, p. 37.

[7] *The Economist*, Feb 7, 2002.

23.3.3 *The WorldCom Scandal (Auditor: Arthur Andersen)*

WorldCom (currently known as MCI) used to be the US second-largest long distance phone company, prior to its bankruptcy filing on July 21, 2001. From 1999 to 2002, the WorldCom management engaged in a series of accounting frauds to mask the company declining earning in order to prop up the price of the company's stock. WorldCom has fraudulently recorded its lease expenses as assets, reporting a profit of $2.4 billion instead of a $662 million loss. Over the years, WorldCom fraudulently inflated its profits by more than $11 billion. WorldCom used its cash flows statement to hide expenses by marking operating costs, which should have been booked as expenses, as capital investments. In so doing, WorldCom inflated cash flow by $3.8 billion for 2001 and 797 million for the first quarter of 2002. WorldCom posted quarters of positive performance when it really lost money. In 2003, the company and the SEC settled for a civil penalty of $2.25 billion.

23.3.4 *The Waste Management Scandal (Auditor: Arthur Andersen)*

Waste Management, Inc. is in the business of waste, recyclables, yard debris, hazardous materials collection, hauling, treatment and disposal, dumpster rental, portable toilet rental and security services. For its fiscal years from 1992 to 1998, the company engaged in accounting improprieties by augmenting the depreciation time length for their property, plant, and equipment. Waste Management eliminated and deferred current period expenses in order to meet its earnings' targets. In so doing, it inflated its after-tax profit by $1.7 billion.

Waste Management engaged in accounting manipulations known as "netting" and "geography". Intercompany netting is the offsetting of accounts receivable and accounts payable between two business entities owned by the same parent, so that payment is only made for the net difference between their receivables and payables. Waste Management used netting to eliminate approximately $490 million in current period operating expenses and accumulated prior period accounting misstatements by offsetting them against unrelated one-time gains on the sale or exchange of assets; and used geography entries to move tens of millions of dollars between various line items on the company's income statement to, in Koenig's words, "make the financials look the way we want to show them.[8]"

The SEC complaint charged that defendants[9]:

- avoided depreciation expenses on their garbage trucks by both assigning unsupported and inflated salvage values and extending their useful lives,
- assigned arbitrary salvage values to other assets that previously had no salvage value,
- failed to record expenses for decreases in the value of landfills as they were filled with waste,
- refused to record expenses necessary to write off the costs of unsuccessful and abandoned landfill development projects,
- established inflated environmental reserves (liabilities) in connection with acquisitions so that the excess reserves could be used to avoid recording unrelated operating expenses,
- improperly capitalized a variety of expenses, and
- failed to establish sufficient reserves (liabilities) to pay for income taxes and other expenses.

In 2001, the company settled a shareholder class-action lawsuit for $457 million, and its auditor, Andersen paid $7 million to the SEC for its assistance to the fraud. Indeed, Andersen agreed to a plan to cover up Waste Management's financial misstatements by reversing them over a period of years rather than correcting them immediately.[10]

The following corporate governance shortcomings have been identified: the SEC disclosures revealed that the executives had received large salary increases, hefty stock options, and golden parachute arrangements. Sixteen members of senior management were awarded $13 million in restricted stock that would vest if the employee was terminated. Mr. Rooney himself was blessed with a new five-year contract, a 25% increase in base salary, plus options on 350,000 shares—twice the grant he'd

[8]Waste Management Founder, Five Other Former Top Officers Sued for Massive Fraud-Litigation Release No. 17435 (2002).

[9]SEC Press Release (March 26, 2002) at http://www.sec.gov/news/headlines/wastemgmt6.htm9

[10]William F. Messier (2012): *Auditing & Assurance Services*, McGraw Hill, 8th Edition, p. 715.

received the year before. Also, a revolving door was created between the auditor and Waste Management: approximately 14 former employees of Andersen switched to Waste Management, occupying key financial and accounting positions.

23.3.5 *The Adelphia Scandal (Auditor: PricewaterhouseCoopers)*

Adelphia Communications Corporation was the US six-largest cable-television company prior to its dissolution in 2002. The Rigas family collected $3.1 billion in off-balance-sheet loans backed by Adelphia; overstated results by inflating capital expenses and hiding debt. The loan to the Rigas revealed to be shame transactions with the aim purpose to hide the true wealth and health of the Company. John Rigas, the former head of Adelphia Communications, and two of his sons were arrested and charged with looting Adelphia assets to pay for luxury condos, golf courses and more. The majority of Adelphia's revenue-generating assets were acquired by Time Warner Cable and Comcast on July 31, 2006. The following corporate governance failures were found:

- Lack of integrity by the top management; and
- Lack of transparent corporate reporting

23.3.6 *The AIG Scandal (Auditor: PricewaterhouseCoopers)*

AIG is a US-based multinational Insurance Corporation. AIG was bailed out by the US Federal Reserve in 2008. From 1999 to 2005, AIG was involved in a wide-ranging accounting fraud culminating in a $3.9 billion restatement in May 2005 that included numerous different types of transactions, and allegations relating to a $500 million no-risk fraudulent reinsurance transaction that AIG entered into with General Reinsurance Corp. in order to artificially boost AIG's reported claims reserves. Further, AIG paid tens of millions of dollars in undisclosed contingent commissions to insurance brokers and participated in a bid-rigging scheme with insurance brokers and certain insurance companies in order to divide the market for certain types of insurance. AIG settled for almost a $ billion and its auditor, PwC settled for $97.5 million for abetting the fraud.

23.3.7 *The Tyco Scandal (Auditor: PricewaterhouseCoopers)*

Tyco International Ltd used to be a US-based corporation. It went through corporate inversion to become a Switzerland corporation with United States operational headquarters in Princeton, New Jersey. In the 1970, Tyco went ton to acquire several companies, most of them outside its field of business. Between 1991 and 2001, Tyco under the leadership of Dennis Kozlowski acquired over thousand companies. For many acquisitions, Tyco incurred extensive losses. In 2002, Dennis Kozlowski and its former chief financial officer, Mark H. Swartz were accused of looting more than $150 million from the company. Both men are serving a jail time up to 25 years. In May 2007, a district judge approved a class action whereby Tyco agreed to pay $2.9 billion (in conjunction with $225 million by PricewaterhouseCoopers) to defrauded shareholders.

The following corporate governance shortcomings have been identified:

- too much company power is put into the hands of a single individual;
- leadership style combined with the firm's decentralized corporate structure meant that few people, including members of the board of directors, accurately understood the firm's activities and finances;
- The CEO making major payments without informing the board members;
- Several board members have been cited for conflict of interest:
  - (i) Frank Walsh pleaded guilty and agreed to repay $20 million plus an additional $2 million in court costs.
  - (ii) Jerry Boggess, the president of Tyco Fire and Security Division, was fired and accused of creating a number of "bookkeeping issues" negatively impacting earnings of shareholders.
  - (iii) Richard Scalzo, the PricewaterhouseCoopers' auditor who signed off on Tyco's 2002 audit, was fired.

23.3.8 *The HealthSouth Scandal (Auditor: Ernst & Young)*

In 2003, HealthSouth, the largest U.S. operator of rehabilitation-hospitals, was under investigation by the Securities and Exchange Commission and the Justice Department for overstating its earnings by $2.5 billion since 1999. In 1996, Scrushy instructed the company's senior officers and accountants to falsify company earnings reports in order to meet investor expectations and control the price of the company's stock. In certain fiscal years, the company's income was overstated by as much as 4700%. The $1.4 billion represents more than 10% of the company's total assets. At the company's height in 2003, it recorded nearly $4.5 billion in revenue, dominated the rehabilitation, surgery and diagnostic services market. By the end of 2003, the company had most of its finances reorganized and was able to avoid Chapter 11 bankruptcy.

23.3.9 The New Century Financial Case (Auditor: KPMG)

New Century was the US second-largest subprime lender, based in Irvine California. It had been one of the largest U.S. providers of home loans to people with poor credit. From 2002 to 2006, New Century's loan originations had risen from $14 billion to about $60 billion. On 2 April 2008, New Century filed for Chapter 11 bankruptcy protection. New Century engaged in a number of significant improper and imprudent practices related to its loan originations, operations, and financial reporting. New Century was "brazen" in increasing its loans and extending them to borrowers who were increasingly unlikely to repay. It had insufficient loan loss reserves to sustain its operations. New Century reported a profit of $63.5 million in the third quarter of 2006 when it should have reported a loss. The company also reported an increase of 8% in earnings per share during the second quarter of 2006 when it should have reported at least a 40% decline.

The auditor, KPMG contributed to some of these accounting and financial errors by enabling them to persist and, in some instances, precipitating the company's departures from applicable accounting standards. The KPMG engagement team acquiesced in New Century's departures from prescribed accounting methodologies and often resisted or ignored valid recommendations from specialists.[11]

Former CEO and co-founder Brad A. Morrice, former CFO Patti M. Dodge and former controller David N. Kenneally consented to the settlement with the Securities and Exchange Commission. Likewise, New Century's former auditor KPMG settled a lawsuit with the New Century

[11] Amanda Beck, Reuters, Mar 27, 2008.

Liquidating Trustee in August 2010 for merely $45 million. Several corporate governance failures were single out, inter alia:

- Strained relationship between the board and senior management;
- Failure to analyze enterprise risk management;
- Limited focus of the audit committee and the company's internal audit department.[12]

23.3.10 Penn West Petroleum Ltd. (Auditor: KPMG)

- Penn West is one of the largest conventional oil and natural gas producers in Canada. The Company is headquartered in Calgary, Alberta. Penn West is cross-listed in the NYSE.
- Penn West Company improperly reclassified approximately $181 million in operating expenses as capital expenditures, and had incorrectly reclassified approximately $200 million in additional operating expenses as royalty expenses for 2012 and 2013. All of the reclassifications of operating expense to capital expenditure occurred at the corporate level and lacked justification or support.
- The scheme artificially reduced the Company's operating costs and, in turn, falsely increased its reported funds flow, netbacks, and other measures of profitability. The misconduct artificially inflated the Company's capital expenditures, thus making it appear as though Penn West was investing more money in oil wells to drive future production.
- In 2012 and 2013, Penn West understated its operating expenses by about 16%.
- Penn West wrote down $48-million of goodwill in 2013's fourth quarter instead of writing off its entire $2 billion goodwill balance.
- In 2016, Penn West settled for $53 million, to be split evenly between Canadian and U.S. investors.

23.3.11 Marrone Bio Innovations (Auditor: E&Y)

- The company develops, manufactures and sells biologically-based products to replace chemicals used to manage agricultural pests.

[12] Michael J. Missal and Lisa M. Richman (2008): New Century Financial: Lessons Learned, Mortgage Banking, October.

- Mr. Hector Absi, Marrone's chief operating officer at the time, had misled the company in its accounting for sales with a scheme that netted him $350,000 in bonuses and stock options. In fact, he inflated sales to earn a higher bonus and boost the value of his stock options. More, he inflated financial results to meet projections that the company would double revenues in its first year as a public company.
- Mr. Absi inflated Marrone Bio's revenues by offering distributors "inventory protection," a concession that allowed distributors to return unsold product. Moreover, Mr. Absi also inflated Marrone Bio's revenue by directing his subordinates to obtain false sales and shipping documents and intentionally ship the wrong product to book sales.
- Marrone Bio agreed to pay a $1.75 million penalty to settle the SEC's charges. The SEC alleges that former COO Hector M. Absi Jr. hid various sales concessions offered to customers from Marrone Bio's finance personnel and independent auditor, leading the Davis, Calif.-based company to improperly recognize revenue on sales.
- Mr. Absi resigned in August 2014 shortly before the alleged fraud came to light and the company's stock price plunged more than 44%.

23.3.12 Weatherford (Auditor: KPMG Auditor)

- Weatherford is an oil and gas service company with a presence in every major oil and gas region of the world.
- Weatherford issued false financial statements between 2007 and 2012 that inflated its earnings by more than $900 million in total.
- Weatherford orchestrated a fraud that spanned four fiscal years and falsely lowered Weatherford's year-end provision for income taxes by $100 million to $154 million each year.
- On March 8, 2011 Weatherford filed its first restatement aimed to address a four-year income tax accounting fraud allegedly perpetrated by James Hudgins, the vice president of tax, and Darryl Kitay, the tax manager and later senior tax manager who reported to Hudgins.
- The restatement reduced previously reported net income by approximately $500 million in total.

- In September 2016, Weatherford agreed to pay $252.6 million to settle the SEC's charges and related actions by four other agencies.
- The SEC also charged the EY partner who coordinated the audits, Craig Fronckiewicz, and a former tax partner who was part of the audit engagement team, Sarah Adams. Both agreed to suspensions to settle charges that they disregarded significant red flags during the audits and reviews. The external auditor knew about post-closing adjustments made by Weatherford in order to lower its year-end provision for income taxes each year, but failed to perform appropriate audit procedures thereof. They relied on the Weatherford management unsubstantiated explanations.
- EY agreed to pay disgorgement of $9 million, prejudgment interest of more than $1.8 million, and a penalty of $1 million. The two partners agreed to be suspended from appearing or practicing before the SEC, including participating in the financial reporting or audits of public companies.

23.4 Diagnosis of the Scandals

Though accounting and auditing frauds describes above have or may have various causes, a close analysis reveals some common characteristics that can be summed up as follow:

23.4.1 Corporate Greed

Presumably, senior executives in the corporations and auditing industry expect to get away with their misfeasance. Being caught is seen like an unfortunate accident that should not happen, or it does happen is due to over-regulations and governments' intrusion in the business affairs. As we have seen, the US stands as the leader in accounting frauds. Some of them used sophisticated approaches expecting to blur the regulators (i.e., SEC, Federal Reserve).

23.4.2 Unfettered Deregulation

Two industries were particularly prominent in the scandals: the energy companies, telecommunications, and the Banking. Deregulation allowed the businesses in some specific industries, mainly the energy and the banking to take excessive risks above their managerial skills. Enron, for instance morphed from a natural gas transmitting to become high-tech energy traders using sophisticated derivatives and structured-finance deals. The short-term result was giant profits for the lenders. For Enron and others it also meant hiding the losses, inflating revenues, manipulating inventories, and other creative accounting devices. The various investment bank scandals are included because their deceptive practices encouraged earnings management and an environment of fraud. The recent mortgage-related scandals have exposed major commercial and investment banks.

23.4.3 *Excessive Compensation*

Excessive executive compensation, incentive packages based solely on the "Profits realized" have also contributed to the corporate accounting and auditing scandals. Managements become short-termed in the race for profit maximization. The end justifies the means.

23.4.4 *Ineffective Boards of Directors*

Most companies are led by ineffective boards, eager to please either the chairman or the CEO. In so doing, most boards are more and less mere rubber-stamping boards of directors. The concentration or excessive powers that these chairmen or CEOs enjoy contributes to such collapse, mainly in jurisdictions were a single person combines both offices.

23.4.5 *Lack of Continuous Training*

This is exacerbated in the US, where most directors lack basic knowledge of accounting, finance, management. Boards are full of lawyers who did not understand business models they pretend to apply. A sound approach would require to provide continuous training of directors, and gatekeepers alike to help them live up to the public and social expectations.

Appendix

- The Effect of Corporate Governance on Auditor-Client Realignments, by Cory A. Cassell, Gary A. Giroux, Linda A. Myers, and Thomas C. Omer; *AUDITING: A Journal of Practice & Theory*, February 2012, Vol. 31, No. 1, pp. 127–146.

- The Role of Incentives to Manage Earnings and Quantification in Auditors' Evaluations of Management-Provided Information, by Urton Anderson, Kathryn Kadous, and Lisa Koonce; *AUDITING: A Journal of Practice & Theory*, March 2004, Vol. 23, No. 1, pp. 29–52.

CHAPTER 24

Auditor Legal Liability

24.1 General

Like other professionals such as physicians, architects, auditors are liable both civilly and criminally. Civilly, an auditor can be found liable either under the common law or a statutory law liability. Common law liability arises from negligence, breach of contract, and fraud. Statutory law liability is the obligation that comes from a certain statute or a law, which is applied, to society. The scope of both common law liability and statutory liability has been expanded to include certain third parties, mainly the foreseen or foreseeable users of audited financial statements. Also, a lawsuit in a state court provides greater protection than the one brought before the federal court.

24.2 Auditor Contractual Liability: The Engagement Letter

An Engagement Letter is, in many respects, a written contract between the CPA and the client, stating both parties' understanding of the professional relationship. It states the responsibilities of the engagement for the CPA and the client. The agreed-upon terms of the audit engagement should be documented in an audit engagement letter or other suitable form of written agreement and should include the following[1]:

[1] AU-C Section 210; Source: SAS No. 122, Par. 9 and 10.

F. I. Lessambo, *Auditing, Assurance Services, and Forensics*,
https://doi.org/10.1007/978-3-319-90521-1_24

a. The objective and scope of the audit of the financial statements;
b. The responsibilities of the auditor;
c. The responsibilities of management;
d. A statement that because of the inherent limitations of an audit, together with the inherent limitations of internal control, an unavoidable risk exists that some material misstatements may not be detected, even though the audit is properly planned and performed in accordance with GAAS;
e. Identification of the applicable financial reporting framework for the preparation of the financial statements; and
f. Reference to the expected form and content of any reports to be issued by the auditor and a statement that circumstances may arise in which a report may differ from its expected form and content.

Suit in Contract is based on privity of contract and the auditors alleged breach of the agreement (the engagement letter). While an engagement letter will not make the CPA immune to lawsuits, the letter can be the "first line of defense" if a client makes a claim against the CPA.

The roles of management and those charged with governance in agreeing upon the terms of the audit engagement for the entity depend on the governance structure of the entity and relevant law or regulation. Depending on the entity's structure, the agreement may be with management, those charged with governance, or both. When the agreement on the terms of engagement is only with those charged with governance, the auditor is required to obtain management's agreement that it acknowledges and understands its responsibilities.[2]

When a third party has contracted for the audit of the entity's financial statements, agreeing the terms of the audit with management of the entity is necessary in order to establish that the preconditions for an audit are present.[3]

The auditor should not agree to a change in the terms of the audit engagement when no reasonable justification for doing so exists.[4] If, prior to completing the audit engagement, the auditor is requested to change the audit engagement to an engagement for which the auditor

[2] AU-C Section 210; Source: SAS No. 122, Par. 20.

[3] AU-C Section 210; Source: SAS No. 122, Par. 35–39.

[4] AU-C Section 210; Source: SAS No. 122, Par. 20.

obtains a lower level of assurance, the auditor should determine whether reasonable justification for doing so exists.

If the terms of the audit engagement are changed, the auditor and management should agree on and document the new terms of the engagement in an engagement letter or other suitable form of written agreement.

If the auditor concludes that no reasonable justification for a change of the terms of the audit engagement exists and is not permitted by management to continue the original audit engagement, the auditor should:

a. withdraw from the audit engagement when possible under applicable law or regulation,
b. communicate the circumstances to those charged with governance, and
c. determine whether any obligation, either legal, contractual, or otherwise, exists to report the circumstances to other parties, such as owners, or regulators.[5]

24.3 Auditor Common Law Tort Liability

Common law refers to unwritten or case-made law (judge made laws) that evolves from prior or precedent cases. Under common law, an auditor can be held liable to its clients for negligence, gross negligence, constructive fraud, and fraud. Due to the substantive amount of damages that a client can collect in a tort action, clients of auditor would be well-advised to gear into tort claims rather than contractual ones. In order to recover from an auditor under common law tort, the client (the aggrieved party) must prove the basic elements of negligence: (1) duty; (2) a breach of duty; (3) an injury; (4) causation (the breach that was the proximate cause of the injury); and (5) damages suffered by the injured party. The audit standards established by both the AICPA and PCAOB require that the auditor plan and perform the audit to obtain reasonable assurance about whether the financial statements are free of material misstatement.

[5] AU-C Section 210; Source: SAS No. 122, Par. 14–17.

24.3.1 Duty

The auditor agrees to perform its audit and other attest services in accordance with the AICPA and/or the PCAOB auditing standards: (i) general standards, (ii) standards of fieldwork, and (iii) standards of reporting. Any tort claim based in tort laws derives from the aforementioned standards of duty set forth by the AICPA and the PCAOB.

- General Standards

  (1) The audit is to be performed by a person or persons having adequate technical training and proficiency as an auditor.
  (2) In all matters relating to the assignment, an independence in mental attitude is to be maintained by the auditor or auditors.
  (3) Due professional care is to be exercised in the performance of the audit and the preparation of the report.

- Standards of Field Work

  (1) The work is to be adequately planned and assistants, if any, are to be properly supervised.
  (2) A sufficient understanding of internal control is to be obtained to plan the audit and to determine the nature, timing, and extent of tests to be performed.
  (3) Sufficient appropriate evidential matter is to be obtained through inspection, observation, inquiries, and confirmations to afford a reasonable basis for an opinion regarding the financial statements under audit.

- Standards of Reporting

  (1) The report shall state whether the financial statements are presented in accordance with generally accepted accounting principles (GAAP).
  (2) The report shall identify those circumstances in which such principles have not been consistently observed in the current period in relation to the preceding period.
  (3) Informative disclosures in the financial statements are to be regarded as reasonably adequate unless otherwise stated in the report.

(4) The report shall contain either an expression of opinion regarding the financial statements, taken as a whole, or an assertion to the effect that an opinion cannot be expressed. When an overall opinion cannot be expressed, the reasons therefor should be stated. In all cases where an auditor's name is associated with financial statements, the report should contain a clear-cut indication of the character of the auditor's work, if any, and the degree of responsibility the auditor is taking.

24.3.2 *Breach of Duty*

The auditor's liability would attach any time his performance in any Engagement Letter falls below the ten standards aforementioned. However, client must point to the specific standard breached rather than alleging vague breach of auditing standards.

A breach of duty occurs when one person or company has a duty of care toward another person or company, but fails to live up to that standard. When considering whether a defendant in a torts case has breached his duty toward the plaintiff, the court asks several questions, inter alia: "did the defendant have a duty of care toward the plaintiff?" If so, was it a duty of reasonable care, or was it based on professional liability, premises liability, or another type of relationship between the plaintiff and defendant? Under the AICPA and the PCAOB standards, an auditor owes a duty of professional care (professional due diligence) to its client and any other aggrieved third party. Thus, an auditor would be in breach of his duty of professional due diligence when he fails to act with the same reasonable care an ordinary person ("CPA") would use in the same circumstances.

24.3.3 *Injury, Loss, or Damages*

Plaintiff seeking to recover loss or damages from an auditor must assert his claims with particulars. Auditing malpractice differs from medical malpractice in that auditors know how to challenge the amount of damages sought against them. Most of the time, CPA would argue that the plaintiff damages sought are mere hindsight fantasy that the amounts accepted by the auditors were unreasonable. Thus, identifying, measuring each items of the harm suffered is key. Failing to do so will tend to make the plaintiff seem greedy and overreaching in the mind of the jury.

Some approaches have helped or assisted the jury to visualize the compilation of the bottom-line amount claim:

- Comparing the statements before and after the auditor' alleged negligence;
- Comparing the profits or operations of a closely comparable business operation to the plaintiff's business for the period at stake; and
- Comparing the numbers from the restated financial statements, free from error or fraud, with the previous statements.[6]

For instance, World Radio v. Coopers & Lybrand,[7] the engagement auditor failed to detect an error resulting from an overstatement of the company's statement of financial position. An amount of $890,000 from a debt payable was not integrated. The company claimed that the auditor's negligence resulted in lost profits and decreased its value. Word Radio through an analytical identification, measurement of a series of particulars[8] computed its damages around $18 million, and the jury found with the company granting it more than $17 million, almost all the damages sought.

24.3.4 *Causation*

To recover in an auditing or accounting negligent case, the plaintiff must establish that the auditor actions or lack of actions cause his loss. Generally, the test employed to decide the causation issue is known as

[6] Cerillo (1990): *Proving Business Damages.*

[7] World Radio v. Coopers & Lybrand, 251 Neb. 261, 557 N.W.2d 1 (1996).

[8] World Radio alleged damages in the following particulars:

- Inability to obtain or raise equity capital for expansion.
- Inability to expand its business by opening new stores and increasing credit lines.
- The making of operating decisions based on false financial information.
- Inability to conduct normal business operations.
- Lost revenues.
- Lost discounts, rebates, and advertising allowances and participation credits.
- Inventory losses.
- Decrease in employee morale.
- Attorney, accounting and polygraph fees.

the "but for test". Put differently, the plaintiff would never such a loss or damage but for the conduct of the auditor. As discussed under the auditor defenses, the action of the management can be a superseding cause that annihilates the auditor conduct.

24.4 Auditor Liabilities Vis-À-Vis Third-Party Claimants

In general and except in situations where the court appoints an auditor to provide its independent and expert opinion concerning the financial statements at stake, the auditor enters rarely into a contract (Engagement Letter) with third parties. Thus, the bulk of the third-party actions or claims against an auditor would be based under the laws of torts. To initiate a common law suit against an independent auditor, a third party must establish the following elements: (i) the existence of a duty of care, (ii) the failure to provide the duty, (iii) the causation, and (iv) the damage. Prima facie, one may say that the common law tort elements required are the same for both the client and the aggrieved third party. In fact, four standards have been developed over the times to assess the auditor's liability vis-à-vis a third party, not in privity of contract with him: (i) the privity approach; (ii) the near-privity approach, (iii) the restatement of torts, approach, and (iv) the foreseeability approach for Courts have developed several approaches in apprehending auditor liability to third-party plaintiff.

24.4.1 The Privity Approach

Under the privity theory, auditor has no liability vis-à-vis a third party who is not in contractual relationship with him. Courts have relied upon the doctrine of privity as a convenient means of limiting the liability of auditors, though this same doctrine has been consistently swept aside in other areas of tort law in order to obtain a duty standard more in keeping with justice and the economic-social needs of society. Shareholders of other victim of auditor mishap would have to prove a fraudulent conduct on behalf the auditor in the absence of privity. Privity, a dated concept in tort law, provides that a contract cannot confer rights or impose obligations arising under it on any person or agent except the parties to it.

- Ultramares v. Touch

In 1924 the auditors of Touche Niven (Touche, Niven & Company) gave the rubber importer, Fred Stern and Company, an unqualified audit certificate, having failed to detect that management had falsified entries to overstate accounts receivable. The auditors knew that the accounts when certified would be used to raise money and for that purpose supplied 32 certified and serially numbered copies. On the faith of one of those copies, given to it on its demand, the plaintiff, Ultramares Corporation, lent Fred Stern and Company money. Stern declared bankruptcy in 1925. Ultramares sued Touche Niven for the amount of the Stern debt, declaring that a careful audit would have shown Stern to be insolvent. The audit was found to be negligent, but not fraudulent. The judge set this finding aside based on the doctrine of privity, which protects auditors from third-party suits. An intermediate appellate court reinstated the negligence verdict. The case then went to the New York Court of Appeals, Judge Benjamin Cardozo presiding held that the claim in negligence failed on the ground that the auditors owed the plaintiff no duty of care, there being no sufficiently proximate relationship. Justice Cardozo stated that "an investor, not in privity, could recover only if the accountant's negligence was so gross as to sustain an inference of fraud."

Likewise, in Cogen, where the plaintiff was one of two shareholders in a corporation, and the audit set the price of stock for a sale to the other shareholder. The purpose and the parties were known to the auditor. The court held that the auditor had no duty to exercise reasonable care and in the absence of privity between the shareholder and the auditor the shareholder would have to prove fraudulent conduct.

A string of recent decisions in a majority of states points to a continued erosion of the requirement of privity in order for a third party to bring a legal action for negligence against an auditor.

24.4.2 The Near-Privity Approach

Before accountants may be held liable in negligence to non-contractual parties who rely to their detriment on inaccurate financial reports, certain prerequisites must be satisfied: (1) the accountants must have been aware that the financial reports were to be used for a particular purpose or purposes; (2) in the furtherance of which a known party or parties was intended to rely; and (3) there must have been some conduct on the part of the accountants linking them to that party or parties, which evinces the accountants' understanding of that party or parties' reliance. In several cases, courts have rejected the strict privity rule and granted recovery to plaintiffs in near-privity.

- In Ryan v Kanne,[9] the court rejected the accountants' contention that a strict privity doctrine governed accountants' liability for negligence. Recovery was permitted where the audit report was used as the accountants had contemplated, by a known non-privy party, to whom one of the accounting partners personally explained the report at meetings they both attended.
- In Larsen v United Fed. Sav. & Loan Assn.,[10] the same court granted recovery to a non privity party who had actually paid for the accountant's appraisal, and was specifically designated on the appraisal itself as the one for whose benefit it was being prepared.
- In Shatterproof Glass Corp. v James[11] the court held that the accountants were under a duty to exercise due care toward the third party who had loaned money to the accountants' client in reliance on the financial statements. The accountants knew that their reports would be issued to and relied upon by a particular creditor. Moreover, the accountants had furnished information directly to the third party creditor as authorized by their client and, indeed, they had charged their client a separate and additional amount for rendering such services.
- In Coleco Indus. v Berman,[12] the non-privy parties who relied upon the financial statements had, in fact, chosen the accountants, explained to those accountants the role they were to play in the ongoing transactions, and had direct dealings with them. The court concluded that the "lack of strict privity" should not preclude a negligence claim against the accountants. The relationship existing between the accountants and the non-privy parties was found to be "'so close as to approach that of privity, if not completely one with it.'"

[9] Ryan v. Kanne (170 NW 2d. 395 [Iowa]).

[10] Larsen v United Fed. Sav. & Loan Assn. (300 NW2d 281 [Iowa]).

[11] Shatterproof Glass Corp. v James (466 SW2d 873 [Tex Civ App]).

[12] Coleco Indus. v. Berman (423 F Supp 275 [ED Pa]).

- In European Am. Bank & Trust Co. v. Strauhs & Kaye, where the facts as alleged by EAB clearly show that S & K was well aware that a primary, if not the exclusive, end and aim of auditing its client, Majestic Electro, was to provide EAB with the financial information it required. Moreover, the accountants' awareness of a particular purpose for their services and certain conduct on their part creating an unmistakable relationship with the reliant plaintiff. It was also established that the parties remained in direct communication, both orally and in writing, and, indeed, met together throughout the course of EAB's lending relationship with Majestic Electro, for the very purpose of discussing the latter's financial condition and EAB's need for S & K's evaluation. Furthermore, the external auditor, S & K Moreover, made repeated representations personally to representatives of EAB, on these occasions, concerning the value of Majestic Electro's assets.
- The Court held that parties' direct communications and personal meetings resulted in a nexus between them sufficiently approaching privity under the principles of Ultramares, Glanzer and White to permit EAB's causes of action.

24.4.3 The Restatement of Torts Approach

Expansion of third-party liability began to gain further acceptance as courts moved away from a contractual theory of liability to one based upon the Restatement (Second) of Torts. Restatement (Second) of Torts §552, entitled "Information Negligently Supplied for the Guidance of Others," states:

1. One who, in the course of his business, profession or employment, or in any other transaction in which he has a pecuniary interest, supplies false information for the guidance of others in their business transactions, is subject to liability for pecuniary loss caused to them by their justifiable reliance upon the information, if he fails to exercise reasonable care or competence in obtaining or communicating the information.
2. Except as stated in Subsection (3), the liability stated in Subsection (1) is limited to loss suffered (a) by the person or one of a limited group of persons for whose benefit and guidance he intends to supply the information or knows that the recipient intends to

supply it; and (b) through reliance upon it in a transaction that he intends the information to influence or knows that the recipient so intends or in a substantially similar transaction.

3. The liability of one who is under a public duty to give the information extends to loss suffered by any of the class of persons for whose benefit the duty is created, in any of the transactions in which it is intended to protect them.

Under the Restatement (Second) approach, individuals may be liable when they supply false information for the guidance of others.

24.4.4 *The Foreseeability Approach*

For a plaintiff to articulate a cause of action based upon negligence misrepresentation theory, the plaintiff must establish: (1) a negligent misrepresentation, (2) by a service provider, (3) that results in economic loss, and (4) to a person not in privity with the service provider. In other words, an incorrect statement or opinion negligently made and justifiably relied upon by a foreseeable user of the audited financial statements provides a cause of action for recovery of damages for economic loss or injury sustained as a consequence of that reliance. That is, when an independent auditor furnishes an opinion with no limitation in the certificate as to whom the company may disseminate the financial statements, he has a duty to all those whom that auditor should reasonably foresee as recipients from the company of the statements for its proper business purposes, provided that the recipients rely on the statements pursuant to those business purposes.

The auditor's function has expanded from that of a watchdog for management to an independent evaluator of the adequacy and fairness of financial statements issued by management to stockholders, creditors, and others. Certified financial statements have become the benchmark for various reasonably foreseeable business purposes and accountants have been engaged to satisfy those ends. In those circumstances accounting firms should no longer be permitted to hide within the citadel of privity and avoid liability for their malpractice. Whenever he certifies a financial statement the certified public accountant is potentially, at least, rendering a service to two or more parties whose interests may come into conflict—management and stockholder, borrower and lender, purchaser and seller. He may, and often does, serve simultaneously competitors in the same line of business, without fear on the part of either client that he will favor the one or the other. It is the peculiar obligation of the certified public accountant, which no other profession has to impose on its members, to maintain a wholly objective and impartial attitude toward the affairs of the client whose financial statements he certifies.

The principle is spelled out clearly in the Rosenblum v. Adler case[13] The relevant facts under the case can be summed up as follow:

- The plaintiffs Harry and Barry Rosenblum entered into a merger transaction with Giant Stores Corporation, whereby they acquired Giant common stock in conjunction with the sale of their business to Giant.
- Plaintiffs relied on the correctness of the audit opinion issued by Touche Ross & Co., the external auditor which audited the financial statements of Giant before the transaction.
- These stocks subsequently proved to be worthless, after findings that the financial statements were fraudulent.
- Plaintiffs claimed that Touche Ross & Co. negligently conducted the audits and that Touche's negligence was a proximate cause of their loss.
- Giant had manipulated its books by falsely recording assets that it did not own and omitting substantial amounts of accounts payable so that the financial information that Touche had certified in the 1971 and 1972 statements was incorrect.
- Touche's opinion affixed to those financials stated that it had examined the statements of earnings and balance sheets "in accordance with generally accepted auditing standards" and that the financial statements "present[ed] fairly" Giant's financial position. Similar data had been incorporated in Giant's annual report for the year ending 30 January 1971. Further, Touche began its audit of Giant's financials for the year ending 29 January 1972. This audit was completed on 18 April 1972. The attached Touche opinion bore the same language affixed to the 1971 statements.
- The plaintiffs' four-count complaint, predicated on the audited financials for the years ending 30 January 1971 and 29 January

[13] Rosenblum v. Adler, 93 N.J 324 (1983) 461 A.2d 138.

1972, charged fraudulent misrepresentation, gross negligence, negligence and breach of warranty.

- Touche moved for partial summary judgment. It sought to have the court dismiss the claims based on alleged negligence in making the audit for the year ending 30 January 1971 and on alleged negligence, gross negligence and fraud in making the audit for the year ending 29 January 1972.
- The trial court granted the motion with respect to the 1971 financials and denied it as to the 1972 financials.
- Both the trial court and the Appellate Division ruled that the plaintiffs' claim based on negligent preparation of the 1971 audit could not be sustained because the accountants were not aware at the time the audit was prepared of the existence of the plaintiffs or of a limited class of which the plaintiffs were members. The defendant's audit had been completed on 16 April 1971 and Giant's merger discussions with the plaintiff did not begin until the following September. Therefore the defendants had no knowledge of the Rosenblums or the prospective merger at the time of the preparation of the audit and there could be no liability under Ultramares or the Restatement.
- The NJ Supreme Court disagreed. The NY Supreme Court found that when the defendants prepared the Giant audit, they knew or should have known that Giant would probably use the audited figures for many proper business purposes. They knew that it was to be incorporated in Giant's annual report, a report that would be transmitted to each Giant stockholder, and would be filed with the SEC in conjunction with Giant's proxy solicitation material for its annual stockholder meeting. The defendants also knew or should have known that the audited financial statements would be available and useful for other proper business purposes, such as public offerings of securities, credit, and corporate acquisitions. These were clearly foreseeable potential uses of the audited financials at the time of their preparation. Giant and the defendant auditors knew that these financial statements would be used at least until the next financial statements had been audited and released.
- Further, the NJ Supreme Court held that the defendants knew that the merger agreement included a representation that the prospectus used for the public offering in December 1971 contained no untrue statement of a material fact and did not omit to state any

material fact. The defendants knew that this prospectus included their opinion that the financials had been prepared in accordance with generally accepted accounting principles and fairly presented Giant's financial condition. The defendants' representations were of a continuing nature and their obligation was a continuing one. That there was no limitation in the accountants' opinion. They could reasonably expect that their client would distribute the statements in furtherance of matters relating to its business. Having inserted the audit in that economic stream, the defendants should be responsible for their careless misrepresentations to parties who justifiably relied upon their expert opinions.

- Finally this court held that irrespective of whether the defendants had actual knowledge of Giant's proposed use of the 1972 audit in connection with the merger, it was reasonably foreseeable that Giant would use the audited statement in connection with the merger and its consummation.

24.5 The Auditor Defenses

External auditors often use two defensive arguments to shield themselves against third-party actions: (i) the In pari delicto, the (ii) the Imputation doctrine. (iii) the absence of negligence, and (iv) the contributory negligence.

24.5.1 The In Pari Delicto: An Equitable Defense

24.5.1.1 The Principle Rationale
Elaborated in 1905 with a case known as Smith v. London Assurance Corporation, the doctrine of in pari delicto mandates that courts will not intercede to resolve a dispute between two wrongdoers. Put differently, the doctrine bars one coconspirator in a fraud from suing another conspirator. Where the plaintiff is a corporation, the predicate for the imputation defense is that the management acted as an agent of the shareholders. The equitably-oriented doctrine of in pari delicto provides a strong shield or line of defense to auditing firms despite their reckless opinions. It is quite different from the doctrines of comparative fault or contributory negligence.

24.5.1.2 The Adverse Interest Exception

Whenever the management of a corporation is acting adversely to the corporation interest it would be improper to impute their acts to the corporation. This exception is known as the "adverse interest doctrine" and its scope is somehow narrow by the courts. That is, whenever the court found that the corporation has benefitted from the actions—though fraudulent—of its agents, the exception becomes inapplicable. The profit or benefit to the corporation is a moot point among jurisdictions. Also, the adverse interest exception requires an utmost careful drafting of the claim on behalf the claimant. The scope of the exception has been broadened since the AHERT case explained below. The "any benefit" used to avoid the exception seems to requires more than a "peppercorn of benefit". Also, a mere continuation of a bankrupt corporation by fraudulent management would not be considered a benefit at all to be used against the corporation.

24.5.1.3 The Inconsistencies of the Defense: Conflicts Among States

- The NCP Case
  - Physician Computer Network (PCN), was a publicly traded New Jersey corporation. From 1993 until mid-1998, PCN retained KPMG as its independent accounting and auditing firm. Throughout the term of the engagement, two PCN officers, John Mortell and Thomas Wraback, served as the primary liaisons between KPMG and PCN.
  - During the mid-to-late 1990s, Mortell and Wraback engineered a plan to fraudulently inflate PCN's earnings and decrease its liabilities. On April 1, 1996, PCN filed its annual report for the year ending 31 December 1995, and reported revenues of $20.5 million in 1994, and a 584% increase from its reported revenues of $6 million in 1993. The inflated revenues effectively reduced PCN's net loss to $11 million, before extraordinary items.
  - In 1997, PCN filed its annual report for 1996 with the SEC, which reported revenues of $96 million-more than double the revenues of the previous year. These revenues were fraudulently exaggerated by numerous sham transactions, including inter alia:

    (i) The record of $4,791,290 pre-paid marketing fees pursuant to an agreement entered into between PCN and Equifax Healthcare EDI Services, Inc. ("Equifax");

(ii) Failure to defer revenue a $1.5 million on maintenance contracts; and
(iii) Failure to properly accrue bonus and vacation.

The 1995 and 1996 financial statements were accompanied by an unqualified audit opinion by KPMG stating:

In our opinion, the consolidated financial statements referred to above present fairly, in all material respects, the financial position of Physician Computer Network, Inc. and subsidiaries as of 31 December 1995 and 1994, and the results of their operations and their cash flows for each of the years in the three-year period ended 31 December 1995, in conformity with generally accepted accounting principles. Also in our opinion, the related financial statement schedule, when considered in relation to the basic consolidated financial statements taken as a whole, presents fairly, and in all material respects, the information set forth therein.

- On 2 April 1996, PCN announced in a press release that it had filed a registration statement and prospectus with the SEC to offer seven million shares of PCN's common stock for sale to the public. On 7 May 1996, PCN filed an amended registration statement with the SEC, lowering the seven million share offering to 5.6 million shares. The registration statement and prospectus contained a copy of the corporation's audited financial statements for 1995 and KPMG's accompanying audit report, which was included with KPMG's express consent.
- On 7 December 1999, PCN filed for bankruptcy under Chapter 11. On May 9, 2002, plaintiff, NCP Litigation Trust (the "Trust"), the successor-in-interest to, inter alia, the claims of PCN against KPMG, filed suit against KPMG alleging that KPMG's breach of contract, negligence, negligent misrepresentation, and breach of fiduciary duty injured PCN.
- On 22 November 2002, this court issued an oral opinion granting KPMG's motion to dismiss. The court based its decision solely on the issue of standing, holding that, because the wrongdoing of PCN's corporate officers had to be imputed to PCN, PCN (and, thus, the Trust) was barred by the doctrine of in pari delicto from bringing this action. Plaintiff appealed.

- On 3 May 2004, the Appellate Division reversed in part, affirmed in part, and remanded the action to this court. The Appellate Division affirmed the court's dismissal of the Trust's breach of fiduciary duty claims. However, the Appellate Division held that the imputation defense is not available to one who contributes to the misconduct sought to be imputed, and that KPMG's alleged conduct-negligence, negligent misrepresentation, and breach of contract-could be considered culpable conduct that contributed to the fraud of PCN's managers. The Appellate Division concluded that the Trust's complaint alleged sufficient facts to form the basis for an equitable fraud claim as well as claims for negligence, negligent misrepresentation, and breach of contract. KPMG sought and obtained certification from the New Jersey Supreme Court.
- On 28 June 2006, the Supreme Court issued an opinion which both affirmed and modified the Appellate Division's earlier decision to reinstate the amended complaint. The Court held that because KPMG's alleged negligence contributed to the misconduct of Mortell and Wraback, KPMG was barred from raising the in pari delicto defense. In the closing paragraph, the opinion states that the Supreme Court was remanding the case to this court "for discovery[,] to allow the Trust an opportunity to present evidence to support its claims that KPMG was negligent and that such negligence proximately caused damage to the corporation." The Court did not make a ruling on any of KPMG's remaining arguments to dismiss.
- The NJ Supreme Court addressed KPMG's in pari delicto argument coupled with the imputation doctrine pursuant to its jurisprudence. The NJ Supreme Court found that KPMG's argument ignores the basic tenets of the imputation doctrine. The Court went on to elaborate that the imputation doctrine is based on the presumption that the agent has discharged his duty to disclose to his principal all material information which the agent obtained through the course of his agency. However, when the agent is engaged in acts that are entirely adverse to his principal, then the presumption dissolves. The presumption that knowledge held by the agent was disclosed to the principal fails because [the agent] cannot be presumed to have disclosed that which would expose and defeat his fraudulent purpose.
- The gravamen of the New Jersey Supreme Court's opinion is that by virtue of its own alleged negligence, KPMG is estopped from

raising the imputation doctrine as a defense against innocent shareholders. The presence of auditor negligence arguably could be called an 'exception' to the imputation doctrine. The court rejects KPMG's position that the knowledge of PCN's rogue managers should be imputed to PCN without further inquiry. Instead, the court holds that the adverse interest exception governs, and denies this portion of KPMG's motion without prejudice.

- AHERF v. PwC, 989 A. 2d 313 (Pa 2010)
  In Aherf, the Pennsylvania Court ruled that in pari delicto applies if "is an active, voluntary participant in the wrongful conduct or transactions for which it seeks redress and bears substantially equal or greater responsibility for the illegality".
  The facts of the case can be summarized as follow:

  - Allegheny Health, Education, and Research Foundation ("AHERF") as a non-profit organization which operated health care facilities. AHERF pursued a business model under which it acquired hospitals, medical schools, and physicians' practice. The business model was a failure.
  - To hide the losses incurred, AHERF management colluded with the external to fraudulently misstate AHERF's financial statements in 1996 and 1997.
  - After AHERF bankruptcy, the Committee of unsecured Creditors initiated a claim against PwC, under Pennsylvania law, for breach of contract, professional negligence, aiding and abetting a breach of fiduciary duty. The committee sought damages for over a billion US dollar.
  - PwC moved for summary judgment under the imputation and the In pari delicto doctrines.
  - The District court ruled in favor of PwC on the sole ground of the imputation and in pari delicto imputing the fraudulent acts of AHERF management to the company, because the management fraudulent acts were committed in the course of their employment and have, to some extent benefited the company.[14]
  - The Committee launched an appeal before Third Circuit.

[14]AHERF Creditors' Comm v. PwC, No. 2000 cv 684 (W.D. Pan. Jan. 17, 2007).

- To clarify Pennsylvania law concerning the extent to which the fraudulent act of a management is imputable to the principal ("the Corporation"), the Third Circuit certified the question to the Pennsylvania Supreme Court:

Does the doctrine of in pari delicto prevent a corporation from recovering against its accountants for breach of contract, professional negligence, or aiding and abetting a breach of fiduciary duty, if those accountants conspired with officers of the corporation to misstate the corporation's finances to the corporation's ultimate detriment?

- The Pennsylvania Supreme Court responded that where the auditor colludes with management to commit fraud the traditional rationale for imputing the acts of agents to the principal ("corporation") is no longer applicable. This Court went on to elaborate that while the imputation doctrine operates to protect third parties on account of their reliance on the agent actual or apparent authority, such reliance does not exist where there is a secret agreement to collude and the actions of the officers are not properly sanctioned by the rules governing the corporation.
- Upon these clarifications from the Pennsylvania Supreme Court, the Third Circuit Court of Appeals vacated and remanded the case to the District Court for a determination of whether PwC acted in good faith in its dealings with AHERF.

24.5.2 *The Absence of Negligence*

The standard of care for accountants' liability for malpractice requires accountants to exercise the degree of skill and care commonly exercised by others professional auditors within the same community. Keeping in mind that auditors perform targeted procedures designed to provide reasonable assurance on whether a client's financial statements are free of a material misstatement, whether caused by error or fraud, plaintiff must establish that the auditor departs from the standard of care aforementioned. A financial-statement audit is not designed to unearth all misstatements made by the management in the financial statements audited.

While an auditor may be liable for malpractice if he fails to detect signs that an employee of the client is embezzling, or if he fails to inform a client of the tax consequences associated with selling a business, a properly conducted audit exculpates an auditor if he complies with all the auditing procedures. Under AICPA AU 230 (PCAOB 339) audit documentation should provide (i) the evidence of the auditor's basis for reaching to its conclusions; and (ii) the evidence that the audit was planned and performed in accordance with the Generally Accepted Auditing Standards.

Jurors perceive auditors' actions to be less reprehensible when they comply with the auditing standards. Audit work-papers must provide sufficient detail to enable a clear understanding of the purpose of the test performed, the source of the evidence obtained, and the conclusions reached. Working papers or audit documentation is the record off the audit procedures performed, relevant audit evidence obtained, and the conclusions the auditors reach. Undoubtedly, plaintiff's expert would examine auditor documentation to find any flaws that may sustain their malpractice claim. To protect against malpractice claim, no other strategy is more reliable that complying with the GAAS and properly documenting any performed audit.

24.5.3 The Contributory Negligence Doctrine

The common law contributory negligence rule foreclosed recovery by any plaintiff who was the slightest bit negligent. It bars a slightly negligent plaintiff from recovery against a greatly negligent defendant. The oldest known invocation of the affirmative defense of contributory negligence as to auditors' liability relates back to the national Surety case.[15]

In National Surety v. Lybrand, plaintiff (National Surety) brought professional malpractice and breach of contract claims against Lybrand (the auditor) for failure to detect an embezzlement committee by the plaintiff's employee, in the course of its audits. The complaint alleged that had the auditor discovered and reported the embezzlement, National Surety could have fired the employee and would not have sustained the subsequent loss. The auditor asserted as an affirmative defense that the audit client had conducted its business so as to make the embezzlement possible and was therefore contributorily negligent. The auditor asserted that they were not liable—even if they were negligent, the client's claim was barred by its contributory negligence. The appellate

[15] National Surety v. Lybrand, 256 A.D. 226 (1939).

court disallowed the defense on the theory that audit clients rely on their auditors to detect such wrongdoing:

We are, therefore, not prepared to admit that accountants are immune from the consequences of their negligence because those who employ them have conducted their own business negligently. The situation in this respect is not unlike that of a workman injured by a dangerous condition which he has been employed to rectify. Accountants, as we know, are commonly employed for the very purpose of detecting defalcations which the employer's negligence has made possible.... Negligence of the employer is a defense only when it has contributed to the accountant's failure to perform his contract and to report the truth.

Since then courts were reluctant to absolve auditing firms where clients also contributed a bit to the damages, by for instance not properly applying its own internal control.

In Shapiro v. Glekel, the S.D.N.Y held that:

> Contributory negligence must be accepted as a theoretical defense, but it applies only if the plaintiff's conduct goes beyond passive reliance and actually affects defendant's ability to do his job with reasonable care.[16]

Thus, client's negligence would be an affirmative defense only in cases when a client has contributed to the auditor's failure to perform his contract and to report the truth.

Several states moved from strict contributory negligence to comparative negligence.

24.5.4 The Comparative Negligence Doctrine

Under comparative negligence, a plaintiff would not barred from recovery simply by virtue of it being partially at fault. Rather, its damages may be reduced prorate to its percentage of fault. However, most jurisdictions would bar a plaintiff from recovery where its share of fault equals or exceeds a certain percentage—50 or 51%.

Under the doctrine of comparative negligence both parties bear responsibility based on their respective roles and faults, and provides an important incentive for all parties to exercise due care. Indeed, under the Generally Accepted Auditing Standards, or GAAS, both the auditor

[16]Shapiro v. Glekel, 380 F. Supp. 1053, 1056 (S.D.N.Y. 1974).

and the client have independent obligations and responsibilities under the applicable professional standards. Failure by either party to live up to those responsibilities should be considered when assessing fault for any particular loss. The audit client is responsible for designing internal controls that prevents and detects fraud, and allows it to initiate, authorize, record, process, and report transactions accurately. The audit client is also responsible for ensuring that its employees follow those internal controls. This allocation of responsibility makes sense given that the audit client is responsible for its own financial statements, for supervising its employees throughout the year, and generally for running its business day in and day out. On the reverse, the auditors is responsible for detecting fraud risks by applying all available tools: tests of details, substantive analytical tests (trends or ratios) with critical and objective mindset. It independence, objectivity, integrity, and sense of serving the public would assist him in detecting fraud and mitigation to the lowest levels possible, inherent and control risks. For instance, if the auditor becomes aware of a significant deficiency or material weakness in the company's internal control over its financial reporting, the auditor should raise the issue to the audit committee or to the management.

24.6 Auditor Federal Statutory Liability

24.6.1 The Securities Act of 1933

The Securities Exchange Act of 1933 enacted in the aftermath of the great depression regulated the disclosure of material facts in a registration statement for any new or additional public offering of securities. Under the 1933 Act, the plaintiff has to prove that he suffered a loss by investing in the registered security, and that the audited financial statements contained a material misstatement of omission. Section 11 of the 1933 Act is more favorable to plaintiff who can prove even a mere ordinary negligence on behalf of the auditor to push his case through the federal court. An inference of fraud suffices.

Under the Securities Laws of 1933, third-party users do not have the burden of proof that they relied on the financial statements or that the auditor was negligent or fraudulent in doing the audit. Instead, the auditor bears the burden of demonstrating as a defense that:

- An adequate audit was conducted in the circumstances; or
- All or a portion of the plaintiff's loss was caused by factors other than the misleading financial statements.

24.6.2 The Securities and Exchange Act of 1934

Once a company becomes a publicly trade or registered, it must comply with the ongoing reporting of its financial statement under the Securities Exchange Act of 1934. To initiate a legal suit against an auditor under the SEC 1934, the plaintiff must establish (i) the existence of a material, factual misrepresentation or omission; (ii) his reliance upon the financial statements; (iii) damages suffered as the result of his reliance; and (iv) scienter.

While the three first requirements are often meet easily by plaintiff, establishing scienter is more challenging. Scienter refers to a mental state embracing intent to deceive, manipulate, or defraud.

- Ernst & Ernst v. Hochfelder

Ernst & Ernst, an accounting and auditing firm was retained by First Securities Company of Chicago, from 1946 through 1967 to perform periodic audits of the firm's books and records. First Securities was a small brokerage firm and member of the Midwest Stock Exchange and of the National Association of Securities Dealers., to perform periodic audits of the firm's books and records. In connection with these audits, Ernst & Ernst prepared for filing with the Securities and Exchange Commission the annual reports required of First Securities under §17(a) of the 1934 Act, 15 U.S.C. §78q(a). It also prepared for First Securities responses to the financial questionnaires of the Midwest Stock Exchange.

Leston B. Nay, president of the firm and owner of 92% of its stock, induced respondents to invest funds in "escrow" accounts that he represented would yield a high rate of return. Respondents did so from 1942 through 1966, with the majority of the transactions occurring in the 1950s. In fact, there were no escrow accounts, as Nay converted respondents' funds to his own use immediately upon receipt. These transactions were not in the customary form of dealings between First Securities and its customers. The respondents drew their personal checks payable to Nay or a designated bank for his account. No such escrow accounts were reflected on the books and records of First Securities, and none was shown on its periodic accounting to respondents in connection with their other investments. Nor were they included in First Securities' filings with the Commission or the Exchange.

This fraud came to light in 1968 when Nay committed suicide, leaving a note that described First Securities as bankrupt and the escrow accounts as "spurious".

The customers of the Brokerage firm filed an action for damages lawsuit against Ernst & Ernst in the United States District Court for the Northern District of Illinois under §10(b) of the Securities Exchange Act of 1934 (1934 Act), which makes it unlawful to use or employ "any manipulative or deceptive device or contrivance" in contravention of Securities and Exchange Commission (SEC) rules. The complaint charged that Nay's escrow scheme violated §10(b) and Commission Rule 10b-5, and that Ernst & Ernst had "aided and abetted" Nay's violations by its "failure" to conduct proper audits of First Securities. Put differently, the investors' cause of action rested on a theory of negligent nonfeasance. The premise was that Ernst & Ernst had failed to utilize "appropriate auditing procedures" in its audits of First Securities, thereby failing to discover internal practices of the firm said to prevent an effective audit. At the center of the contention was the question whether rule 10(b) and Rule 10b-5 require that plaintiff establishes scienter on behalf an auditor in order to win civil litigation under the aforementioned SEC rules.

The District Court granted Ernst & Ernst's motion for summary judgment and dismissed the action. The court rejected Ernst $ Ernst's contention that a cause of action for aiding and abetting a securities fraud could not be maintained under §10(b) and Rule 10b-5 merely on allegations of negligence. It concluded, however, that there was no genuine issue of material fact with respect to whether Ernst & Ernst had conducted its audits in accordance with generally accepted auditing standards.

The Court of Appeals for the Seventh Circuit reversed and remanded, holding that one who breaches a duty of inquiry and disclosure owed another is liable in damages for aiding and abetting a third party's violation of Rule 10b-5 if the fraud would have been discovered or prevented but for the breach, and that there were genuine issues of fact as to whether petitioner committed such a breach and whether inquiry and disclosure would have led to discovery or prevention of the president's fraud.

The Supreme Court held that 10(b) and Rule 10b-5 might be held to require proof of more than negligent nonfeasance by Ernst & Ernst as a precondition to the imposition of civil liability.

24.6.3 The Private Securities Litigation Reform Act of 1995

The Private Securities litigation Reform Act (PSLRA) was enacted in 1995 as a check against abusive litigation by private parties. Put differently, the PSLRA aims to curb perceived abuses of the 10(b) private action targeting deep pocket defendants, vexatious discovery requests and manipulation by class action lawyers. PSLR Act sets proportionate liability among auditors involved in a lawsuit. The Act requires plaintiffs to state with particularity both:

i. Specify each statement alleged to have been misleading [and] the reason or reasons why the statement is misleading; and
ii. State with particularity facts giving rise to a strong inference that the defendant acted with the required state of mind.

If the first requirement is easy to satisfy, courts have been divided as to the scope of the second requirement, concerning the required state of mind.

- The Tellabs, Inc. case
  - Tellabs, Inc., a manufacturer of specialized equipment for fiber optic cable -networks.
  - The plaintiffs Shareholders filed a class action alleging that Tellabs and its Chief executive officer (Mr. Notebaert) had engaged in securities fraud in violation of §10(b) of the Securities Exchange Act of 1934 and Securities and Exchange Commission Rule 10b-5 by misrepresenting the strength of its products and earnings in order to conceal the declining value of the company's stock.
  - Under the Private Securities Litigation Reform Act of 1995 (PSLRA), plaintiffs bringing securities fraud complaints must allege specific facts that give rise to a "strong inference" that the defendant intended to deceive investors. Tellabs moved to dismiss the complaint on the ground that the Shareholders had failed to plead their case with the particularity the PSLRA requires.

- The District Court agreed, dismissing the complaint without prejudice. The Shareholders then amended their complaint, adding references to 27 confidential sources and making further, more specific, allegations concerning Notebaert's mental state.
- The District Court again dismissed the case, this time with prejudice.

The court held that the plaintiff's allegations were too vague to establish a "strong inference" of scienter on the part of Tellabs.

- On appeal, the U.S. Court of Appeals for the Seventh Circuit reversed one of the lower court's dismissals in relevant part. Like the District Court, it found that the Shareholders had pleaded the misleading character of Notebaert's statements with sufficient particularity. Unlike the District Court, however, it concluded that the Shareholders had sufficiently alleged that Notebaert acted with the requisite state of mind. In evaluating whether the PSLRA's pleading standard is met, the Circuit said, courts should examine all of the complaint's allegations to decide whether collectively they establish an inference of scienter; the complaint would survive, the court stated, if a reasonable person could infer from the complaint's allegations that the defendant acted with the requisite state of mind.
- The Seventh Circuit ruled that a plaintiff need only allege "acts from which, if true, a reasonable person could infer that the defendant acted with the required intent." The Court of Appeals decided to consider only the plausibility of the inference of a guilty mental state, and not any competing inferences of an innocent mental state.
- The Seventh Circuit's ruling conflicted with those of other Courts of Appeals, which required plaintiffs to show that the inference of scienter supported by the alleged facts was more plausible than any competing inference of innocent intent.
- The US Supreme Court held that in determining whether the pleaded facts give rise to a "strong" inference of scienter, the court must take into account plausible opposing inferences. The Seventh Circuit expressly declined to engage in such a comparative inquiry. That the strength of an inference cannot be decided in a vacuum. The inquiry is inherently comparative. The Supreme Court stated that to determine whether the plaintiff has alleged facts giving rise to the requisite "strong inference," a court must consider plausible

non-culpable explanations for the defendant's conduct, as well as inferences favoring the plaintiff. The inference that the defendant acted with scienter need not be irrefutable, but it must be more than merely "reasonable" or "permissible"—it must be cogent and compelling, thus strong in light of other explanations. A complaint will survive only if a reasonable person would deem the inference of scienter cogent and at least as compelling as any plausible opposing inference one could draw from the facts alleged. That a plaintiff alleging fraud under §10(b) must plead facts rendering an inference of scienter at least as likely as any plausible opposing inference. At trial, she must then prove her case by a "preponderance of the evidence." The Court found that neither the District Court nor the Court of Appeals had the opportunity to consider whether the Shareholders' allegations warrant "a strong inference that Notebaert and Tellabs] acted with the required state of mind."

24.6.4 The Racketeer Influenced and Corrupt Organization Act (RICO)

The organized Crime Control Act of 1970 constitutes another area of civil liability against external auditors. Section 1962(c) makes it unlawful "for any person employed by or associated with any enterprise ... to conduct or participate, directly or indirectly, in the conduct of such enterprise's affairs through a pattern of racketeering activity ...." However, the House Judiciary Committee that voted RICO out in 1970, described §1962(c) as proscribing the "conduct of the affairs of a business by a person acting in a managerial capacity, through racketeering activity." Furthermore, the legislative history confirms that one is not liable under that provision unless one has participated in the operation or management of the enterprise itself. Racketeering activities include, inter alia: mail fraud and fraud in the sale of securities. Plaintiff successful under RICO Act can reap triple damages in civil cases against a faulty auditor. However, plaintiff should establish that the auditor knew or should have known of the material misstatements in the financial statements. In Reves v. Ernst & Young,[17] the US Supreme Court has held hold that "to conduct or participate, directly or indirectly, in the conduct of such

[17] Reves et al. v. Ernst & Young, 507 US 170 (1993).

enterprise's affairs," §1962(c), one must participate in the operation or management of the enterprise itself.

24.6.5 *The Sarbanes-Oxley Act of 2002*

Under the Sarbanes-Oxley Act of July 2002, management of a publicly traded company is responsible for the production and certification of financial statements. The CEO and the CFO must certify that, to the best of their knowledge, annual (Form K) and quarterly (Form Q) reports submitted to the Securities and Exchange Commission (SEC) materially represent the financial condition of the corporation. Also, the management is responsible for ensuring that the internal control over financial report works effectively.

The Public company Accounting Oversight Board requires auditors to provide "reasonable assurance" that the financial statements reviewed materially conform to the GAAP.

24.7 Auditor State Liability

Auditors may be held liable under states statutory laws. Statutory laws refer to written law as established by federal or state legislative bodies.

As many federal routes for legal action against auditors have been restricted, auditors' clients and aggrieved third party are more and more turning into state legal systems to pursue their suits against auditors. The bulk of legal actions, at the state level, against continue under statutory provisions—contract and tort laws—and are subject to jury trial, where the level of damages cannot be predicted and punitive damages may be awarded. There are several reasons to this shift: (i) state law claims provide broader scopes of liability and remedies against auditor defendants beyond that provided under the federal securities laws,[18] (ii) pleading standards with respect to §10(b) actions initiated under the Securities Exchange Act of 1934 have become more demanding, a hurdle to many plaintiff, (iii) while auditor liability in connection with federal securities claims is generally limited to the issuance of false financial statements within a relevant period, several important state law claims provide for liability well beyond this limitation, (iv) the standard for alleging and

[18] Blair A. Nicholas (2008): Auditor Liability: Institutional Investors Pursue Opt-Out—Actions to Maximize Recovery of Securities Fraud Losses, p. 9.

proving liability under these state statutes is generally less onerous than with similar federal claims, and (v) the loss causation of presumed under §10(b) actions.[19]

Audit firms are attempting to circumvent these legislations and reduce their exposure at state level by including restrictive clauses in their engagement letters to limit the cost of litigation and avoid punitive damages. These clauses vary but may include provisions requiring the client companies to agree to alternative dispute resolution, jury trial waivers, limitation of liability to the company, and indemnification of auditors against management fraud. These steps represent direct or indirect contractual limitation of liability.

24.8 Auditor Criminal Liability

During the course of audit, auditor may commit various offenses and be criminally held liable. That might be the case if (i) the auditor knowingly makes, permits or directs another to make materially incorrect entries in a client's financial statements, (ii) fails to correct statements that are materially false or misleading when the member has such authority, and (iii) signs, permits or directs another to sign a document containing materially false or misleading information. There are several statutes under which criminal liability may be imposed on accountants. The six more cited statutes and of particular significance for those involved in making up financial statements sent through the mails or filed with the government are: the false statement, mail fraud, aiding and abetting, and conspiracy statutes, and the criminal provisions of the Securities Act' and the Exchange Act, explained below in the Continental Vending Machine case.

- Continental Vending[20]

Continental Vending is one of the first major criminal cases successfully brought against auditors. The three auditors[21]: Carl Simon, Robert Kaiser, and Melvin Fishman were convicted of conspiracy to violate 18

[19] Blair A. Nicholas, Idem, p. 11.

[20] Continental Vending [U.S. v. Simon, 425 F.2d 796 (2d Cir. 1969)].

[21] Ronald M. Mano, Matthew Maurissen, and Ryan Pace (2006): Principles-Based Accounting: It's Not new, It's Not the Rile, It's the Law, *The CPA Journal*.

U.S.C. §100,126 (false statements to a government agency), 18 U.S.C. §134,127 (mail fraud), and 15 U.S.C. §78ff (criminal violation of the Exchange Act), as well as two substantive counts of mail fraud, in connection with their respective roles as a senior partner, junior partner, and senior associate on Lybrand, Ross Bros. & Montgomery's audit of the financial statements of Continental Vending Machine Corporation ("Continental").

The Lybrand firm was retained by Roth as auditor of Continental since 1956. Three Lybrand auditors were selected on Continental Vending Machine Corporation. A Continental affiliate, Valley Commercial Corporation, borrowed a large sum of money from Continental. Valley then loaned the funds to a dominant officer and significant shareholder of both Valley and Continental. The auditors learned that the dominant officer would not be able to repay Valley, and the auditors knew that as a consequence Valley would be unable to repay Continental. Nevertheless, the Continental financial statements showed the receivable from Valley as an asset, with only a relatively obscure footnote, which reads:

The amount receivable from valley Commercial Corp. (an affiliated company of which Mr. Harold Roth is an officer, director, and stockholder) bears interest at 12% a year. Such amount, less the balance of the notes payable to that company, is secured by the assignment to the company of Valley's equity in certain marketable securities. As of February 15, 1963, the amount of such equity at current market quotations exceeded the net amount receivable.

Continental never did collect payments from Valley on the receivable in question; in fact, Continental went bankrupt shortly after the financial statements were issued.

The SEC brought a legal action against the named auditors, arguing the three auditors were aware of the fraud, but failed to disclose, that $3.9 million, shown on Continental's financial statements as loans receivable from an affiliate named Valley Commercial Corporation ("Valley"), were uncollectable because Valley had in turn loaned approximately the same amount to Harold Roth, Continental's President.

Roth was unable to repay the loan and belatedly "secured" his obligation to Valley with collateral that consisted mostly of Continental common stock.

In their effort to rebut the SEC charges, the auditors argued that they properly followed generally accepted auditing standards (GAAS) during the audit and that the footnote also complied with applicable standards. To that end, the auditors provided several experts testified that the footnote disclosure explaining the receivable from Valley complied with generally accepted accounting principles (GAAP) and that the auditors had followed GAAS.

At their jury trial, the defendants called eight independent accounting experts, who testified that the treatment of the Valley receivable described in Note 2 was not inconsistent with either GAAP or generally accepted auditing standards (GAAS), and that neither required that the auditors disclose the make-up of the collateral, or the fact that the receivable had increased after the closing date of the financial statements. All eight also testified that the Roth borrowings from Valley did not need to be disclosed, and seven of the eight stated affirmatively that disclosure would have been inappropriate. The jury found the three auditors guilty.

On appeal, the defendants made two arguments based on their accounting experts' testimony. First, they contended that the trial judge had erred in refusing to instruct the jury that the defendants could be found guilty only if, according to GAAP, the financial statements as a whole did not fairly present Continental's financial condition, and then only if the defendants' departure from accepted professional standards was due to willful disregard with knowledge of the statements' falsity and intent to deceive.

The Second Circuit rejected this argument, holding instead that the judge had properly instructed the jury that "the 'critical test' was whether the financial statements as a whole 'fairly presented the financial position of Continental as of [their date],'" and if they did not, the issue was whether defendants had acted in good faith, as to which proof of compliance with GAAP and GAAS was "'evidence which may be very persuasive but not necessarily conclusive.' " In language that, as highlighted below, contains some important qualifications, the appellate court said: We do not think the jury was… required to accept the accountants' evaluation whether a given fact was material to overall fair presentation, at least not when the accountants' testimony was not based on specific rules or prohibitions to which they could point, but only on the need for an auditor to make an honest judgment and their conclusion that nothing in the financial statements themselves negated the conclusion that an honest judgment had been made. Such evidence may be highly persuasive, but it is not conclusive, and so the trial judge correctly charged.

Second, defendants next attacked the verdict on the ground that the evidence was insufficient as a matter of law to allow the jury to consider the charges against them, particularly in light of the expert testimony. Here, the Second Circuit focused not on the abstract issue of whether compliance with GAAP and GAAS is a defense, but instead on the particular fact that Continental was being looted (in response to which, in the court of appeals' view, GAAP and GAAS themselves required the defendants to do more than they did): We join defendants' counsel in assuming that the mere fact that a company has made advances to an affiliate does not ordinarily impose a duty on an accountant to investigate what the affiliate has done with them or even to disclose that the affiliate has made loan to a common officer if this has come to his attention. But it simply cannot be true that an accountant is under no duty to disclose what he knows when he has reason to believe that, to a material extent, a corporation is being operated not to carry out its business in the interest of all the stockholders but for the private benefit of its president. For a court to say that all this is immaterial as a matter of law if only such loans are thought to be collectible would be to say that independent accountants have no responsibility to reveal known dishonesty by a high corporate officer. If certification does not at least imply that the corporation has not been looted by insiders so far as the accountants know, or, if it has been, that the diversion has been made good beyond peradventure (or adequately reserved against) and effective steps taken to prevent a recurrence, it would mean nothing, and the reliance placed on it by the public would be a snare and a delusion.

The Second circuit went on to elaborate that:

Generally accepted accounting principles instruct an accountant what to do in the usual case where he has no reason to doubt that the affairs of the corporation are being honestly conducted. Once he has reason to believe that this basic assumption is false, an entirely different situation confronts him.

Then, as the Lybrand firm stated in its letter accepting the Continental engagement, he must "extend his procedures to determine whether or not such suspicions are justified." If as a result of such an extension or, as here, without it, he finds his suspicions to be confirmed, full disclosure must be the rule, unless he has made sure the wrong has been righted and procedures to avoid a repetition have been established. At least this must be true when the dishonesty he has discovered is not some minor peccadillo but a diversion so large as to imperil if not destroy the very solvency of the enterprise. The foregoing discussion suggests two important limiting principles on Simon's holding with respect to the dispositive nature of GAAP compliance: (i) first, that the persuasive nature of GAAP will vary depending on whether it explicitly supports-or, as in Simon, simply does not prohibit the disclosure at issue; and (ii) that GAAP compliance is a weak defense if the government can show that the defendants deliberately misled investors about an extraordinary fact, such as the looting of a corporation by its officers, but not otherwise.

Finally, the Sarbanes-Oxley Act of 30 July 2002 also contains several sections that provide causes of criminal actions against auditors. Sections 802, 805, 806, 1107 of the Sarbanes-Oxley Act of July 30, 2002 contain specific criminal liability for auditors in their business conduct.

- Section 802 requires auditors to maintain all audit or review work-papers for a period of five years. Accountant who knowingly and willfully violates this record keeping requirement faces a maximum prison sentence of ten years. Section 802 has also set up a twenty years criminal penalty against any auditor for destruction, alteration, or falsification of records in Federal investigations.
- Section 805, which requires the US Sentencing Commission to review its sentencing guidelines for any violation of the SOX Act may lead to harsh jail sentencing or criminal liability.
- Section 806 increases the maximum sentence for securities fraud to 25 years in prison.
- Section 1107 makes it a crime to retaliate against whistleblowers. Any confirmed act of retaliation on the part of an auditing firm is susceptible of 10 years of imprisonment. Section 1107 defines retaliation to include "any action harmful to any person, including interference with the lawful employment or livelihood of any person, for providing to a law enforcement officer any truthful information relating to the commission or possible commission of any Federal offense."

24.9 Conclusion

For decades, and against common sense, and outcry from the legal scholars, judges almost blindly dismissed the cases against auditors under the "in pari delito" doctrine and its narrowly drafted exceptions. Recent decisions have reframed the debate, opening the doors for more jury indictments in auditors' malpractice claims. The profession needs to integrate the new reality and live up to its professional due care. Auditors are gatekeepers of the markets and investors and meet that expectation.

Appendix

- Auditors' Strategies to Protect Their Litigation Reputation: A Research Note, by Susan A. McCracken; *AUDITING: A Journal of Practice & Theory*, September 2002, Vol. 21, No. 2, pp. 7–20.
- Debiasing the Outcome Effect: The Role of Instructions in an Audit Litigation Setting, by Peter M. Clarkson, Craig Emby, and Vanessa W.-S. Watt; *AUDITING: A Journal of Practice & Theory*, March 2002, Vol. 21, No. 1, pp. 11–27.

Practice

Question 1

Which of the following factors does not contribute to corporate governance failure?

(a) Unfettered Deregulation
(b) Excessive Compensation
(c) Ineffective Boards of Directors
(d) Lack of Continuous Training
(e) None

Question 2

Which factor is not included in the triangle of fraud?

(a) The pressure or incentive
(b) The above-the-law attitude
(c) The opportunity
(d) The rationalization of fraudulent behavior

Question 3

The following corporate governance shortcomings were found in the Enron scandal, except?

(a) Non-executive directors lacked independence to perform their duties
(b) Conflicts of interest involving members of the firm's internal audit committee
(c) Lord Wakeham who sat on the audit committee had a consulting contract with Enron
(d) Several top executive, particularly its chief executive officer (CEO) and the financial director had poor moral character
(e) None

Question 4

Which one of the below assertions concerning Section 802 of the SOX Act is inaccurate?

(a) Section 802 requires auditors to maintain all audit or review work-papers for a period of five years
(b) Accountant who knowingly and willfully violates this record keeping requirement faces a maximum prison sentence of ten years
(c) Accountant who knowingly and willfully violates this record keeping requirement faces a maximum prison sentence of twenty years
(d) Section 802 has also set up a twenty years criminal penalty against any auditor for destruction, alteration, or falsification of records in Federal investigations

Question 5

Which one of the below assertions concerning Section 1107 of the SOX Act is inaccurate?

(a) Section 1107 makes it a crime to retaliate against whistleblowers
(b) Any confirmed act of retaliation on the part of an auditing firm is susceptible of 20 years of imprisonment
(c) Any confirmed act of retaliation on the part of an auditing firm is susceptible of 10 years of imprisonment
(d) Section 1107 defines retaliation to include "any action harmful to any person, including interference with the lawful employment or livelihood of any person, for providing to a law enforcement officer any truthful information relating to the commission or possible commission of any Federal offense."

CHAPTER 25

Forensic Auditing

25.1 Introduction

Forensic Accounting can be, at best, defined, as the use of auditing in investigative skills to examine financial statements in preparation to be used in a court of law.[1] Forensic auditing is the integration of specialized accounting knowledge and positive mental attitude to resolve legal issues. The profession can be traced back around the early 1900s and has greatly altered the way fraud is discovered and handled. However, the term "forensic accounting/audit" was coined in 1946, by Maurice Peloubet and won acceptance.[2] Recently, the Sarbanes-Oxley Act of July 2002 highlighted the needs for forensic accounting in several of its provisions. Section 404 of the SOXs, for instance, requires management (both the CEO and the CFO) to certify that their financial statements are free from material misstatement and fraud. SOX Section 409 accelerates the SEC filings for Form 10-Q and annual report Form 10-K.

Forensic auditing as a specialty has better days ahead. It is predicted that growth of the industry, based on the amount of jobs, will reach 6.7% for the years between 2013 and 2018. The revenue the industry

[1] Kristen Dreyer (2014): *A History of Forensic Accounting*, Grand Valley State University, p. 3.

[2] Brown, M. (2008, June 1): Forensic Accounting-Past, Present, & Future. It's All About Money. Retrieved April 17, 2014 from http://www.envoynews.com/rwcpas/e_article001108198.cfm.

F. I. Lessambo, *Auditing, Assurance Services, and Forensics*,
https://doi.org/10.1007/978-3-319-90521-1_25

brings in is also steadily increasing as time goes on. In 2013 the industry brought in $4.5 billion and is expected to bring in $6.3 billion by 2018.[3] The Association of Certified Fraud Examiners (ACFE) estimates that occupational fraud losses cost organizations $994 billion annually.[4]

A recent Cornerstone Research report shows that accounting fraud cases, increased sharply over the past year, due in part to the agency's heightened focus on accounting-related fraud. The 2014 Review and Analysis, shows allegations of accounting fraud surged 47% in securities class-action lawsuits last year over 2013.[5] That partly reflects a corresponding 46% increase in accounting fraud enforcement cases brought by the SEC for the 2013–2014 fiscal year that ended September 30.

25.2 The PCAOB Objectives of Forensic Audit

Although forensic audits examine financial reporting and internal control matters, the objective of a forensic audit is not expressly articulated in an established set of standards. Instead, users of forensic audits establish their objectives on a case-by-case basis.[6] Nonetheless, it is commonly agreed upon that Forensic audits can be performed to achieve various objectives and can include a variety of different procedures.[7] The POB's Panel on Audit Effectiveness ("PAE") reported back in 2000 that:

> This new forensic-type phase should become an integral part of the audit, with careful thought given to how and when it is to be carried out. A forensic-type fieldwork phase does not mean converting a generally accepted auditing standards ("GAAS") audit to a "fraud audit." Rather, the characterization of this phase of a GAAS audit as a forensic-type phase seeks to convey an attitudinal shift in the auditor's degree of skepticism.

[3] Chiang, J. (2013, August 21): Accountants Uncover Opportunity In Forensics. Media Center RSS. Retrieved April 13, 2014 from http://www.ibisworld.com/media/2013/08/21/accountants-uncover-opportunity-inforensics/.

[4] ACFE 2008 Report to the Nation.

[5] Terry Sheridan (2015): Number of Accounting Fraud Cases Continues to Rise, AccountingWeb.

[6] PCAOB (2007): Standing Advisory Group Meeting-Panel Discussion: Forensic Audit Procedures, p. 2.

[7] PCAOB (2007): Standing Advisory Group Meeting-Panel Discussion: Forensic Audit Procedures, p. 4.

> Furthermore, use of the word phase does not mean that the work cannot be integrated throughout the audit.[8]

In 2002, the AICPA's Auditing Standards Board considered the PAE's recommendation and developed the standard on financial fraud, Statement on Auditing Standards No. 99, Consideration of Fraud in a Financial Statement Audit, codified as AU sec. 316.[9] In 2004, the International Auditing and Assurance Standards Board issued an International Standard on Auditing ("ISA"), The Auditor's Responsibilities Relating to Fraud in an Audit of Financial Statements. The standard contains forensic-type procedures similar to those in AU sec. 316, the PCAOB's interim auditing standard. Among others, ISA 240 requests that the engagement team makes inquiries of management, internal audit, those charged with governance, and others within the entity to determine whether they have knowledge of fraud.

Recent Research papers show that "incorporating more forensic course work for auditors will only increase their skills and better serve the public."[10]

25.3 The International Auditing and Assurance Standards Board (ISA 240)

ISA 240 states that the primary responsibility for the prevention and detection of fraud rests with both those charged with governance of the entity and management.[11] However, ISA 240 goes on the add that:

> An auditor conducting an audit in accordance with ISAs is responsible for obtaining reasonable assurance that the financial statements as a whole are free from material misstatement, whether caused by fraud or error.[12]

[8] Public Oversight Board, The Panel on Audit Effectiveness ("PAE"), Report and Recommendations (2000).

[9] PCAOB (2007): Standing Advisory Group Meeting—Panel Discussion: Forensic Audit Procedures, p. 5.

[10] Michele Leonard (2014): *The Impact of Fraud Education on Fraud Detection*, University at Albany, State University of New York, p. 16.

[11] ISA 240 (Redrafted), Par. 4.

[12] ISA 240 (Redrafted), Par. 5.

25.4 Forensic Auditing Services

The AICPA has recognized forensic accounting services to generally involve:

- The application of specialized knowledge and investigative skills possessed by CPAs
- Collecting, analyzing and evaluating evidential matter
- Interpreting and communicating findings in the courtroom, boardroom or other legal/administrative venue.[13]

Fundamental forensic knowledge includes[14]:

- Professional responsibilities and practice management
- Laws, courts and dispute resolution
- Planning and preparation
- Information-gathering and preservation (documents, interviews/interrogations, electronic data)
- Discovery
- Reporting, experts, and testimony.

25.5 Forensic Audit and Fraud Detection

Fraud can take different forms including internal financial fraud, bribery, corruption, and embezzlement. Fraud is the reason Forensic Accounting exists. In a survey done by Kroll provided by Georgetown University for their 2013/2014 Global Fraud Report it was discovered that over 70% of companies were affected by at least one type of fraud in the past year.[15]

[13] Durkin and Ueltzen (2009): The Evolution of the CFF Credential, The Practicing CPA, July/August.

[14] Durkin and Ueltzen (2009): The Evolution of the CFF Credential, The Practicing CPA, July/August.

[15] Kristen Dreyer (2014): A History of Forensic Accounting, Grand Valley State University, p. 10.

25.5.1 Brainstorming

Prior to or in conjunction with the information-gathering, members of the audit team should discuss the potential for material misstatement due to fraud. The discussion should include[16]:

- An exchange of ideas or "brainstorming" among the audit team members, including the auditor with final responsibility for the audit, about how and where they believe the entity's financial statements might be susceptible to material misstatement due to fraud, how management could perpetrate and conceal fraudulent financial reporting, and how assets of the entity could be misappropriated.
- An emphasis on the importance of maintaining the proper state of mind throughout the audit regarding the potential for material misstatement due to fraud.

The discussion should include a consideration of the risk of management override of controls. The discussion among the audit team members should emphasize the need to maintain a questioning mind and to exercise professional skepticism in gathering and evaluating evidence throughout the audit. It should also lead audit team members to thoroughly probe the issues, acquire additional evidence as necessary, and consult with other team members and, if appropriate, experts in the firm, rather than rationalize or dismiss information or other conditions that indicate a material misstatement due to fraud may have occurred.

25.5.2 Identification of Fraud Factors

Auditors examine the financial statements in accordance with GAAP and GAAS, while the Forensic Accounting Investigators deal with fraudulent financial reporting and misappropriation of assets.[17]

There are four elements to any fraud[18]:

[16]AU Section 316—Consideration of Fraud in a Financial Statement Audit, §14.

[17]Jagdish S. Gangolly (2015): Lecture Notes on Forensic Accounting Investigations, State University of New York at Albany, Department of Accounting & Law, p. 7.

[18]Jagdish S. Gangolly (2015): Lecture Notes on Forensic Accounting Investigations, State University of New York at Albany, Department of Accounting & Law.

- A false representation of a material nature (either misstatement or omission of a material fact)
- Scienter: Knowledge that the representation is false, or reckless disregard for truth
- Reliance: The person receiving the representation has reasonably and justifiably relied on it
- Damages: Such receiving party has sustained.

Financial Statement Frauds include: overstatement of revenue, inventory misstatements, investments misstatements, and others.

Investigation steps include:

- Background investigation,
- Conducting interviews,
- Gathering and documenting evidence
- Explaining the theory of the case

Because fraud is usually concealed, material misstatements due to fraud are difficult to detect. Nevertheless, the auditor may identify events or conditions that indicate incentives/pressures to perpetrate fraud, opportunities to carry out the fraud, or attitudes/rationalizations to justify a fraudulent action. Such events or conditions are referred to as "fraud risk factors." Fraud risk factors do not necessarily indicate the existence of fraud; however, they often are present in circumstances where fraud exists.

The auditor's identification of fraud risks also may be influenced by characteristics such as the size, complexity, and ownership attributes of the entity.[19]

25.5.3 Major Types of Fraud

The forensic accountant performs different types of fraud investigations. By and large, the three major types are: (i) corruption, (ii) asset misappropriation; and (iii) financial statement fraud. Among the three, corruption is the most widespread.

- Corruption

[19] AU Section 316—Consideration of Fraud in a Financial Statement Audit, §37.

There are three types of corruption fraud: conflicts of interest, bribery, and extortion. In a conflict of interest fraud, the fraudster exerts their influence to achieve a personal gain which detrimentally affects the company. The fraudster may not benefit financially, but rather receives an undisclosed personal benefit as a result of the situation. For example, a manager may approve the expenses of an employee who is also a personal friend in order to maintain that friendship, even if the expenses are inaccurate.

Bribery is when money (or something else of value) is offered in order to influence a situation.

Extortion is the opposite of bribery, and happens when money is demanded (rather than offered) in order to secure a particular outcome.

- Asset misappropriation

By far the most common frauds are those involving asset misappropriation, and there are many different types of fraud which fall into this category. The common feature is the theft of cash or other assets from the company, for example: Cash theft—the stealing of physical cash, for example petty cash, from the premises of a company.

Fraudulent disbursements—company funds being used to make fraudulent payments. Common examples include billing schemes, where payments are made to a fictitious supplier, and payroll schemes, where payments are made to fictitious employees (often known as 'ghost employees').

Examples of misappropriation of assets include the following

- Skimming, forgery, kiting, phony refunds, larceny, fraudulent disbursements
- Lapping, fictitious write-offs, duplicate payments, nonexistent vendor, kickbacks
- misdirected shipments, theft, unauthorized personal use of assets, fictitious burglary
- phantom employees, falsified time cards

- Financial statement fraud

This is also known as fraudulent financial reporting, and is a type of fraud that causes a material misstatement in the financial statements. It can include deliberate falsification of accounting records; omission of transactions, balances or disclosures from the financial statements; or the misapplication of financial reporting standards. This is often carried out with the intention of presenting the financial statements with a particular bias, for example concealing liabilities in order to improve any analysis of liquidity and gearing.

Examples of fraudulent financial reporting include the following

- Fictitious revenues, asset overstatement, unrecorded liabilities, improper disclosure
- Corruption, conflict of interest, bribery, illegal gratuities, economic extortion

25.5.4 The Forensic Mindset

The skeptical mindset is something that has long been inherent in forensic accountants and other internal investigators when looking for evidence of fraud. The investigator historically has asked a set of questions different from those of conventional auditor, who is monitoring the financial statements to see whether they are in compliance with generally accepted accounting principles (GAAP) and thereby fairly represent the financial conditions of the company.[20] The process of forensic accounting is also sometimes more intuitive than deductive, although both intuition and deduction play important parts. Financial auditing is more procedural in many regards and is not intended to work as effectively as the tenets of fraud auditing and forensic accounting.[21]

[20] Fatma Ulucan Ozkul and Ays,e Pamukcu: Fraud Detection and Forensic Accounting, Springer 2012, p. 31.

[21] Idem, p. 32.

25.6 Forensic Audit Procedures

The performance of forensic audit procedures shall be a part of an audit of financial statements.[22] There are several commonalities between financial statements' audit and forensic audit.[23] Forensic thinking is used throughout the audit. To perform adequately the fraud detection procedures in an audit of financial statements, the forensic auditor must have or collect critical background information about the company, its business and its environment. In a sense, forensic audit procedures are more specific as geared toward detecting the possible material misstatements in financial statements resulting from fraudulent activities or error.

25.6.1 Computer Forensic

Computer forensics is the branch of forensic science pertaining to legal evidence, such as financial databases, spreadsheets, e-mails, journals and SMS messages, found in computers and digital storage mediums. It examines the context, the status (active or deleted), location and usage of this evidence, and is a tool used to achieve electronic discovery, which deals with the use of digital information before a trial starts in a lawsuit.[24]

Electronic evidence including e-mails, user files in the suspect's computer hard drives, files on the corporate network and any shared workspace, and archived data in the backup system along with relevant financial data in the accounting system should be quarantined and secured by forensic technology. The most important questions are: How the information was collected, how it was documented, where the photographs were, and which machines, or computers, held the evidence. This ensures data is not altered during the acquisition phase and chain of custody issues are addressed. This is a critical step if the electronic evidence will be used in any court proceedings.[25]

[22] PCAOB (2007): Standing Advisory Group Meeting—Panel Discussion: Forensic Audit Procedures, p. 1.

[23] Popoola, O. M.J. (2014): Forensic Accounting Knowledge and Mindset on Task Performance Fraud Risk Assessment, *International Journal of Business and Management*, Vol. 9, No. 9, p. 122.

[24] Carol Ko (2009): The Digital Smoking Gun, in Computer Forensics.

[25] Carol Ko (2009): The Digital Smoking Gun, in Computer Forensics.

The job of computer forensics experts is to analyze recovered data and evidence, then match the information found in e-mails against those in spreadsheets to determine if fraud has been committed and if yes, how and by whom.

Forensic accountants can certainly help to explain the nature of the fraud, but as for [an] understanding of the bigger picture, I think it needs a computer forensics analysis and analysts to be able to look at all the elements of the computer usage that surrounds the fraud.

25.7 Investigation Techniques and Digital Evidence

25.7.1 Investigation Techniques

1. Preparation

To prepare for the interview, interviewers should thoroughly review the appropriate data, documents, and information relating to the subject matter of the interview. Some documents may be found in public domain (i.e., EDGAR) while others are private. An interview plan and theme should be developed before conducting the actual interviews. Ideally, interviews should be conducted by two people. And, the plan should outline the goals of the interview, who will be the lead interviewer, who will be taking notes, the role of the second interviewer, the subject areas and key points to cover, as well as safety considerations.

During the preliminary, the interviewer must outline the nature of the case; list of potential witnesses; a preliminary order of interviews; key issues to resolve; appropriate data, documents, and information to obtain; and investigative measures that should be conducted before interviews begin.

The interviews usually should begin with neutral witnesses and move to corroborating witnesses. The actual suspects of the case normally are interviewed toward the end of the interview process; however, other options may be considered depending on the nature of the case. In some circumstances, interviews with suspects may be conducted early in the investigation if it appears that evidence may be destroyed, if the suspect is leaving the company, or if threats to other witnesses are being made.

With each successive interview, the interviewers should obtain background information about the witnesses, the subject matter of the investigation, and the potential suspects. Interviewers should be prepared for a wide variety of circumstances in a forensic engagement and should remain objective, fair and act with integrity. To be successful, an interview should be thorough. It requires strategic planning, relevant questions, and an objective interviewer. By remaining objective and fair, the interviewers can better gain the confidence of the interviewee. Interviewers can develop rapport by exhibiting objectivity, fairness, and professionalism at all times. The interviewers should be non-threatening in their demeanor, particularly in the introductory phase. When arranging an interview, a location should be chosen to ensure privacy and to minimize interruptions.

2. Building up a rapport

Interviewers should begin by asking simple questions to put the witness at ease and help to build a rapport. Background questions should include asking their name, address, phone number, title, how long they have been in that position as well as what their duties are. Forensic accountants may also want to consider asking the person being interviewed if anyone has talked to them about the reason for the interview or if allegations have been made.

- Who should be present at the interview

Depending on the type of witness or where in the investigative process, an attorney representing the company may want to be present. Regardless, the ideal situation would be to have two interviewers who conduct the interviews, one person at a time. In some circumstances, only one interviewer will be present, or the person being interviewed will be represented by an attorney or other company representative. The identity of the interviewers should be disclosed and the identity of the person interviewed and others present should be confirmed.

- Approaching sensitive question

Interviewers should approach sensitive questions very carefully and should not react to statements made by the interviewee. Interviewers should not express shock, disgust or similar emotions. And, interviewers should remain nonjudgmental, fair and objective. While the interviewers are observing the verbal and nonverbal actions of the interviewees, it should be remembered that the interviewers also can demonstrate powerful messages by their own verbal, nonverbal and physical actions.

3. The questioning styles

The interviewers must be more meticulous in questioning the interviewees. The following are most found types of questions:

- Informational Questions
- Open Questions: Open questions encourage a monologue and narrative type response. Open-ended questions always are encouraged to keep people talking; however, most interviews will use a combination of open and closed questions.
- Closed Questions: are designed to require a precise answer, usually "yes" or "no."
- Leading Questions: are questions that contain an answer as part of the question. Leading questions can be used to confirm facts that already are known. Leading questions often are not allowed in courtroom situations, but they can be an effective technique during the interview process.
- Double-Negative Questions: Double-negative questions should be avoided.
- Attitude Questions: are those in which the attitude of the interviewer is conveyed by the structure of the question. The attitude of the interviewer can be conveyed by a tone of voice or by intentionally altering body language exhibited by the interviewers.
- Admission Seeking Questions

4. Concluding an interview

In closing, the interviewers should try to close an interview on a positive note and leave the door open for additional contact. Therefore, it is desirable to leave the interview on a positive note so that additional contact is encouraged.

5. Collecting and documenting

A forensic accountants should weigh the benefits of relying on the evidence against the risk of potential damage to the case if the information proves false. To the extent possible, information received from confidential sources should be corroborated through independent investigation.

Written records of an interview should be prepared as soon as possible following the conclusion of the interview. It should be determined if original notes should be retained. Law-enforcement officers generally are required to retain original notes. The notes may be requested by opposing counsel pursuant to discovery requirements. It is recommended that narrative reports be written in third person. Keep in mind that written records and written notes may be disclosed to opposing counsel in the future and interviewers may be questioned about the contents of the report and notes.

25.7.2 Digital Evidence[26]

The information contained in computers, mobile phones, personal data assistants and a myriad of other electronic devices is increasingly playing a major role in legal matters. Digital evidence is being employed effectively in all types of litigation. Electronic discovery, more commonly referred to as e-Discovery, is the gathering, analysis, and production of electronic documents in litigation discovery. In e-Discovery, the information collected usually only includes active and archived data that is easily accessed and has not been deleted, encrypted or hidden. Typical data repositories include backup disks or tapes, email servers, and network server storage. In e-Discovery data is accessed, but not analyzed.

The commonly accepted definition of digital forensics is "The use of scientifically derived and proven methods toward the preservation, collection, validation, identification, analysis, interpretation, documentation and presentation of evidence derived from digital sources." More plainly, digital forensics is the art and science of finding, analyzing, preserving and the precise documentation of digital evidence, wherever it may be found, and then interpreting those findings in a way that makes it meaningful to any client or trier of fact. It is a science in the sense that a digital forensic examiner's approach uses the investigative method as well as certain industry-recognized protocols and standards. It is also called an art because each examination involves the skills, techniques and abilities of the examiner to find the deleted and hidden files or other

[26] L. Scott Harrell (2010): Digital Forensics in Anticipation of Litigation, in IRB Seach, LLC.

bits of information that would surely be missed through e-Discovery; every examination is unique (although each should produce the same results). An even simpler definition might simply be summed up this way, "Digital forensics is the transformation of raw data into intelligible information that meets the minimum standards of legal admissibility."

Forensic imaging, or copying, involves the following critical phases:

- Securing and preserving the data source;
- Imaging the items;
- Documenting the approach and methods used to copy data;
- Validating the accuracy of the evidence.

The essence of computer forensics begins with the procedures utilized to create a forensic image. A proper forensic imaging process insures the integrity of the evidence by preserving it.

Sources of digital evidence include personal computers, mobile communication devices (smartphones and mobile cellular telephones) and digital storage mediums including tape, floppy disks, compact disks, digital video disks, external or network hard drives, flash memory cards and USB "thumb" drives. Increasingly, digital forensic examiners are beginning to specialize in extracting data from often overlooked digital sources such as digital cameras, images and photographs, computer peripherals (printers, fax machines, scanners, and copiers) as well as satellite navigation devices, automobile "black boxes" and web pages. In fact, anything with a memory chip installed in it might store critical evidence!

Digital evidence comes in many forms depending upon its source. Computers will generally produce the following types of information:

- Hidden, deleted, temporary and password-protected files can be recovered
- Documents and spreadsheets
- Contact information and calendars
- Email and Deleted Email
- Internet browsing history and habits
- Pictures, graphics, videos, and music
- Event logs, hacker activity, and break-in attempts
- Software installed (illicit, pirated and legitimate).

The work of the digital forensic examiner falls into three broad categories:

First and foremost comes forensic imaging. There are specific tools for acquiring forensic images of digital storage media without changing the contents. It is not acceptable to merely copy and paste data files; the entire disk must be copied bit for bit.

Second, digital forensics incorporate established protocols for identifying and preserving digital files. The standard involves applying numeric procedures to the disk to produce a number, called a hash that is for all purposes unique to the disk. Digital forensic experts use and validate these techniques each time they access the data to demonstrate its veracity.

The *third* task of the forensic examiner is to interpret hidden, deleted, partial and temporary files. This analysis requires specific knowledge of how digital devices and the various software applications handle the storage of data. The specialist must be able to clearly explain his findings to the Court.

25.7.3 Evidentiary Rules

The issues regarding the admissibility of electronic records is a fact-intensive issue. If the records are merely stored in a computer, they raise no computer-specific authentication issues. On the other hand, if the computer processes data rather than storing it, authentication issues may arise depending on the complexity and novelty of the computer processing.[27] Judge Weinstein concludes the degree of foundation required to authenticate computer-based evidence depends on the quality and completeness of the data input, the complexity of the computer processing, the routineness of the computer operation, and the ability to test and verify results of the computer proceedings.[28]

For example, in Safavian,[29] the court allowed e-mails, which were not clearly identifiable on their own, to be compared to other e-mails alleged

[27] Eric S. Eissenstat (2008): Making Sure You Can Use ESI You Get: Pretrial Considerations Regarding Authenticity and Foundation of ESI, p. 7.

[28] Eric S. Eissenstat (2008): Making Sure You Can Use ESI You Get: Pretrial Considerations Regarding Authenticity and Foundation of ESI, p. 7.

[29] Safavian, 435 F. Supp. 2d at 40.

to be from the same sender, which had been authenticated under Rule 901(b)(4).

With respect to electronically-stored records, the attorney should locate and prepare a witness who can testify (1) regarding their familiarity with the computer-stored records and explain the basis for his or her familiarity; (2) that the witness recognizes the paper records as being a printout of the computer-stored records; and (3) that the paper records accurately reflect the computer-stored records. "In general, electronic documents are records that are merely stored in a computer and raise no computer-specific authentication issues."

25.8 Case Study

25.8.1 The Centennial Technology, Inc. (1996)

- The CEO of Centennial Technologies, Mr. Pinez and other Centennial executives, including the former chief financial officer, James Murphy, had "cooked the books," creating a phony list of receivables.
- Centennial employees fabricated record sales, from which the firm experienced a 451% surge in value to $55.50 per share on the NYSE.

25.8.2 Taylor Bean v. PwC[30]

- The lawsuit arose out of PwC's work for the Alabama-based Colonial Bank Group Inc., where Taylor Bean was the largest client.
- Bean & Whitaker Mortgage (TBW) was a subsidiary for Colonial Bank that also traded with its parent company.
- Taylor Bean & Whitaker (TBW) was formerly a top U.S. mortgage lender. In 2009, the firm filed for Chapter 11 bankruptcy protection after a federal investigation uncovered a seven-year fraud scheme between TBW and Colonial Bank Group, Inc.
- PricewaterhouseCoopers failed to spot for seven years a multibillion dollar fraud that led to the demise of Taylor Bean & Whitaker Mortgage Corp. PwC adequately vetted documents that Taylor

[30]Taylor Bean & Whitaker Plan Trust V. PricewaterhouseCoopers LLP, Case Number 2013-33964-CA-01, in the 11th Judicial Circuit Court of the State of Florida.

Bean gave to the bank, it would have spotted a multi-year fraud by executives at both firms far earlier and put an end to it, the trustee claims. Instead, federal regulators uncovered it in 2009 and Taylor Bean and Colonial went bankrupt. The bankruptcy trustee sued in 2013 seeking $5.6 billion in damages.

- In 2013, Taylor Bean's trustee filed a legal proceedings against PwC.
- The fraud scheme arose in Taylor Bean's business with Colonial's Mortgage Warehouse Loan Division, which provided short-term, secured financing to mortgage originators.
- The Mortgage Warehouse Loan Division provided short-term, secured financing to mortgage originators. The division's largest customer was Taylor Bean, whose executives colluded with a Colonial employee to shuffle money to cover up overdrafts and shortfalls.
- Beginning in at least 2002, Taylor Bean shuffled money in its Colonial Bank accounts to cover up overdrafts and shortfalls. Later, as the shortfalls mounted, executives sold worthless mortgage loan assets to the bank for more than $1 billion in the scam. The assets were based on loans that didn't exist.
- Taylor Bean recycled the fake loans and trades and fed the bank false documents to cover its tracks with help from co-conspirators at Colonial Bank.
- Taylor Bean's trustee argued that PwC was negligent in its audits of the parent company of Colonial Bank, which was used by Taylor Bean executives to carry out the multibillion dollar fraud that eventually led to the sixth-largest bank collapse in U.S. history. PwC certified the existence of more than $1 billion of Colonial Bank assets that did not exist and should have discovered the fraud, according to the trustee.
- The trustees claim that Colonial Bank bought $1 billion of worthless assets that were concocted by rogue TWB executives. Put differently, PwC certified the existence of more than $1 billion of Colonial Bank assets that did not exist and should have discovered the fraud, according to the trustee.
- For six years from 2002, PwC auditors consistently gave Colonial Bank a clean bill of health, until the bank collapsed. Despite six years of scrutinizing the books, the auditors did not even raise a red flag. TWB is arguing that PwC had a responsibility towards them to

report any evidence of fraud. Given their intimate understanding of Colonial Bank and the size of involves monies, it would have been almost impossible to miss the fraud.

- The trustee has argued that auditors like PwC owe a duty to the public. The trustees base their case around the Supreme Court's 1984 decision that asserts an auditor "assumes a public responsibility transcending any employment relationship with the client" and "owes ultimate allegiance to the corporation's creditors and stockholders, as well as to the investing public".
- PwC claims that sophisticated frauds are difficult to detect and audits are no guarantee of exposure. PwC maintains that it could not have been expected to pick up on a fraud that eluded detection by Colonial's internal auditors and bank regulators as well as by Taylor Bean's own auditors.
- Experts called in the case found among other things that:
  - auditors relied on woefully inadequate evidence in testing the balance of a loan facility
  - auditors relied on a confirmation prepared and received by the client
  - the auditors failed to test a major account balance for existence
  - the audit partner failed to comply with the standard of due care
  - On August 26, 2017, in a Miami courtroom. PwC settled for $5.5 billion as things did not look promising in the courtroom.

25.8.3 The Toshiba Case in Japan (Auditor: Ernst & Young)

- Toshiba one of Japan's top companies and a global company was caught in a $1.9 billion accounting scandal. The inappropriate accounting practices happened over the course of seven years. Toshiba booked future profits early, pushed back losses, pushed back charges and other similar techniques that resulted in overstated profits. Employees were pressured into inappropriate accounting by postponing loss reports or moving certain costs into later years.
- The conglomerate operates business units on a worldwide scale in a variety of diverse industries, including semiconductors, personal electronics, infrastructure, home appliances and medical equipment. Toshiba reported net worldwide sales of more than $63 billion for the fiscal year ending March 31, 2015. It employs more than 200,000 people worldwide.

- The consumer electronics and engineering giant had overstated operating profits by a total of 151.8 billion yen ($1.22 billion) since 2008, claiming numbers that were up to three times the actual level.
- Toshiba's executive and president Hisao Tanaka stepped down after an independent investigation found he had been aware the company had been inflating its profits over a number of years.
- By concentrating power in the role of the president, the corporate governance structure of Toshiba has undermined the surveillance function of its audit committee and outside directors.[31]
- Weak corporate governance and a poorly functioning system of internal controls at every level of the Toshiba conglomerate. Internal controls in the finance division, the corporate auditing division, the risk management division and in the securities disclosure committee did not function properly to identify and stop the inappropriate behaviors.
- In the US, the Securities commission and justice department are examining Toshiba's US Units for any accounting irregularities.
- Toshiba has sought 200 billion yen to 250 billion yen ($1.75 billion to $2.19 billion) in loans from three lenders to cover the cost of restructuring of its home electronics and semiconductor businesses and has obtained a credit line of 400 billion yen from lenders in September 2016.
- When asked about criticism of its role in the scandal, Ernst & Young official Hiroyuki Sato alleged that E&Y could not comment the fraud because of a confidentiality clause in the client's contract.
- Meanwhile, Japan's financial regulator has fined Ernst & Young 2.1 billion yen ($17.4 million) after the firm's audit of Toshiba Corp's accounts failed to spot irregularities in the country's worst accounting scandal in years. The Financial Service Agency has suspended Ernst & Young ShinNihon LLC from taking on new business contracts for three months.

[31] Atsuko Fukase (2015): Toshiba Accounting Scandal Draws Record Fine From Regulators, The WSJ, Dec 7, 2015.

25.8.4 *The Tesco Accounting Scandal in the UK (Auditor: PwC)*

- Tesco, which controls about 29% of Britain's grocery market, struggled with falling sales and a strong commercial identity as premium grocers and big discounters have taken away market share.
- In October 2014, Tesco had overstated its first-half profit by 263 million pounds, about $420 million. Tesco accounting irregularities took place between February and September 2014.
- Profits for the six month to the end of August, 2014 were overstated by £250 m due to the "accelerated recognition of commercial income and delayed accrual of costs".
- Tesco was boosting profits by £200 m by deducting cash from suppliers' trading accounts or extending payment dates without notice.
- Tesco pushed up its numbers to make things appear healthier than they actually were.
- The fraudulent accounting recording was disclosed by Tesco's staff, who triggered the alarming accounting trends, during the final preparations for Tesco latest interim results in 2014.
- On September 9, 2016, three former Tesco executives have been charged with fraud in connection with an accounting scandal that rocked the British supermarket giant.
- The Tesco scandal highlights the perils and pressures of being a publicly traded company with a focus fixed on the short-term.

Practice

Question 1

One of the primary differences between a Financial Statement auditor and a Forensic Accountant lies on this factor?

(a) Financial statement auditors are likely to follow leads suggested by immaterial items whereas Forensic Accountants often must restrict their efforts in searching for material misstatements
(b) Forensic Accountants are likely to follow leads suggested by immaterial items whereas financial statement auditors often must restrict their efforts in searching for material misstatements
(c) Forensic Accountants must focus on specific legal areas that produce fraud charges under the courts of law whereas

financial statement auditors focus their attention on the Generally Accepted Accounting Principles

(d) Forensic Accountants are likely to ask individuals to fix discrepancies found in financial statements whereas financial statement auditors will fail a corporation's financial statement certification, therefore having repercussions with the SEC

Question 2

Forensic Accounting is defined as:

(a) The practice of applying defined financial ratios to investigate a company's financial health
(b) The use of law enforcement to subpoena financial records to determine unlawful actions
(c) The application of investigative and analytical skills for the purpose of resolving financial issues in a manner that meets standards required by courts of law
(d) The investigatory arm of the Securities and Exchange Commission

Question 3

If your actions are the result of misleading, intentional actions or inaction (including misleading statements and the omission of relevant information) to gain an advantage, then you have committed:

(a) Perjury
(b) Contempt
(c) Treason
(d) Fraud

Question 4

Which of the following does a forensic accountant investigate?

(a) Purchases of Businesses
(b) Valuation of divorce assets
(c) Calculation of lost profits
(d) All of the above

Question 5

Forensic accounting can be broken into how many categories?

(a) Two: Investigative and Litigation
(b) Two: Internal and External
(c) Three: Investigative, External, Preventative
(d) Three: Internal, Litigation, Certified

Glossary of the Terms

A

Acceptance sampling: sampling to determine whether internal control compliance is greater than or less than the tolerable deviation rate.

Adverse opinion: an audit opinion which states that the financial statements as a whole are not in conformity with U.S. GAAP.

Advisory services: refer to consulting services in which the CPA develops the findings, conclusions, and recommendations presented for client decision-making.

Affiliate of the accounting firm (or "affiliate of the registered public accounting firm"): includes the accounting firm's parents; subsidiaries; pension, retirement, investment or similar plans; and any associated entities of the firm.

Agreed-upon procedures: an engagement where the client specifies procedures and the accountant agrees to perform those procedures. An accountant may accept an engagement to apply agreed-upon procedures to financial statement elements, where the scope of the engagement is not sufficient to express an opinion, if the users assume responsibility for sufficiency of the procedures, and use of the report is restricted to specified users.

Analytical procedure: a comparison of financial statement amounts with an auditor's expectation.

Assurance engagement: an engagement in which an accountant issues a report designed to enhance the degree of confidence of third parties

F. I. Lessambo, *Auditing, Assurance Services, and Forensics*,
https://doi.org/10.1007/978-3-319-90521-1

and management about the outcome of an evaluation or measurement of financial statements (subject matter) against an applicable financial reporting framework (criteria).

Audit adjustment: a correction of a financial information misstatement identified by the auditor, whether recorded or not.

Audit committee: means a committee (or equivalent body) established by and among the board of directors of an entity for the purpose of overseeing the accounting and financial reporting processes of the entity and audits of the financial statements of the entity.

Audit evidence: information used by the auditor in arriving at the conclusions on which the auditor's opinion is based. Audit evidence includes both information contained in the accounting records underlying the financial statements and other information.

Audit client: means the entity whose financial statements or other information is being audited, reviewed, or attested and any affiliates of the audit client

Audit planning is developing an overall strategy for the audit.

Audit risk: the risk that the auditor expresses an inappropriate audit opinion when the financial statements are materially misstated. Audit risk is a function of the risks of material misstatement and detection risk.

Auditor: term used to refer to the person or persons conducting the audit, usually the engagement partner or other members of the engagement team, or, as applicable, the firm.

B

Business risks: risks that could adversely affect an entity's ability to achieve its objectives and execute its strategies or from the setting of inappropriate objectives and strategies.

Business units: refer to subsidiaries, divisions, branches, components, or investments.

C

Carrying broker: a broker that maintains custody of customer funds and securities. The carrying broker typically agrees to receive and hold the customer's cash and securities, clear transactions, make and retain records relating to the transactions and the receipt and holding of assets, and extend credit to the customer in connection with the customer's securities transactions.

Client: the person or entity with whose financial statements a covered member is associated.

Collusion: a secret agreement (or arrangement) between two or more parties for fraud or deceit.

Comfort letter: a letter written by the auditor to an underwriter of securities, which expresses an opinion about whether the audited financial statements and schedules in the registration statement comply as to form with applicable accounting requirements of the SEC Act of 1933 and related rules and regulations adopted by the SEC. Procedures performed are specified by the underwriter.

Compliance audit: A program-specific audit or an organization-wide audit of an entity's compliance with applicable compliance requirements.

Contingency: an existing condition involving uncertainty as to possible gain (gain contingency) or loss (loss contingency) that will be resolved by future events. Estimates, such as the useful life of an asset, are not contingencies. Eventual expiration of the asset's utility is not uncertain.

Contingent fee: any fee established for the sale of a product or the performance of any service pursuant to an arrangement in which no fee will be charged unless a specified finding or result is attained, or in which the amount of the fee is otherwise dependent upon the finding or result of such product or service.

Control risk: the risk that a misstatement that could occur in an assertion about a class of transaction, account balance, or disclosure and that could be material, either individually or when aggregated with other misstatements, will not be prevented, or detected and corrected, on a timely basis by the entity's internal control.

Cutoff test: An auditor uses tests of cutoff to obtain evidence that transactions for each year are included in the financial statements of the appropriate year.

D

Detection risk: the risk that the procedures performed by the auditor to reduce audit risk to an acceptably low level will not detect a misstatement that exists and that could be material, either individually or when aggregated with other misstatements.

Detection risk of noncompliance: The risk that the procedures performed by the auditor to reduce audit risk of noncompliance to an acceptably low level will not detect noncompliance that exists and that could be material, either individually or when aggregated with other instances of noncompliance.

Disclaimer: a statement that the auditor is unable to express an opinion as to the presentation of financial statements in conformity with U.S. GAAP

Dual-purpose test: audit procedures are classified as substantive tests or tests of controls. If a procedure provides both types of evidence it is a dual-purpose test.

E

Encryption: scrambling data so it is meaningless to anyone but the intended recipient, who has the key to unscramble the data.

Engagement letter: a letter that represents the understanding about the engagement between the client and the CPA. The letter identifies the financial statements and describes the nature of procedures to be performed. It includes the objectives of the procedures, an explanation that the financial information is the responsibility of the company's management, and a description of the form of report.

Engagement partner: the partner or other person in the firm who is responsible for the audit engagement and its performance and for the auditor's report that is issued on behalf of the firm and who, when required, has the appropriate authority from a professional, legal, or regulatory body.

Engagement quality control reviewer: a partner, other person in the firm, suitably qualified external person, or team made up of such individuals, none of whom is part of the engagement team, with sufficient and appropriate experience and authority to objectively evaluate the significant judgments that the engagement team made and the conclusions it reached in formulating the auditor's report.

Estimation uncertainty: the susceptibility of an accounting estimate and related disclosures to an inherent lack of precision in its measurement.

F

Field work: the performance of audit procedures outside the CPA's office. Much field work, but not all, is done in the client's offices after the balance sheet date.

Financial forecasts: are prospective financial statements that present expected future financial position, results of operations, and cash flows based on expected conditions. A financial forecast is of the most likely future scenario.

Fraud: is an intentional act that results in material misstatement of the financial statements.

G

Going concern assumption: assumes the company will continue in operation long enough to realize its investment in assets through operations (as opposed to sale). Presenting assets at historical cost is justified by assuming productive assets will be used rather than sold. This makes market values irrelevant and supports accounting methods that match the actual cost of an asset to periods benefited.

H

Hardware control: computer controls built into physical equipment by the manufacturer.

Historical financial information: information expressed in financial terms regarding a particular entity, derived primarily from that entity's accounting system, about economic events occurring in past time periods or about economic conditions or circumstances at points in time in the past.

I

Information systems: consist of infrastructure (physical and hardware components), software, people, procedures (manual and automated), and data.

Inherent risk: the susceptibility of an assertion about a class of transaction, account balance, or disclosure to a misstatement that could be material, either individually or when aggregated with other misstatements, before consideration of any related controls.

Inherent risk: the susceptibility of a balance or transaction class to error that could be material, when aggregated with other errors, assuming no related internal controls.

Interim audit procedures: procedures done during the year under audit, before year-end.

Internal control: Policies and procedures designed to provide reasonable assurance that specific entity objectives will be achieved. It consists of the control environment, risk assessment, control activities, information and communications, and monitoring.

Introducing broker: broker that agrees to act as the customer's account representative (for example, by providing the customer with account opening documents, ascertaining the customer's investment objectives, and making investment recommendations)

J

Journal: book of original entry in a double-entry system. The journal lists all transactions and the accounts to which they are posted.

K

Key engagement team members: include all engagement team members who have significant engagement responsibilities, including the engagement partner.

Kiting: is possible when internal control weaknesses permit one person to issue and record checks or collusion exists between the two people who are responsible for the two functions. Kiting may be detected by obtaining and using a bank cutoff statement because a kited check clearing in January will not appear on the list of outstanding checks for December and performing a cash cutoff test because the last check issued in December will not be recorded in the check register.

L

Lapping: a scheme design to cover an embezzlement by using payments made by one customer to reduce the receivables balance of another customer.

Lead schedule: the schedule at the beginning of audit documentation that summarizes the detailed schedules.

Lockbox (bank lockbox): speeds the availability of funds from cash collections by reducing the time from the customer mailing the check until the funds are available to spend. Remittances are sent to a bank near the customer and the bank deposits funds speedily to the payee's account.

M

Management: the person(s) with executive responsibility for the conduct of the entity's operations. For some entities, management includes some or all of those charged with governance for example, executive members of a governance board or an owner-manager.

Management bias: a lack of neutrality by management in the preparation and fair presentation of information.

Material noncompliance: In the absence of a definition of material noncompliance in the governmental audit requirement, a failure to follow compliance requirements or a violation of prohibitions included in the applicable compliance requirements that results in noncompliance that is quantitatively or qualitatively material, either individually or when aggregated with other noncompliance, to the affected government program.

Management's specialist: an individual or organization possessing expertise in a field other than accounting or auditing, whose work in that field is used by the entity to assist the entity in preparing the financial statements.

Material weakness: a deficiency in internal control such that there is a reasonable possibility that a material misstatement of the entity's financial statements will not be prevented, or detected and corrected on a timely basis.

Misstatement: a difference between the amount, classification, presentation, or disclosure of a reported financial statement item and the amount, classification, presentation, or disclosure that is required for the item to be in accordance with the applicable financial reporting framework.

Monitoring: A process comprising an ongoing consideration and evaluation of the firm's system of quality control, including inspection or a periodic review of engagement documentation, re- ports, and clients' financial statements for a selection of completed engagements, designed to provide the firm with reasonable assurance that its system of quality control is designed appropriately and operating effectively.

N

Negative confirmation: A request to the recipient to respond only if he or she disagrees with the information stated on the request.

Non-sampling risk: audit risk not due to sampling. An auditor may apply a procedure to all transactions or balances and fail to detect a material misstatement. Non-sampling risk includes the possibility of selecting audit procedures that are not appropriate to achieve a specific objective. For example, confirming recorded receivables cannot reveal unrecorded receivables. Non-sampling risk can be reduced to a negligible level through adequate planning and supervision.

O

Occurrence: assertions about occurrence deal with whether recorded transactions have occurred during a given period. For example, management asserts that sales in the income statement represent the exchange of goods or services with customers for cash or other consideration.

P

Parity bit: a redundant bit added to a string of bits to increase the accuracy of data transmission.

Per diem: an allowance for daily expenses.

Piecemeal opinion: an expression of an opinion on an item in financial statements is not permitted as part of a disclaimer or adverse opinion on the financial statements as a whole because it would tend to overshadow or contradict a disclaimer of opinion or an adverse opinion.

Positive confirmation: A request to the respondent to indicate whether he or she agrees with the information stated on the request. Other positive forms, referred to as blank forms, do not state the amount (or other information) on the confirmation request, but request the recipient to fill in the balance or furnish other information.

Professional judgment: the application of relevant training, knowledge, and experience, within the context provided by auditing, accounting, and ethical standards, in making informed decisions about the courses of action that are appropriate in the circumstances of the audit engagement.

Professional skepticism: an attitude that includes a questioning mind, being alert to conditions that may indicate possible misstatement due to fraud or error, and a critical assessment of audit evidence.
Pro forma: the objective of pro forma financial information is to show effects on historical financial information as if a proposed event had occurred earlier.
Pronouncements of the FASB and GASB: rules that determine the principles for external financial reporting and disclosure.

Q

Quality control systems: provide a CPA firm with reasonable assurance that personnel comply with professional standards and the firm's standards of quality, independence, integrity, and objectivity. It covers personnel management, acceptance and continuance of clients, engagement performance, and monitoring.

R

Reasonable assurance: a high, but not absolute, level of assurance.
Relevant assertion: is a financial statement assertion that has a reasonable possibility of containing a misstatement or misstatements that would cause the financial statements to be materially misstated. The determination of whether an assertion is a relevant assertion is based on inherent risk, without regard to the effect of controls.
Revenue Cycle: Process of receiving a customer's order, approving credit for a sale, determining whether goods are available for shipment, shipping the goods, billing the customers, collecting cash, and recognizing effect of this process on other related accounts.
Review evidence: information used by the accountant to provide a reasonable basis for the obtaining of limited assurance.
Roll-forward period: The systematic establishment of a new accounting periods balances by using (rolling forward) prior accounting period data.
Roll-forward procedures: Procedures are used when acceptable levels of detection risk are high or assessed levels of controls risk are low. Roll forward procedures are useful in testing accounts receivable and revenue because controls are usually strong over revenue transactions and accounts receivables balance.

S

Sampling risk: refers to the possibility that conclusions drawn from the sample may not represent correct conclusions for the entire population.

Segregation of duties: means assigning different people the responsibilities of authorizing transactions, recording transactions, and maintaining custody of assets. Segregation of duties reduces the opportunities for one person to both perpetrate and conceal errors or fraud.

Simulation: representation of the operation or features of one process or system through the use of another. Computer simulation of waiting lines can determine the number of employees needed to serve customers at a particular time.

Specialist: an expert at activities not usually done by auditors (i.e., an appraiser for valuation).

Staff: Professionals, other than partners, including any specialists that the firm employs.

Subsequent events: events that occur between the balance sheet date and issuance of the financial statements. Some such events provide additional evidence about conditions that existed at the balance sheet date, such as the bankruptcy of a customer with a history of financial difficulty.

Substantive audit procedure: a direct test of a financial statement balance designed to detect material misstatements at the assertion level. Substantive procedures comprise tests of details (classes of transactions, account balances, and disclosures), and substantive analytical procedures.

Suitably qualified external person: an individual outside the firm with the competence and capabilities to act as an engagement partner (for example, a partner of another firm).

T

Tolerable deviation rate: the maximum rate of deviation from an internal control that will allow the auditor to place the planned reliance on that control.

Trial balance: a statement of open debit and credit accounts in a ledger to test their equality.

U

Unqualified opinion: an audit opinion that the financial statements are in conformity with U.S. GAAP.

V

Valuation: an assertion made by management that each asset and liability is recorded at an appropriate carrying value.

Variable sampling: the characteristic tested has many possible values (such as dollar value of inventory).

W

Window dressing: refers to actions taken or not taken prior to issuing financial statements in order to improve the appearance of the financial statements.

Working papers: records kept by the auditor of procedures applied, tests performed, information obtained, and pertinent conclusions in the engagement.

Write-off: cancellation of part or all of a balance. Costs incurred that have no future utility are charged (written-off) to an expense or loss account, not carried forward as an asset.

Write-up: an intentional increase in the carrying value of an asset. In narrative terms a write-up is a description of something or some event.

Bibliography

ACFE. (2008). Report to the Nation.

AHERF Creditors' Comm v. PwC, No. 2000 cv 684 (W.D. Pan., 2007, January 17).

Allison, I. (2015). Deloitte, Libra, Accenture: The Work of Auditors in the Age of Bitcoin 2.0 Technology.

American Accounting Association Committee on Basic Auditing Concepts. (1973). *A Statement of Basic Auditing Concepts, American Accounting Association*. Sarasota, FL.

American Institute of Certified Public Accountants: Code of Professional Conduct, Paragraph 53, at http://www.aicpa.org.

Bean, T., & Whitaker. Plan Trust v. PricewaterhouseCoopers LLP, case number 2013-33964-CA-01, in the 11th Judicial Circuit Court of the State of Florida.

Beck, Amanda, Reuters, 27 March 2008.

Blair, A. N. (2008). Auditor Liability: Institutional Investors Pursue Opt-Out—Actions to Maximize Recovery of Securities Fraud Losses, p. 9–11.

Brown, M. (2008, June 1). Forensic Accounting-Past, Present, & Future. It's All About Money. Retrieved April 17, 2014, from http://www.envoynews.com/rwcpas/e_article001108198.cfm.

Cerillo. (1990). Proving Business Damages.

Chiang, J. (2013, August 21). Accountants Uncover Opportunity in Forensics. Media Center RSS. Retrieved April 13, 2014, from http://www.ibisworld.com/media/2013/08/21/accountants-uncover-opportunity-inforensics/.

Coates IV, J. C. (2007). The Goals and Promise of the Sarbanes-Oxley Act. *Journal of Economic Perspectives*, *21*(1), 94.

Coffee, J. C. (1999). *Gatekeepers: The Professions and Corporate Governance*. Oxford: Oxford University Press.

F. I. Lessambo, *Auditing, Assurance Services, and Forensics*,
https://doi.org/10.1007/978-3-319-90521-1

Coleco Indus. v. Berman, 423 F Supp 275 [ED Pa].

Continental Vending [U.S. v. Simon, 425 F.2d 796 (2d Cir. 1969)].

Dreyer, K. (2014). *A History of Forensic Accounting*, Grand Valley State University, p. 3.

Eissenstat, E. S. (2008): Making Sure You Can Use ESI You Get: Pretrial Considerations Regarding Authenticity and Foundation of ESI, p. 7.

Eun, C. S., & Resnick, B. G. (2015). *International Financial Management* (7th Ed., p. 102). New York: McGraw Hill.

Fukase, A. (2015, December 7). Toshiba Accounting Scandal Draws Record Fine from Regulators. *The WSJ*.

Gangolly, J. S. (2015). *Lecture Notes on Forensic Accounting Investigations*. Department of Accounting & Law, State University of New York at Albany, p. 7.

Harris, S. B. (2014, November 24). *The Rise of Advisory Services in Audit Firms*. PCAOB. Tysiac, K. (2013, December 9). Effects of Non-audit Services at Audit Firms Concern PCAOB, SEC. *Journal of Accountancy*.

Healy, P., & Palepu, K. G. (2003, July 1). How the Qwest for Efficiency Undermined the Market. *Harvard Business Review*.

Howard, G. (2015). Blockchain Technology Is Our Chance to Rebuild the Internet in a Way That Benefits Creators.

IAASB. (2010, March). *Assurance and Related Services on Financial Statements Other than Audits*, p. 2.

Kiviat, T. I. (2015). Beyond Bitcoin: Issues in Regulating Blockchain Transactions. *Duke law Journal, 65*, 569, page 578.

Larsen v United Fed. Sav. & Loan Assn. (300 NW2d 281 [Iowa]).

Lessambo, F. (2013). *The International Banking System: Capital Adequacy, Core Businesses, and Risk Management*. Basingstoke: Palgrave Macmillan, Chapter 1.

Levitt, A. (2002). Accounting and Investor Protection Issued Raised by Enron and Other Public Companies, available at http://www.iasplus.com/resource/levitt.pddf.

Mano, R. M., Maurissen, M., & Pace, R. (2006): Principles-Based Accounting: It's Not New, It's Not the Rile, It's the Law. *The CPA Journal*.

Messier, W. F. (2012). *Auditing & Assurance Services* (8th Ed., p. 715). New York: McGraw Hill.

National Surety v. Lybrand, 256 A.D. 226 (1939).

Ozkul, F. U., & Pamukcu, A. (2012). *Fraud Detection and Forensic Accounting* (p. 31). Berlin: Springer.

PCAOB Auditing Standard No. 2: An Audit of Internal Control Over Financial Reporting Performed in Conjunction with an Audit of Financial Statements.

PCAOB. (03/2006). A Layperson's Guide to Internal Control Over Financial Reporting (ICFR). Overview of Trust Services (CICA), 2013.

PCAOB. (2007). Standing Advisory Group Meeting—Panel Discussion: Forensic Audit Procedures, p. 5.

Popoola, O. M. J. (2014). Forensic Accounting Knowledge and Mindset on Task Performance Fraud Risk Assessment. *International Journal of Business and Management, 9*(9), 122.

Public Oversight Board. (2000). *The Panel on Audit Effectiveness ("PAE")*. Report and Recommendations.

Reves et al. v. Ernst & Young, 507 US 170 (1993).

Robert, K., & Pallais, D. M. (1997). Are You Ready for New Services? *Journal of Accountancy*, 49.

Rosenblum v. Adler, 93 N.J 324 (1983) 461 A.2d 138.

Salterio, S. E. (2000). Expanding Assurance Services: An Update from the Assurance Services Executive.

The Sarbanes-Oxley Act of 2002, Section 104.

SAS No. 122 Effective for Audits of Financial Statements for Periods Ending on or After December 15, 2012.

Scott Harrell, L. (2010). Digital Forensics in Anticipation of Litigation, in IRB Seach, LLC.

SEC, In the Matter of the Application of Wendy McNeeley: CPA, AAER No. 3427, at 15 (December 13, 2012), http://www.sec.gov/litigation/opinions/2012/34-68431.pdf.

SEC Press Release (March 26, 2002) at http://www.sec.gov/news/headlines/wastemgmt6.htm9.

Shapiro v. Glekel, 380 F. Supp. 1053, 1056 (S.D.N.Y. 1974).

Shatterproof Glass Corp. v James (466 SW2d 873 [Tex Civ App]).

Sheridan, T. (2015). Number of Accounting Fraud Cases Continues to Rise, AccountingWeb. PCAOB. (2007). Standing Advisory Group Meeting—Panel Discussion: Forensic Audit Procedures, p. 2–4.

Solomon, J. (2010). *Corporate Governance and Accountability* (3rd Ed., p. 37). New Delhi: Wiley. *The Economist*, 7 February 2002.

TeaMate Analytics—Kluwer Wolters at http://www.teammatesolutions.com/analytics/summary-of-tools.aspx.

Teck-Heang, L., & Ali, A. M. (2008). The Evolution of Auditing: An Analysis of the Historical Development. *Journal of modern Auditing and Accounting, 4*(12), 1–4.

Waste Management Founder, Five Other Former Top Officers Sued for Massive Fraud- Litigation Release No. 17435 (2002).

Whittington, R. (2012). *Principles of Auditing & Other Assurances Services* (18th Ed., p. 47). New York: McGraw Hill.

Yolanda and Cathy: Developments in Auditing and Assurance (2010), Corporate Financial Reporting, NJ, p. 93.

Answers to Chapter Questions

Chapter 1

1. D
2. E
3. A
4. A
5. B

Chapter 2

1. E
2. C
3. B
4. B
5. C

Chapter 3

1. E
2. E

F. I. Lessambo, *Auditing, Assurance Services, and Forensics*,
https://doi.org/10.1007/978-3-319-90521-1

Chapter 4

1. C
2. B
3. E

Chapter 5

1. E
2. F
3. B
4. F
5. D

Chapter 6

1. E
2. D
3. D
4. C

Chapter 7

1. C
2. C
3. C
4. C
5. E

Chapter 8

1. C
2. E
3. A
4. D
5. D

Chapter 9

1. C
2. E
3. D
4. B
5. E

Chapter 10

1. E
2. B
3. D
4. D
5. C

Chapter 11

1. D
2. D
3. A
4. C
5. D

Chapter 12

1. C
2. D
3. E
4. C
5. E

Chapter 13

1. D
2. E

Chapter 14

1. B
2. E
3. E

Chapter 15

1. C
2. B

Chapter 16

1. E
2. B
3. E

Chapter 17

1. B
2. D
3. D
4. D

Chapter 18

1. D
2. E
3. C
4. E
5. E

Chapter 19

1. C
2. B
3. E
4. A
5. E

6. B
7. A
8. C
9. E

Chapter 20

1. E
2. D
3. D
4. C
5. E

Chapter 21

1. E
2. E
3. D
4. B
5. B

Chapter 22

1. C
2. B
3. B
4. B
5. B

Chapter 24

1. E
2. B
3. E
4. C
5. B

Chapter 25

1. B
2. C
3. D
4. D
5. A

Index

F. I. Lessambo, *Auditing, Assurance Services, and Forensics*,
https://doi.org/10.1007/978-3-319-90521-1